The Nationalist Ferment

The Nationalist Ferment
The Origins of U.S. Foreign Policy, 1789–1812

Marie-Jeanne Rossignol

Translated by Lillian A. Parrott

The Ohio State University Press
Columbus

Library of Congress Cataloging-in-Publication Data

Rossignol, Marie-Jeanne.
[Ferment nationaliste. English]
The nationalist ferment : the origins of U.S. foreign policy, 1789–1812 /
Marie-Jeanne Rossignol ; translated by Lillian A. Parrott.
p. cm.
Originally published in French under the title: Ferment nationaliste.
Includes bibliographical references (p.) and index.
ISBN 0-8142-0941-6 (hardcover : alk. paper)
1. United States—Foreign relations—1789–1809. I. Title.
E310.7.R67 2003
327.73'009'033—dc22
2003017257

Paper (ISBN: 978-0-8142-5750-0)

Cover design by Dan O'Dair.

Contents

Acknowledgments vii
Introduction ix

Part 1. A Nation Divided
1. Between Border and Frontier: The Quest for Sovereignty 3
2. From Factions to Political Parties: The Rise of Partisan Divisions over Foreign Policy Problems, 1789–1793 25
3. Liberties and the Republic: The Division of the Nation over Foreign Policy Issues 45

Part 2. Foreign Policy Goals Shared by the Entire Nation
4. Commercial and Territorial Expansion 69
5. National Greatness, War, and Peace: The Ambiguities of Isolationism 92

Part 3. Implementing Foreign Policy Goals: Ambitions and Ambiguities
6. The United States and Haiti: Rejecting the Other American Republic 119
7. The Louisiana Purchase: American Expansion and Its Problems from 1803 to 1812 141
8. From Tripoli Harbor to the 1812 Declaration of War: Identity and Recognition 169

Conclusion 195

Notes 201
Bibliography 249
Index 265

Acknowledgments

I wish to thank all who made this book possible: Elise Marienstras, who guided me throughout my doctoral research; my colleagues from the Centre de Recherches sur l'Histoire des Etats-Unis [Center for Research on the History of the United States] of the University of Paris 7—Denis Diderot; Denis Lacorne, who encouraged me to publish my work; and finally, Jean Heffer and François Weil, who greatly contributed to improving the manuscript through their pertinent remarks and advice.

This book, however, would probably not have existed if it were not for a one-year exchange scholarship I had at Duke University in Durham, North Carolina, for which I thank the University of Paris 7. At the history department at Duke, I profited from the stimulating teaching of Peter Wood and Barry Gaspar, who helped me deepen my reflection and engage it onto more daring tracks.

The English translation of *Le ferment nationaliste* was made possible by the Organization of American Historians, which rewarded in this way a book that it had deemed worthy of the Foreign Book Prize in 1996. This English publication also owes a great deal to The Ohio State University Press, which has taken it upon itself to support this prize, and to the translator's conscientious work. During the translation process, the translator and I made certain very minor modifications, but these do not amount to a revised edition of the original work.

Introduction

Nationalism: French Nationalism versus American Nationalism

In the wake of the wars of the late nineteenth century and the first half of the twentieth century, a large part of European public opinion has come to view nationalism as an evil.[1] In post–World War II Eastern Europe, however, intellectuals kept trying to define and legitimize one or another national claim, but this went largely unnoticed.[2] As a result, the independence movements that took hold of former Eastern bloc countries starting in the late eighties were originally rejected by commentators as being reincarnations of a monster that was thought to have disappeared forever. The Yugoslav conflict in the early nineties was labeled "archaic," and an alarm was sounded over the rise of nationalist trends. The question was raised whether nationalism did not actually "constitute in itself a regressive utopia," with the implication that in fact it did.[3]

There were, however, journalists and critics who tried to avoid automatically applying ready-made interpretations of past nationalism to the current situation. In view of its highly negative connotations, they did not dare use the term "nationalism"; rather, they made a distinction between "national democratic movements in Czechoslovakia, Armenia or Slovenia, and the strictly nationalist agendas that inspire[d] the leaders of Serbia and Georgia."[4] This distinction was suggested by Gérard Malkassian, a critic of Armenian descent, who has styled himself as the advocate of the national aspirations of small nations. In his view, the rise of nationalism is no obstacle to universal cosmopolitanism; it is merely a necessary spiritual and cultural stage. In his view, nation does not automatically entail state, power, or denial of diversity; rather, a nation can also recognize itself in "its minority status, or in its essential fragility."[5]

In contrast, the legacy of French nationalism makes it difficult to promote this type of analysis, or, for that matter, any dispassionate study of the question. According to Pierre-André Taguieff, the reason why "the scholarly literature on these issues, with few exceptions, has remained very close to the level of newspaper controversy, [is] notably because ideology and polemics are so pervasive." One reason why nationalism is so controversial in France, even—and indeed especially—in scholarly discourse, is that "the history of French nationalism has been written sometimes by nationalists and sometimes by antinationalists." Hence, there is a great theoretical opposition between antinationalist definitions of nationalism, which hold it to be a xenophobic phenomenon or a device for social exclusion and ultimately for war (cf., the equation "nationalism = racism"), and nationalist definitions (as a "normative theory of identity as self-defense"[6]).

In analyzing the way American nationalism was established through the early republic's (1789–1812) foreign policy, either school of thought could be invoked. On the one hand, as a xenophobic phenomenon leading to war, American nationalism was indeed linked, during this period, to five years of Indian wars, three years of undeclared war against France, and lastly to a declaration of war against Great Britain in 1812. On the other hand, as a phenomenon of collective identity defense, American nationalism allowed the early republic, small in population and fragile in its unity, to defend its sovereignty against attacks by the great powers of the period—powers whose colonial possessions surrounded the early republic's poorly controlled territory. Such an ideological reading of the concept of "nationalism" is relatively fruitless, however, and probably reflects the ambiguities of the national form and the false clarity of nationalism.[7] A number of concepts that play a role in this controversy will be retained in the present study, as they are essential for understanding the phenomenon of nationalism (concepts such as sovereignty, xenophobia, patriotism, national feeling, and national identity). Yet in order to avoid polemics, the problem will be situated in its own peculiar context, that is, that of the North American continent at the end of the eighteenth century. In the wake of recent events that have put the issue of nation in the spotlight, this study of American nationalism from 1789 to 1812 is intended as a way of putting things into perspective, or as a dose of "culture shock."[8]

Unlike French nationalism, American nationalism has not been widely studied. Moreover, instead of the end of the eighteenth century, the second half of the nineteenth century is generally considered to be the crucial period of the history of nationalism.[9] The term "nationalism" did, however, appear in France at the time of the French Revolution, and the idea of nationalism cannot be separated from the rise of great modern nations at the end of the eighteenth century.[10] Meanwhile, in the United States, the term "nation" was rarely used after the American Revolution. "People" was preferred (as in the opening words of the Constitution [1787]: "We, the people"), or "the Union," in order to spare the rights-conscious states the centralizing connotations of the word "nation."[11] Supporters of strong federal institutions and a powerful nation nevertheless adopted the name "nationalists" from 1781 to 1787, during the period of the Confederation, although they abandoned it once the new institutions were in place.[12] This first meaning of the term "nationalism," limited as it was to the cause of a stronger central government, is not, however, broad enough to cover the topics that will be examined here. In order to define American nationalism at the end of the eighteenth century, it is necessary to start from a wider, less restrictive definition of nationalism, such as that outlined in John Breuilly's set of three basic assertions of nationalist discourse:

a) There exists a nation with an explicit and peculiar character.
b) The interests and values of this nation take priority over all other interests and values.
c) The nation must be as independent as possible. This usually requires at least the attainment of political sovereignty.[13]

Similarly, one can also draw upon the following definition of nationalism given by the specialist Raoul Girardet: "On the political level, and within the context of a nation-state that has already been established historically, nationalism can also be defined as the priority given to preserving independence, maintaining full sovereignty, and asserting the greatness of that nation-state. On the moral and ideological level, it may seem merely to amount to extolling national feeling."[14] This last definition is useful in that it distinguishes nationalism from national feeling and shows the dynamic relation between these two concepts, which are often confused.

The Distinctiveness of American Nationalism at the End of the Eighteenth Century

These definitions clearly pose a problem for the study of American nationalism. In 1776, at the time of the creation of the American nation, one cannot say that "there existed" in the United States a nation endowed with an explicit, specific character; the United States did not constitute a "nation-state already established historically." American historians are divided over the issue of how much diversity and cultural specificity there was among the different British colonies of North America.[15] Nevertheless, it is certain that at the time of the War of Independence, cultural homogeneity had not been firmly established from Vermont to Georgia, but it was emerging.[16] And after the war, such homogeneity could by no means be founded upon a colonial past that the recent fighting had repudiated.

It is this peculiarity of American nationalism—namely, an original perspective on the founding of a nation—that has been analyzed by French historian

Elise Marienstras in two pioneering works, *Les Mythes fondateurs de la nation américaine. Essai sur le discours idéologique des Etats-Unis à l'époque de l'Indépendance (1763–1800)* [The founding myths of the American nation. An essay on the ideological discourse of the United States at the time of independence (1763–1800), 1776] and *Nous, le peuple. Les origines du nationalisme américain* [We, the people. The origins of American nationalism, 1988]. Marienstras defines the political and the ideological as the principal forces behind American nationalism, as distinguished from its French counterpart. Indeed, in her view, the identity of the French nation was at that time anchored in geographical, historical, and cultural features that the abstract definition of revolutionary nationalism could not have replaced;[17] the same was not true for the United States, however, where the national geography, history, and culture were in the midst of being created. In order to assert its identity, the young American nation could only count on the new institutions that it had just endowed itself with, unlike revolutionary France:[18] "Since the justification [for nationalism] could not be found in the usual factors of other nations—that is, in the past, culture, history, or its own territory—it found a home in ideology. Nationalism, which emerged at the very moment when the state and the nation were being born, sought to make up for the lack of tangible and historical components by substituting an institutional and ideological characterization."[19]

From 1789 to 1812 nationalism in the United States could not therefore be restricted to "preserving independence, maintaining full sovereignty," or "extolling national feeling." It also had to bring out the national character, stir up patriotic feeling, and create a core to be elaborated and preserved. By the establishment of nationalism in the United States, I will thus mean here the construction and affirmation of the nation, in the sense of a community linked by "a common destiny and a common character."[20] Once the Constitution of 1787 was passed and ratified, Americans found themselves endowed with national institutions around which the forms of a civic religion were to be organized. This civic religion was intended to enlist the citizens in the cult of the nation.[21]

Owing to the key positions that they occupied in society, the elite played a major role in this spread of nationalism. They were the ones who provided the impetus for the Philadelphia Convention that was to lead to the drafting of the Constitution; in fact, only a minority of Americans took part in the vote on the ratification of the Constitution.[22] Nevertheless, the ideological work of the elite would have been pointless without the consent of the citizens.[23] In this regard, Ernst Gellner's model of the emergence of nations and of nationalism can be usefully applied to the United States. For Gellner, the key to this phenomenon is a revolution in communication systems, a sort of "cultural revolution" that necessarily accompanies the transition to the industrial era. He believes that, in traditional societies, numerous factors contribute to great cultural diversity between regions and social groups, whereas as soon as a given society begins to evolve toward industrial capitalism, communication between groups increases, and there is bound to be a shift toward cultural homogenization. For example, citizens who refused to give in to the demands of a national educational system would quickly find themselves excluded from society, since society needs citizens who are mobile and adaptable to the demands of an evolving employment market, and who therefore have a common cultural background.[24]

In the period examined in this book, American society indeed started to adopt the structures of free-market capitalism;[25] one can also observe the beginnings of an information revolution, which was to assume its full magnitude in the decades that followed. Already a proportionally greater number of U.S. citizens were literate than in European countries.[26] In addition, at the turn of the nineteenth century, nearly all big American cities had one or several daily newspapers. Although the circulation remained low, information began to circulate quite well as newspapers changed hands in taverns and in city reading rooms, while favorable postal rates enabled publishers to send the news from one end of the country to the other.[27] Thus there existed an informed public opinion in the United States, which the elite could reach by the press, and which could express itself through voting or by writing in the newspapers.[28] According to Benedict Anderson, the development of the press gave a sense of belonging to an "imagined community."[29] At the end of the eighteenth century, American society thus lent itself readily to the spread of a nationalist ideology, which aimed at transforming regions that were still diverse into one indivisible nation.

Nationalism and Foreign Policy

According to Breuilly's third condition for nationalism given above, "[t]he nation must be as independent as possible," which "usually requires at least the attainment of political sovereignty." As Elise Marienstras observes, "in order to assert itself, every nation must distinguish itself from other nations."[30] After achieving its independence, the American nation, in order to truly exist, had to be recognized by the international community, and it also had to assert itself as a nation distinct from other nations. The present book investigates this dimension of American nationalism, a vital dimension in the period that began in 1789, when the federal institutions created by the Constitution of 1787 were put into place, and ended with a highly symbolic war against the former homeland, the War of 1812, often called the "second War of Independence." This study is thus essentially devoted to the expansion of a "secondary" patriotism, that is, one formulated "in those terms of general interest, diplomacy, conflicts, and glory that are proper to state powers." This contrasts with "primary" patriotism, which is characterized by attachment to one's roots and by family and community memory.[31]

The members of the Constitutional Convention of 1787 wanted to create a nation out of former British colonies, which the War of Independence had not managed to unite in a stable manner. The establishment of a civic religion and reverence for the institutions were not enough: as long as the outside world did not perceive the specific identity of the new nation, the elite could not force the unity and consistency of such an identity on its own inhabitants. Moreover, as a former settlement colony, the American nation could not assert itself on the international scene by invoking a glorious past or a preexisting identity that was clearly distinct from that of the homeland.[32] In order for the undertaking of the writers of the Constitution to succeed, their country had to deal with other countries in a sufficiently firm and distinctive manner, so that foreign countries would contribute to the construction of America's national character through a mirror effect, that is, by reflecting back to Americans the image of themselves as a people bound through unity and solidarity. In 1789 the issue was thus the following: if the federal government could assert its altogether new authority and new sovereignty over the states, over its own citizens, and with regard to other nations, then America would be recognized and accepted by other powers; these powers would in turn reflect back to America the image of a mature nation.

It is hard for a nation to exist on the international scene if it is not endowed with a government that is represented abroad by a single authority (i.e., embassy or consulate), one that is recognized by other countries. When exactly the American nation truly came into being is thus debatable (in 1776, 1783, 1787, 1798, or 1812), as is the moment when the American national feeling finally reached maturity. The date when the American nation truly began to belong to the international community is, however, difficult to challenge. Of course, as historians L. S. Kaplan and J. T. Lowe explain, already in the prerevolutionary period, the thirteen colonies maintained some sort of diplomatic relations with one another, as well as with Great Britain and the Indian nations; they did not, however, form an independent nation that was recognized as such by the great European powers.[33]

During the American Revolution, the American envoys in Paris represented the thirteen colonies and made decisions binding the entire nation. After the war, however, despite the presence of plenipotentiaries in London (John Adams) and in Paris (Thomas Jefferson), America did not present a unified front abroad, since the different states reserved the right to make decisions (for example, on tariffs) that were only binding for themselves; for several years Vermont even had its own diplomatic relations with London. The United States of America could thus not be perceived abroad as a single entity or as a stable partner. Although the new nation was officially recognized, it had not yet achieved true international recognition as one indivisible nation. This essential element for the formation of its identity was still lacking.

From 1787 on, the new institutions engendered by the Philadelphia Convention provided the early republic with the means for assuming its place among the nations of the world. The ambassadors no longer depended on the Continental Congress, but on a president, the head of the executive branch, who could be rightly expected to make firmer and quicker decisions. The president was, moreover, in charge of treaties as well as in command of the army, the navy, and the state militias. Since foreign trade was the responsibility of the federal Congress, interference between the jurisdiction of the states and that of the federal government in matters of foreign relations no longer seemed possible. The birth of the young nation as a full-fledged member of the international community, on equal footing with other nations, could finally take place.

Far from being a matter of indifference to citizens, and of interest only to diplomats and those in power, this process was to occur at the height of a period of popular enthusiasm for foreign events. To read American newspapers between 1789 and 1812, no matter which political party they supported, was to learn first and foremost about the state of the world and foreign relations. Even if domestic policy was of major interest to Americans, it could not compete with the stories of revolutionary battles, and later Napoleonic battles, that filled the bulk of the newspapers.[34] Domestic policy often seemed even subordinate to foreign policy debates, which had considerable influence on its very discourse and on the issues at stake. This infatuation with foreign events and the role of their country in the world could be viewed as a mere relic of the colonial heritage of the citizens of the early republic. Such a view would imply that Americans were fascinated by foreign policy out of a lack of interest in anything that concerned only their country. In fact, such was not the case. In the American passion for foreign policy, one must discern a manifestation of the nationalist process rather than a colonial remnant. Owing to the new status of the United States in the international community, as well as to the impetus of the French Revolution and its consequences on the early republic—in terms of memory, political life, economy, social structure, and collective imagination—Americans were placed in the midst of international events; these events were to give a central role to foreign policy in defining the national identity. In a world context that was radically transformed from 1789 on, the American nation was to define and identify itself in the eyes of the world through the foreign policy objectives it would be able to set forth and implement.

Toward a Cultural History of International Relations

In order to study how American nationalism was put into effect in the early republic's foreign policy, it is important to study diplomatic history sources of the period. As the Comte de Garden wrote in 1833, "[d]iplomacy is the science of external relations or foreign affairs of states: in a more specific sense, it is the science or the art of negotiation. It comprises the entire system of interests arising out of established relations between nations, the goal being their respective security, tranquility, and dignity."[35]

Many American diplomatic historians, the most famous of which is Samuel Flagg Bemis, examined these sources closely during the first half of the twentieth century. It thus seems unnecessary to go back over the exact same ground that has been so adeptly explored by other scholars, especially considering that methodological advances in the history of international relations have now made traditional diplomatic history obsolete. This means that it is no longer possible to rely solely on the work of diplomats and political leaders for the study of relations between nations. In the United States, traditional diplomatic history methods were notably called into question by the historian William Appleman Williams in his book *The Tragedy of American Diplomacy* (1959), which assessed the formulation of foreign policy on the basis of economic interests, and not only in terms of the role of the elite.[36] In 1965, in the introduction to his book *Empire and Independence: The International History of the American Revolution,* historian Richard W. Van Alstyne clearly distinguished his work from that of diplomatic historians: "International history . . . is not diplomatic history. I have not in this book confined myself to diplomacy, much less to foreign policy. I have searched for deeper currents in my effort to understand basic attitudes and motivations that come to light only after long study and detached thought. Hence I have not hesitated, whenever occasion demanded, to stray from the well-worn path of diplomatic history and venture into fields commonly labeled domestic or internal history."[37] The methodological innovations described by Van Alstyne (bringing domestic history into the analysis of a country's foreign policy; searching for "deeper currents" that allow one to understand "basic attitudes and motivations") met with little success. Indeed, in 1980 an American historiographic assessment deplored that the history of international relations, be it the history of American or foreign diplomacy, could not be counted among the innovative currents in the field in the 1970s.[38]

Since the early 1980s, however, American historians have been renewing this area of historical research by paying more attention to nonpolitical aspects of the past, such as culture, bureaucracy, and gender relations.[39] Interest in the classic problems of American diplomatic history, such as isolationism or the opposition between realism and idealism, has been on the wane. As a result, perhaps the name of the discipline is no longer clear-cut: "diplomatic history" is still used, "international history" is favored by historians who no longer want to focus their study on the United States, and "history of foreign relations" appears to reflect the aspirations of historians who wish to extend the study of foreign affairs to nonpolitical forces (e.g., businessmen, missionaries, and travelers) while focusing their work on the United States.[40]

New Aspects, New Forces

The present study of how nationalism was enacted through the foreign policy of the early American republic relies somewhat traditionally on the discourse and actions of American leaders, and on the work of diplomats. It does not, however, consider these leaders and diplomats separately from the political, social, economic, and cultural forces of their nation—as cold strategists, advancing the pawns of the interests of their country on the international chessboard. As French historian Lucien Febvre suggested in 1931, foreign policy is motivated not by mood, psychology, or the interplay of competing diplomatic strategies; rather, it is motivated by geographical, economic, social, and intellectual factors.[41] Accordingly, a guiding principle of this study is that foreign and domestic policy cannot be analyzed independently from each other.[42]

To this end, one must first and foremost be familiar with the views of American leaders and with the political stakes at the time, so as to see to what extent partisan disputes influenced foreign policy orientations. The correspondence and personal papers of politicians between 1789 and 1812 provide an abundant and passionate source of information about the development and management of foreign policy. By reading the papers of opposition leaders, who took a critical view of the work of men in power, one can bring to light the ambiguities and contradictions inherent in the policies. Next, it is important to ascertain the range of public opinion and the views and reactions of citizens. Instead of attempting to analyze countless personal journals of men and women of all "sections," of all ages, and of all social classes, I have undertaken an exhaustive reading of several representative newspapers that were published in different regions. These papers (such as the *Boston Columbian Centinel* or the *Richmond Enquirer*) reflect the views of one party or another and therefore display contrasting opinions. In addition to reports of European wars and polemical editorials, one can in fact find in these papers correspondents' letters, political tracts, toasts made on the occasion of national holidays, such as the Fourth of July, the texts of Citizens' Addresses and Resolutions sent to the president of the United States during exceptional crises (neutrality in 1793, the XYZ Crisis in 1798, the bombing of the *Chesapeake* in 1807), and sometimes patriotic songs that testify to the important place that foreign policy occupied at that time in popular culture and in the minds of Americans. Other documents, such as the sermons of New England ministers, and journals or correspondence of observers who were not directly linked to the higher spheres of politics, make it possible to know the views of individuals, influential or not, who expressed their opinion far from the realms of power.

In addition to individual agents, that is, American citizens who could express themselves through the press or various public events, one should not fail to consider the huge mass of silent agents who, although present on the

American scene at the time, have never been given their just due in the classical historiography of international relations. I am referring above all to the black slaves, that is, 20 percent of the American population at the turn of the century. Whether or not they had access to newspapers, they could always hear the news when they went into town, listen to conversations when serving their master at table, and transmit this information to the slaves who worked the land. The means of communication were numerous: although they may have been silent, the slaves were nonetheless active. Indeed, the increase in the number of slave insurrections in the southern United States must be attributed to the example of the successful insurrection of the slaves of Santo Domingo, which was to lead to Haiti's independence in 1804. In this particular case, only a knowledge of the social contradictions of an early republic that was both democratic and slaveholding can explain the ambiguous attitude of American leaders toward Haiti. The silence of classical diplomatic historians on the subject points clearly to the degree to which this question hinges on interpretation.

The slaves are not the only neglected foreign policy agents of the United States; the same is also true of the indigenous nations of the North American continent, who are generally not included among the international partners of the United States in the period under consideration. When diplomatic history studies deal with U.S.–Native American relations, they present the North American Indian nations as (manipulated) intermediaries of those European powers established on the North American continent, such as Great Britain in Canada or Spain in Florida. Indeed, generally speaking, when historians examine the foreign policy of the early republic, they do so from a very Eurocentric point of view: they assume that the early republic's foreign policy was limited to its relations with European countries. Not only do they overlook the regular relations that it had with the indigenous peoples of North America, but they likewise make very little of U.S. relations with non-European powers, such as the Barbary Coast.[43] Nevertheless, the intensity of diplomatic relations between Native Americans and settlers is well documented. The first interactions between settlers and an Indian nation were always followed by the drafting of treaties that were necessary for land acquisition and for arrangements between the two groups. These treaties were not concluded verbally by smoking the peace pipe but were always written up.[44] As long as the Native Americans were powerful enough to be respected as independent nations, negotiations were conducted very formally, often according to the wishes and the protocol of the Native Americans, as in the case of the Catawbas.[45] Thus, the fact that documents relating to U.S.–Native American relations have traditionally fallen under the domain of Indian Affairs, and not of foreign policy, does not mean that one must accept a distinction that was not justified before the War of 1812. Until that date, the American Indian nations constituted a real threat for the early republic.

This book not only seeks to analyze a particular dimension of American nationalism, and to introduce new agents in the field of foreign policy at the end of the eighteenth century and at the beginning of the nineteenth; it is also an attempt at writing a chapter of the cultural history of the international relations of the United States. Nationalism is defined in this work as an ideology that aims to create a lasting nation: in this regard, the study of nationalism belongs to the study of culture, which is conceived here as "the sharing and transmission of memory, ideology, emotions, life-styles, scholarly and artistic works, and other symbols."[46] More specifically, a cultural approach to international relations, in the words of Akira Iriye, "explores the ideological or intellectual underpinnings of a nation's behavior toward other nations."[47]

Thus presented, the cultural history of international relations encompasses the history of foreign policy ideologies, construed as a "set of beliefs and values, sometimes very poorly and partially articulated, that make international relations intelligible and decision making possible."[48] Such an approach allows one to understand and interpret types of discourse and attitudes that inform the foreign policy decisions in light of the society's evolution.[49]

Putting American Nationalism into Effect: The Different Stages

The Nation Divided over Foreign Policy

In 1789 the American nation had just endowed itself with a state, that is, strong federal institutions that were to allow it to anchor its citizens' national feeling in a civic religion. The nation as artefact was to cure the shortcomings of the "organic" nation.[50] It was a gamble that the Founding Fathers made, the success of which strictly depended upon the reaction of other countries. This ambitious but abstract program appears to have overlooked the fact that the American nation was already an organic one. More than twenty years of national history had forged the outlines of a national character, which was to be quickly defined and shaped through foreign conflicts. If one is to follow Pierre Nora's definition of memory as something "permanently at stake" ("enjeu toujours disponible"), and as a "set of strategies,"[51] then the American national memory was above all the Revolution, which was the source of national identity and the political legitimacy thereof. Then, from 1789 on, the French Revolution came along to wake up American revolutionary memories by posing an essential question, one to which the end of the fighting had not provided an answer: assuming that the American Revolution was the source of American identity, what exactly did it signify? Was the French Revolution the daughter of the American Revolution, and did Americans define themselves as democrats—that is, as Jacobins? Or were there in fact few links between the two events, and was the American Revolution merely an outburst of violence and radicalism necessary for the establishment of an elitist and conservative social system? Before this question could be answered, ten years of intense political conflict were to tear the nation apart. Partisan hatred was to sweep away hopes for recognition by other powers, which would have reinforced the image of a nation bound by unity and solidarity: until 1800 Americans were perceived everywhere as a divided nation, and they perceived themselves in the same light.

Foreign Policy Objectives Common to the Entire Nation

This perception is not false, but it obscures the fact that despite their conflicts and political hatreds, Americans were in the process of shaping the elements of their national identity. Owing to partisan struggles, bipartisanship was established in the United States from 1789 to 1800; this was an institutional system that had not been intended by the Founding Fathers. The system, along with Thomas Jefferson's victory in the presidential election of 1800, marked the irreversible decline of an ideological model (i.e., classic republicanism) that had been pervasive in the political discourse of revolutionary America. These developments also marked the advent of a social and political perspective in which the citizen—far from privileging the common good and taking pride in republican virtues—placed above all else the defense of personal liberties and interests, and especially of property. In America the interest of the nation had to be preceded by each individual's prosperity: government was at the service of the citizen, with whom it shared and anticipated foreign policy objectives. The end of the Federalist era thus marked the beginning of the era of economic liberalism in the United States.[52]

These years of political conflict also witnessed the emergence of foreign policy objectives that were shared by all. Expansion was the nation's first objective; this was furthered by the wars that were tearing Europe apart, and it manifested itself at sea (i.e., commercial expansion) as well as on land (i.e., territorial expansion).[53] Indeed, American citizens—from those in power to pioneers on the frontier—came together in the same grandiose vision of their nation's future, which guided and fed their nationalism. For them, the American "empire" was destined to expansion and to an unprecedented development.[54] This national vision belonged to the collective imagination, at times without any direct connection to reality or the near future (for example, Thomas Jefferson readily pictured his people spreading out over both continents). This vision did, however, coincide with a real upsurge in expansionism. Tireless shipowners took advantage of Europe's wars to develop a neutral American trade and to give their country the status of a great economic power. The pioneers moved toward the Mississippi, hoping to use the river to take their goods to port. Striving first and foremost to obtain navigation rights on the Mississippi, Thomas Jefferson kept constant pressure on the Spanish diplomats; in 1795 the Americans finally achieved their goal thanks to Pinckney's Treaty, which guaranteed outlets for the product of the new western territories.

Implementing Foreign Policy Objectives; Ambivalent Ambitions

Americans' growing interest in the West went hand in hand with an increasing lack of interest in Europe's quarrels: the more the American nation defined itself through its expansionist will, the less it wanted to see itself as linked to Europe. Far away and different, it perceived itself, moreover, as being better. Foreign crises, which certain leaders used to their advantage, exacerbated the nascent chauvinism of American citizens and led them to see their own country in an ever more idealized light and then to display their attachment to it. From this point of view, the various crises that pitted the United States against Europe between 1793 and 1814 constituted an essential element in the development of American nationalism. These crises also enabled the leaders to outline the doctrine of isolation. This notion was called for in the name of American superiority and pacifism; it did not, however, apply to Native Americans or to non-European nations: in their dealings with these groups, Americans did not shy away from aggressive behavior.

Bit by bit America had thus forged an identity that made it indeed different from European countries. Nothing indicates, however, that its particular character actually made it as free of ambivalence as it claimed. There remained a gap between the leaders' discourse on the nation (which the white population supported without much opposition after 1800) and the actual situation. This gap was brought to light by certain foreign policy problems, and it contributed to the shift in the country's foreign policy orientations after 1803. The proclamation of independence in Haiti in 1804 and the installation of a black government led Thomas Jefferson to break all relations with that country, even though American government circles (regardless of party affiliation), as well as business circles, coveted the riches of Santo Domingo. In order to avoid confronting the problem of slavery, the nation agreed to transfer its expansionist will to the West. Here as well, however, ambiguities persisted and multiplied: although they were carried out in the name of progress and the Enlightenment, the expeditions sent by President Jefferson encroached upon the geographic claims of other nations. The expeditions did not tolerate other Europeans unless they Americanized, and they sentenced Native Americans to "civilizing" themselves or to disappearing. Although the conquest of the West allowed Americans to define themselves as citizens of a continent, it was at the cost of the impending elimination of the indigenous tribes.

Between 1789 and 1812 the American nation thus forged a geographic, political, economic, and racial identity through foreign policy conflicts and events.

In 1812 the American citizen (i.e., the white male) was the citizen of a continent; for him, his country's borders were not definitely set: he had seen them change, and he expected they would change again. His motherland was thus a vision or a promise as well as a reality; his patriotism did not manifest itself so much in a commitment to the current territory as in a belief in the coming expansion of his country. He did not like the fact that Florida belonged to Spain, and he already considered himself the quasi-legitimate owner of the Northwest Coast. To this end, he counted above all on himself (expansionism had popular support), but also, when necessary, on his government. His democratic and economically liberal views stipulated that the government respond to citizens' expectations without directing them too much or ever neglecting their economic interests. He was proud of his country and ready to defend it (if a good argument was given); he did not much care about matters in Europe, a continent he deemed morally inferior. He was driven by a grandiose vision of his nation's future, and thus he devoted himself completely to building it; this for the moment entailed conquering the North American continent and increasing everyone's wealth. Nevertheless, one last obstacle remained: as long as Great Britain refused this new image of the United States, Americans would feel deprived, and their credibility would remain incomplete in their own eyes. Even if they preferred to push westward, for several years Americans would continue to look back eastward, in order to secure from their former colonizing power the recognition they needed for the full affirmation of their national identity.

PART 1

A Nation Divided

CHAPTER 1

Between Border and Frontier: The Quest for Sovereignty

For the authors of the *Federalist Papers,* two issues were at stake in the Philadelphia Convention: the disappearance of the confederal structures established by the Articles of Confederation in 1781, and the replacement of those structures by a federal constitution that, in addition to reinforcing national unity, would better preserve the role of the elite. The different essays that are contained in the *Federalist Papers* were thus mostly devoted to political and institutional questions; only a few dealt with the advantages of the new constitution for resolving the early republic's foreign policy problems.[1] Although only a small part of this collection of tracts focused upon this aspect of the debate, Alexander Hamilton nevertheless was moved to deliver a vehement diatribe against the disastrous consequences of the foreign policy conducted by the Continental Congress since the end of the Revolution. In Hamilton's words:

> We may indeed with propriety be said to have reached almost the last stage of national humiliation. There is scarcely any thing that can wound the pride or degrade the character of an independent nation which we do not experience. Are there engagements to the performance of which we are held by every tie respectable among men? These are the subjects of constant and unblushing violation. Do we owe debts to foreigners and to our own citizens contracted in a time of imminent peril for the preservation of our political existence? These remain without any proper or satisfactory provision for their discharge. Have we valuable and important posts in the possession of a foreign power which, by express stipulations, ought long since have been surrendered? These are still retained, to the prejudice of our interests, not less than of our rights. Are we in a condition to resent or to repel the aggression? We have neither troops, nor treasury, nor government. Are we even in a condition to remonstrate with dignity? The just imputations on our own faith, in respect to the same treaty, ought first to be removed. Are we entitled by nature and compact to a free participation in the navigation of the

> Mississippi? Spain excludes us from it. Is public credit an indispensable resource in time of public danger? We seem to have abandoned its cause as desperate and irretrievable. Is commerce of importance to national wealth? Ours is at the lowest point of declension. Is respectability in the eyes of foreign powers a safeguard against foreign encroachments? The imbecility of our governments abroad are the mere pageants of mimic sovereignty.[2]

It is easy to understand how such an assessment could spawn the belief that the period of the Articles of Confederation was "the critical period of American history." Not everyone shares this view, however; Merrill Jensen, for example, strongly disagrees.[3] And it must be conceded that the assessment made by Alexander Hamilton was not completely straightforward. It is true that in 1787 the Continental Congress had still not come up with the money to pay off the public debt accumulated during the war years, nor had it found the means to force American citizens to reimburse their English creditors from the pre-war period, despite a clause to this effect in the peace treaty with Great Britain (cf., in the Hamilton text above: "Do we owe . . ."). This could not, however, prevent Americans from protesting "with dignity," as Hamilton says, against the unjustified presence of the British in the Northwest ("a foreign power . . ."). After the war, when some states stopped paying back their debts to British subjects (hence "the just imputations" that detracted from Americans' "faith," according to Hamilton), the British had already decided to keep their military posts for as long as possible. According to Samuel Flagg Bemis, it should be kept in mind that as early as April 8, 1784, the Governor General of Canada had been instructed not to withdraw British garrisons from frontier posts since, in using the phrase "with all convenient speed," the treaty had not set any specific date for their evacuation.[4] The word of honor of the British was to be taken with as much caution as that of the Americans.

When speaking of Spain's ban on navigation ("Spain excludes us from it"), Hamilton forgot to mention that the United States had indeed begun negotiations with Spain over this in 1785 and that they had failed not only because of the "imbecility" of the American government, but also because of the irreconcilability of the two countries' positions, which made any negotiation, and therefore any resolution, difficult. Yet the ambassadors, whom Hamilton referred to with such scorn, did in fact accomplish a great deal in the form of treaties that they managed to conclude with Holland and Sweden (1783), and then with Prussia (1785) and Morocco (1787) on the basis of the Franco-American treaty of commerce of 1778.[5]

No matter how exaggerated they were, Hamilton's remarks nonetheless reflect legitimate concerns, at least on the part of those who were worried about the new nation's apparent weakness on the international scene and its seeming inability to assert its sovereignty, either at home or abroad.[6] As historian Forrest McDonald suggested, it was a "critical" period in American history only for those who had faith in the American republic.[7] In this extract from the *Federalist Papers,* Hamilton speaks above all as a "nationalist"[8] keen on building a truly independent nation, one endowed with a strong executive and respected by other countries.

Indeed, the reputation of the United States abroad as an independent nation declined throughout the period of the Articles of Confederation. The French began to consider the possibility that the Confederation might be dissolved; the British gradually came to neglect the American plenipotentiary in London, John Adams, as a representative of a nation that did not stand up for itself; and Barbary Coast pirates kidnapped American sailors without fear of retaliation since the American government had neither its own income, nor a national army or navy worthy of such a name.[9] In short, the Confederation was incapable of making other countries respect its sovereignty.

In the eyes of Hamilton and the nationalists of the Philadelphia Convention, the reason for this weakness was simple: the cause lay in the existing institutions. As Hamilton explained in *The Federalist* no. 23, these institutions needed to give way to a new constitution that would allow a strong executive to control and coordinate the republic's foreign policy (defense, trade, and diplomacy): "The principal purposes to be answered by union are these—the common defence of the members; the preservation of the public peace, as well against internal convulsions as external attacks; the regulation of commerce with other nations and between the States; the superintendence of our intercourse, political and commercial, with foreign countries."[10] That is, if the federal government managed to affirm the existence of the United States as a nation in relation to other nations, the republic would finally take its true place on the international scene. The situation would now be straightforward: foreign countries would know who really had authority and who had the means to exert it. It was this challenge that the nationalists wanted to take on when they came to power in 1789.

In order to assert the independence of their country, however, the nationalists had first of all to assert the federal government's sovereignty over the territory that had been ceded to it and formally granted in the peace treaty of 1783. On the surface, the "frontier" that they were concerned about was the border of international treaties and diplomatic negotiations, and not the one that Frederick Jackson Turner would write the history of. Nevertheless, the borders of the United States were in fact on the "frontier." As a matter of fact, one can no longer adhere to the ethnocentric definition that Turner gave to the "frontier" at the turn of the century—that is, as the scene of white "civilization" pushing away indigenous "savagery." The notion of frontier, which is a cornerstone of American history and historiography, must nonetheless be maintained in reference to a particular zone of colonization and development, one where cultures meet, trade, and come to terms with each other.[11]

Indeed, even though the American border was a line drawn on a map as European borders were, it did not look like them in actuality. As Frederick Jackson Turner said, "The American frontier is sharply distinguished from the European frontier—a fortified boundary line running through dense populations."[12] In contrast to European borders, the borders that the American negotiators obtained in Paris in 1783 were quite far from the densely settled areas of the East Coast. The American borders ran along the outermost settlement zone, where pioneers and speculators were preparing the way for larger waves of arriving settlers, and where they lived in constant contact with the local Indian tribes. Isolated from the centers of power by the Appalachians, the frontier people would be quite willing to take their destiny into their own hands. Meanwhile, the Indian nations had regrouped after the end of the War of Independence and were not much afraid of the budding nation, which seemed to have a hard time getting organized. For the new American government, gaining respect for itself and for its borders was not simply a matter of geopolitical clarification with Spain and Great Britain. It also needed to assert itself in relation to the Indian nations, as well as with regard to some of its own citizens.

The Aftermath of the War of Independence

In 1789 the American government was not in complete control of the territory that had been attributed to the United States in the "Definitive Treaty of Peace between Great Britain and the United States of America," which had been signed at Versailles on September 3, 1783. In the North and Northwest, as in the South and Southwest, the borders that had been assigned to the United States during the peace negotiations were not respected by their neighbors, Spain and Great Britain, the two biggest colonial powers at the end of the eighteenth century. Both of them encroached upon American territory, where they maintained military outposts. This failure to respect the legal borders angered American nationalists, for it showed that their government's authority was not recognized by other powers.

Great Britain in the Northwest

In order to put distance between the United States and France at the end of the War of Independence, British negotiators had made an irresistible offer to Benjamin Franklin, John Jay, and John Adams: the land beyond the Appalachians, from the Great Lakes to Florida, over to the Mississippi was to be ceded to them.[13] Still, the British did not want to make things too easy for the former insurgents. By 1784 British colonial officials in Canada had decided to delay evacuation of the posts that they occupied in the area (namely Detroit, Pointe Aufer, Mackinac, Niagara, Oswego, Oswegatchie, and Dutchman's Point); this decision soon received support in the form of secret instructions from London. This enabled the British to keep up the profitable fur trade with American Indians.[14] When the Continental Congress proved to be incapable of forcing the states to pay off their prewar British debts, the British used this as a pretext to maintain the status quo and continue occupying the posts, since the United States was thus violating one of the clauses of the peace treaty.[15]

Spain in the Southwest

The Spanish, who continued to occupy military posts on American territory after the Revolution, were not, strictly speaking, violating the peace treaty. They were, rather, simply taking advantage of the contradictions that existed between the Anglo-American treaty and the Anglo-Spanish treaty of 1783 concerning the south-southwest border of American territory, as well as the navigation of the Mississippi. In this regard one should keep in mind that Spain was not an ally of the United States during the War of Independence, but was only an ally of France against Great Britain, which explains the inconsistencies between the different treaties that ended the conflict. Although Spain had supported the American effort, it had not become a U.S. ally because, already at that time, the two countries were unable to agree on the navigation of the Mississippi.[16]

In the Anglo-American treaty, Great Britain granted the United States a southern limit set at the 31st parallel, whereas the Anglo-Spanish treaty, although signed the same day, did not specify the northern limit of the Floridas, which allowed Spain to claim that it was still set at 32° 28', as during the British occupation of the region.[17] Likewise, the Anglo-American treaty stated that the navigation of the Mississippi was open to all citizens of the United States, whereas the Anglo-Spanish treaty said nothing about this, which allowed Spain to close off navigation of the river to Americans in 1784.[18]

In 1785 the Spanish minister plenipotentiary, Don Diego de Gardoqui, attempted to solve the various problems with John Jay, the secretary of foreign affairs. In return for commercial advantages, Jay, a New Yorker, agreed to give up the navigation of the Mississippi for twenty-five or thirty years. This proposition ran up against opposition from the southern delegates to Congress and was the source of long-lasting western mistrust of easterners. Indeed, for western pioneers, the Mississippi was the natural route for exporting their products. Closing off the river would be tantamount to paralyzing their economic development.[19]

After these negotiations failed, the American Southwest remained in Spanish hands, with the Spanish advance posts of Natchez and St. Stephens well above latitude 31°; Fort Nogales was added in 1792 and Confederacion

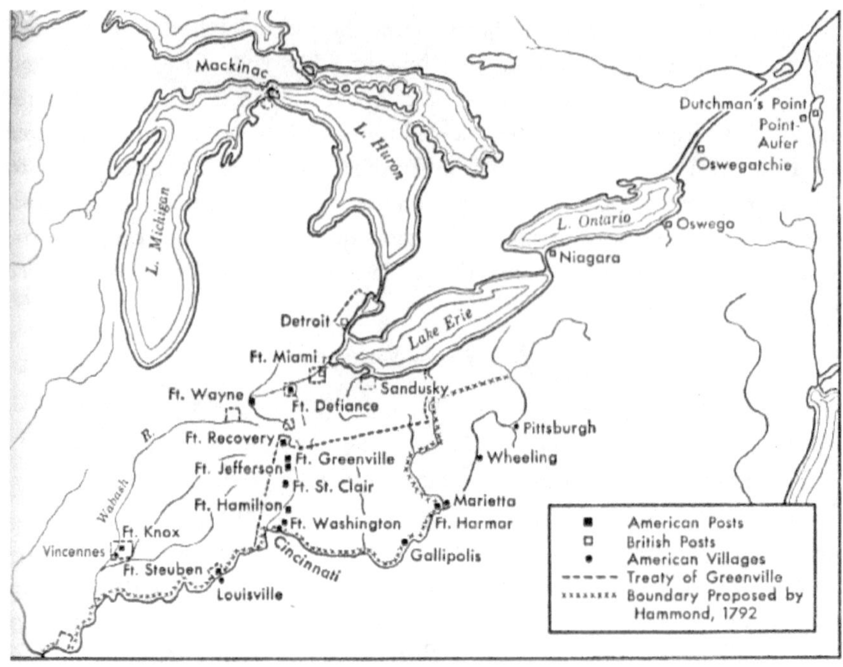

Situation in the Northwest (Ray Allen Billington, *Westward Expansion,* p. 223)

in 1793, which showed that Spain was anxious to consolidate its expansion into U.S. territory.[20] Such military presence indicated that Spain also felt that the border of the United States need not be respected. Spain considered that the early republic was above all a bad example of emancipation for its own colonies, and it only half-heartedly recognized American independence.[21]

Native American Sovereignty

In 1768, in the treaty of Fort Stanwix, which was signed by the superintendent of Indian Affairs, Sir William Johnson, and the Six Nations of Iroquois, the British had guaranteed that the land north of the Ohio would constitute Indian territory, and the thirteen colonies were never supposed to encroach upon this land. The British were thus reaffirming the steps taken by the king of England in the Proclamation of 1763, which set the Appalachians as the westernmost limit for settlement, and which had thereby infuriated the colonists.

For the Iroquois the treaty of 1768 meant that the British officially recognized their sovereignty over this territory, against colonists' claims. It is thus not surprising that they sided with the British (with the exception of the Oneidas and the Tuscaroras) during the War of Independence, as did the Cherokees,

Chickasaws, Choctaws, and Creeks in the South.[22] These nations as well were only too aware of the colonists' greed, since the Creeks, in 1773, and the Cherokees, in 1775, had had to cede large chunks of their territory to them.[23] In 1783 the former rebels were again victorious, and the Iroquois were subjected to the "law of the winner" in the new treaty of Fort Stanwix (1784), where they were forced to give up large chunks of the Old Northwest.[24]

The true occupants of the Northwest, however, were mostly Algonquian, as one can see on the adjoining map; thus, in signing the treaty of Fort Stanwix, the Iroquois had spoken for them without authorization. Driven out of territory further to the west by the Iroquois during the seventeenth century, these Algonquian nations (Ojibwas, Miamis, Hurons, Petuns, etc.) had taken refuge around the Great Lakes. There, with the help of the French, they had later managed to push back the Iroquois, thus avoiding Iroquois domination. During the War of Independence, the Algonquians had ended up siding with the British, and, in contrast to the Iroquois, they had not suffered a major defeat.[25] When speaking of the Old Northwest, or of the Northwest, and of the way the British ceded it to the United States, the Algonquians should be kept in mind, and not only the Iroquois. The Algonquians did not consider themselves vanquished at the end of the War of Independence and did not give up any part of their territory.

Nevertheless, during the peace negotiations, the British ignored Native American sovereignty, whether Iroquois, Algonquian, or Cherokee, and ceded to the new nation huge tracts of land without consulting the owners; in the end, Indian independence could only be subordinate to non-Indian sovereignty.[26] The peace treaty of 1783, which was incomprehensible from the Native American point of view, subjugated the Indians to the United States, which chose not to recognize Native American sovereignty over their own territories, and treated them as a conquered people, as punishment for having sided with the British. After 1783 Congress sought to apply a unilateral policy toward the Indian nations: peace would only be granted to them if they accepted to pay reparations in the form of territorial transfers.[27] For the Indians of the Northwest, this meant that they had to move back beyond the borders of the 1768 treaty: the Ohio River would no longer be the line separating their territory from that of the colonists. Federal authorities thought they had reached their goal when, between 1784 and 1786, they signed six peace treaties with various Indian nations, whereby those nations gave up large chunks of their territory.[28] In the Southwest, the states themselves took charge of dispossessing the great Indian nations, that is, the Creeks, the Chickasaws, the Choctaws, and the Cherokees. In 1783 North Carolina decreed that the Indians living on its territory—the Cherokees and the Creeks—had lost all rights over their land. And during its short existence, the independent state of Franklin (the eastern part of Tennessee) took the same action.[29]

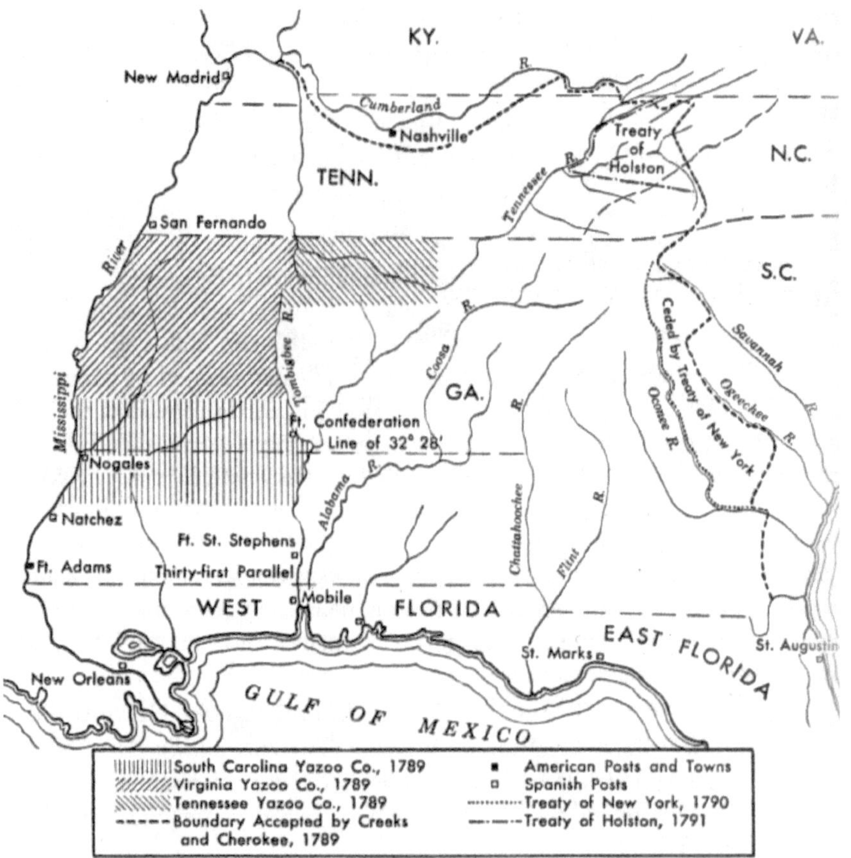

Situation in the Southwest (Ray Allen Billington, *Westward Expansion,* p. 234)

In 1786 hostilities resumed on the frontier.[30] The Indians of the Northwest chose to fight rather than to lose their territory without resisting, whereas the American government, which had just organized pioneer settlements on newly acquired lands, had no intention of giving in. But the stakes were high, for it was clear that the British were going to support the Indians in order to protect their own interests and maintain their unjustified presence in the region.[31] In the Southwest, the tribes went to battle again, with a determination that was multiplied tenfold by Spanish aid and by the charisma of chiefs such as the Creek Alexander McGillivray.

In 1789 the American government thus had to face a double challenge to its sovereignty: as an independent nation, equal to the great European nations, but also as a colonial power, which refused to admit the sovereignty of Native Americans over their own territory. Not only did it have to establish its authority on two fronts, that is, the Northwest and the Southwest—

the former being in complete turmoil—but it also faced opposition from three sides, which were quite likely to help one another or even openly join forces against the new republic.[32]

Toward a Resolution of the Conflicts?

War in the Northwest

When the Revolution was over, many American pioneers rushed into the newly acquired territories and crossed the Ohio River. Native Americans responded to the pioneers' raids and brutality with violent attacks.[33] Indeed, they wanted to force the pioneers back across the river and to discourage similar encroachment by others, in order to guarantee the de facto preservation of Indian territory north of the Ohio. The new government could not fail to react to this outburst of violence, which undermined its ability to ensure territorial integrity and to control its citizens' anger. A redefinition of its relations with the Indian nations was in order. Although U.S.–Native American relations still revolved around the issue of land acquisition, the government had to give up the doctrine of conquest as well as the claim to total sovereignty over Indian land. As Great Britain had done before, the American government chose to keep a monopoly over relations with the Indian nations; these relations were to be regulated by treaties negotiated according to international diplomatic custom. The Indian nations were thus once again recognized as sovereign and independent nations.

Thus, after long negotiations, the governor of the Northwest, Arthur Saint-Clair, managed to conclude the Treaty of Fort Harmar in 1788; according to this pact, the chiefs of the Confederacy of Northwestern Tribes agreed to respect the land transfers made just after the war and therefore to move back beyond the Ohio. By the time the treaty was signed, however, the Petun-Huron chiefs who had been involved in the negotiations had already lost almost all their influence, and in 1789 the Shawnees worked out a consensus among the various tribes in favor of resistence.[34] Armed confrontation thus seemed inevitable, which was bound to pose a problem for the new federal government, since it was obliged to defend pioneers whose actions it otherwise disapproved of, and to engage in a rather uncertain show of force. In June 1789 the secretary of war, Henry Knox, ordered General Harmar, who was in charge of operations in the Northwest, to go on the attack. The first campaign took place in October 1790 and ended in failure. This failure was the result of a lack of preparation and discipline on the part of the American army, which was confronted with determined Native Americans (Shawnees, Miamis, Ottawas, Sauks, and Delawares).

The Indians were able to win not only because they were formidable warriors but also because they were well armed and equipped by British agents.[35]

The Indian Nations of the Southeast (Alice Kehoe, *North American Indians: A Comprehensive Account,* p. 152)

This material aid, which had already been offensive to American sovereignty in peacetime, became intolerable in wartime. It was difficult enough for the new nation to admit that its army could not hold out against Indian warriors, but it was even more humiliating to see a great nation support hostile tribes with complete impunity. Thomas Jefferson, who was secretary of state from 1790 to 1793, expressed his indignation over this during a meeting of George Washington's cabinet in April 1791. He proposed that, since there was no official representative of Great Britain in Philadelphia, the U.S. protests be addressed to Colonel Beckwith, a British secret agent who enjoyed a semiofficial status in Philadelphia.[36] Alexander Hamilton, who was secretary of the treasury, answered that he had broached the topic with Beckwith, who had in return assured him that nothing except the yearly gifts at the usual period had been distributed to the Indians.

For those who knew about Native American diplomatic customs, such distribution of gifts was not at all reassuring. It was through such practices that the French had been able to establish a strong, albeit stormy, alliance with the Algonquians of the Northwest, from the middle of the seventeenth century to the end of the Seven Years' War.[37] Jefferson was not reassured by Hamilton's statements and wanted to go further, for which he obtained the cabinet's support. James Madison lived in the same house as Beckwith, and so Jefferson asked Madison to explain to Beckwith that although such presents were innocent enough in peacetime, they were not in wartime, and that it violated neutrality laws for a neutral country to provide one of the warring parties with weapons. Beckwith appeared shaken: he claimed that neither he nor Lord Dorchester[38] knew about the distribution of presents, and he said that he would write to his government about it. According to Jefferson, the British agent understood that his apologies to Hamilton had not been sufficient.[39]

But what could be the effect of a secretary of state's diplomatic arguments when victory was no longer on his side? For the British, the American army's defeat in October 1790 constituted a ray of hope: their territorial losses of 1783 were perhaps not irreparable if the federal government proved incapable of imposing its authority in the Northwest Territory. The Americans' position was indeed so weak that they might in fact be forced to accept the British diplomatic plan for that area. When George Hammond, the first British minister plenipotentiary to the United States, arrived in Philadelphia, the United States had just suffered one of its worst defeats at the hands of Native Americans. On November 4, 1791, the American army, led by General Saint-Clair, was almost destroyed by the joint forces of Little Turtle (Miami) and Blue Jacket (Shawnee): nine hundred officers and soldiers perished in the blood bath. Conditions now seemed ripe for the young British emissary's proposals to be received by a distraught federal government.

The plan that was contained in Hammond's instructions, and which was proffered as an effort at mediation between the United States and Native American tribes, sought in fact to create a neutral Indian barrier state. This state would have included the territories north of the Ohio and east of the Mississippi, as well as a strip of New York State extending over to the forts on the other side of Lake Champlain. This plan was immediately rejected by American officials, who correctly sensed in it a wish to create a "British protectorate" (as S. F. Bemis put it) over the Northwest Territory.[40] In 1792, having failed in its overtures toward American leaders, the British government ceased to advocate openly the sort of tacit union between the Northwest and the Crown that the creation of a barrier state would have implied. Nevertheless, the British did not abandon their plan, and Canadian officials took anything but a passive stance, especially after Lord Simcoe, a particularly belligerent lieutenant governor of Upper Canada, took office.[41] Once Simcoe had taken charge, the British objective became clear: since the Northwest could not be recovered through negotiation, the Indians had to be provided with the means to enforce their sovereignty over the territory so that British influence and interests could be maintained there.[42] From July 29 to August 16, 1793, a last attempt was made at conciliation between the Indian Confederacy and federal representatives over the issue of boundaries, but British agents saw to it that no accord could be reached between those two parties.[43] British influence aside, it is questionable whether any sort of accord could have been reached at that time between the United States and the Northwest Confederacy, given the mounting divisions among the tribes over the issue of the Ohio as border.[44]

During the fall and winter of 1793, fear of an American offensive against British posts added to the tension that reigned on the frontier. Relations between Great Britain and the United States had deteriorated to the point where a war between the two powers became a distinct possibility. Shedding his characteristic reserve, Lord Dorchester, who was governor of Upper Canada, was so bold as to address the Indians directly with words of war on February 10, 1794. Shortly thereafter, as he was concerned about defending Detroit, Lord Dorchester ordered a new fort (Fort Miami) built on the banks of the Maumee; this amounted to foreign aggression on U.S. soil.[45] The war between the federal government and Native Americans seemed likely to turn into a war between two colonial powers: with England protecting the Northwest in the name of Indian sovereignty (sovereignty that it had not defended in 1783), and the United States safeguarding its own sovereignty over the same land (sovereignty that was based exclusively on force).

On August 20, 1794, the area near Fort Miami witnessed the final confrontation between Native American forces, commanded by the Shawnee chief Blue Jacket, and the American army, led by General Anthony Wayne. When the Indians retreated in the direction of Fort Miami, the British garrison denied them any help whatsoever. This betrayal came as a surprise to the Native Americans, for they had benefited from ample British supplies and equipment during the winter and spring, and that morning they had seventy Canadians in their ranks.[46]

Wayne's victory over the Indian Confederacy at Fallen Timbers was also a victory over the British. Indeed, after the battle Americans symbolically set fire to the trading post of the British agent McKee. The United States had managed to assert its sovereignty over its territory by pushing back an enemy who had paid little heed to its newly acquired independence. Even more than the signing of Jay's Treaty (November 19, 1794), the Battle of Fallen Timbers marked the beginning of British withdrawal from the region.[47] By defeating the overconfident Native Americans, the federal government had managed to put into effect its conception of U.S.–Indian relations: although in theory the Indian nations were independent and sovereign, they were in fact subject to the authority of the federal government. However, even though the vanquished and famished northwestern tribes seemed to accept allegiance to the United States at the Treaty of Greenville in 1795, they had not lost all hope. Beginning in 1808, the Shawnee chief Tecumseh sought the support of all the northwestern and southwestern tribes, and he launched a general offensive during the War of 1812, thereby making use of British logistical help.

In the Southwest: Indian Wars and International Negotiations

In the Southwest, two goals dominated the new government's foreign policy: first, to secure navigation rights on the Mississippi for its western citizens (who had had such rights when they were subjects of the British Crown), and second, to impose its authority over the territory it had been granted by the treaty of 1783. Like the British in the Northwest, the Spanish wanted to wait as long as possible before withdrawing from the military posts they occupied on territory ceded to the United States by Great Britain. Ever since the end of the War of Independence, they too had been striving to create an "Indian barrier" with this intention, by capitalizing on the poor relations between the United States and the great tribes of the Southwest. In the mind of Floridablanca, the Spanish minister of foreign affairs, this Indian barrier was to extend from the Atlantic to the Mississippi, and it would have consisted of the contiguous territories of the Creeks, Choctaws, and Chickasaws.[48] Moreover, in order to stay on good terms with these tribes, Spain let the British firm Panton, Leslie and Company keep up their profitable trade with Native Americans in Pensacola when Florida came back into Spanish hands after a short period of British rule (1763–1783).

Spain did not, however, want to enter into full-fledged war with the United States just to back up Indian demands. In 1790 the Creek representative Alexander McGillivray was compelled to negotiate with the new federal government. Under threat from northwestern tribes, the government gave a triumphant welcome to the Creek chief and reached an agreement with him (on August 7, 1790) that amounted to a compromise between the claims of the Creeks and those of the state of Georgia. According to this treaty, the Creek chief also recognized U.S. sovereignty.[49] Nevertheless, by not upholding the territory clauses of the treaties that Georgia had forced upon the Indians after the Revolution, the Treaty of New York was bound to bring about renewed fighting, since the pioneers would not tolerate being chased away from their land.[50] Thus, the Treaty of New York did not resolve all the problems that existed between the United States and Native Americans in the Southwest. Furthermore, as long as Native Americans could take advantage of the rivalry between the United States and Spain, get their supplies from Spanish-approved merchants, and maintain their sovereignty over land disputed by the two powers, the United States would not have total sovereignty over the territory it had acquired in the 1783 treaty with Great Britain. The key to the problem lay with Spain and the renewal of negotiations.

How, then, could Spain, which ignored the new republic, be forced to resume negotiations that had proved to be so ineffectual during the war and again from 1785 to 1787? In June 1790 Thomas Jefferson thought he had found the right pretext to launch a great diplomatic campaign that would lead Spain into discussion with the United States. The year before, British merchants in search of furs had settled at Nootka Sound, on the Northwest Coast, and Spain had reacted violently to what it considered a violation of its territory. As the situation deteriorated, the two nations were on the brink of war in the spring of 1790. Jefferson believed that the United States could take advantage of the international crisis that pitted its two neighbors against each other, and on August 2, 1790, he wrote to the American chargé d'affaires in Spain, William Carmichael, urging him to resume talks with the Spanish government. Jefferson also contacted William Short, the American chargé d'affaires in Paris, so that the latter could enlist the support of the French government in favor of American interests.[51] Jefferson thought that Spain would settle its differences with the United States so as not to add to its problems.

At the very moment when Jefferson thought he had found haughty Spain's weak spot, the crisis between the two colonial powers was resolved by diplomatic means. Even so, in 1791, shortly after receiving a memorandum from William Short concerning American rights to the navigation of the Mississippi, Floridablanca offered to resume negotiations with the United States.[52] At that time monarchist Spain believed that it could no longer count on its traditional ally, France, and it felt the need to thwart any possible alliance between the United States and its powerful competitor, Great Britain, by adopting a more conciliatory attitude toward the new republic. Jefferson was very pleased when the news of these overtures reached him in December 1791, and on March 18, 1792, he named William Short and William Carmichael envoys to the Court of Madrid.[53] Short, however, only reached Spain a year later, when the balance of power between European countries had been completely upset. Spain was now allied with Great Britain in war against France, and as a result, its position on the American continent was strengthened. As long as it had British support, Spain had nothing to fear from the United States.

The two envoys quickly realized that the situation had changed. When they finally had their first meeting with the Spanish negotiator Gardoqui on March 23, 1793, the latter assumed an uncompromising stance toward both aspects of the issue. Gardoqui supported Spain's right to the borders that it claimed in the Southwest and contested the right of the United States to the navigation of the Mississippi: no negotiation was possible. Short and Carmichael did not, however, want negotiations to end when they had only just begun. If Spain's position at that time was dictated by its alliance with Great Britain, who could say what changes a new balance of power in Europe might bring about? Short and Carmichael said they preferred to wait and see what was to follow, as no one knew how quickly the international situation in Europe might deteriorate. They counted on a resurgence of Spanish fears of Great Britain, fears that they had witnessed at the time of the Nootka Sound incident, and which they felt would be instrumental in bringing about real negotiations with Spanish authorities.[54]

While the negotiations being conducted in Spain by Short and Carmichael were at a standstill, the situation in the Southwest was turned upside down at the end of 1791 when a new governor, the Baron de Carondelet, took office. Carondelet renewed a strategy that his predecessor Esteban Miro had downplayed since 1787, namely, actively supporting Indian tribes against Americans. It appears that in 1792–93 Carondelet sought to organize a Confederacy of Southwestern Tribes, similar to that of the Northwest, and just as effective against the U.S. Army. On July 6, 1792, Alexander McGillivray signed a treaty with the Spanish governor that was very favorable to his nation, but he took pains to avoid committing himself to any military action whatsoever against the United States. Far from seeing his dreams of an Indian Confederacy come into being, Carondelet then learned that the Chickasaws (who were pro-American) had gone to war with the Creeks.[55] This war likewise displeased the federal government, but it did allow the secretary of state to give new impetus to the controversy over the Southwest frontier even before negotiations had really begun in Spain. Jefferson hastened to demand clarification for Spanish support to the Creeks. He accused Spanish officers on the frontier of hostile behavior toward Americans, and he went so far as to claim that Carondelet himself was responsible for the Indian attacks since he provided them with weapons and ammunition. In his dispatch to Short and Carmichael, Jefferson concluded: "In short, [Carondelet] is the sole source of a great and serious war now burst upon us."[56]

Jefferson also contacted two Spanish diplomats posted in Philadelphia, Jaudenes and Viar. Jaudenes and Viar were in a strong position because of the Anglo-Spanish alliance. They did not simply justify the actions of the Spanish officers; they accused the Americans in turn. The quarrel escalated and came to a head on May 25, 1793. In a letter addressed to the secretary of state, the two diplomats threw the ball back into Jefferson's court: although the Creeks had initiated the fighting, it was because the Americans had provoked them by supporting the Chickasaws. Jefferson summarized this letter for Short and Carmichael as follows:

> This letter charges us, and in the most disrespectful style with
>
> 1. exciting the Chickasaws to war on the Creeks
> 2. furnishing them with provisions and arms
> 3. aiming at the occupation of a post at the [illegible]
> 4. giving medals and marks of distinction to several Indians
> 5. meddling with the affairs of such as are allies of Spain
> 6. not using efficacious means to prevent these proceedings [. . .]

The threats of war contained in the letter (i.e., if the United States continued to help the Chickasaws, Spain would openly take sides with the Creeks) convinced Jefferson to cease communication with the two diplomats. He only refuted their attacks so as to give leverage to Short and Carmichael, who now had to settle this new case in Madrid alone: "This is indeed so serious an intimation, that the President has thought it could no longer be treated with subordinate characters, but that his sentiments should be conveyed to the Government of Spain through you."[57] Nevertheless, once Gardoqui was taken off the case by the new Spanish prime minister Manuel Godoy, Duke of La Alcudia,[58] Godoy and the two American envoys began corresponding. At first this correspondence reassured Carmichael and Short about Spanish intentions: they believed that the Spanish Court would no longer support any interference with American interests on the frontier and that the United States no longer had any reason to fear that Spain would support their Indian enemies.[59] On January 21, 1794, William Short was able to give his government more specific reassurance about the Spanish attitude toward Native Americans: Short and Carmichael had received a letter from the Spanish prime minister to the effect that the king had now ordered his Florida and Louisiana governors to cease assisting the Indians, as proof of the Spanish sense of justice, and as a gesture of friendship to the United States, and the American envoys were supposed to forward this information to the president.[60]

By officially disavowing Carondelet's policy of aid to Native Americans in the Southwest, Godoy was seeking to ingratiate himself with the federal government. The American government got the impression that—for once—a great colonial power was taking their claims into consideration and was taking pains to respect their sovereignty, but this was brought about by the balance of power in Europe being again in a state of flux. The Spanish military suffered setbacks at the end of 1793, and the alliance with Great Britain was gradually called into question. As a result, Spain had to humor the United States, as in 1790–91, in order to prevent the new republic from forming an alliance with Great Britain, which would open up Spain's North American possessions to the British.

It was only in July 1794 that things really started moving, and a true upheaval occurred in the balance of power among European countries, as Short and Carmichael had been expecting since the time of their very first dispatches in 1793. After John Jay arrived in London on May 8, 1794, an isolated Spain began to fear that what it dreaded most for the kingdom and its possessions in America would materialize, namely: an Anglo-American alliance that would threaten its possessions in North America. William Short was aware of Spain's fears, and in the fall of 1794, he anticipated a positive outcome from the Spanish-American talks. Assuming that Jay's negotiations led to the end of all diplomatic quarrels between the United States and Great Britain, Short reasoned, the Spanish ministry would grant Americans their "rights" and would give in on the navigation of the Mississippi.[61]

When Godoy found out in December 1794 that a treaty had been concluded between the United States and Great Britain, he could not hide his fears or his disappointment.[62] He anxiously waited for the arrival of Thomas Pinckney, who was to take over from Short and Carmichael, but Pinckney only reached Madrid in January 1795. During this long wait, Godoy was able to make sure that Jay's Treaty contained no alliance clause between the United States and Great Britain, but in spite of this, Pinckney's delay did not undermine the opportunity that the Anglo-Spanish rift presented to the United States. Indeed, in March 1795 Godoy concluded a separate peace with France in the Treaty of Basle, thus violating the 1793 treaty of alliance with Great Britain. Retaliation was to be feared, and Godoy did not want to make a bad situation worse by continuing to annoy the United States. This was what set the stage for Pinckney's Treaty, in which Spain gave in on the points of contention: Spanish troops were to clear out of the disputed territory, and the United States was granted navigation rights on the Mississippi as well as the privilege of having a depot in New Orleans for three years (renewable).

On paper, Spain's disengagement in Native American country was complete.[63] Both of the contracting parties were forbidden to conclude any treaty whatsoever with Native Americans living in the other's territory. Each of the two powers had to prevent the Indians living in its territory from attacking the Indians living in the other's territory, or from attacking the citizens of the other's territory. Since the thirty-first parallel finally became the official boundary of the United States, recognized as such by Spain, the sovereignty of nine-tenths of the southwestern tribes became subordinate to U.S. sovereignty, and the ambiguity that had existed since 1783 disappeared. Yet in the field, paradoxically, Carondelet's endeavors since 1792 were succeeding, and in October 1793 the four southwestern tribes (Creek, Cherokee, Chickasaw, and Choctaw) formed a confederacy allied with Spain, thus remaining loyal to the only power that traded with them and provided them with supplies.[64]

Hailed as a victory of American diplomacy, the advantages attained through Pinckney's Treaty were nevertheless due in large part to Spain's fears in Europe.[65] Given that Spain was in command of the situation in the Southwest, and that Native American tribes knew their new protectors were first and foremost seeking to encroach upon their land, it came as no surprise that the treaty was only carried out very grudgingly by Spain and the Native American tribes. In December 1796 navigation of the Mississippi was indeed opened to American boats, but the dismantling of the Spanish forts (i.e., Natchez, Nogales, San Fernando, and St. Stephens), which had begun in February 1797, was resumed only in March 1798. Moreover, Spain retained a position of influence in Native American country. In his book *The Mississippi Question,* Arthur Preston Whitaker made the following observation about Pinckney's Treaty: "Five years after its conclusion, the Governor of Louisiana was able to say with some justice that the Choctaw, Chickasaw, and Creeks still constituted a barrier against American aggression."[66] Nevertheless, the end of the War of the Chikamauga (the Cherokee of the Lower Towns) in 1794 meant that the tribes of the Southwest had to come to terms with pioneers and local leaders. In 1798 the Cherokees were forced by the Treaty of Tellico to make significant territorial concessions, and then in 1805–1806 they had to relinquish their hunting grounds through a series of hotly contested treaties.[67] In Georgia the Creek nation was made to cede large tracts of territory in 1796 and in 1805; Creek warriors did not, however, lose hope of reconquering that land, and many of them were to join Tecumseh when the War of 1812 broke out.

Sovereignty Attacked from Within

After its victory over Great Britain, the early republic was caught in the grip of centrifugal forces: citizens whose patriotic feeling was still weak were ready to renounce their allegiance to the nation in order to pursue their own agenda. In certain areas the feeling of belonging to the new nation proved at times to be shaky and indeterminate—even after the new federal government had been formed, which meant putting the newly born union at risk. This was particularly true of the western frontier, where people felt that their interests were not taken seriously enough in the East, and where they were at times prepared to join forces with a nation that was an enemy of the United States.

In 1777 the state of Vermont, whose admission to the Continental Congress was blocked by the state of New York, decided to proclaim its independence, and from that time on it issued its own currency and maintained its own diplomatic relations with other powers.[68] In the West, Spain's closing off of the Mississippi to American navigation in 1784 was a true disaster for those who lived on that side of the Appalachians. The Spanish minister plenipotentiary, Don Diego de Gardoqui, realized that he could use this discontent to weaken the early republic and win over the inhabitants of those areas to the Spanish cause. In fact, westerners themselves contacted Madrid's envoy in order to obtain favors that their fellow citizens in the East did not appear willing to grant them.

In April 1787 negotiations between Jay and Gardoqui remained at a standstill, but western pioneers were afraid that Jay was ready to give up the navigation of the Mississippi once and for all. James Wilkinson, an audacious and unscrupulous man from Kentucky, chose this moment to head for New Orleans on his own. There he met with the governor, Esteban Miro, and he told Miro that once Kentucky was independent, it would seek Spain's protection. Before leaving New Orleans, Wilkinson swore allegiance to the king of Spain, and he soon began drawing a colonel's salary from the Spanish king.[69] In New York Gardoqui was first contacted in 1786 by James White, another Kentuckian, and then in 1787 by John Brown, a delegate to the Continental Congress whose mission was to seek Kentucky's entry into the Confederation. Brown and Wilkinson were two of the driving forces behind the "Spanish conspiracy," which sought to sever the region from the

American fold.[70] The Gardoqui-Jay negotiations did not even come close to reaching an accord acceptable in western eyes, and instead the outcome was a treaty draft that only exacerbated the westerners' feeling of being abandoned. By 1788 secessionist unrest was at its peak: in what is now eastern Tennessee, John Sevier became the governor of the unrecognized state of Franklin, and Kentucky, whose admission was once again turned down by the Continental Congress, was on the verge of secession.[71]

Fortunately for those who lived in the West, the treaty draft was dropped, and as soon as the new federal institutions were set up, both Kentucky and Vermont were admitted into the Union (1791). The federal government was able to win back erstwhile secessionist leaders from the area through the creation in 1790 of a "Territory south of the Ohio river." Tension abated for a time thanks to other factors as well: Spain started opening up the Mississippi to American river navigation by granting commercial passports to influential Kentuckians and by allowing them to convey their exports in transit through New Orleans for a 15 percent fee in taxes.[72] Former conspirators, such as John Sevier, were assigned to high-ranking posts, and they appeared to develop ties to the American government, which they now supported and vouched for. It is also likely that they felt culturally closer to Americans in the East than to the Spaniards.[73]

In the 1790s there was unbridled land speculation, especially in Georgia, which led some influential frontiersmen to overlook or overstep the federal government's authority, even though the government alone had the power to negotiate with Native Americans and to organize the nation's westward expansion. Although new and more powerful institutions had been created, some citizens still ignored them, just as they had done before with the Confederal Congress. Such was notably the case with Dr. O'Fallon, a representative of the Yazoo Company in South Carolina, who in 1790 sought to settle on land that was claimed by both Georgia and the federal government in an area that was still under Spanish control. O'Fallon was willing to betray his country in order to avail himself of the land in question, and he even considered creating an independent state on the Mississippi for which he sought Spanish aid and support. When Spain turned him down, he threatened to join forces with Great Britain to mount an attack on New Orleans.[74] On March 19, 1791, George Washington countered with a proclamation denouncing O'Fallon's schemes, but that did not prevent O'Fallon, in 1792, from contemplating an expedition to Spanish territory, this time with French aid. Dr. O'Fallon's brother-in-law, George Rogers Clark, went so far as to propose his services to France. This took place before the new French minister plenipotentiary Genêt had left for the United States, and it affected the directions that Genêt received. Although Genêt was recalled and disavowed by the French authorities at the end of 1793, the conspirators kept up their plotting in the Carolinas, Georgia, and Kentucky until May 1794, despite George Washington's proclamation of March 24, 1794, which forbade them from fitting out men for expeditions directed against neighboring countries.[75] Once again the American government had to disavow its citizens' private political activities in order to preserve its credibility.

Moved by the urge to control western land, even the most influential public figures, and those who were closest to the government, conspired with foreign nations. Such was the case with Sen. William Blount. Blount was a member of the Constitutional Convention in Philadelphia in 1787, and in return for his loyalty to the Federalist cause, he was awarded the position of governor of the Southwest in 1790. He was then elected senator of Tennessee when it was admitted into the Union in 1796.[76] When he found out that same year that France wanted to get Louisiana back, he feared that France as a hostile power would close off the navigation of the Mississippi to pioneers and thereby cause the price of land to fall. He decided to prevent such a catastrophic transfer by organizing, with British consent, the attack on the Spanish colonies. He joined forces with Chisholm, a former loyalist who was on friendly terms with the Native Americans; Chisholm then contacted Liston, the British minister in Philadelphia. An outline of this outlandish project was made for the Spanish minister plenipotentiary by General Collot, a French officer who visited the West:

> According to the deposition made by Squire Michel, a resident of Tennessee, it appears:
>
> 1) that 1000 inhabitants of this province have been enlisted by a man named Chisholm, an British agent and resident of Tennessee; these men are supposed to attack the posts in Baton-Rouge, New Gales and the Ecors à Magot, which belong to His Catholic Majesty;
> 2) that Chisholm has done all the surveys of Louisiana and both Floridas and has convinced the Creek and Cherokee nations to turn their arms against the Spanish possessions;
> 3) that Chisholm has obtained a list of 1500 Tories or English loyalists from the Natchez, who have vowed to take up arms on the side of the English as soon as they come to attack lower Louisiana and, from that conquest, to march on Santa Fe.[77]

Collot rightly felt that this plan was implausible because it linked irreconcilable interests (i.e., speculators and Indians, and American speculators and the British), but the fact remained that contacts had been made, and goals had been set, which bore witness to the determination of these men, and their lack of consideration for the American government. The plan was crushed when, in March 1797, a letter from Blount containing instructions fell into the hands of the administration. This occurred when Chisholm was leaving for England in order to obtain official support, as Liston had not been able to give him a definitive answer. William Blount was chased out of the U.S. Senate, but he managed to make it to Tennessee, where his popularity remained intact.[78]

Although the British did in fact drop the project, one wonders what exactly their role was. To judge by Liston's letters, one might think that the British minister plenipotentiary simply let himself be manipulated by a crafty plotter, but that is only a superficial reading.[79] The American minister in London, Rufus King, investigated the case and got the solution to the puzzle straight from the horse's mouth, namely from Chisholm. Chisholm confessed in exchange for a bit of money, which clarified everything: the plan was to mount a military operation involving both western pioneers and British troops, after which Florida and Louisiana would become British colonies, and Great Britain would guarantee navigation of the Mississippi for the western states. The problem was that neither Liston nor Grenville, the British minister of foreign affairs, showed any interest in this project.[80] Although the direct responsibility of the British in this conspiracy cannot be established, one should note that Liston was more embarrassed than annoyed by Chisholm's propositions, and that the British government took Chisholm the adventurer under its wing for six to eight weeks before presenting him with a final refusal. Great Britain was probably not opposed to an attempt that would have allowed it to create division in the United States and to put a stop to the new nation's expansion southwestwards. Indeed, the British were at the same time supposedly contemplating an attack on Louisiana from Canada.[81]

What is striking about these conspiracies is the fact that the plotters got away with almost no punishment. Although often indicted, James Wilkinson was never convicted; he managed to remain in the federal government's confidence even though it was fairly well known that he had ties to Spain.[82] As for William Blount, who showed that he had no qualms about ignoring the American government's authority and setting up his own personal foreign policy, an impeachment procedure was in fact brought against him, but it failed, and the former senator was elected to the state senate of Tennessee in 1798.[83] The federal government's authority seemed ill equipped to deal with the activities of people who flouted the law and yet did not consider themselves real traitors to their country. The government went easy on them and even overlooked their doings, perhaps because it was trying to keep them in its fold, or because it felt that the conspirators' territorial claims, although premature, were in the best interest of the nation as a whole in the long term. In condemning the conspiracy while at the same time trying to accommodate the conspirators (through Pinckney's Treaty and Jay's Treaty), was the government truly overwhelmed or was it not instead using the expansionist threat contained in the plotters' illegal activities to obtain more favorable treaties? This question would be raised again in 1805 when Jefferson, the leader of a much more powerful and stable country, seemed just as reluctant to counter the activities of his enemy Aaron Burr, who in turn proved willing to appropriate Spanish territory on his own initiative. There was thus a subtle interplay between expansionism on the part of citizens and expansionism on the part of the government, and in this one can discern the foundations of an original expansionism, peculiar to the United States, where the government preferred to follow the people's expansionist will rather than anticipate it. At any rate, during this decade the ruling elite accomplished a great feat in managing to keep and anchor in the Union a regionalist population with questionable national feeling.

The writers of the Constitution wanted a strong central government, one that could assert its sovereignty on the territory that was attributed to it in the international treaties of 1783, so that the United States could fend off attacks from abroad as a unified nation. From 1790 to 1800 the new government fought on all fronts, asserting its authority and sovereignty on its neighbors, Native Americans, the states, and its citizens. All told, the successes (e.g., Jay's Treaty, Pinckney's Treaty, and the Battle of Fallen Timbers) outnumbered the failures, but the failures (e.g., Saint-Clair's defeat) were tremendous and the problems could come back again. The federal government managed to enforce its sovereignty as well as its authority over the territory that the treaties of 1783 had attributed to it; union could thus be achieved around a single territory. The national territory had been won through a hard-fought struggle with the various neighboring powers as well as with the uncontrolled expansionist tendencies of groups of citizens in the West, and it was therefore the best symbol of true national sovereignty. Nevertheless, this process of building the nation through national territory was threatened, in the nation's fiber, by profound political discontent.

CHAPTER 2

From Factions to Political Parties: The Rise of Partisan Divisions over Foreign Policy Problems, 1789–1793

Few of the *Federalist Papers* were devoted to foreign policy, but the "nationalists" of the Philadelphia Convention, according to Frederick W. Marks III, nevertheless cleverly used this topic as a unifying theme, one that would allow them to rally a majority of delegates. In Marks's view, the delegates, who were divided over economic and regional questions, were able to forego their differences for a common cause, namely, how the United States could assert itself effectively as an independent nation and commercial power in relation to European countries.[1] When one examines the history of the early republic's political life, however, it seems that, from 1789 on, foreign policy had the opposite effect on the construction of the American nation: it appears to have gone from being a unifying force to a very powerful factor of division. This could be seen as surprising: in the eighteenth century, weren't foreign policy problems restricted to discussion among experts, negotiations between professional diplomats, and, at most, parliamentary debates? Such a view overlooks the fact that 1789, which was the year the Constitution took effect, also marked the beginning of the French Revolution, and 1792 was the year the revolutionary wars began. In this light, the interest that the American public lent to foreign policy events is understandable.

As a revolutionary nation itself, the early American republic, moreover, could not help being especially fascinated by a revolution that shared the same revolutionary spirit. Nonetheless, far from being united in celebration of French revolutionary events, Americans (and first and foremost, the political elite) found in it a point of long-lasting contention. This was accompanied by the reincarnation of an institution that had hitherto existed under the pejorative label of factions: the party system. This paradoxical phenomenon appears to indicate that the political perspective that had dominated American debates up until the writing of the Constitution—that is, classical republicanism—was gradually being displaced by a modern perspective, one emphasizing the democratic content of the American Revolution.

During the War of Independence, the American revolutionary leaders had to worry not only about establishing a republican regime in the United States, but also about making the republican spirit dominant in the society at large. The theory of republicanism, which was inherited from classical thought, had been rediscovered during the British Commonwealth by James Harrington and was used as the principal source of inspiration by British opposition theoreticians and pamphleteers after the Restoration. This theory not only advocated the abolition of the monarchy and the aristocracy; it also emphasized each citizen's civic virtue, which was supposed to make the fulfillment of the common good possible.[2] The war years, however, and then the period of the Articles of Confederation, engendered real disenchantment among many of the political leaders of the Revolution. The republic, where each person was only supposed to care about the common good, became the battleground of interest groups. The legislative assemblies of the states, which were dominated by whatever group was in control at the moment, voted in laws that had the obvious goal of favoring the group in power and that would of course only last until a new "faction" took over. Civic virtue and the common good: these two concepts did not last long; as many revolutionaries feared when rejecting England, corruption had indeed emigrated to America.[3] No matter what their region and interests were, the intellectuals of the Revolution sought therefore to save the republican ideal by overhauling the institutions; this is what James Madison showed in the famous *Federalist* paper no. 10. In this pamphlet Madison echoed those who were disenchanted with the Revolution: "Complaints are everywhere heard from our most considerate and virtuous citizens, equally the friends of public and private faith, and of public and personal liberty, that our governments are too unstable, that the public good is disregarded in the conflicts of rival parties, and that measures are too often decided, not according to the rules of justice and the rights of the minor party, but by the superior force of an interested and overbearing majority."[4] By "party" Madison meant "faction," which for him was an interest group. These "factions," which were based solely on interest, were thus not parties in the modern sense, that is, they were not organized and structured parties, but they were nonetheless effective. Since they could not be curbed without depriving the citizens of their freedom, it was necessary, in Madison's view, simply to "control" their "effects" in order to "secure the public good and private rights against the danger of such a faction, and at the same time to preserve the spirit and the form of popular government."[5] In order to achieve such control of factions, it was not enough for the republic to be small and the citizens' interests to be similar, as Montesquieu and later Rousseau had thought. The small size of a republic did not guarantee that the common good would be sought out more widely; Madison in fact claimed the contrary: "Extend the sphere and you take in a greater variety of parties and interests; you make it less probable that a majority of the whole will have a common motive to invade the rights of other citizens."[6]

Faced with the tyranny of the majority in the state legislatures, the "nationalists" reacted by allowing the different selfish interests to balance themselves out in the various levels of representation that were provided for in the new constitution. Indeed, despite appearances, the Constitution was not inspired by the British theory of mixed government and the balance of social orders but was, rather, a true innovation in that it relied solely on popular sovereignty and representative democracy.[7] Thus, the federal government, protected as it was by the size of the republic and the nature of the Constitution, supposedly could not fall prey to factions, which, it would seem, could only develop in the states. In *The Federalist* no. 10, James Madison expressed his certainty in this regard: "The influence of factious leaders may kindle a flame within the particular States, but will be unable to spread a general conflagration through the other States."[8] If the factions were unable to develop beyond the state level, the citizens of the states, that is, the nation, were supposed to be united through the Constitution. Nevertheless, starting with George Washington's first presidency, national union degenerated into national dissension, and it was precisely over topics of national interest, that is, topics of foreign policy, that oppositions arose.

The scenario that Madison envisaged in *The Federalist* no. 10 predicted that once the political sphere assumed national proportions, local opposition groups would lose their impact on national political life. An unforeseen consequence, however, was that new topics of discord emerged.[9] Foreign policy was one of the great common interests that Madison believed could not cause dissent, but in fact, from 1789 to 1793, it was the domain that polarized and even exacerbated the nation's internal opposition the most. Just where the union was supposed to be cemented, disunion was born. This process did not simply result from the new institutions that the Constitution introduced, nor from the struggles for influence among rival politicians. Rather, it reflected real ideological struggles over the very meaning of the American Revolution and of the new nation.

The Rise of Conflicts in Congress and the Executive Branch

Customs and Tonnage Duties; the Nootka Sound Affair

When George Washington came to power, he wanted to limit the emergence of factions and the opposition between geographical sections as much as possible, in keeping with the "nationalist" spirit. For this reason he drew up a cabinet of men from different regions. Thomas Jefferson, the secretary of state, and Edmund Randolph, the attorney general, were Virginians, as was the president himself, whereas the other cabinet members (i.e., Henry Knox, the secretary of war, and Alexander Hamilton, the secretary of the treasury) came from the state of New York, a middle state. The vice president, John Adams, was from Massachusetts and thus represented New England. At the highest level then, no region dominated the others. Moreover, the necessary conditions for smooth coordination between the executive branch and the legislative branch appeared to be met since James Madison, who was both a friend of Jefferson's and coeditor of the *Federalist Papers* along with Alexander Hamilton and John Jay, presided over the House of Representatives.[10] It therefore seemed equally impossible that any one of the branches of government would be monopolized by a group that was opposed to the other groups. Nevertheless, from the very first Congress, rifts appeared between the supporters of Hamilton's financial program and its opponents. Foreign policy considerations were soon added to these disputes over domestic economic policy, and bit by bit foreign policy issues came to dominate the debate.[11] This phenomenon is especially apparent in the discussions in the House of Representatives over the bills concerning customs and tonnage duties.

Insofar as most of the manufactured goods that were consumed by Americans were imported, customs and tonnage duties seemed the most likely candidates for producing sufficient revenue for the federal government. This economic calculation had significant consequences for the early republic's foreign policy. Indeed, in view of the fact that Great Britain had remained the chief supplier of the United States after the Revolution, healthy finances thenceforth called for good relations with the former home country. As Joseph Charles has explained, friendly relations with England had become essential for the federal government's credit since England was the major trading partner of the United States, and since a high level of imports was needed by the Treasury.[12] Favoring Great Britain, however, made it seem that seven years of war were being swept under the carpet and that Great Britain's refusal to negotiate a commercial treaty with John Adams during the period of the Articles of Confederation was being forgotten.[13] Furthermore, it seemed that the aid given by France was being overlooked. In April 1789 James Madison therefore presented in the House of Representatives a bill on customs duties in which he proposed establishing a policy of discrimination against Great Britain, and favoring countries such as France that had concluded a commercial treaty with the United States. Alexander Hamilton, who was not yet secretary of the treasury (only in August 1789 did he take office), fought against such a plan.[14] James Madison's proposals, which were adopted by the House of Representatives, had their discriminatory clause removed by the Senate. Members of Congress had clashed over the choice of which country they preferred the United States to trade with: this was the first time that foreign policy—the preference for a particular country—was the decisive factor in a domestic policy debate. But one could not yet say that these oppositions reflected serious ideological differences.

In the course of the year 1790, differences of opinion over foreign policy came to undermine the very unity of the cabinet, which George Washington had wanted to make a symbol of the unity of the entire nation. The conflict pitted Thomas Jefferson against Alexander Hamilton. Their first direct confrontation occurred over the Nootka Sound affair, which opposed Great Britain and Spain with regard to a site on the island of Vancouver used for wintering and trade with local Indians, and known as Nootka Sound. This site was claimed by both countries (see chapter 7). On August 27, George Washington, who was concerned about the tense situation between Spain and Great Britain, conferred with his cabinet on the issue of American neutrality. If the British asked to cross the western part of the United States in order to attack Spanish posts from Detroit, how should the United States respond? The president feared the worst from such an expedition.[15] Thomas Jefferson gave his answer the very next day, on August 28. For Jefferson, there was a middle ground between refusing and accepting: avoid responding. He knew, as did Washington, that this would most likely not deter Lord Dorchester from moving forward. But then, the secretary of state maintained, the United States would be in a strong position for negotiating: "They will proceed notwithstanding, but to do this under our silence, will admit of palliation, and produce apologies."[16]

This response, which emphasized above all the preservation of American neutrality, contrasted with Alexander Hamilton's view. For the secretary of the treasury, it would be better to cultivate British friendship by giving in to their request, even if it meant clashing with Spain.[17] Two different conceptions of U.S. foreign relations were thus emerging within the cabinet: on the one hand, Alexander Hamilton stressed friendly relations with Great Britain; on the other hand, Thomas Jefferson insisted that American neutrality be preserved. The cabinet was divided, or at least division was setting in, for the lines were not yet definitively laid out for each member. John Jay and John Adams had answered in the negative, whereas Henry Knox did not express a clear opinion.[18] For the time being, only Alexander Hamilton systematically sided with the British. Until then, his positions reflected an economic choice rather than an ideological stance, but the question nonetheless arises whether Hamilton was not overly concerned with pleasing Great Britain. Did the young nation, which had just won its independence, need to put all its effort in that direction? Did the separation from the mother country only reflect a desire for independence, or was there an opposition between a pure, republican, and revolutionary America and a corrupt, tyrannical, and monarchical Great Britain? Hamilton's political activity implicitly contained a new interpretation of the American Revolution, one that erased its democratic and revolutionary content.

Two-Headed Foreign Policy

The rivalry between Jefferson and Hamilton in matters of foreign policy became obvious at this point, although the secretary of the treasury had in fact already been carrying out a foreign policy that was different from that of the president and the secretary of state. In 1789, as soon as he became secretary of the treasury, Hamilton took it upon himself to shape the orientation of the foreign policy of the United States by undermining Jefferson's and Washington's initiatives; he was able to do this thanks to his privileged relationship with Colonel Beckwith. During his meetings with the British agent, Hamilton gave out parallel information, which he guaranteed to be more official than the official information itself.[19]

Hamilton's goal was to improve Anglo-American relations gradually, and to this end, he tried in 1790 to control the discussions that Gouverneur Morris had entered into with the British government in London. Before Jefferson became head of the State Department in charge of foreign affairs, George Washington had indeed instructed Morris to use his stay in Europe to try to reopen the negotiations concerning the unresolved points of the Anglo-American treaty of September 3, 1783.[20] At first Hamilton was very much in favor of this endeavor, since it sought to strengthen the links between Great Britain and the United States, but he was afraid of the tone that the highly nationalistic Gouverneur Morris might assume. In his conversations with Beckwith in October 1789, Hamilton assured the British agent that the American administration was well disposed to Great Britain, but he nevertheless encouraged the British to be conciliatory.[21] For this reason, when Gouverneur Morris arrived in London, he found himself in a position not of negotiating, but of asking.[22] To make matters worse, Hamilton took away Morris's other weapons for negotiation: he explained to Beckwith in April 1790 that the American military preparations in the Northwest were directed solely against the Indians and not against the British troops.[23] These remarks were all the more detrimental to Morris's efforts since, as Jefferson would soon foresee, the Nootka Sound crisis forced the British to reconsider their attitude toward the United States and to adopt a more moderate tone in their dealings with them. At the very moment when the British were softening their discourse toward Washington's envoy so as not to offend the sensibilities of a country whose support they might need in case of conflict with Spain, they received assurances from Beckwith and Dorchester concerning the pro-British neutrality of the United States. It was thus not in their best interest to give up anything, and their position was thus strengthened. For the most part, then, the failure of Gouverneur Morris's mission in the spring of 1790 can be blamed on Hamilton's unofficial diplomacy, which undermined Morris's bargaining power.

The secretary of the treasury next turned to Thomas Jefferson's decision to send secret memoranda to Great Britain and Spain. As we saw in the preceding chapter, the tension between Spain and Great Britain in the spring of 1790 gave Jefferson hope. For the secretary of state, the situation was a godsend, and he wanted to make the most of it. In exchange for settling the points of contention between each of the two countries and the United States, Jefferson sent them both assurances of American neutrality in case war actually broke out. This diplomatic bluff could only succeed, however, if hostilities began: Jefferson thus wrote dispatches giving Carmichael and Short instructions on how to act in case of war, and he entrusted them to David Humphreys, who was to assume the position of chargé d'affaires in Portugal, and whose job it was to protect these letters and to take them to their destination.[24]

Jefferson's undertaking ran counter to Hamilton's ideas: instead of courting Great Britain in order to win its favor, as the secretary of the treasury was doing through Beckwith's intermediary, the secretary of state sought to make the most of the great power's momentary weakness in order to gain advantages. He expected nothing from the former parent country and sought to act independently, as befitted the secretary of state of a young nation in the face of a great country that had long been considered to be the oppressor. This was the reason why Hamilton defused Jefferson's explosive project as soon as he could. He first waited for the official representatives of American diplomacy (Jefferson and Washington) to leave Philadelphia, and then on August 31, 1790, he spoke to David Humphreys about the goal of his mission. Hamilton asked Humphreys to make sure, once he was in England, that Great Britain was favorably disposed toward the United States.[25] He knew that Humphreys would thereby reveal the official nature of his questions and consequently of his mission, and this turned out to be the case.[26] Even if the crisis between the United States and Great Britain had not been resolved soon thereafter, Humphreys's mission could only have failed, for once the secret of his operation had been disclosed, the force of Jefferson's strategy was broken.

The two-headed foreign policy of the cabinet reflected the fundamental difference of opinion between Jefferson and Hamilton. In 1789 and 1790 the activity of the secretary of the treasury remained mostly secret, but the opposition between the two men came out in the open during the congressional debates from December 1790 to 1791. During this last session of the first Congress, the conflict over foreign policy often appeared to turn to the advantage of the secretary of state, who was supported by the president. But Hamilton's influence over the Senate majority was to prove decisive.

Thomas Jefferson's Reports

Hostilities began with the president's annual message to Congress (December 8, 1790).[27] In a note dating from November 29, which was intended as preparation for the president's message, Jefferson expressed his concern over foreign trade and American fishermen, and he recommended that legislative measures be taken to protect them.[28] This text was retained in the president's message, and it allowed James Madison to reintroduce in the House of Representatives the issue of American trade protection. In the face of opposition from Hamilton's supporters, Madison demanded that measures be taken regarding trade and navigation. A committee set about drafting a bill modeled after the British Navigation Acts, which had been efficiently protecting the British merchant marine since the seventeenth century.[29]

Thomas Jefferson added to this campaign by submitting three reports (on December 28, a report concerning trade in the Mediterranean and a report on the prisoners in Algeria; on February 1, 1791, a report on cod and whale fishing).[30] The last report was an outright indictment of the British: Jefferson had no trouble showing that British sailors and fishermen were the chief rivals of Americans, and, in particular, that the British had a closed market, whereas the French market was much more open. Jefferson scored one last point on February 14, 1791, the day when the president's message was passed on to Congress. The message had been put together by George Washington and his secretary of state, and it dealt with the outcome of Gouverneur Morris's mission in London.[31] The tone and content of the message were very clear: the friendly overtures made by the new republic had been haughtily rejected by powerful England. More than the preceding reports, this message had a powerful effect on members of Congress, who had not reacted strongly to the previous reports. Less than a week later (on February 21, 1791), James Madison's navigation bill was approved by the committee in charge, which had hitherto only halfheartedly dealt with the issue.[32]

Nevertheless, after January 20, 1791, Hamilton and Beckwith gradually became less worried and more optimistic. It seemed that the British government was finally convinced that they should not neglect the United States and was on the verge of sending a minister to Philadelphia, thereby reaching out to the United States.[33] Jefferson's satisfaction was thus short-lived: the navigation bill was scrapped at the end of the session when it was announced that George Hammond had been nominated as the first British minister plenipotentiary in the United States. Still, this nomination meant that Jefferson's strategy had been a success of sorts, since only the fear of trade reprisals had driven the British to make a decision. The fact remained, however, that the bill no longer existed, and by way of compensation, Jefferson was asked to present a report to Congress on the nature and extent of privileges and restrictions of U.S. foreign trade.[34]

Perhaps more seriously, the pro-British stance that marked all of Alexander Hamilton's actions—his secret meetings with George Beckwith, his opposition to discriminating or reciprocal legislation, and his open conflict with Thomas Jefferson whenever the issue of making demands on Great Britain came up—began to bear fruit as well as to irrevocably affect the relations of the United

States with other countries. Indeed, France was indignant about being treated like Great Britain. Not only had France signed a trade treaty with the United States, but in 1787 it had granted specific privileges to the new republic without asking for anything in return.[35] In December 1790 Louis-Guillaume Otto, the French chargé d'affaires in the United States, received an order from the minister of foreign affairs, Montmorin, to make an official protest to the American government. Jefferson passed on the French demands for reciprocity to Hamilton, who of course found a way to reject them even though the French were putting on more pressure and were threatening to retaliate at the beginning of January 1791. The secretary of state then submitted a report on French protests to George Washington, and on January 17, 1791, he presented it to the Senate, which was composed mostly of Hamilton supporters, and was therefore hostile.[36] While considering all possible American reactions (favorable to France or not), this report suggested that only a friendly gesture toward France could head off the prospect of retaliation. This time, however, George Washington's support and personal influence had no effect. The committee that dealt with the report in the Senate was close to Hamilton and did not follow the secretary of state's proposal.[37]

At the end of the last session of the first Congress, the cabinet's division over foreign policy meant that Jefferson's projects were systematically defeated in the Senate. Although the secretary of state was the official source of the new republic's foreign policy, and although he was almost always supported by the president, in the Senate he ran up against a majority that was favorable to Alexander Hamilton. Within the cabinet, there was only a semblance of unity, and what unity there was could now be attributed entirely to George Washington's personality; as Jefferson noted with concern: "The prudence of the President is an anchor of safety to us."[38] The passion that everyone showed in the beginning for building the new nation gave way to a bitter weariness on the part of the secretary of state: "I long for pursuits of this kind [natural history] instead of the detestable ones in which I am now labouring without pleasure to myself, or profit to others."[39]

It was not the feigned unity that really defined American political life at this time, but rather the highly visible divisions that separated Congress into two camps: those who supported Hamilton (the Senate majority) and those who supported Madison (the House majority). The political consensus on the national level that Madison had dreamed of in the *Federalist Papers* and that Washington had wanted in his cabinet was now just a thing of the past. Although in the composition of the Constitution every effort had been made to maintain a balance between the different interest groups and to prevent political parties from emerging, the debates of the first Congress crystallized the formation of two groups, one of which was consistently favorable to Hamilton's ideas and the other unfavorable; these would soon be called "Federalists" and

"Republicans," respectively. Abandoning the "nationalist" consensus, the ruling elite became divided and then formed distinct camps in the context of a new institution: the two-party system.

From its inception, the chief characteristic of this system was, paradoxically, its national dimension. Indeed, what originally brought about the division between the two parties, and what fueled it thereafter, was disagreement over foreign policy decisions more than economic differences or regional oppositions. In 1927 Charles Beard described the political opposition between Federalists and Republicans as a reflection of the economic and regional conflict between capitalists (concentrated in the North) and agrarians (led by the landed aristocracy of the South).[40] The historian John R. Nelson Jr. has refuted this hypothesis by drawing upon studies of the two parties at the local level and using an analysis of the social background of the various members of Congress. As it turns out, some big merchants from northern and central states were indeed members of the Republican Party (e.g., James Nicholson of New York and Stephen Girard of Philadelphia), whereas farmers from Maryland and Delaware supported the Federalist Party. In New York State, "mechanics" (workers and craftsmen) were the chief supporters of the Republican Party while farmers were split between the two parties. Whether at the grassroots level or among those elected to Congress, the same socioeconomic groups were represented in each party, with one small exception: more merchants than planters supported the Federalist Party.[41] This leads one to think that the opposition that arose in Congress and in the executive branch was ideological in nature and had to do more with differing conceptions of the new nation's identity than with economic or regional differences.

The French Revolution as Bone of Contention between the Parties

In 1791 the meaning of the rift that divided Congress and the executive branch slowly came to light: while it was clear that Hamilton was on the side of cooperating with Great Britain, Jefferson little by little emerged as the upholder of French-American amity. The contrast between the two countries came to symbolize the opposition between two conceptions of the young nation. For Jefferson the United States was first and foremost the heir to the Revolution of 1776 and the sister of the French Revolution; for Hamilton the United States was the daughter—formerly rebellious but now faithful—of aristocratic Great Britain. In moving closer to Great Britain, Hamilton was not only clashing with Thomas Jefferson, he was also running counter to the people's enthusiasm, which had warmly greeted the French Revolution.

Grassroots Enthusiasm versus Mistrust on the Part of Certain Political Leaders

From the very beginning, the entire nation was enthusiastic about the French Revolution.[42] Newspapers all over the United States hailed the advent of the French Revolution as the victory of a freedom and liberation movement that had its roots in America. This was symbolized in the father-son type of relationship that existed between George Washington and Lafayette. On October 14, 1789, the *Pennsylvania Gazette* claimed that the political emancipation of French citizens must be credited to the Marquis de Lafayette, rather than to any other "patriotic" figure. The *Gazette* maintained that Lafayette learned everything about the rights of the governed versus the rulers from his correspondence with George Washington.[43]

Despite assertions to the contrary on the part of the editors of *The Federalist,* Americans had been afraid that republics might be more fragile than monarchies, and therefore they viewed the French Revolution as an event that not only benefited the French, but themselves as well. Indeed, when France actually became a republic, they welcomed the birth of a regime that was similar to theirs and that was prepared to fight against all the European monarchies together.[44] In the French political upheavals they saw the seeds of a fundamental transformation of U.S.–European relations. The United States was no longer alone, for they had a "sister republic" on the other side of the Atlantic. The precarious isolation that had characterized America up until then thus came to an end.

The French Revolution was not only proof of the durability of the American experience; it also confirmed its validity: for Americans, the French experience legitimized their own revolution. As David Brion Davis has explained, the fact that republican principles could be exported justified the illegal—some called it treacherous—cause that the Declaration of Independence had defended.[45] In his preface to *The Rights of Man,* which was dedicated to George Washington, Thomas Paine glorified this feeling of solidarity and continuity: "I present you a small treatise in defense of those principles of freedom which your exemplary virtue has so eminently contributed to establish. That the rights of man may become as universal as your benevolence can wish, and that you may enjoy the happiness of seeing the New World regenerate the Old."[46] The fate of the French Revolution was seen as a test measuring the success of American revolutionary principles: if they spread in Europe, America would thereby be justified and rewarded. According to Philippe Raynaud, for Paine the French Revolution confirmed the interpretation he had given of the American Revolution in *Common Sense,* namely that the British constitution was not essential to the defense of freedom, but popular sovereignty was.[47]

Thomas Jefferson had already been paying close attention to the events in France at the end of his stay in Paris, and he shared the enthusiasm of the American people when he heard about the proclamation of the republic in France. In a letter to John Francis Mercer dated December 19, 1792, he wrote: "[T]he republicans are rejoicing and taking to themselves the name of Jacobins which two months ago was affixed on them by way of stigma."[48] Supporters of Jefferson and Madison were more and more referred to as Republicans: they advocated a republic that, through its identification with the French Revolution, asserted its revolutionary and democratic character. For Jefferson, the fate of both the French and American nations was inextricably linked in a common fight for republicanism and freedom. In expressing his enthusiasm in a letter to Gouverneur Morris, who was at that time the American minister plenipotentiary in Paris, Jefferson went so far as to propose an exchange of citizenship between the two countries: "Indeed we wish to omit no opportunity of convincing them how cordially we desire the closest union with them. Mutual good offices, mutual affection and similar principles of government seem to have destined the two people for the most intimate communion, and even for a complete exchange of citizenship among the individuals composing them."[49] Jefferson's optimism was nevertheless tempered by the lukewarm revolutionary attitude, if not altogether aristocratic prejudice, that he sensed on the part of a number of other American leaders. Thomas Paine's work *The Rights of Man,* which was written in response to Edmund Burke's *Reflexions on the French Revolution,* was published in the United States in May 1791, with a preface by Thomas Jefferson. The remarks made by the secretary of state included a very clear attack on Americans who opposed the French Revolution. As he subsequently explained to George Washington: "I added that I was glad to find it reprinted, that something would at length be publicly said against the political heresies which had lately sprung up among us, that I did not doubt our citizens would rally again round the standard of common sense."[50] In later years, Jefferson would always deny that he knew his text was going to be published. At the time, he apologized to the vice president for its publication, saying that he had not wanted to hurt him.[51] Nevertheless, in expressing in the preface his delight at the prospect of the controversy that Paine's book was sure to stir up in America, he made it clear that he hoped *The Rights of Man* would incite the opponents of John Adams's pro-British ideas to make a counterattack. After all, the "heresies" that Jefferson spoke about did in fact refer to the "Discourses on Davila," thirty-one essays by John Adams that had appeared in John Fenno's *Gazette of the United States,* which was a Federalist paper. They were written in reaction to the Marquis de Condorcet's *Four Letters from a New Haven Bourgeois.* In them, Adams defended the notion that there could be no freedom without a "scientifically determined" constitutional balance between passions and interests, that is, without a mixed constitution where "the few" and "the many" would be represented by different houses. He concluded by saying that liberty had all but vanished from the surface of the earth, with the exception of one island and North America.[52]

In thus linking the political systems of America and England, Adams seemed to be putting them in the same category and implying that they shared the same political philosophy. For Jefferson, Adams's ideas were a dangerous hodgepodge that tended to bring together the forms of the U.S. government and those of the British Constitution.[53] Adams's misinterpretation lay in his likening American institutions to British institutions based on the common denominator of a balance of power. In Jefferson's view, Adams was not alone in making this error, for other high-ranking figures also sought to undermine the genuine foundations of the American republic by substituting England's hybrid regime ("a half-way house"), that is, neither monarchic nor republican, for a regime founded on the sovereignty of the people.[54]

Adams and Hamilton were not the only American leaders to be wary of the path that events in France were taking from 1791 on. The king's imprisonment and the September massacres sowed the seeds of doubt in the minds of those who called themselves republicans but who feared the excesses of democracy. Was France not slipping into anarchy or moving toward tyranny of the majority?[55] In a letter to Lafayette on June 10, 1792, George Washington insisted that, in avoiding despotism, it was important that license not take the place of freedom, nor confusion that of order.[56] The cabinet members who were close to Hamilton, namely John Jay and Henry Knox, shared his concern over the issue. After Lafayette fled to Austria (August 1792), Washington became even more skeptical about the French Revolution, an attitude that was reinforced by the critical dispatches that Gouverneur Morris sent him from Paris. On February 14, 1793, Morris, who was minister plenipotentiary in Paris, wrote to Washington: "You will find that events have blackened more and more in this country. Her present prospects are dreadful. It is not so much, perhaps, the external force; great as that may be, for there are always means of defence in so vast a nation. The exhausted state of resources might also be borne with, if not remedied; but the disorganized state of the government seems irremediable. The venality is such that if there be no traitor, it is because the enemy has no common-sense."[57]

The Conflict Takes on a National Dimension: The Beginnings of a Partisan Press and Debates over Official Relations with France

As we have seen, there was an ideological confrontation between those who supported the French Revolution, considering it to be the heir to American freedom, and those who refused to recognize the American political heritage in the direction that French politics were taking. With the conflict between

John Adams and Thomas Jefferson, this ideological confrontation was to exceed the limited context of Congress and the meetings of the executive committee members. The vice president took Jefferson's criticism as an unpardonable offense. In June 1791 the pamphleteer Publicola (the author was none other than John Quincy Adams, John Adams's own son) came to the defense of the vice president in the *Boston Columbian Centinel.* But he was not the first to launch a public debate. Already on May 8, 1791, Jefferson had written: "Paine's answer to Burke's pamphlet begins to produce some squibs in the public papers. In Fenno's paper they are Burkites, in the others, Painites."[58] Set off by the reactions to Paine's pamphlet and Jefferson's preface, pamphlet war was declared. This war would rage on in the press until 1800. The division even took hold of the dailies and gave rise to a partisan press, that is, papers specializing in political commentary. This new kind of press set out to rally the interest of the American public, either in support of the ideas put forth by Jefferson and his friends, or those put forth by Hamilton and his friends. The French Revolution, which was supposed to bring all Americans together in celebration of the values they had fought for, became a symbol that they had to take a stand on. During the summer of 1791, Thomas Jefferson and James Madison managed to convince the poet Philippe Fréneau to start a Republican daily newspaper in Philadelphia, a newspaper that was intended to oppose John Fenno's *Gazette of the United States.* The first issue of the *National Gazette* came out on October 31, 1791.

Until the beginning of 1793, the debate that divided supporters and critics of the French Revolution remained strictly within the realm of professional politics and did not have an influence on the administration's management of foreign affairs. In April, however, when Jefferson learned that Great Britain was at war with France, the situation became very touchy for the new republic's administration. Would it have to make a choice between its best trading partner and greatest source of revenue, that is, Great Britain, and its only real ally, that is, France—in other words, between the former colonial power and the "sister republic"? An answer to this question would be all the more difficult for Washington's cabinet members to find since their individual preferences for one country or the other were now known.

Without clearly taking sides, George Washington nevertheless opened the debate by submitting to his cabinet members a series of questions that dealt with U.S. foreign relations.[59] The first had to do with the advisability of proclaiming neutrality. All the cabinet members were in favor of neutrality, but they certainly did not all agree on what neutrality meant. As was the case during the Nootka Sound affair, Jefferson wanted active neutrality, which would allow the United States to play upon European rivalries in order to reap the greatest benefits. For this purpose, the United States needed to play hard to get, maintain its power of negotiation, and not reveal its intentions. But Hamilton opposed this view of neutrality. He wanted to reassure his British friends formally about the attitude that the United States would adopt during the hostilities, considering that the United States was allied to France and might therefore contribute to the French war effort. In this second outright clash with Jefferson over foreign relations, it was Hamilton who emerged victorious. By April 19, 1793—the questions had been put forth on the eighteenth—the decision was taken to issue a proclamation of neutrality. The proclamation itself was dated April 22.[60]

Another issue was resolved at the April 19 session: Edmond-Charles Genêt, who was the new French minister plenipotentiary, was to be received officially. With regard to this issue, it was Jefferson who won. In December 1792 he had shown that the French republic was a regime that the United States ought to recognize, "considering the Convention, or the government they shall have established as the lawful representatives of the Nation and authorized to act for them."[61] Siding with Jefferson, the American administration received Genêt and officially recognized the French republic as the only legitimate government in France, at a time when all of Europe joined together against the French republic in order to reinstate the ancien régime. Alexander Hamilton had wanted things to go differently,[62] but he did not manage to convince George Washington. He did not admit defeat, however, and a few days later he attempted to counteract the administration's decision, and thereby undermine Franco-American friendship, through lengthy argumentation in response to another question from the president (namely, were the treaties concluded with France in 1778 still valid?). In this text, Hamilton did not go so far as to say that the treaties concluded with France were no longer valid, but he maintained that they should be suspended. Indeed, they had been concluded between the United States and King Louis XVI, and not with the republic that had followed. According to Hamilton, the United States needed to wait for a stable regime to be established in France before deciding whether to renew relations with it.[63]

Following the line of reasoning put forth by the Swiss jurist Emer de Vattel, Jefferson countered by developing the principle that he had laid out in a letter to Gouverneur Morris dated December 30, 1792, and he declared that: "Upon the whole I conclude that the treaties are still binding, not withstanding the change of government in France."[64] Although Hamilton did not share the concerns inspired by Vattel's enlightenment philosophy, he knew Vattel's work and was familiar with his opinion on alliances. Paradoxically, Hamilton also used an excerpt from Vattel's work, where it was explained that an alliance between two countries could be broken if there had been a change of government in one of the two countries and "if that change of government made the alliance useless, dangerous or disagreeable" for the other country.[65] Hamilton put forth the danger argument in order to justify suspending the treaties, but Jefferson rebelled: what danger could there be in recognizing the French republic? What would be dangerous, he concluded, would be not to recognize it. That would give France a good reason to go to war with the United States.

What made Hamilton so reluctant to recognize the French republic was the fact that France was at war with Great Britain. He did not see a "sister republic" in the ally of 1778, but rather a great danger: what would happen if Genêt asked for American aid? It would dash in one fell swoop all the hopes for an understanding with Great Britain that Hamilton had been cultivating for the past four years. As Jefferson observed, Hamilton's line of reasoning was more clever than it was consistent. George Washington and the other cabinet members did not follow the secretary of the treasury's lead on this issue: the treaties were maintained.[66]

Even though Jefferson's ideas won out, Hamilton's conservatism and his promonarchy and antidemocracy stance caused the secretary of state to worry about the fate of American democracy. Didn't a refusal to recognize the French republic amount to repudiating the American republic itself? The promonarchy leanings that he also suspected in John Adams and many other Federalists seemed to call into question the very existence of the American nation as both a republic and a democracy. Quarrels over foreign policy thus revealed the political differences between Jefferson's and Madison's supporters, on the one hand, and Hamilton's, on the other. Indeed, Hamilton himself was no less concerned about the consequences on the American nation of Jefferson's pro-French stance.

The secretary of state felt isolated in the cabinet, but he could be happy about one thing: like Jefferson, most Americans saw in the French republic a continuation of the American republic. As an example, consider this Address of the Citizens of Philadelphia:

> We cannot hide our joy at the sight of a nation that, after establishing America's freedom, has finally managed to establish its own with so much grandeur and glory. . . . There is another point of interest, that of liberty and equality, which further contributes to the strength of our affection, and which makes the French cause an interesting one for all republics and endears it to mankind. Rest assured that, as we rightly regard the spread of republican principles as the best means for ensuring that our government of the people will last, our greatest hopes lie with France and the course she takes at this critical moment.[67]

Citizen Genêt

The French minister plenipotentiary Edmond-Charles Genêt received a hero's welcome,[68] and Jefferson openly expressed his enthusiasm for the "revolutionary spirit" that it rekindled in the United States.[69] The popularity of the French Revolution brought about a new awareness throughout the country: not only were festivities planned in Genêt's honor, but people got together in democratic-republican societies, the goal of which was to let all citizens actively take part in political life. The fact that these societies resembled similar societies in France and other places in Europe was no coincidence: their members, like their counterparts in Europe, felt that they were taking part in a freedom movement that transcended national borders and that was in the process of giving birth to a new world order. As historian Eugene Link explained, however, the societies in the United States were also expressions of a distinctly American political tradition: they were the descendants of the Sons of Freedom, that is, societies that were active during the American Revolution.[70] After a decade devoted to strengthening national institutions and fearing their experiment would fail, most Americans finally grasped the revolutionary dimension of their own revolution thanks to the impact of the French Revolution. Indeed, they had been the first to break once and for all with a traditional society, one based on deference, in order to adopt a modern society and political regime.[71] With the success of the French Revolution and the arrival of Citizen Genêt, Americans adopted a "radical" interpretation of the American Revolution as a revolution of the people. As a result, the secretary of state disapproved of the reserved manner in which the president and the other cabinet members received the French minister, who arrived in Charleston in April 1793. This reserve revealed an unfortunate rift between most American leaders and public opinion.[72] Taking their cue from Alexander Hamilton, those in power distanced themselves from what was the true source of their mandate in Thomas Jefferson's eyes: the will of the people.[73] With Genêt's arrival, Jefferson saw his fears confirmed, namely, a powerful executive branch in open opposition to the American people, that is, to the source of its constituency. For the secretary of state, it was only thanks to the president's moderating influence that the executive branch was not entirely cut off from the rest of the nation.[74]

Genêt's intentions were, however, entirely peaceful, to the point that they could only reconcile the people and their leaders, as Jefferson explained to Madison when telling him about his first meeting with Genêt:

> It is impossible for anything to be more affectionate, more magnanimous than the purport of his mission. "We know that under the present circumstances we have a right to call upon you for the guarantee of our islands. But we do not desire it. We wish you to do nothing but what is for your own good, and we will do all in our power to promote it. Cherish your own peace and prosperity. You have expressed a willingness to enter into a more liberal treaty of commerce with us; I bring full powers (and he produced them) to form such a treaty, and a preliminary decree of the National Convention to lay open our country and its colonies for every purpose of utility, without your participating [in] the burthens of maintaining and defending them. We see in you

> the only person on earth who can love us sincerely and merit to be so loved."
> In short he offers everything and asks nothing.[75]

Beyond the grandiloquent tone of the professions of friendship that the declaration contained, it was a great relief to all those (such as Jefferson) who were afraid that France would ask the United States to help them protect their possessions in the Caribbean, as provided for in the treaty of 1778, in case of attack by the British.[76] While offering the United States significant trade advantages, the declaration left American neutrality intact.

Although Genêt's words delighted the secretary of state, his actions clearly constituted a real danger for the neutrality of the United States. In April Jefferson had reviewed the risks that maintaining the alliance entailed—his goal being to show that there were no risks—and he had been careful to mention Article XXII of the Treaty of Amity and Commerce between France and the United States (1778): "Is the danger to be apprehended from the 22d Article of our treaty of commerce, which prohibits the enemies of France from fitting out privateers in our ports, or selling their prizes here?" For Jefferson the situation was clear: "But we are free to refuse the same thing to France, there being no stipulation to the contrary, and we ought to refuse it on principles of fair neutrality."[77]

Edmond-Charles Genêt, however, interpreted Article XXII in a very different way from Jefferson. When he arrived in Charleston on April 8, 1793, he received a warm welcome from South Carolina leaders, and this encouraged him to raise troops in the West in order to attack Spanish holdings. This was exactly what western speculators were hoping for: they wanted to chase out the Indians and Spaniards with the help of the French.[78] Genêt then created a prize court so that the ships captured by the frigate that brought him over would be tried and sold. He then began to fit out other captured ships as privateers that would seize British ships off the American coast.[79]

The British minister George Hammond immediately lodged a complaint. If the United States was going to accept such behavior, then American neutrality would be called into question. Jefferson realized that Genêt needed to be called to order, which he proceeded to do on June 5, 1793.[80] Genêt, however, persisted in ignoring Jefferson's warnings and his interpretation of Article XXII.[81] During the month of June, the secretary of state and Genêt corresponded in vain over the captured ships.[82] The situation took a sharp turn for the worse in early July over the *Little Sarah* affair. On July 6, the cabinet members found out that the French prize was being transformed into a privateer and was about to set sail. Genêt was ordered to cease operations, but he refused to do so. Whereas Jefferson suggested they wait and see, Hamilton and Henry Knox wanted to fire at the ship if it actually set sail, which would amount to war with France.[83]

Although the threats were not carried out, Genêt was permanently discredited in the eyes of the whole cabinet, including Jefferson. The policy of "fair neutrality," which Jefferson had managed to sustain until then in opposition to Hamilton's "English neutrality," was likewise discredited.[84] In fact, it was in order to prevent his "party" from collapsing that Jefferson willingly supported the decision to request Genêt's recall: "We have decided unanimously to require the recall of Genet. He will sink the republican interest if we do not abandon him" (Jefferson was here referring to other Republicans).[85] The secretary of state was speaking here more as a party man than as an ideologue. Genêt had placed Jefferson in a difficult position—both with regard to George Hammond and with regard to the cabinet as a whole—in his insistence on his peculiar interpretation of Article XXII of the Franco-American treaty, as well as through his clashes with the other cabinet members. This had weakened Jefferson politically by diminishing the credibility of "fair neutrality." Overnight the British minister plenipotentiary went from being the accused to the victim, and the pro-British members of the government became the true champions of national independence. Indeed, Genêt, through his acrimonious remarks against George Washington from July on, swung public opinion in favor of the president, whereas it had been supporting Genêt in his capacity as representative of the "sister republic." Jefferson had to disassociate himself publicly from the French minister plenipotentiary in order not to lose support of the "Republican interest," because this "Republican interest," albeit pro-French, was first and foremost American, and it condemned "this interference on the part of a foreigner."[86] George Washington was the icon of the republic and the symbol of a united nation, and he was still so far above the nascent party politics that an attack on him was tantamount to an attack on the new nation. Nevertheless, Jefferson's moderate and strategic attitude did not reflect the feelings of all the militant Republicans. Indeed, the democratic-republican societies preferred ideological rigor over the political gambling that was meant to ensure access to power, and they continued to support Genêt even after he had been dismissed.[87]

Jefferson felt out of place in the administration, which he considered biased, and he resigned from his position at the end of December 1793. Before resigning, however, he had publicly relaunched the debate over the choice of France or England as trading partner. On December 16, the secretary of state submitted to Congress the *Report on the Privileges and Restrictions on the Commerce of the United States in Foreign Countries,* which had been requested of him on February 23, 1791. Like the report on fishing of February 1, 1791, this report made clear that France had good intentions in matters of trade, whereas Great Britain had only bad intentions. Jefferson concluded by requesting that a real navigation system be put in place. This report came at the right moment to feed the disputes in Congress between those who favored maintaining good relations with France and those who favored Great Britain; meanwhile, the international situation was becoming more and more tense.[88]

When the first administration came to power in 1789 under George Washington, everyone believed that the Constitution would guarantee stability and prevent "factions" and "parties" from forming. But by 1791 it was clear at the highest levels of political life that the national consensus was crumbling away. Opposing groups began to form in the cabinet and in Congress, and their antagonistic opinions filled the pages of the nascent partisan press. Initially, however, the American people remained united, and they rediscovered the democratic meaning of their own revolution through their fascination with the first years of the French Revolution. Foreign policy was clearly the catalyst for dissension among the political elite. The crucial choices that Americans had to make during this critical time divided the political leaders into pro-British and pro-French camps. This polarization reflected the emergence of an institutional structure that the Founding Fathers had not foreseen: the two-party system. And within this system an important ideological battle was to be played out, a battle that was to come out in the open after 1793 and inflame the whole nation.

CHAPTER 3

Liberties and the Republic: The Division of the Nation over Foreign Policy Issues

From 1793 to 1800 the party struggles that had so inflamed congressional debates from 1791 on spread to the whole nation by means of a fervid press. At a time when monarchical Europe was joining forces against the French republic, foreign policy was more than ever an ideological battleground: on one side, there were Republicans, who had confidence in the future of a democratic American republic (and were thus close to France), and on the other, there were Federalists, whose main goal was to ensure that the nation's elite continued to prosper (and who were thus close to Great Britain).[1] While the divisions in Congress grew stronger and became institutionalized, the ideological oppositions spread to the whole nation.[2] Three stages punctuated this process of increasing polarization and confrontation: the year 1794, marked by the suppression of the Whiskey Rebellion and the signing of Jay's Treaty; 1796, marked by the excesses of the presidential campaign; and 1798, marked by the passing of the exception laws.

For five years the whole country was up in arms over issues of national interest that should have sealed the nation's unity. The failure to maintain a consensus was, however, offset by restructuring on the national level, even though such restructuring was not altogether clear to those involved. Indeed, far from being simply the reconstruction of an ideology that had been developed in another time and place, as Lance Banning claims in *The Jeffersonian Persuasion,*[3] the two-party system that emerged in Congress and then spread to the whole country was the first manifestation in the United States of a modern political life of the liberal type. But although American politicians—both Federalists and Republicans—were involved in this development, they did not possess the analytical tools to comprehend it. They made it up as they went along, without having the full picture, and often without approving of it since it called to mind a "party spirit" that the still dominant classical republican ideology had hitherto condemned.[4]

At a time when the tradition of legitimate political opposition was only just beginning, it was not surprising that each party called the legitimacy of the other party into question.[5] For the party in power, it was very tempting to take control of the democracy before it had even emerged in its modern form, to refuse to allow political opposition in times of crisis, and to adopt authoritarian practices that were hardly compatible with the spirit of a republican government as had been inherited from the American Revolution. For Madison and Jefferson, who wrote the Virginia and Kentucky Resolves of 1798, it was clear that infringement on the part of the administration upon the liberties inscribed in the Bill of Rights amounted to rejecting the democratic heritage of the Revolution and thereby jeopardizing the nation's identity and principles.

The Ideological Turning Point of 1794

Jay's Treaty

At the end of 1793 and the beginning of 1794, the Federalists had not yet fully taken over the administration. Although Jefferson had left George Washington's government at the end of 1793, he was replaced by another Republican, Edmund Randolph. For the time being, the president remained above the political scuffles.[6] Meanwhile, for Hamilton and his allies, controlling the government did not simply mean checking the political orientation of cabinet members; it was also a matter of enacting a particular program based on good relations between the United States and Great Britain. At the end of 1793 and the beginning of 1794, however, instead of friendship, dissension appeared to set in between the two countries, and this had the potential of tipping the balance in favor of the pro-French policy of the Republicans.

The disagreement between the United States and Great Britain arose in part because of the aid provided by the British to the Indians of the Northwest, as we have already seen. Another factor was France's declaration of war on Great Britain on February 1, 1793, and the outbreak of hostilities between the two nations. As a maritime power, Great Britain had every intention of using all the means at its disposal in the fight against its enemy France. The British were aware of the fact that the French wanted to buy the staples they lacked from the United States, not only because the United States was a large producer of grain and other food products, but also because it was a neutral country.[7] In the 1778 treaty of commerce between France and Great Britain, it was stipulated that "free Ships shall also give a freedom to Goods."[8] The French government thus counted on American goods reaching France without incident, especially in view of the fact that this rule had been adopted since 1778 in treaties the United States had signed with the United Provinces and with Prussia; this rule had thus acquired a certain weight at the international level. France had not taken Great Britain into consideration, however. Great Britain refused to recognize the new rule and followed, rather, the previous custom (*consolato del mare*), which allowed warring nations to inspect neutral ships if they carried goods belonging to the enemy or products listed as contraband.[9] The American merchant marine received its first blow on June 8, 1793, when the British cabinet decreed an Order in Council according to which all neutral ships headed to France and carrying wheat or flour were to be brought into British ports so that the cargo could be seized and purchased by the British government. This Order in Council, which constituted a threat to the American merchant marine, also endangered the interests of American farmers. Jefferson had barely had the time to make official representations to the London government when news reached the United States that another Order in Council had been passed, one that was even more unpalatable to the American merchant marine.[10] The point of this new order, which was dated November 6, 1793, was to sever economic relations between France and its colonies by prohibiting neutral powers from transporting colonial products: "all ships laden with goods [that are] the produce of any colony belonging to France, or carrying provisions or other supplies for the use of any such colony" were to be stopped and detained, and brought in "for prize-court adjudication."[11] This order was unacceptable for two reasons. First of all, it was made public only in December, which meant that British war vessels had time to reach the Caribbean before American ships could withdraw to the U.S. coast. Secondly, this order was based on a rule of international law that was peculiar to the British—the rule of 1756—according to which trade that was closed in peacetime could not be opened up in wartime without being subject to sanction. Although France did open up its colonies more to American trade after hostilities had broken out, much of the French Caribbean trade had already been open to Americans before.[12] The British had thus defied their own rule: it was clear that in wartime no law mattered to them.

In Congress news of the inspection of more than 250 American vessels came at the perfect time for the Republicans. Jefferson had just presented his final report on the economic relations between the United States and its major partners, and it was thus in the midst of the uproar over the situation of the American merchant marine in the French Caribbean that the House of Representatives immediately set about examining Jefferson's report. Madison could once again propose discriminatory measures, as he had done before—to no avail—in 1789 and 1790.[13] Once again, however, the debate was short-lived. The measures that Madison proposed were to appear insufficient in the wake of a speech pronounced by Lord Dorchester to the Indians of the Seven Villages of Lower Canada on February 10, 1794, in which he declared that the actions of the American people would most likely lead to war between Great Britain and the United States, and in that event the "warriors" would draw the line.[14] This speech contained a two-pronged threat of war: with England, and also with the Indians, whom the American army had not yet come close to defeating.

According to John Jay, passions were roused, both in the public at large and in Congress: "There is much irritation and agitation in this town, and in Congress. Great Britain has acted unwisely and unjustly; and there is some danger of our acting intemperately."[15] There was a threat of war. Hamilton, however, managed to turn the situation to his advantage by proposing to send to London a envoy extraordinary, in the person of John Jay.[16] This measure, which was presented as the last attempt at conciliation with Great Britain before war broke out, was approved by the Senate.[17] Hamilton had thus found a way of avoiding both war and Madison's proposals. All that remained to be done was to make sure that this conciliatory attempt was successful and that it led to the signing of a treaty that would seal the agreement that he had been working on from 1789 to 1793. In order to avoid any chance of the negotiation failing, the true intellectual leader of American diplomacy had to make sure that John Jay's orders contained no demands that the British would find hard to meet. Hamilton managed this perfectly since he essentially drafted them himself. In intent, Jay's orders followed the Federalist view expressed by Hamilton in George Washington's cabinet, with some minor points added by Edmund Randolph.[18] As to the wording of the orders, it was particularly flexible and thus quite unconstraining: there were nineteen recommendations but only two sine qua nons.[19] Whereas the secretary of state in charge was a Republican, in fact "the ideas of Hamilton dominated the negotiation." As Samuel Flagg Bemis observed, in the realm of foreign policy "Hamilton's influence was now practically unlimited."[20] In only four months after Jefferson's departure, Hamilton had managed to take control over U.S. foreign policy. He could now redirect this policy the way he wanted, namely, toward increased cooperation with Great Britain. Insofar as the Federalists were ready to give in on virtually every front in order to achieve an agreement, all that was required was for England to find the agreement worth its while.[21] This was precisely the turn the events took when John Jay reached London. Faced with the spectacular victories scored by the French armies, the first coalition that had been formed against France was beginning to weaken, and England stood to find itself alone in the fight.[22] England could not afford to lose a special economic partner and to scatter its army. John Jay was therefore well received, as he confided to Edmund Randolph and more pointedly to Alexander Hamilton.[23] On the one hand, Secretary of State for Foreign Affairs Lord Grenville went back on the Orders in Council of June and November 1793. Meanwhile, the negotiations made headway, and on September 30, 1794, John Jay transmitted to Lord Grenville a draft of the final version of the treaty. This draft was actually much more ambitious than the treaty that was eventually signed on November 19, 1794. Indeed, it included among other clauses the rule that "free ships make free goods," which was not included in the final draft.

How can one account for the new inflexible stance that was adopted by the British starting on September 30 and carried over into the final treaty? This stance was in fact the unintended by-product of Hamilton's persistent efforts at parallel diplomacy meant to better ensure the success of John Jay's mission. Indeed, on September 20, Lord Grenville had learned from George Hammond in Philadelphia that Hamilton had assured him that the United States would not join in armed neutrality. Suddenly the Americans' wrath no longer seemed so menacing to the British government. Whereas the negotiation had gotten off to an auspicious start for Jay, it ended up favorably for the British, as can be seen from the terms of the treaty that was signed on November 19, 1794.[24]

Most historians who have analyzed the treaty draw a negative assessment of it. One such assessment is that of L. S. Kaplan:

> When Jay was dispatched to London, his major mission was to end British depredations on the high seas. The treaty he signed not only had nothing to say on the subject but also appeared to accept the British depredations of neutral rights and freedom of the seas. British interpretations of international law were written into the treaty. Nor did Jay secure the commercial treaty Hamilton had wanted or the privileges such a treaty would have accorded American commerce, with the exception of a limited entry into the West Indies which was so inadequate that Article XII, in which it was embodied, was deleted by the Senate. Conspicuous by its silence in the treaty was the flaming issue of impressment. . . . Westerners were upset over Jay's failure to gain a British commitment against interference in Indian affairs in the Northwest, while Southerners were angry over his failure to provide compensation for loss of slave property carried away by the British army during the war.[25]

In fact, even S. F. Bemis conceded in his own way that diplomacy had not played a primary role in the signing of Jay's Treaty: he observed that this was the best treaty Jay could get if he really wanted a treaty.[26] What the Federalists and Alexander Hamilton wanted was a treaty, any treaty, not with a view to solving all the issues between the United States and Great Britain, but in order to avoid a falling out between the two countries.

Through this treaty Hamilton believed that his policy of Anglo-American rapprochement was given substance and recognition. And through this victory in foreign policy, he hoped to establish the preeminence of the Federalist Party line. He succeeded on the first score: the last chance mission was changed into a "quasi alliance" with Great Britain, with several aspects and provisions of the treaty clearly trampling over the 1778 treaty with France in both spirit and letter and actually jeopardizing Franco-American friendship.[27] This clearly constituted a reversal of alliances, however, and for most Americans, who less than a year before had thought they were on the brink of war with Great Britain, and who felt very close to the French "sister republic," such a reversal amounted to exchanging something certain for something uncertain. In South Carolina, for instance, all strata of the population were incensed at the British decision not to reimburse the planters for slaves captured or freed during the War of Independence, against the stipulations of the 1783 peace treaty. Senator Jacob Read, whose vote made the ratification of Jay's Treaty possible, could not go back home to Charleston for fear of the riots that would follow from too speedy a return.[28] The Republicans in particular were determined not to go along with this. They now knew, however, that they could no longer count on George Washington's support.

The Whiskey Rebellion

Until 1794 the president had managed to stay above partisan squabbles and remain the symbol of nascent national union, centered on the Constitution. Now, however, the protests of western pioneers (from western Pennsylvania, Maryland, Kentucky, North Carolina, Virginia, and the Northwest Territory) against the 1791 excise tax on whiskey were pushing him toward the Federalist side.[29] Indeed, the political unrest of the 1790s was matched by forms of social unrest that revealed the deep tensions within American society. In the cities, the emergence of new, capitalistic types of work relations altered the old structures of the craftsman's world and resulted in social conflicts.[30] In the country, and especially on the frontier, the 1790s witnessed a growing opposition between two social categories: on the one hand, there were small farmers who sought free or cheap access to the virgin lands, and on the other hand, there were great landowners who used political connections to acquire large land grants.[31] In this context, the whiskey tax constituted a war cry for the pioneers, squatters, and small landowners; these groups resented having to pay a tax that weighed much more heavily on themselves than on the eastern seaboard, home of the Federalist leaders and the great landowners. Indeed, the price of whiskey was much lower in the West than in the East, whereas the tax was uniformly set at seven cents per gallon.[32] Moreover, in the West whiskey was a common drink, a token of exchange, and an indispensable component of social and economic life, which was not the case elsewhere.

Instead of gradually receding, the troubles that this new tax caused intensified with time, especially in western Pennsylvania, where, under the aegis of democratic societies, various assemblies of citizens strongly condemned the federal tax in 1794. These peaceful protests were accompanied by outbreaks of violence that were typical of frontier life: tax collectors were threatened or chased away, ambushes and raids were organized, and houses were burnt down. Such a climate of insurrection was intolerable for George Washington, who was himself a great landowner in absentia in this area,[33] and who, as a statesman and man of law and order, could not bear to see the authority of the state and the social order being jeopardized. Although the rebels fought against the tax in the name of the revolutionary tradition of 1776, that is, the rights of citizens to oppose the powers that be, George Washington clearly meant to impress upon them the fact that he no longer abided by that tradition. In his Proclamation of August 7, in which he condemned the rebellion, he declared that such "combinations" were "proceeding in a manner subversive equally of the just authority of Government and of the rights of individuals."[34] George Washington did not doubt for a moment that the true impetus behind this social movement came from the democratic-republican societies, which were inspired by Genêt and, through him, by the principles of the French Revolution:

> That these societies were instituted by the *artful* and *designing* members . . . primarily to sow the seeds of jealousy and distrust among the people, of the government, by destroying all confidence in the Administration of it; and that these doctrines have been budding and blowing ever since, is not new to anyone. . . . I early gave it as my opinion to the confidential characters around me that, if these Societies were not counteracted . . . or did not fall into disesteem from the knowledge of their origin, and the views with which they had been instituted by their father, Genet, for purposes well known to the Government; that they would shake the government to its foundation. Time and circumstances have confirmed me in this opinion. . . . I see, under a display of popular and fascinating guises, the most diabolical attempts to destroy the best fabric of human government and happiness.[35]

At the end of August, the president initiated a military campaign, the goal of which was to end unrest in the area. This decision was not only meant to restore the government's authority over the frontier, but it was also geared at putting down once and for all a political and social movement that he saw as linked to the Republican Party; moreover, from the mere fact that this movement was rebelling against the administration, he also believed that it constituted a fatal threat to the government. By so openly siding with the Federalists and refusing to allow for opposition, George Washington lost his status as "Father of the Nation," and his political action lost its unifying dimension. In trying to further the nation's unity in the direction he wanted, George Washington ended up undermining the pioneers' loyalty to the federal government, which was now Federalist.

At the end of this military campaign, which was totally lacking in greatness, the president himself emphasized the political nature of the operation.[36] In his message to Congress on November 19, 1794, he publicly linked the Whiskey Rebellion to "certain self-created Societies."[37] It was clear to everyone what this obscure expression referred to: the democratic societies, which were linked to the Republican Party. For the president, a sector of public opinion as well as a political party (i.e., the Republicans) had thus ceased to be simply the opposition and had become the enemy. The nation was now divided into two hostile camps, one conservative and elitist (i.e., the Federalists), and the other closer to the people and their demands (i.e., the Republicans); from that moment on, George Washington made no attempt to hide his Federalist sympathies.

In emphasizing a narrow connection between the democratic societies (and by implication the Republican Party) and the western rebels, George Washington considerably overstated these societies' agenda. Although Republican politicians did express outrage at the strong-arm tactics of the government's campaign against the Whiskey Rebellion, they cannot seriously be considered the direct instigators of this farmer revolt. In the West itself, the democratic societies, which had supported the movement in the beginning, distanced themselves from it, and their leaders tried in vain to appease the farmers' anger when the revolt turned into an insurrection.[38] A good illustration—almost to the point of caricature—of the "radical" limits of the Republicans' democratic ideology as revealed by the Whiskey Rebellion is the case of lawyer Hugh Henry Brackenridge. An ambitious lawyer with Republican leanings, Brackenridge joined the rebellion of the Pennsylvania farmers in order to temper their anger. Soon overtaken by the mob, he derived from this experience a lasting disgust of the simple frontier citizens.[39] The Republicans were not interested in satisfying the egalitarian aspirations of farmers and craftsmen; they sought first and foremost to rally their energies and votes in support of their own moderate political agenda.[40] The Republican leaders' democratic commitment did not mean that they intended, once in power, to end social inequalities in the new republic, be it in New York or in South Carolina.[41] While the Whiskey Rebellion was, in the words of Thomas P. Slaughter, the "last violent battle over the meaning of the Revolution,"[42] it was not waged in the name of goals that could easily be endorsed by the Republican leaders.

Driving Out the Last Republicans from the Administration

When the treaty Jay had concluded reached Philadelphia, the only motive that could have prevented George Washington from signing it was his mistrust of the former enemy in the War of Independence; indeed, that mistrust was doubtless strengthened in the spring of 1795, when the British renewed their measures of June 1793. Neither the fierce press campaign that the Republicans launched nor the opposition of Republican voters could affect him.[43] Seeing that the treaty was likely to be sent back to Great Britain for further negotiation, Edmund Randolph, the secretary of state who was the last Republican member of the cabinet, wrote in hopeful terms to James Monroe, on July 14,

1795: "The treaty is not yet ratified by the president nor will it be ratified, I believe, until it returns from England, if then."[44] Little could Randolph imagine then that barely one month later he would help bring about what he feared most, that is, the signing of the treaty by George Washington. Indeed, at the end of July, George Hammond forwarded to Secretary of War Timothy Pickering a dispatch from Joseph Fauchet, the French plenipotentiary in Philadelphia, which had been intercepted by the British during the preceding winter. Written at the time when George Washington was preparing to put down the Whiskey Rebellion, Joseph Fauchet's dispatch contained disclosures that incriminated the secretary of state on two counts: it mentioned criticism leveled by Randolph at other members of the American cabinet during past discussions with Fauchet, and, more importantly, it hinted that Randolph had requested financial aid to rekindle the Republican ardor of western political leaders. The virtuous French minister cried, "Thus a few thousand dollars would have been enough for the French republic to decide the issue between civil war and peace!" Then he added, without being able then to perceive the irony of the remark: "It is true that the certainty of these painful conclusions will remain indefinitely within our archives."[45]

For the American president, such remarks were unquestionable proof that Edmund Randolph was in cahoots with the western rebels; on August 19, without investigating the matter, he showed the letter to Randolph and refused to accept his explanations. The secretary of state denied ever having betrayed his government, but nonetheless had to resign.[46] The political changes that the administration had initiated in putting down the Whiskey Rebellion thus came to a head: now that the Republicans had no representatives in George Washington's cabinet, they became the de facto opposition. The myth of an executive branch embodying national unity crumbled—at the very moment when Congress was clearly splitting into two groups: those who supported Jay's Treaty and those who were opposed to it; meanwhile, the Republican base was growing stronger in the areas where the administration had come down hardest.[47] For the Federalists to achieve their goal of total control of government, all that remained to be done was to oust the last Republican in a high-ranking position, namely, James Monroe, the American minister in Paris.

Monroe had left the United States in the spring of 1794, at the height of the Anglo-American crisis. From his instructions, which were written by Randolph, one easily perceives a desire to keep up close relations with France, the only great power that was a U.S. ally.[48] The secretary of state knew that John Jay's departure for London would most likely make the French uneasy, and he advised Monroe to depict the political opposition between Federalists and Republicans in a softer tone than what the French might have hitherto imagined.[49] Indeed, the French justifiably felt that the American government was more eager to cultivate a friendship with Great Britain than to strengthen Franco-American ties.

By producing statements in favor of France and the revolutionary spirit uniting the two nations,[50] Monroe managed to redress a state of affairs that had deteriorated partly because of the aristocratic discourse of his predecessor Gouverneur Morris and the added circumstance of John Jay's departure for London.[51] Through Edmund Randolph, George Washington even congratulated Monroe.[52] The French were now convinced that the American government supported France and that the United States belonged to the side of democratic republics along with France.

When the news of the signing of Jay's Treaty reached Monroe and the Committee of Public Safety, the American minister in Paris sought at all costs a way to silence accounts according to which: "Mr. Jay had not only adjusted the points in controversy, but concluded a treaty of commerce with that government. Some of those accounts state that he had also concluded a treaty of alliance, offensive and defensive."[53] Monroe also was anxious to quell the doubts that arose in his own mind as he wondered whether he was not the "organ of . . . a double and perfidious policy," sent to Paris to allay French suspicions until an Anglo-American treaty was signed.[54] He therefore asked Jay to give him the text of the treaty, but Jay refused to do so.[55] Jay placed no trust in the Republican, who, in his view, only wanted to sell out the United States to France. Monroe also did not receive any further instructions from his government, and he thus became an impotent witness to the rising anger of French leaders against the Federalist administration. After wanting to believe as long as possible that the treaty would not be ratified, the French gave free rein to their wrath once the bad news was announced. In the pages of the *Moniteur,* one editorialist exclaimed: "Indeed, there were dangers for you to face; but was there not also a sacred debt to be paid off, and national honor to be defended? Who held up your forts and captured your vessels? England did. Who sought to enslave you? Who brought you war with the Algerians and the Indians? England did. And who defended you when you broke your chains? France did. Who, for her own sake, wants you to preserve your liberty? France does."[56]

After the president ratified the treaty, it was all too easy for Timothy Pickering, successor to Edmund Randolph, to send James Monroe long explanatory dispatches and to incriminate the American minister in Paris for his misinterpretations.[57] How could Monroe have given an accurate interpretation of a treaty he was denied access to? In spite of Monroe's efforts to avoid a rift between the United States and France in the spring of 1796, Pickering notified him of his recall in a letter dated August 22, 1796.[58] For the Federalists, Monroe was a convenient scapegoat; they pointed to him as the sole cause of the misunderstanding that now existed between the United States and France. The last influential Republican was thus eliminated. As the undisputed holders of power, the Federalists could now implement their policies.

The 1796 Presidential Campaign: The French Faction vs. the English Party

Political Passions and Conspiracy Theories

In this period, that is, the end of the eighteenth century, the political life of the United States foreshadowed that of modern capitalist democracies. Under pressure from ideological struggles and events in foreign policy, Americans went through political conflicts in the heat of passion, without moderation and reason, or even strategic planning and negotiation. For Marshall Selmer, the Federalist period was the "age of passions," the three dominant passions being, in his analysis, hatred, anger, and fear.[59] As was the case with George Washington's indictment of the democratic societies during the Whiskey Rebellion, politicians, whether Republican or Federalist, could not bring themselves to treat their opponents as respectable citizens, merely professing different views. Any opponent was bound to be an enemy, or worse a traitor, a conspirator, or even a foreign agent. Foreign policy had contributed to fashioning the parties; it now became the principal ingredient of the political hatreds that made up the bulk of public debate in the United States after Jay's Treaty. Passions were fully unleashed during the presidential campaign of 1796, with verbal slander reaching a climax.

Each party's press was in search of sensation and allotted a good deal of space to all kinds of denunciation of the other party. Politicians' correspondence was also laden with virulent quarrels. The Federalist *Gazette of the United States* charged Thomas Jefferson, the Republican candidate in the 1796 presidential election, with failure to comply with the president's authority in his dealings with Genêt, the former French minister. In this view, Jefferson had forsaken his patriotism. He and his friends were also corrupt, according to the Federalist *Minerva.* For this paper, giving free rein to that clan would amount to electing Genêt president and turning the United States into "a French colony."[60] The Republicans were not considered to be worthy opponents, but rather traitors who once in office would sell out the country to foreign interests. Just as the Federalists viewed the Republicans as a "French party" and more globally as a band of traitors to the country, the Republicans similarly denounced the Federalists as an "English party." According to the Republican *Aurora,* John Adams, who was the Federalist candidate in the 1796 election, was "the friend of hereditary power." Federalist pamphleteers were reputedly in the pay of Great Britain. With regard to the chief editor of the *Gazette of the United States,* John Fenno, the *Aurora* wrote: "his modes of acting and thinking are entirely English." No better treatment was granted to Noah Webster, the chief editor of the *Minerva:* "Noah is patronized by old Tories and British agents." In the opinion of Republican editorialists, the hidden influence of British thinking and the supposed role of British agents were geared at dismantling a national edifice that, in their view, rested on the Constitution and on republicanism. The Republican *National Gazette* thus logically interpreted John Adams's ideas and Federalist vociferation as signaling a will to destroy the nation's founding principles. It claimed, for example, that Adams preferred a limited monarchy to the federal form of government.[61]

John Adams, on the other hand, felt that the Republicans' "zeal for France" was "greater than their love for the United States."[62] Once he was elected, that opinion found further confirmation in his correspondence with his son John Quincy Adams, the American minister plenipotentiary in The Hague and then in Berlin. The young Adams learned about events in the United States with a delay of several months. Meanwhile, he witnessed the European expansion of revolutionary France under the Directory, and at the same time he was avidly reading European counterrevolutionary writers; this was to shape his thinking in a significant way.[63] If one were to believe John Quincy Adams, the Republicans were not only "the enemies to the government of the United States" but also traitors to the nation and sowers of civil war. The president's eldest son considered the corruption of Jefferson's party to be less serious than its lack of patriotism and its revolutionary internationalism. The true danger that lay within the secret alliance of the Republicans with France was civil war and the destruction of the national edifice. A Republican, according to John Quincy Adams, would hold that "his countrymen are his enemies and France is his ally."[64] The young diplomat regarded the Republican Party as a French fifth column, made up of men who had lost all national feeling; in agreement with France, these men were plotting to overthrow the government and transform the United States into a French satellite.

The 1796 presidential campaign thus set the stage for a form of political debate that was highly dangerous for the nation's unity, as both parties accused each other of being in the pay of the enemy and denied each other any kind of legitimacy. From that moment on, and until 1800, the political debate was to be impregnated and fed by this obsession with conspiracy, which took on the same forms as those of the conspiracy narratives that Raoul Girardet has discussed (i.e., fear of a fifth column and of a "foreign party" conspiring to take over, insurrections supposedly plotted by secret organizations under foreign guidance, etc.).[65] In the presidential election of 1796, all of John Adams's supporters called Thomas Jefferson a traitor to his country, while all of Jefferson's supporters charged Adams with monarchism. Thus, these accusations were not specific to isolated, marginal, or socially victimized groups; instead, they were shared by the entire political class, the press, and probably a large part of public opinion. Indeed, the Federalist political press was no longer alone in trying to instill mistrust of the French Revolution in the minds of American citizens. Preachers, especially in New England, watched France fall into the fallacy of deism, an even worse evil than papism, from which they had thought the Revolution would save the country. Borrowing from counterrevolutionary thought, they then started to propagate the myth of conspiracy in fiery sermons that, as in the case of the Boston minister David Osgood, denounced the abolition of all religion in France, and called the French Republicans "infernal" creatures and "demons" in human form.[66]

Insofar as it permeated all of political life, the conspiracy theme cannot be equated with a mere rhetorical trick, but at the same time it does appear as a political myth. As a matter of fact, although the nation was tearing itself apart, a study of the factual foundations of this myth reveals that neither one of the two opposing parties was actually aligned with a foreign power. The Federalists certainly wanted to maintain the best relations with Great Britain, but that did not make them "Tories," ready to betray their country and turn it into a British satellite, as the Republicans claimed. As we have seen, John Adams had been suspected of monarchism by the Republicans ever since his *Defence of the Constitutions of Government of the United States* and *Discourses on Davila.*[67] The Republicans construed his admiration for British institutions as renunciation of the principles of 1776 and a desire to restore the monarchy. This suspiciousness was strengthened by the aristocratic habits and conservative principles that prevailed in Federalist circles; thus, the Republicans concluded, a monarchist conspiracy was being fomented by their political enemies. In point of fact, the president was a devout nationalist, whose handling of the XYZ crisis would lead the United States toward true independence from European powers.

As for the Federalists, they did not doubt for a moment that the French enjoyed Republican support in the United States for their alleged expansionist plots.[68] As concerns French expansion, Genêt's sole mission was to propagate revolutionary principles in Spanish Louisiana so as to destabilize the area (Spain was an British ally at that time); this was supposed to be achieved with the help of the pioneers, whose ambitions Genêt knew about. France had no intention of setting up secret military operations unbeknownst to the American government; it simply wanted to work toward goals common to both countries, with the tacit agreement of the United States.[69] Moreover, had France actually wanted to conduct operations for its own benefit, it would have been barred from doing so by its local allies, that is, the western pioneers, whose help, which was essential, was only dictated by the need to defend their own interests. Finally, far from regarding Republicans as mercenaries in the pay of France, Joseph Fauchet, the successor to Genêt, viewed them as "respectable citizens" with a concern for the future of their country: "The men we have just mentioned [i.e., Jefferson and Madison] unquestionably desire no more, as do a great many respectable citizens, than that the spirit of a government which is believed to be guided by anglomania become more congenial to republicanism."[70]

When Jay's Treaty was discussed in the House of Representatives, James Madison was not the one who led the fight against the president. In 1796 Pierre-Auguste Adet, Fauchet's successor who was then trying to influence the presidential campaign, held interviews with local leaders rather than with the major leaders of the Republican Party. As Fauchet observed, the great leaders of the Republican Party defended first and foremost their conception of U.S. national interest, and not the French conception. Still, because of a clumsy maneuver, some Republican leaders did in fact lend credence to the story of a Franco-Republican conspiracy. Indeed, by inciting the French minister plenipotentiary to interfere in the 1796 presidential campaign, they drove public opinion away from the Republican cause that it had hitherto espoused.

Adet's Intervention in the Presidential Campaign

The Republicans had hoped to capitalize on public hostility to Jay's Treaty in order to prevent the financial clauses from being implemented in the House of Representatives, but the signing of Pinckney's Treaty on October 27, 1795, which fulfilled the expectations of the entire western population, frustrated their plans. In the spring of 1796, as they held the majority in the House, they demanded that the president submit to them the documents pertaining to the negotiation of Jay's Treaty before they would authorize the necessary expenditures for its execution. George Washington refused to comply and instead linked the fate of Jay's Treaty to Pinckney's Treaty, which was very popular among Republican voters.[71] While the debate dragged on in vain, neither treaty could be implemented, and the House was inundated with petitions hostile to it, which swayed the majority of representatives.[72] With the 1796 presidential election in mind, the Republican leaders wanted to keep their voters, whom they had angered. Some Republicans, however, who were aware of the oversimplified view of American politics that French leaders had, decided to request French interference in U.S. domestic policies. They communicated their plan to Pierre-Auguste Adet, the French minister in Philadelphia after Fauchet's departure, who commented: "Our friends have no doubt of succeeding if the rumor now circulating here is confirmed, if the Executive Directory in France makes known its opinion on the conduct of the federal government, if it thereby imparts new strength to the men who are devoted to us."[73] The French minister did not hesitate to embark on a campaign:

> Our friends in Massachusetts were especially dejected—they had interpreted the French government's silence as unfavorable to them, and they were almost resolved to give up the upcoming election to their adversaries. I boosted their dwindling morale, I rekindled their hopes, I announced to them that the French Republic, far from deserting them as they feared, had felt bitter

indignation at the news of the treaty being concluded with Great Britain; that it had measured the price of the efforts made by the friends of liberty and that it would certainly not abandon them to the mercy of England; and that was enough to bolster their zeal again.[74]

In order to fully "bolster their zeal again" and to marshal the support of public opinion, Adet's "friends" counseled him on the policy to follow: "They told me that it was necessary for France to adopt such measures as would make merchants concerned about their property, so that they would be compelled to place at the head of the government a man whose known character would inspire trust in the French republic and enable him to serve as mediator between the republic and the United States."[75] In compliance with this policy, so as to make a stronger impression upon voters and incite them to "vote right," Adet announced on the eve of the election the measures taken by France against the United States: diplomatic relations between the two countries were suspended, and France would henceforth treat the American merchant marine the same way Great Britain would.[76] A few days later, the *Aurora* published a translation of a long letter from Adet to Timothy Pickering, enumerating all the French grievances against the American government.[77]

In the name of Republican solidarity, the French stance was supposed to rally a majority of votes for the candidate favored by France, but this scheme failed. The plotters who urged Adet to act miscalculated the consequences of such a move, mistakenly reasoning that a French intervention in favor of Thomas Jefferson would better underscore the profound difference between Jefferson and John Adams. Jefferson was supposed to emerge as the candidate of the people and the one who would bring about reconciliation with France, in short as the democrat par excellence, whereas John Adams stood for conservative forces and an elite that opposed the power of the people.[78] But the scheme actually had the opposite effect: such an interference in U.S. national politics tarnished France's image in the eyes of the American public, and aroused or even exacerbated patriotic feelings. As France persisted in this analysis of the American political situation, U.S. public opinion soon warmed up to the Federalists, who had previously been out of favor because they were deemed too close to Great Britain. This new Federalist sympathy did not arise from a consensus on their politics, but from the assumption that they truly embodied national resistance to foreign interference.

Liberties Threatened: The Special Laws of 1798

In January 1797 France refused to receive James Monroe's successor, General Charles Cotesworth Pinckney, and this gave the Federalists an opportunity to strengthen their hold on public opinion. France was no longer the ally, but a great power that sought to humiliate the new American republic. In addition, on March 2 the Executive Directory promulgated an order that violated the treaty of 1778 insofar as it annulled the principle of freedom of the seas for neutral countries.[79] This act also held that any American serving under an enemy flag would be considered a pirate, and that any American vessel without a muster roll would be free game. From this moment on, French privateers based in Guadeloupe zeroed in on ships from the American merchant fleet that maneuvered in the Caribbean.[80] This plundering had in fact begun soon after Jay's Treaty was signed, but now it took on unprecedented proportions. President Adams convened a special session of Congress for May 15, 1797.[81] Adams did not think that the time had come for a split; rather, he was seeking to obtain approval for a conciliatory mission to France, as well as for several defense measures. Led by Hamilton, the Federalists felt that this program, which was firm but peaceful, could only help them win over an even bigger portion of public opinion, while waiting until the public was ready to accept open war with France.[82]

The orders that John Marshall, Charles Cotesworth Pinckney, and Elbridge Gerry received from Timothy Pickering were therefore completely devoid of any sort of conciliatory tone, and in this regard they reflected the secretary of state's true motives, for Pickering was probably the most pro-British of the Federalists.[83] These orders stressed the need to obtain compensation for U.S. trade losses resulting from French decrees, as though the Americans were free of blame. With regard to the treaty of 1778, the United States asked to be officially relieved of its obligation to defend the French Caribbean in case of attack. They also requested that the Franco-American treaty be altered on the basis of Jay's Treaty, which amounted to an admission that Jay's Treaty violated the clauses of the Franco-American Treaty. The United States was demanding a great deal but was offering almost nothing in return.

The French still believed that only a cynical policy could ensure Republican success and renew good relations between France and the United States.[84] In fact, they played into the hands of the ultra-Federalists by granting quite an original welcome to President Adams's envoys. On October 14, 1797, after the three envoys had been waiting for an official audience since the fifth, Talleyrand explained to them that they would only be granted such an audience on the condition that they would provide clarification on "certain topics that were mentioned in the President's speech."[85] That condition was, of course, not sufficient. On October 17, the Swiss banker Hottinguer, who was the first of Talleyrand's secret emissaries to make contact with the Americans, disclosed the other prerequisites to them. Once accepted, these conditions were to "form the basis of a treaty between the two nations to negotiate which [the envoys] should be publicly received." In the words of one of the "XYZ" envoys, these conditions were the following:

> It was absolutely acquired [i.e., taken for granted] that we should give satisfaction to the honor of France wounded by the speech of the President, that we should pay the debts due by contract from France to our citizens, that we should also pay for the spoliations committed on our commerce for which France should be adjudged liable by commissioners to be appointed as in the British treaty and that we should make a considerable loan to an extent not defined in the proposition. Besides this . . . there must be something for the pocket. On being asked to explain himself he [Hottinguer] said that there must be a considerable sum for the private use of the Directoire and minister under the form of satisfying claims which did not in fact exist.[86]

Two points in these propositions deserve special attention. The first is the secret loan as a prerequisite to negotiation. Talleyrand's special emissaries, Hottinguer and also Bellamy and Hauteval, were to return time and again to this point, alternating sweet talk and threats as means of persuasion. Provision for such a loan was not included in the envoys' orders, and this presented an insurmountable obstacle to them. Lending money to France in wartime seemed tantamount to siding with France in the hostilities, a turn of events that the Americans wanted to avoid at all costs.

The other crucial point was Talleyrand's request for "something for the pocket." In April 1798, when the correspondence of the three envoys extraordinary was published in the United States, this condition more than any other caused a stir of nationalist feeling throughout the country. After Adet's abuses and in a time of increasing attacks on the American merchant marine by French privateers, it was the ultimate and most intolerable show of humiliation. Talleyrand's demand provoked massive rallying of public opinion in favor of the Federalist Party, which seemed to be the best defender of the nation's honor. The envoys' mission failed and ended in March 1798. As far as the Federalists were concerned, it primarily served to bring France's ruthlessness and hostility toward the United States out in the open.

In preparation for imminent war, the Federalists took several military measures. Then on July 7, 1798, the United States abrogated its treaties with France. As early as April 1798, the publication of documents relating to the XYZ affair had revealed to the American public the dishonest proposals of Talleyrand and his emissaries; as a result, the entire American population joined together to back John Adams and the Federalist Party, in a surge of patriotic feeling.[87] Even though this national consensus meant that the Federalists were certain to have the backing of public opinion and silence from the Republicans, they did not take advantage of the situation to establish themselves as the party of national unity, to cement the Union, and to appease passions.[88] Instead they sought above all to put the "quasi war" toward partisan use, thus furthering the nation's divisions.[89]

Meanwhile, the Franco-American crisis facilitated the diplomatic plans that the Federalists had long had in mind for their country. The policy of rapprochement with England, which Alexander Hamilton had unfalteringly advocated since 1789, finally bore fruit: the former enemy of 1776 now proposed a military "quasi alliance" to its former colony. In Bradford Perkins's bold appraisal, the period between the publication of the XYZ dispatches and the Convention of Mortefontaine was characterized by a level of military cooperation that was to remained unmatched for the next century.[90]

Cooperation was first established on the material level, with the British supplying arms to the United States.[91] But there was also cooperation on the logistical level, since the British quite willingly agreed to escort convoys of American merchant ships so as to ward off easy capture by French privateers.[92] Finally, there was a strategic aspect, since the two navies divided up the tasks of watching the coasts and seas: thus, it fell to the powerful British navy to oversee the Atlantic Ocean, while the small American navy, with its more manageable vessels, was to operate in the Caribbean and near the coasts.[93] Although this cooperation was to a large extent the outcome of Federalist foreign policy, and especially that of Alexander Hamilton, it still did not satisfy the Federalist thirst for power. It is unclear whether the Federalist attitude was dictated by aristocratic mistrust of public opinion, which they judged inconsistent, or by their own lack of political maturity, or by an authoritarian rejection of the rules of democracy.[94] The fact remains in any case that for the Federalists it was not enough to control both the administration and Congress. Although they were beginning to enjoy some popular support, they wanted to silence the opposition, so as not to have to face challenges in the following election. At the height of the Franco-American crisis, the slogan "Millions for Defence, not one cent for tribute"—a proud proclamation of American independence—became very popular.[95] It was during this period that the Federalists proposed a series of special laws, which they managed to have passed by Congress, still under the spell of the XYZ affair: the Naturalization Act (passed June 18, 1798), the Alien Act (June 25), the Act Respecting Alien Enemies (July 6), and the Sedition Act (July 14).[96]

Only the Act Respecting Alien Enemies was a war measure: it allowed the American government, in case of war or foreign invasion, to capture or deport any citizen of the enemy nation.[97] This law reflected the paranoid concerns about "French agents" that the Federalists had been voicing since the mid-1790s. However, in her study of French émigrés in the United States during this period, Frances Childs concluded that the refugees contributed to their own bad press by making their quarrels too public.[98] Meanwhile, other groups of foreign residents were targeted by the other three acts, which clearly revealed the Federalists' goal in domestic policy, that is, to exclude foreigners from political life in the United States. Such was indeed the Federalists' rather undemocratic dream;

for them, immigrants, who were often poor and destitute, did not deserve to become full-fledged citizens. Thus, the Naturalization Act set the longest required length of stay for obtaining citizenship in the entire history of the United States.[99] Rather than xenophobia,[100] however, political scheming was the real motive behind these laws. In fact, an influx of political refugees from Great Britain and Ireland had been thickening the Republican ranks since 1793.[101] These new voters not only provided extra weight in elections; they were also very active in their commitment to democracy. In the decade 1790–1800, immigrants edited one-fourth of Republican newspapers. As historian Michael Durey observes, the immigrants were all the more influential as some of them controlled certain of the best-known, most widely read, and most strategically located papers in the years leading up to Jefferson's victory in 1800.[102]

In order to keep these foreigners from supporting the Republican cause, it was not enough to keep them from voting; their actions also needed to be curtailed. As the Act Respecting Alien Enemies could only apply to French émigrés, Congress resolved to take measures that could affect foreigners even in the absence of a conflict between the United States and their home countries.[103] This new law was called the Alien Act, and it reflected the obsessive fear of conspiracy that consumed Federalist political thought. If every Republican was a traitor and a potential French agent, what could be said of an Irishman, who had been driven out of Great Britain for having attempted a revolution there with French support, such as Wolfe Tone, who had landed in the United States in 1795? The Alien Act was drafted and voted on at a time when the Federalists had both power and public support at their disposal. The first article, which was inspired by the political hatred of the times, allowed the president of the United States to order those foreigners he deemed dangerous to the nation or the government to leave American territory.[104] The same obsession with conspiracy permeated yet another legislative text, namely, the Sedition Act, which aimed at eradicating criticism by U.S.–born Republicans; the word "conspiracy" appeared twice in the first article. In the Federalist view, the opposition sought to raise insurrections and riots; it could therefore not be legitimate and must be annihilated.[105]

By passing this series of acts, the Federalists shamelessly trampled on civil liberties that were written into the Bill of Rights, especially the Fifth and Sixth Amendments (with the Alien Act), and the First and Tenth Amendments (with the Sedition Act). They thus confirmed their authoritarian, conservative, and antidemocratic biases.[106] It was more and more obvious that the Federalists were intent on erasing the whole democratic and liberal heritage from the American political tradition. During the congressional debates, Republicans came to the defense of the civil liberties that were being crushed, and once the bills were passed, they did not give up the fight.[107] Thomas Jefferson, the true leader of the Republican Party since his return to Washington, D.C., in 1796 as vice president,[108] drafted various resolutions attacking these blackguard laws, which were adopted by the Kentucky legislature in November 1798.[109] Then in collaboration with James Madison, he wrote another set of resolutions, which were approved by the Virginia assembly. The Kentucky and Virginia Resolutions sought to contain the power of the federal government within those limits defined by the Constitution; these resolves are often considered to be the foundation of the theory of states' rights in opposition to the federal government. The resolves demonstrated that in passing the acts of June and July 1798, Congress had overstepped the constitutional framework. The resolves claimed to safeguard the Constitution and the Union (Kentucky resolution no. 7), called for enforcing the civil liberties that were written into the amendments (Kentucky resolutions nos. 6-3-4), and, in keeping with the American revolutionary tradition, protested the excessive powers assumed by the executive.

Although these resolves had only a limited impact, with no other state following the example of Virginia and Kentucky, the Republicans did not let themselves be overwhelmed by the authoritarian impulse of the Federalists. In spite of the fact that, under the Sedition Act, lawsuits were brought against owners of Republican-leaning newspapers (such as Benjamin Bache and his successor as head of the *Aurora,* William Duane) and members of Congress (such as Matthew Lyon, a Vermont representative), Republicans actively prepared for the 1800 election.[110] Republican newspapers increased in number from twenty to fifty, and naturalized American voters of foreign origin showed their objection to the Alien Act by voting en masse for the Republicans.[111] After Thomas Jefferson won the presidential election in 1800, the threat of alien and sedition acts vanished.

How should one assess the domestic reaction of the Federalists to this foreign crisis? Their uneasiness is clearly discernible from the fact that they did not shrink from actions that were bound to split the nation further, and did not respect the rights of the opposition. The acts passed in the summer of 1798 shocked American citizens, who rejected them by voting the Federalists out in the 1800 election. These acts made it clear to American voters that their lawmakers refused to abide by the rules of liberal democracy that had gradually set in from 1789 to 1800. The Federalist defeat was a defeat of an archaic vision of political relations, as much as Thomas Jefferson's success was that of a democratic and liberal conception of American society. In lieu of the classical perspective of republicanism, there had now risen an opposition between a conservative side (the Federalists, who were close to the ideas of the European counterrevolution) and a democratic one, whose members advocated true sovereignty of the people, which they saw as the authentic legacy of the American Revolution. The year 1800 was no longer the time of the virtuous citizen, but that of the citizen, period. No matter what that citizen's occupation or place in society was, the Republican Party gave him the opportunity to voice his concerns.

This last assertion, however, needs one qualification: Thomas Jefferson's party still remained a party of the elite. The Republican leaders retained the liberal and democratic heritage of the American and French Revolutions, and not the radical social message that was embodied in the Whiskey Rebellion. Once he took office, Jefferson would no longer invoke the example of the French Revolution to support and justify his own reading of the American Revolution: in the French Revolution he no longer saw anything but its bloody excesses. In contrast, the American Revolution was now defined as a homogeneous political movement that brought democracy without shedding blood. As historian Michael Hunt has observed, Jefferson and Adams later even came to agree that the American Revolution was a "model of revolutionary moderation and wisdom,"[112] a measuring stick for evaluating any other revolution. Although there did exist ideological conflicts in the 1790s, the Republican elite had, by turning democratic energies to its advantage, channeled and diverted social discontent that had not found its full expression. The indifference that the Republicans displayed toward France once they came to power in 1800 foreshadowed the direction of their political evolution.

Part 2

Foreign Policy Goals Shared by the Entire Nation

CHAPTER 4

Commercial and Territorial Expansion

Foreign policy was a realm where national feeling and nationalism were both very prominent, and from 1789 to 1800 it was at the center of especially heated political debate, to the point of impairing the precarious unity of the new republic. Through their conflicting positions, the Republican and Federalist parties actually endorsed one particular view of the American republic. In contrast to the elitist and socially conservative republic of the Federalists, the Republicans favored a democratic republic, faithful to the revolutionary spirit of 1776, which the French Revolution had rekindled. Moreover, in lieu of the traditional concept of deference, which had governed social relations until then, the Republicans preferred the modern value of equality. Although there was real political opposition between the two parties, the fact remains, as historian Joyce Appleby has noted, that both parties were led by men committed to economic change.[1] In spite of their political divisions, the governing elite of the American republic had the same economic goals for the new nation; indeed, they agreed that the best way to ensure unity and strength for the American nation was to push commercial as well as territorial expansion. Although debates over foreign policy raised a good deal of bitterness between Republicans and Federalists, they also set the stage for defining common foreign policy goals. These common goals contributed in a crucial way to the shaping of the nation's identity, even though the two parties did not always agree upon ways to put those goals into effect.

The Growth of Foreign Trade and Commercial Expansion

1776–1789

The obstacles set by British mercantilist policy against American foreign trade had been a major factor in the onset of rebellion in the colonies before 1776. Indeed, the colonies had virtually no domestic market, nor manufacturing, and for them prosperity was highly dependent on foreign trade. Only by funneling their agricultural production into other markets could Americans procure manufactured goods and give a boost to farming.[2] Even prior to the political act of the Declaration of Independence, the colonists had broken free from the economic subjugation that bound them to their former mother country, subjugation that was embodied in the Navigation Acts: in April 1776 they had opened up their ports to ships of all nations, with the exclusion of British ships.[3] The message was clear: without economic independence there could be no political independence. However, in a century that had watched large mercantilist empires emerge and compete, a new nation was likely to experience trouble trying to assert itself on the international scene. Still, the American rebels' economic aspirations were nurtured by the free trade ideas of Adam Smith (whose *Wealth of Nations* appeared in 1776), as well as the exhortations of Thomas Paine. In *Common Sense,* Paine had stated: "Our plan is commerce and that, well attended to, will secure us the peace and friendship of all Europe; because, it is the interest of all Europe to have America a *free port.*"[4] Such language encouraged the rebels to think that their products would be welcome on European markets.

Given that American products were necessities, the designers of the 1776 treaty plan had a firm belief in American economic strength, and thus they envisioned only treaties of friendship and commerce, but no military alliances.[5] The war and its consequences, however, were to teach Americans that although they had obtained political independence, this did not enable them to assert their views of economic exchanges, nor even change their status as a "British colony" in economic terms.[6] As a matter of fact, commercial links between Great Britain and the United States were quite naturally restored after the war, to the great satisfaction of the British government, which was in a position to follow Lord Sheffield's advice in his 1783 book *Observations on the Commerce of the United States:* to exploit American dependence on British products, merchants, and bankers, in order to avoid making any commercial concessions to them. As early as July 1783, an Order in Council barred American ships from the British Caribbean islands. The principle of free trade, on which Americans had hoped to build a new international economic order after the war, also did not appeal to allied or neutral nations. The Netherlands and Denmark opened up their colonies in the Caribbean to American trade, but France, and above all Spain, took longer to offer the United States commercial advantages.[7]

In order to achieve its independence, the new nation had therefore to design a new commercial policy, one that was more dynamic and better adjusted to the reality of a world where mercantilism still reigned. Since the Continental Congress did not seem up to the task, the "nationalists" saw the formation of a federal government as a means to implement a forceful commercial policy, based on reciprocity.[8] This new commercial spirit is perfectly summarized in the following statement from *The Federalist* no. 11, in which Alexander Hamilton advocated adopting protectionist tariffs:

> By prohibitory regulations, extending, at the same time, throughout the States, we may oblige foreign countries to bid against each other, for the privileges of our markets. . . . Suppose, for instance, we had a government in America, capable of excluding Great Britain (with whom we have at present no treaty of commerce) from all our ports; what would be the probable operation of this step upon her politics? Would it not enable us to negotiate, with the fairest prospect of success, for commercial privileges of the most valuable and extensive kind, in the dominions of that kingdom?[9]

Far removed in spirit from the confident free trade outlook of 1776, these propositions stemmed from a wish to exert retaliation and discrimination against Great Britain, as the only means to force it to negotiate the opening of its colonies; furthermore, they were aimed at making economic expansion and prosperity possible for Americans, in the face of European nations that, according to Hamilton, had every intention of standing in their way. *The Federalist* no. 11 was the expression of an inflammatory nationalism, pitting the young promising America against great and jealous mercantilist nations. Hamilton added: "Under a vigorous national government, the natural strength and resources of the country, directed to a common interest, would baffle all the combinations of European jealousy to restrain our growth."[10]

Madison and Jefferson: Discrimination Laws and the Diversification of Markets

Once the new institutions were in place, this ambitious program could be implemented. It was thus quite natural for James Madison, on the occasion of congressional debates upon tonnage and customs duties in April 1789, to ask for a navigation system to be created in the United States that would favor American ships (through tonnage duties) and goods imported into the United States on American ships, as opposed to the same goods when carried by foreign ships (through customs duties).[11] As we saw in chapter 2, Madison, in introducing these measures, included the idea of discrimination, with a view to imposing heavier taxes on countries that had not signed a treaty with the United States. His nationalistic argumentation perfectly echoed what Hamilton had written in *The Federalist* no. 11: "I wish to teach those nations who have declined to enter into commercial treaties with us, that we have the power to extend or to withhold advantages as their conduct shall deserve."[12] Economic discrimination as well as commercial retaliation against Great Britain were, in Madison's view, a show of national pride and the essential step toward achieving an autonomous national identity, one that would constitute a total break from the past colonial identity. In depicting the drafting of the Constitution and the establishment of federal institutions as a "revolution," he clearly signaled that the key to the success of this national undertaking lay in an aggressive commercial policy: "We have now the power to avail ourselves of our natural superiority, and I am for beginning with some manifestation of that ability, that foreign nations may or might be taught to pay us that respect which they have neglected on account of our former imbecility. This language and these Sentiments are the language and the sentiments of our Constituents. The great political revolution now brought about by the organization of the new government, has its foundation in these sentiments."[13] Madison added that the states had separately tried to counter the nefarious influence of Great Britain, but these attempts were in vain. Now they had decided to act together, in order to obtain the reciprocity that justice required. In order to force the former colonial power to respect the new independence and identity of the United States, Madison went so far as to declare that the United States was ready to wage an "economic war" on Great Britain.[14]

In addition to being nationalistic, the commercial policy that Madison propounded was also eminently national in character, for it ignored the specific interests of the various regions and economic groups and instead considered only those of the Union as a whole. In fact, Madison knew quite well that many southern planters would oppose his propositions; their goods were still being transported to Europe on British ships, and the prospect of a shortage of inexpensive freight, or of an increase in their transportation costs, made those planters fear that their goods might no longer be exportable to Europe or might sell poorly on account of higher prices. Did Madison mean to destroy the farming economy of the southern states for the benefit of shipowners of the northeastern states, as Thomas Tudor Tucker of South Carolina and James Jackson of Georgia wondered?[15] Or did he mean to destroy American farming as a whole for the benefit of trade, as Theodorick Bland of Virginia and John Lawrence of New York speculated?[16] Madison responded that neither was the case and stated that he was only interested in the good of the nation. For Madison, farming and commercial interests were "compatible and consistent with each other," as were the interests of southern and northern states.[17] Indeed, he claimed that his proposal to set up an American merchant marine was not only geared at securing revenue for the government and stimulating a sector of the national economy, but also it was aimed in the end at ensuring the security of the nation and at enabling it to counter military threats from other countries. He explained: "[M]y great object is to provide a maritime defence against a maritime danger. . . . The United States can have no commerce without a navy. Whenever a war shall break out, what a situation will this country be in?"[18]

When Thomas Jefferson became secretary of state in April 1790, he was ready to second Madison's efforts at setting American trade free from the colonial chains that bound it to Great Britain. As soon as he took office, he made a special effort at improving commercial relations between the United States and France, Great Britain's major economic competitor. In so doing, Jefferson was not merely following his own personal and political inclinations; he was, above all, seeking to boost American trade by diversifying its markets.[19] He knew it would be no easy task, for Americans were used to credit and to British manufactured goods, and most European countries followed very strict protectionist policies; but in the course of his five-year term in Paris as minister plenipotentiary (from May 1784 to October 1789), he had become aware that the French government was willing to favor Franco-American trade.

In the wake of the war, French merchants had tried to force their way into the American market, although they did not know much about what its needs were or the way it operated. Having failed in this attempt, the French trade world had lost much of its interest in America.[20] In fact, many French merchants had tried to curb the expansion of trade between the United States and French colonies in the Caribbean. An edict issued in August 1784, which was intended to open up more trade opportunities for Americans in the French Caribbean, had occasioned a storm of protest in Bordeaux, Nantes, and La Rochelle.[21] With the help of Vergennes and Lafayette, however, Jefferson had managed to obtain numerous concessions from the French government. The monopoly on the tobacco trade, which had bound Robert Morris to the Farmers-General, had not been renewed in 1787, although some sales did go through the Farm Administration after that date; furthermore, in December 1787 the French government issued a decree that included several concessions in favor of U.S. trade and navigation.[22]

With regard to the specific issue of opening up Franco-American trade, the revolutionary events of 1789 inspired the new secretary of state with renewed optimism: not only did he know and appreciate the new men in power, but also, and most importantly, he was convinced, as was his former secretary William Short, now the U.S. chargé d'affaires in Paris, that the abolition of privileges in France should logically be followed by a similar end to mercantilist barriers. Thus, the United States would no longer be alone in trying to apply modern free trade ideas; in concert with France, it could make a breach in the mercantilist system and strengthen its position.[23] In Jefferson's mind, the first consequence of this change of mood in France should be the liberation of its colonies' trade. Nothing could have been more in keeping with the laws of free trade than to let the French colonies in the Caribbean get their supplies from their neighbors, instead of importing the same products from France at the highest possible price: "The French colonies will doubtless claim in their new constitution, a right to receive the necessaries of life from whomever will deliver them cheapest; to wit, grain, flour, live stock, salted fish and other salted provisions."[24] Thomas Jefferson and William Short did, however, realize that such a change would go against the interests of the merchants of the great harbors on the Atlantic Coast, who had built their wealth upon trade with the colonies, and who were a prominent group in the Constituent Assembly.[25] In order to quell their protests, Jefferson advised Short to encourage the colonies' deputies to take a forceful stance.[26] Jefferson and Short also expected the French Revolution to result in a liberalization of the tobacco trade. They could hardly conceive that such an ancien régime institution as the Farmers-General might be preserved; thus Short, as a true lobbyist before lobbies existed, extolled to the French deputies the advantages of the free sale of tobacco.[27]

Very soon, however, the American representative in Paris understood that there was no way that the French Caribbean would be opened to American trade, given the influence of merchants in the Constituent Assembly.[28] Caught between free trade principles on the one hand, and political and economic realities on the other, the Assembly chose to be pragmatic: "The Assembly were forced here to deviate from their known principles from an apprehension of the large trading towns and the provinces adjoining them."[29] Furthermore, adhering to a strict interpretation of the consular convention between France and the United States, the French minister for foreign affairs, Montmorin, opposed granting exequaturs to American consuls for Martinique, Guadeloupe, and Saint-Domingue.[30] While the French Commerce Committee was debating new customs duties, Montmorin learned that the American discrimination clause had been rejected by the Senate in 1789 and again in 1790. This discrimination clause had been aimed essentially at Great Britain, and Madison had included it in the bill on tonnage. France, a former ally of the United States, was thus not being treated any better than Great Britain, the former colonial power. Such developments could not but reinforce the French merchants' misgivings about Americans, whom they viewed as still too bound up with British trade.[31]

In February 1791 the new French General Customs Tariff struck a terrible blow to the type of commercial relations that had been established between France and the United States by the decrees of 1787. Although rights on whale oil remained low, the transportation of American tobacco on U.S. ships was heavily taxed in order to favor the French merchant marine.[32] Indeed, foreign tobacco imports, no matter what the means of transportation, were subject to heavy taxation. Contrary to Jefferson's long-standing hopes, the end of the tobacco monopoly, which occurred at the same time, was not followed by free trade measures or by a ban on tobacco growing in France. Owing to pressure from Alsatian deputies, tobacco growing was in fact encouraged in France, and the new tariff on imported tobacco was the result of this protectionist step. Gouverneur Morris's protests only resulted in an additional clause to the tariff, stipulating that only tobacco from North America could be imported into France. Such a mediocre compensation, however, was not enough to prevent the irreversible decline of tobacco growing in the Chesapeake Bay area, a decline that was clearly linked to the end of purchase orders from the Farmers-General.[33] Jefferson confided his disappointment to Madison in the following terms: "The French proceedings against our tobacco and ships are very eccentric and unwise."[34] In 1793 Genêt arrived with orders to negotiate a new trade treaty, which briefly rekindled Jefferson's hopes; as we have seen, however, the French minister's unwelcome activities were to shatter the secretary of state's dreams.

In his commitment to developing foreign trade, Jefferson took an interest in all areas of the United States and sought means to help New England fishermen as well as tobacco growers in Virginia.[35] Although clearly national, his economic policy was more subtly nationalistic than that of James Madison. Whereas Madison was ready to put a halt to all trade between the United States and Great Britain as a means of defending the new republic's honor and independence, Jefferson promoted a less flamboyant brand of economic nationalism, albeit no less resolute. From May 1790 to December 1793, Jefferson waged a ceaseless campaign in favor of diversifying and opening up markets. After the General Customs Tariff was decreed in 1791, Jefferson, although a friend of France, became so bitter as to threaten to retaliate against the former ally, France.[36] As he explained to William Short and Gouverneur Morris in January 1792, the most important duty for a diplomat was "the patronage of our commerce, and the extension of its privileges."[37] Like Madison, Jefferson could not conceive of real independence without a prosperous foreign trade, but for the secretary of state, that goal was to be achieved less through confrontation than through timely and realistic use of the international situation. At the time of the Nootka Sound affair, Jefferson declared: "If the war between Spain and England takes place, I think France will inevitably be involved in it. In that case I hope the new world will fatten on the follies of the old. If we can but establish the principles of the armed neutrality for ourselves, we must become the carriers for all parties as far as we can raise vessels."[38] (For details on the Nootka Sound affair, see chapter 7.) No better expression could be found for the priority given to one's country's prosperity, even and especially if such prosperity had to be achieved at the expense of other nations. In Jefferson's writings, one senses his desire not only to assert the independence of the new nation in a hostile world that was dominated by the great mercantilist powers, but also to carve out a spot on the international scene for the United States as an essential partner. Jefferson and Madison did not simply try to assert the new nation's identity in opposition to Great Britain's; their agendas reflected great national pride that was rooted in their faith in the future of the United States.

Alexander Hamilton and James Madison's Opponents

When Madison introduced a discriminatory clause into the tonnage bill, he probably did not foresee so much hostility, especially coming from the author of *The Federalist* no. 11, Alexander Hamilton himself, who was then secretary of the treasury. The Senate was, however, under Hamilton's influence, and Madison's discriminatory measure was rejected both in 1789 and in 1790. In 1794, when Madison once again attempted to introduce his plan, he was again unsuccessful. As in 1789 and 1790, Hamilton managed to counter Madison's offensive, this time by channeling congressmen's anger into other forms of action.[39] What is one to make of Hamilton's about-face? So soon after the war, so soon after *The Federalist,* how did he come to accept the economic domination of Great Britain? How is it that so many members of Congress came to follow his lead?

Because they failed to rebel against ships being captured by the British navy, historian John R. Nelson Jr. has accused Hamilton and his followers of abdicating national independence and pursuing a neocolonial policy, thus supposedly even hurting the American economy by forestalling the development of manufacturing.[40] William Appleman Williams, while considering the drafters of the Constitution to be the heirs to British mercantilism, differs in the analysis of the economic policies at work and does not consider Hamilton's policies to have been a major hindrance to the rise of economic liberalism in the United States. Like Nelson, however, Williams regards the secretary of the treasury's nationalism as lukewarm and as subordinate to his desire to maintain privileged economic relations with Great Britain.[41] But then if such was the case, that is, if Hamilton's ideas were indeed so weakly nationalistic, why did they win over Congress and defeat the ideas of Thomas Jefferson and James Madison?

The first debate on tonnage duties, which was preceded by a closely related debate on import duties, took place in April and May 1789, at a time when the future ideological cleavage between Republicans and Federalists was not yet clearly established. Already at this time, however, the arguments set forth by Madison's opponents formed a coherent whole. Many representatives agreed with Madison in theory, but they recommended caution and moderation. Thomas Fitzsimmons of Pennsylvania doubted whether "it would be politic, at this moment, to adopt a severe remedy for the evil" and suggested making "only a small discrimination for the present." James Jackson of Georgia and Roger Sherman of Connecticut shared this view.[42] For these congressmen, resorting to an aggressive commercial policy would only be justified once caution and negotiation proved vain. John Lawrence of New York also counseled moderation as the "advice of prudence," adding that if this failed, then other measures could be applied.[43]

Whereas Madison was not afraid of the possibility of British retaliation, his opponents appeared persuaded that a conflict between the two countries would be in Great Britain's favor.[44] They did not hide the fact that in this matter they were concerned about the nation. Like Roger Sherman, John Lawrence made this point clear: "I am actuated only by the purest motives for my country's good, in opposing what I consider as prejudicial to her interest."[45] It was James Jackson, however, who most thoroughly expounded on the "national" reasons behind his opposition to Madison's discriminatory clause. The Georgia representative felt the Union was still weak, as some states had not yet even ratified the Constitution. The union of the new republic needed to be cemented, and the new institutions needed to produce a united nation; to this purpose, the federal government had to gain—but not force—acceptance and avoid becoming a symbol of economic turmoil. Or as Jackson put it himself: "The question before the committee appears to me to be, whether we shall draw in, by tender means, the States that are not of the Union, or deter them from joining us, by holding out the iron hand of tyranny and oppression."[46] Jackson's main concern was the durability of the new system and the unity of the new nation. As John Lawrence explained, if the federal government took steps that led toward an economic crisis, it would lose its credibility and destroy the nation's soul, that is, the people's industry; Lawrence thus clearly showed that economic prosperity was one of the foundations of American national feeling.[47]

By 1794 opposition had become more open and positions more marked. Still, if one examines the statements made by Madison's opponents, it is clear that they merely expanded upon the same arguments that had already been used in 1790. In a speech originally inspired and outlined by Hamilton,[48] William Loughton Smith of South Carolina spoke in turn for moderation: "[W]e ought with great caution to attempt any thing at a future day, till we have acquired a maturity which will enable us to act with greater effect, and to brave the consequences, even if they should amount to war. . . . Wisdom admonishes us to be patient, 'to make haste slowly.'"[49] For the time being, Smith added, an aggressive policy toward Great Britain could only lead to war. And who, in a time of full prosperity, would want to start a war?[50] Even in the event of a mere trade war, Uriah Forrest of Maryland said, citing figures, that the United States did not stand a chance: "Who will suffer most? She, by the interruption of one-sixth [of her trade], with the means of getting most of the articles we supply, on as good terms, from other nations, . . . or we, with an interruption of one-half our trade and commerce?"[51] Like William Loughton Smith, other congressmen, such as Richard Bland Lee of Virginia, William Vans Murray of Maryland, and Abiel Foster of New Hampshire, evoked the general prosperity of the United States in trade and agriculture, only to end up speculating on the meaning of measures that were bound to undermine it.[52] The cautious attitude adopted by Hamilton's followers regarding Madison's propositions led them to downplay the hindrance to the development of American trade caused by the British. This, however, did not result from a lack of national feeling or a sudden renunciation of the principles for which these men had fought in 1776 and had changed the Constitution in 1787: indeed, they did not take to Hamilton's ideas out of cowardice, but rather because those ideas seemed better suited to guarantee the existing prosperity, without which it seemed impossible to them to build a strong American nation.

Prosperity and Nationalism

In fact, between 1789 and 1794 the American economy emerged from the period of instability that had set in immediately after the war.[53] Merchants and shipowners in particular had seen their businesses prosper since 1793.[54] Although France and Great Britain closed off their colonies to American trade after the war, the merchants of the early republic managed to get through by resorting to fake documents and changing their ships' names or ports of registry. When he was fighting for French colonies to be officially opened, Jefferson observed: "The revolution in France goes on with a slow and steady step. Their West Indian islands are all in combustion. There is no government in them, consequently their trade is entirely open to us."[55] Whereas Europe was being reluctant, the East was opening up to American ships. During the debate of 1789, John Lawrence informed his colleagues that no fewer than forty-seven ships were at that moment sailing toward countries beyond the Cape of Good Hope.[56]

As a result of the onset of revolutionary wars, American shipowners and traders suddenly came into a controlling position over trade with the European colonies; indeed, thanks to the neutral status of the United States, they were able to keep up transatlantic trade. Having been driven off the seas by Britain's naval power, France opened up its colonies to American ships in February 1793. As for Spain, from the moment it entered the war against Britain in 1796, it also lost its freedom on the seas and, much to its dismay, was forced to open the ports of its Atlantic colonies to American trade by a decree in 1797. As early as January 1794, Great Britain, which until then had been reluctant, allowed the practice of "broken voyage," which meant that Americans could buy goods from the colonies of enemies of England and transport them to the parent country. England posed only one restriction: goods had to be unloaded on U.S. soil before being reshipped. Thus, the American merchant marine gradually came to replace the merchant marines of the warring countries, which England's naval power prevented from trading with their colonies. Britain's willingness to accept the "broken voyage" subterfuge amounted to fostering a new role for the American merchant marine on the basis of its own need for American help.[57] William Vans Murray could rightfully declare: "Our ships visit every part of the world; . . . there is no place to which American enterprises does [*sic*] not convey our various products; . . . so far is our commerce confined, that the most distant ports and oceans in Russia and China, and the Pacific, are its only boundaries."[58] This extraordi-

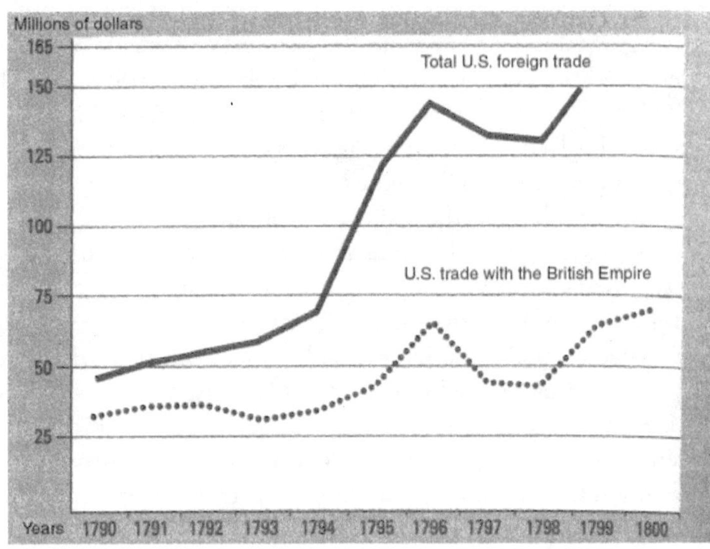

Growth of American Foreign Trade in Millions of Dollars (John R. Nelson Jr., *Liberty and Property*, p. 179)

nary commercial growth stirred up enthusiasm not only on the part of Vans Murray, but also on the part of many other Americans. In 1789, when such a prospect was not yet in view, Madison's appeal to republican civic spirit and disinterested patriotic feeling could still be heard. But soon after that it became clear, through reports about debates on foreign policy, that Madison's opponents wanted first and foremost to preserve the restored prosperity. They would support no economic policy that appeared to hamper the country's commercial development. Like Hamilton, Madison wanted to ensure the nation's prosperity, but his economic policy implied real sacrifices from his fellow citizens, since it was likely to lead to war if Great Britain opposed American actions. From 1789 to 1794 it seemed impossible for any American economic policy geared at national independence to privilege the common welfare over private gain. Giving priority to the common good was no longer an option: the American elite felt that the nation's economic development and the growth of private wealth should now go hand in hand.

Hamilton's about-face and his new, pro-British economic policy therefore caved in to the spirit of the times, in which "interest" was given precedence over "virtue." In supporting Hamilton's economic policy, members of Congress betrayed the growing influence on the American elite of free trade ideology, a new credo that merged public and private interests.[59] In fact, in the early 1790s, the way to ensure the quickest growth of U.S. wealth was an entente with Great Britain, the country's first trading partner, whereas a confrontation would only have resulted in delaying such growth, and might not have been any better guarantee of the nation's independence. Whether or not this argument is valid for the period up to 1793, it undoubtedly applies to the situation after that date, in which the revolutionary wars enabled England to impose once again its hegemony over the seas. Indeed, had Great Britain not been well disposed toward its former colony, the United States could not have become the carrier of all of Europe's colonial goods. True national independence, grounded in national prosperity, required some degree of compromise with Great Britain. It is therefore difficult to agree with historian John R. Nelson Jr.'s criticism of Alexander Hamilton. Even though Hamilton's economic policy was less explicitly nationalistic than Jefferson's and Madison's, it cannot be reduced to a short-sighted program, one geared solely at preserving the secretary of the treasury's tax bill. It is also difficult to agree with Nelson when he claims that Hamilton "abandon[ed] an independent merchant marine and foreign trade."[60] Hamilton only sought to use Great Britain's economic support in order to foster American development.

It is equally impossible, however, to say that Hamilton's policy was the only suitable way of ensuring true national independence and prosperity. Great Britain would certainly not have allowed American trade to grow if the onset of the revolutionary wars had not made an entente with the United States seem more appealing. Hamilton's ideas won the day because, given the international context, they were the most conducive to quick prosperity and thus, in the long term, to the economic independence that was indispensable to true national independence. In point of fact, in order to explain the success of the secretary of the treasury's ideas, one has to invoke external circumstances, along with an American desire for individual wealth. Through the debates on U.S. foreign trade relations, it becomes clear that commercial expansion was a common foreign policy goal; moreover, one can discern a free trade bias in this expansionist agenda, which, although seemingly frustrating the hopes of statesmen such as Jefferson and Madison for immediate economic independence, in fact anchored such independence in a deep-seated desire for personal prosperity.

Territorial Expansion

U.S. Commercial Influence Extended to the Caribbean, South America, and the Far East

For the great mercantilist empires of the eighteenth century, commerce and conquest went hand in hand. The very idea of the "exclusive" reflected a desire to achieve total control over trade with another part of the world and, by extension, to try to conquer that part of the world. The mercantilist system was inseparable from the rise of rival empires. Although Americans began professing free trade ideas in 1776 and sought to break out of the mercantilist mold, they were aware of the ambiguities involved in any desire for commercial expansion in a mercantilist world. In 1791, as he was trying to secure the opening up of all the French Caribbean islands to American trade, Jefferson explained to William Short that commercial expansion did not, in the American mind, rhyme with conquest: "Whenever jealousies are expressed as to any supposed views of ours on the dominion of the West Indies, you cannot go farther than the truth in asserting we have none. If there be one principle more deeply than any other in the mind of every American, it is that we should have nothing to do with conquest. As to commerce indeed we have strong sensations."[61]

The diplomatic campaign Jefferson waged with the French authorities was, in his own words, grounded in the "natural right" to "have commerce and intercourse with our neighbours."[62] In appealing to natural right and casting off every notion of conquest, Jefferson clearly proved his allegiance to Enlightenment philosophers such as Rousseau, Vattel, and d'Holbach. These philosophers had indeed objected to dynastic and colonial wars as well as to the consequences of them, such as extensions of territory that violated the will of individual peoples and their natural right to self-determination, and they had condemned conquest and expansion, which they compared to the law of the jungle.[63] It should be noted, however, that in order to assert this natural right, Jefferson declared himself ready to use force—an unlikely association, and one that had little to do with the peaceful spirit that supposedly was to accompany the rejection of conquest and the desire for free trade: "To suppress this neighborly intercourse is an exercise of force, which we shall have a just right to remove when [we are] the superior force."[64]

Jefferson was in fact not the only one to justify such claims by appealing to both natural right and the right of the strongest. Edward Rutledge, an influential politician from South Carolina, resorted to the same reasoning: "The West Indies are naturally connected with this Country, that they must forever depend upon Us; Her Separation appears to have been effected by a convulsion of nature. . . . . With the Means of a Navy in our Hands, and with the Prospect of a Navy in the Eye of Europe, we may dictate a treaty."[65]

In the minds of the Enlightenment philosophers, a given people's natural right extended to their territory; for Americans, it also extended to adjoining territories. Natural right thus came to justify aims of an expansionist nature. When Americans actually spelled out this particular interpretation of natural right, they justified it in terms of security, evoking the fear of being encircled by great neighboring powers.[66] In 1790, however, their appeal to natural right was strong enough for them to simply assert their right without explaining its exact source. The recourse to natural right was indeed a definitive argument, one that was not up for negotiation nor discussion. In fact, being even less moderate in actions than in words,

Jefferson challenged the views of French authorities by stubbornly insisting upon posting American consuls in the French colonies.[67] American citizens exploited the political and administrative turmoil at Saint-Domingue from 1789 on and established a lucrative business there. According to historian John H. Coatsworth, by 1790 the value of American exports to Saint-Domingue exceeded that of exports to all other Caribbean islands.[68] Once the French islands were officially opened to American trade, the same trend prevailed until 1797.

As is apparent in the example of Saint-Domingue, the aggressive stance of American foreign trade in the Caribbean after 1789 more closely resembles a commercial offensive than the enactment of peaceful ideals. In the name of free trade, Americans wanted to gain control of markets and take part in the competition between nations. As Richard Van Alstyne wrote in 1949: "The years from 1783 to 1860 were the years when the United States created its empire. We are prone to forget that the paths of empire led seaward as well as landward, and we fail commonly to correlate the maritime phase of American expansion with the continental."[69]

The term "empire" had long been part of the American vocabulary. Proud subjects of the British Empire until 1776 (like Benjamin Franklin), Americans had redirected their pride onto the American Empire, which they saw as the heir to the British Empire.[70] For them empire meant not only power and sovereignty, but also the prospect of expansion over land and sea.[71] Once the revolutionary wars had dismantled the mercantilist yoke, Americans logically exploited the new situation by gaining control over the Caribbean trade (which amounted to about one-third of their exports).[72] First it was Saint-Domingue, the richest of all the European colonies, which bought between 39 and 44 percent of all American exports to the Caribbean and South America. Then, at the height of political, diplomatic, and military collaboration between Great Britain and the United States (1798–1801), the British islands took in over 35 percent of American exports to that area.[73] This was sweet revenge on the 1784 Order in Council that had officially closed off those islands from American trade. Likewise, in Spanish America the rise of U.S. trade was spectacular.[74] Timothy Pickering posted consuls there, and American merchants and sailors began to discover the ports of Latin America, which they had previously had almost no commercial links with because the Spanish Empire had been so forbearing. Even in Chile, where in theory Americans were not wanted, the number of U.S. ships that touched land multiplied almost tenfold between 1797 and 1809.[75] Given the fact that smuggling was a national passion with American sailors, the official statistics should be taken with a grain of salt: even before Spain opened all those territories to American trade, American trade had come to them.[76]

Americans did not limit their ambitions to the Caribbean and Europe. By 1789 prospecting for commercial avenues had taken them also to the Pacific

Coast and toward the Far East. As Captain Cook's third journey had shown in 1778, the Northwestern Coast of the American continent was rich in furs that would find a ready market in China. Whoever among the Russians, the Spanish, the British, and the Americans would first claim sovereignty over the Pacific Coast would hold the key to that trade: thus, the extension of the commercial domain and territorial expansion were tightly connected.[77]

The Republicans' Grassroots Territorial Expansionism

Jefferson's correspondence during his term as secretary of state shows that he had two main concerns: foreign trade, but also Spain's opening of the Mississippi to U.S. navigation and international trade. This foreign policy concern was even dearer to Jefferson's heart than getting Spain to respect the southwestern border, and it sheds light on the nature and strength of the young nation's expansionist ambition over territories located beyond its borders.

After the Revolution, neither France nor Spain cared to strengthen the U.S. position on the North American continent.[78] For both countries, the aim of their involvement in the conflict had essentially been to strike a blow at the triumphant British Empire and thus restore a balance of forces in Europe. Spain's latent hostility toward the United States became overt in 1783 with the closing of the Mississippi to American navigation. At a time when there was not yet a network of roads and canals linking the agricultural West to the markets of the East Coast, the Mississippi was the vital artery for the economic development of the new states and the only way for them to get their goods to market. The western states had already toyed with the idea of seceding before the Constitution was ratified, and it was thus possible that they might start thinking again about leaving the Union if the federal government did not obtain for them the same privilege that the British had enjoyed from 1763 to 1778. Speaking on behalf of the Democratic Society of Kentucky in 1793, John Breckinridge expressed the anger of westerners when he explained that, in an age that had proclaimed the triumph of the rights of man, it ought to be obvious that the free navigation of the Mississippi was the natural right of the people who lived in its basin.[79]

In order to further the interests of western states, but also to demonstrate to skeptics the power and efficiency of the federal government, Jefferson wholeheartedly embraced the cause in August 1790. In a memorandum he sent to William Carmichael, he expounded upon the arguments to be used to open negotiations with Spain, flatly declaring: "We have *a right* to the navigation of the Mississippi, 1. by Nature; 2. by Treaty."[80] In order to support his demand for opening the Mississippi to navigation, Jefferson preferred to appeal to natural right rather than treaties and international law, which, according to historian Albert K. Weinberg, would not have supported his claims.[81] Thus, because of its definitive and nonnegotiable character, the natural right argument proved especially useful in this specific case. As with the opening of the Caribbean to American trade, the secretary of state voiced his desire for peace when he declared "conquest not in our principles; inconsistent with our government."[82] To this philosophical discourse, however, he added very pragmatic warnings that seem much more directly inspired by what could be called "realpolitik" than by the spirit of the Enlightenment. With regard to the western population, Jefferson noted that "forty thousand [westerners] bear arms" and added that the federal government would support them "whenever they shall say 'we cannot, we will not, be longer shut up.'" If Spain would not give in on the navigation of the Mississippi in the name of the very philosophical concept of natural right, western pioneers would sweep into Spanish possessions to redress a wrong that existed only in the eyes of the secretary of state. Far from comprehending the unjust and insolent nature of his demands, Jefferson even sketched out the various stages of a military campaign: New Orleans, once taken, could be retaken by the Spaniards, but then: "We can recover it by a counter-expedition, and so as often as the case shall happen. Their expedition will be slow, expensive, and lead to catastrophes. Ours sudden, economical. . . . We should associate the country to our Union. The inhabitants wish this."[83]

Although the spirit of conquest was not one of the explicit principles of the new nation, it surely was part of the American imagination. The only difference between the wars of conquest fought by France and Great Britain on behalf of their empires and the war Jefferson threatened Spain with was that pioneers and citizens started the latter, whereas the former were dictated by the highest spheres of the state. Indeed, Jefferson's expansionism had a grassroots and democratic base, and it derived its ultimate rationale from the will and actions of the citizens; in fact, if one is to believe the secretary of state, the federal government would almost have no choice but to follow the lead of the westerners.[84] Indeed, his point is supported by the facts: the population of Kentucky had doubled between 1783 and 1790, and kept on growing rapidly, doubling once again between 1790 and 1800 to reach 220,000; and Kentuckians made their will known.[85] Before conflicts ended between the Indian nations and the federal government, pioneers also poured into Tennessee, the population reaching 77,000 in 1796.[86] It is thus logical that the justification of expansion by the will of the people should recur as a leitmotiv throughout Jefferson's correspondence on Mississippi navigation. In March 1791 he wrote: "Should any spark kindle these dispositions of our borderers into a flame, we are involved beyond recall by the eternal principles of justice to our citizens, which we will never abandon."[87]

The "eternal principle of justice" invoked by Jefferson was not an ideal criterion for judging human actions; it was a political bond that, in the Jeffersonian conception of American democracy, inseparably tied statesmen to citizens, and bound the former to observe the latter's will. Just as justice legitimized conquest, so the doctrine of natural right enabled Jefferson to voice ever increasing territorial claims. In 1790 he explained that if there was to be any negotiation between the United States and Spain, it could not possibly focus upon Mississippi navigation (for that was a natural, nonnegotiable right), but rather it could only address the issue of obtaining a port for depositing goods at the mouth (i.e., New Orleans): "It may be asked, what need of a negotiation, if the navigation is to be ceded at all events? You know that the navigation cannot be practised without a port. . . . The fixing on a proper port, and the degree of freedom it is to enjoy in its operations, will require negotiation."[88] One week later, the demand for a port was presented in turn as a "natural" necessity with which the Spaniards would eventually have to comply, no matter if they negotiated now or not: "Nature has decided what shall be the geography of that in the end . . . by cutting off from the adjacent countries of Florida and Louisiana, and enclosing between two of its channels, a long and narrow slip of land, called the Island of New Orleans."[89]

Already by August 1790, Jefferson was even thinking that Spain had better give the Floridas over to the United States, in exchange for the new nation's commitment to safeguarding Spanish possessions west of the Mississippi. Between drafting a peace treaty and making an unjustified claim on foreign territory, there was but a thin line that Jefferson could easily cross.[90] Finally, in his report on the negotiations with Spain, dated March 18, 1792, Jefferson came up with another element of natural right to justify American demands: the right for boats going downstream to use the river banks.[91]

Such an aggressive attitude from the secretary of state is worth noting, especially at a time when the United States was far from controlling the territory granted to it by the treaty of 1783, and when Spain and Great Britain thought so little of the new nation that they did not condescend to opening official talks with it before 1791. Jefferson's confidence exceeded the usual limits of diplomatic coolheadedness and, bluff aside, reflected his certainty of being in the right. In addition, his firmness of language and ever increasing claims reveal his optimism and vision, which reflected his trust in the country's future as well as in the pioneers' undertakings.

In 1793 the arrival of the French minister Genêt strengthened Jefferson's ideas and encouraged his expansionist views. "[W]hile waiting for the American government to join [France's] cause," Genêt was instructed "to take all the necessary steps within his capacity to instill principles of liberty and independence in Louisiana and the other American provinces neighboring the United States."[92] Indeed, France had just entered into a war against Spain (on March 7, 1793) and wanted to destabilize it in its colonies. The French knew that the United States would not openly side with them. While they respected such neutrality, they were not unaware of the situation: since Kentuckians had been "long burning with a legitimate desire to enjoy free navigation on the Mississippi," they would probably support France's undertaking. Genêt was thus authorized to act: "to maintain agents in Kentucky, to dispatch some to Louisiana as well, and to spend whatever money he deems appropriate to further the execution of this plan."[93]

As Genêt knew, many pioneers in the West would welcome French aid first and foremost as a chance to launch expeditions that they had long been plotting.[94] Indeed, General George Rogers Clark, who had conquered the Northwest for the United States during the War of Independence, volunteered his services to the French envoy:

> General Clark has informed me of a plan he has long been nurturing, to seize first Upper Louisiana and shortly thereafter the banks of the Mississippi down to the sea. . . . Since the advent of peace his sole preoccupation has been to ascertain the means of the Spanish government in Louisiana and Mexico, the number of men employed in their defence, the situation of ports, the various means of communication, above all the inclination of the people, which he believes in our favor. . . . He thinks that with 400 men he could easily drive Spanish agents out of Upper Louisiana, and with 800 perform the same operation for New Orleans. . . . In the way of naval forces he is only requesting 2 or 3 frigates to support him from the sea.[95]

Such a plan was a perfect match for Jefferson's expansionist projects and did not fail to rouse his interest. Faced with the prospect of a French sea attack on Spanish colonies, Jefferson withdrew his previous offer to safeguard them. He wrote American negotiators Short and Carmichael, who were then trying to settle the Spanish-American dispute: "[Y]ou should not, by any clause of treaty, bind us to guarantee any of the Spanish colonies against their own independence." Jefferson already envisioned an American takeover of the Floridas, for in his mind France would "not object to the receiving those on the East side [of the Mississippi] into our confederation."[96] In contrast, he said nothing about the fate of Louisiana: did he think that once it was "liberated" by French and Kentuckian forces, it should fall into American hands, or should it be reunited with French possessions? The latter option seemed implausible enough, since the Clark-Genêt expedition was to be composed mainly of Americans, and Jefferson was showing restraint in his relations with France, as he had explained to William Short back in 1790: "It is proper to apprize you of a circumstance which may show the expediency of being in some degree on your guard, even in your communications to the court of France."[97]

Although the fate of Louisiana did not seem to be a top priority for the secretary of state in this particular case, his response to botanist André Michaux's journey reveals that, in fact, anything that pertained to the North American continent meant something to him. Already back in 1785, during his stay in Paris, Jefferson had been worried about the true motivations behind the French navigator Jean-François de La Pérouse's journey: were the French not seeking to colonize the Northwestern Coast of North America?[98] At the same time, John Ledyard, an American sailor who had taken part in Cook's voyages, had described to him the value of the Chinese market for American furs.[99] In order not to let the United States fall behind Canadian explorers, Jefferson entrusted Michaux with a scientific mission that came on top of his function as political agitator in the Spanish territories, a function Jefferson was aware of.[100] Anticipating that the great European empires were ready to divide among themselves this last unexplored area of the American continent, Jefferson wanted the United States to play an active role in the battle between the mercantilist empires. To this end he entrusted Michaux with orders "to explore the country along the Missouri, and thence westwardly to the Pacific Ocean." The goal was geopolitical and strategic: "[T]he chief object of your journey is to find the shortest and most convenient route of communication between the United States and the Pacific Ocean," although Michaux, as a devoted naturalist, was also supposed to make an account of all "interesting circumstances" he would happen upon.[101]

Contrary to historian L. S. Kaplan's opinion, Jefferson's aid to Michaux did not reflect naiveté or blindness on his part in the face of French imperial ventures in the American West.[102] Although a report by the Compte de of Moustier, a French diplomat posted in the United States after the American Revolution, had once again brought to light the considerable advantages Louisiana presented for colonization, the French Convention was sincerely trying to liberate Spanish colonies, or at least to destabilize them, but not to conquer them.[103] Jefferson was always suspicious of the designs of other powers on the North American continent, and he was thus able to use Michaux as a scout for American expansion. As a matter of fact, Michaux's orders were to serve as a blueprint for those that Jefferson drafted for Lewis and Clark in 1803.[104]

Rufus King and Alexander Hamilton: The Other Expansionist Dream

In the course of his negotiations with Gardoqui in 1786, John Jay had suggested that Congress temporarily give up on the Mississippi navigation in return for an advantageous commerce treaty with Spain. Since that time there had been a great deal of mistrust among the southern and western states toward the East, which they suspected of being willing to sacrifice continental expansion in favor of developing the interests of New York and Boston merchants. This feeling was not dispelled after Jefferson became secretary of state;[105] and it was even strengthened when the Federalists (many of them from southeastern states) came to power, especially after the Whiskey Rebellion of 1794 increased tensions between East and West. Like Hamilton, however, some Federalist leaders believed that the American nation could only answer its calling and prosper by affirming direct or indirect control over both, North and South America. After consolidating federal power over the territories acquired in 1783 and the foreign nations occupying them (1790–96), they now expected to use the revolutionary wars to replace the declining empires in the New World. Even before he had such strong influence in American politics, Hamilton had made no secret of his ambition to see the United States dominate the American continent. In *The Federalist* no. 11 he wrote: "I shall briefly observe, that our situation invites and our interests prompt us to aim at an ascendant in the system of American affairs. . . . Let Americans disdain to be the instruments of European greatness! Let the thirteen States, bound together in a strict and indissoluble Union, concur in erecting one great American system, superior to the control of all transatlantic force or influence, and able to dictate the terms of the connection between the old and the new world!!"[106]

In 1798, as part of the military preparations brought on by the quasi war with France, Hamilton was thrown into a commanding position in the American army, second only to George Washington. At the same time, in London, the British government was finally lending a willing ear to the propositions of the Venezuelan adventurer Francisco de Miranda. In his drive to free Latin America from Spanish rule, Miranda had suggested that the British help him set up a liberation operation.[107] The British no longer needed to humor Spain, which was now France's ally, and did not care to let the vast Spanish colonial domain fall into the sphere of revolutionary France, which would have put the resources of those colonies at the disposal of the French. As the American minister in London, Rufus King, learned: "If England engages in this plan, she will propose to the United States to cooperate in its execution." The excellent relations between the United States and Great Britain at that time made such a plan seem appealing; as he was convinced that the United States could play an outstanding role on the American continent, Rufus King advised Secretary of State Timothy Pickering to accept such a proposal: "The President may therefore expect the overture of England and will I am persuaded act upon it under the influence of the wise and comprehensive policy which looking forward to the destinies of the new world shall in the beginning by great and generous deeds lay deep and firm the foundations of lasting concord between its rising empires."[108]

Miranda, growing tired of London's procrastination, decided to go directly to President John Adams and ask him to lend some four to five thousand troops to the Anglo-American expedition. In Rufus King's mind, the nature of the undertaking gradually took shape; he wrote Hamilton that the United States should assume the leading role in this liberation war for it could not miss such an opportunity.[109] For Rufus King "opportunity" clearly meant a chance for the United States to stand out and to further its ideas on the American continent; he may have also had in mind a commercial opportunity. As a matter of fact, opening up the trade of all of Spanish America to U.S. merchants and producers would give them an opportunity they had not hoped for. Hamilton had received several letters from Miranda, whom he had known for a long time, and he was enthralled by the projected expedition. Like Rufus King, he thought that the United States ought to play the leading role and not be a mere partner or ally of Great Britain. As the actual commander of the U.S. Army, he already saw himself as the head of the expedition.[110]

Hamilton not only wanted to liberate the Spanish colonies, he also wanted to make sure that future governments would share the political views of the American government. He thus betrayed imperialist designs that aimed at imposing upon the countries that were to be freed conditions that would favor trade with the United States. Once under the protection of the United States and England, the former Spanish colonies in Latin America would thus form a sphere of American influence. Following independence, "moderate" governments would be formed, and these would grant commercial privileges to the countries that had worked together for their liberation.[111]

Neither John Adams nor Timothy Pickering answered Rufus King's dispatches on the subject. In 1799, the end of the near-war situation put an end to the near alliance with Great Britain, bringing about the dismantling of the American army and, by consequence, the crushing of Hamilton's military ambitions. Miranda's plan had met with so much enthusiasm from Hamilton and Rufus King for a specific reason: because it allowed them to combine an ideological justification (liberation) with the goal of real political and commercial supremacy over the whole American continent. In that sense, it was reminiscent of Genêt's planned operations with respect to Louisiana and the Floridas. Thus, what distinguished the expansionism of Rufus King and Hamilton from that of Jefferson was not the geographical goal, but the method. Whereas Jefferson counted upon the unruly drive of the pioneers, Hamilton thought primarily in terms of centralized operations, designed and carried out by the federal government.

Although Miranda's plan had no real follow-up, Rufus King nevertheless soon had a chance, once again from London, to try to further American interests in an area that Americans thought of as "naturally" bound to them, the Caribbean. In September 1793, capitalizing on the opposition between Jacobins and Royalists, British troops had landed in Saint-Domingue in a drive to conquer the island and try to restore slavery there before the example set by the blacks of Saint-Domingue spread to the British islands. Those troops had been decimated by the combined effects of yellow fever and rough handling by Toussaint-Louverture's soldiers.[112] In the summer of 1798 their commanding officer, General Maitland, had to seek out an agreement with Toussaint; a convention was signed on August 31, 1798, by which the Saint-Domingue rebels pledged not to attack Jamaica, while the British committed themselves to providing it with supplies.[113] When Rufus King found out about this convention, in early December 1798, he instantly understood that it threatened a major goal of U.S. foreign policy, that is, the opening of Saint-Domingue to American trade. The dispatch in which he confided his concerns to Henry Dundas, the British secretary of war, was unambiguous: "I am aware that jealousies may be felt among our Merchants from the exclusive commerce secured to Great Britain under this Convention."[114] By the same token, King suggested opening the Saint-Domingue trade to the Americans. Henry Dundas, who at the time saw the United States as a precious friend for Great Britain, could not turn down this proposal; thus, joint action was settled upon with Lord Grenville. The British then decided to negotiate a new convention with Toussaint, this time acknowledging American participation.[115]

Meanwhile, in Saint-Domingue, Toussaint-Louverture, as a good strategist, was keeping several irons in the fire: far from relying solely on the British, he attempted after Maitland's departure to obtain from the American government the reopening of trade between the United States and Saint-Domingue. By then Toussaint's allegiance to French authorities was more and more tenuous; without even waiting for the official termination of the quasi war between France and the United States, he pledged to the American government that the Saint-Domingue–based pirate raids would end. As the American Congress was anxious to resume a lucrative trade and to restore U.S. commercial and political leadership in the area, in 1799 it passed an act enabling the president to reopen commercial relations with French possessions as soon as spoliation ended. As historian Rayford W. Logan has explained, although the law theoretically encompassed all French possessions, in the end it was only applied to Saint-Domingue.[116] The United States posted a consul general in Saint-Domingue, Edward Stevens. Thus, Rufus King and John Adams helped Jefferson's dream come true: protectionist mercantilism, whether British or French, had clearly lost the battle in Saint-Domingue. In order to avoid losing the support of the British fleet, which was helping it in the fight against French privateers, the American government decided not to push its advantage. When Maitland arrived in Philadelphia on April 20, 1799, a cooperation agreement was signed between the United States and Great Britain. Toussaint was initially prepared to admit only American ships, but despite his opposition, Maitland managed to secure the ratification of the final convention, albeit without Stevens's signature. That convention formulated a principle of noninterference (in the sense that it called for continued armistice and provided British and American ships protection from French privateers); above all, it granted rights of trade with Saint-Domingue to British and American ships only.[117] Thanks to Rufus King's watchfulness as well as Timothy Pickering's and John Adams's speed of action, the United States was thus able to maintain its leadership in the area.

Although their methods were different, the main goals of Republicans and Federalists in foreign policy were similar. Both parties sought to found national independence upon commercial and territorial expansion. As to the general direction of foreign trade, Jefferson's and Madison's ideas were less successful than Hamilton's, which were better suited to the economic situation and to the citizens' demands for free trade. In fact, the national feeling appears to have been inseparable from a desire for personal gain that followed two paths: the one over sea (thanks to foreign trade) and the other over the American continent (by way of an explicit expansionist impulse). "We are all Republicans, we are all Federalists," Thomas Jefferson rightly said in his 1801 inaugural address.[118] In the eyes of all those who took part in the economic growth of the late eighteenth century, the two parties uttered the same convictions and set out with the same faith on the road to prosperity. This consensus cannot, however, mask the fact that prosperity bypassed many people, although congressmen and members of government did not pay them much attention: among those, black slaves (20 percent of the population), whites without land or property, small indebted farmers, and widows of private soldiers who had died during the War of Independence (they would only start receiving pensions in 1832)—none of these groups experienced improvement during this period of national growth.[119]

Chapter 5

National Greatness, War, and Peace: The Ambiguities of Isolationism

The portrait of Americans that Moreau de Saint-Méry sketched in his *American Journey* of 1793–98 was a rather unflattering one. Though he acknowledged their generosity, especially toward the French émigrés in Saint-Domingue, he was surprised at what, according to him, was the leading passion of Americans, that is, the lust for wealth. That lust evidently seemed to him incompatible with the virtues one should observe in the citizens of a "great nation": "When their trickiness and their commercialism have been replaced by the virtues that citizens of a great nation should have, the country should enjoy perfect tranquillity."[1] The word "virtue" refers to the ideal way the citizen was portrayed by classical republicanism: as a man devoted first and foremost to the community, and placing his own interests second to those of his country. As we saw with the debates on Madison's proposed commercial discrimination bills, it was pointless to encourage a spirit of sacrifice in citizens without offering them prospects for quick prosperity; for Americans, private interests were inseparable from the love of one's country. But then, should the nation, as Madison feared, suffer in silence the humiliations that more powerful nations would gladly inflict upon it? Would the materialistic concerns of Americans prevent their mobilization when it came to a matter of national honor?

Neither George Washington nor Gouverneur Morris, two determined nationalists, thought so. Both men shared their fellow citizens' aims for personal prosperity, and yet they felt that such a quest could be reconciled with more patriotic values. Committed to the wealth as well as to the greatness of the nation, they wanted to instill in their fellow citizens a spirit of love and worship of one's country, a spirit that they thought was the only means to forge a true American identity and to guarantee the nation's independence. Knowing as they did that those who could get rich preferred to do so more than they cared to defend their country's honor, and seeing that foreign policy crises were breaking the nation up rather than bringing it together, they sought to strengthen the bonds between all Americans. To this end, they wanted patriotism and the worship of national honor to be given priority once again. For, as Gouverneur Morris explained, such was indeed "the true Source and Principle of national Greatness. It is the national Spirit. It is in that high, haughty, generous and noble Spirit which prizes Glory more than wealth and holds Honor dearer than Life." Once American citizens shared in that spirit, "Foreign Powers [would] then know that to withhold a due Respect and Deference is dangerous." Thus Morris anticipated "the Day when to command Respect in the remotest Regions it will be sufficient to say I am an American."[2]

Still, to invoke national spirit in the abstract would not do to bring the nation together. As Gouverneur Morris suggested, American identity and independence had to be attained in opposition to Europe: exploiting foreign crises would contribute to defining national character as well as to bringing out spontaneous American pride, a new patriotism that would rebel against the humiliations inflicted upon the country. Morris's mission in London in 1790 thus gave him—as well as George Washington—the opportunity to display the new nation's independence and dignity. Later, the European wars and the quarrel with Pierre-Auguste Adet enabled George Washington to develop and extol, in his Farewell Address of 1796, the idea of a special destiny for America that would not hinder prosperity: far from Europe, America needed to grow and prosper in neutrality.

Even more credit is due to John Adams, however, than to Gouverneur Morris and George Washington, for the first great upsurge in patriotism after the war, the one that truly brought the nation together. Skillfully exploiting the XYZ dispatches that recounted the misfortunes of American envoys to France in dealing with Talleyrand's dishonest maneuvers, Adams indeed managed to enlist the majority of Americans in a great patriotic movement of self-righteous opposition to France. By the same token, he reinforced the feeling Americans had of their moral superiority over Europe, without ever seeming to lead the country on the road to a war with dire economic consequences. The national spirit was wrought out of these crises, which gave free rein to Americans' patriotic anger, an anger that was thus both an outward expression and cement for national identity.

Nevertheless, while American patriotism rose during the Federalist era by extolling military neutrality and moral superiority over Europe, this development cannot be separated from the more aggressive policy pursued by the country toward non-European nations. Whereas Americans stood on the purity of their principles and practice in order to assert their desire for peace and their rejection of Europe, its wars and its diplomatic methods, they at the same time displayed belligerence and diplomatic maneuvering on those fronts that concerned them more immediately. Arming the nation was not only meant as a way of fending off potential European invasions. The creation of an American army was primarily aimed at fighting the Indians; that of a navy, at getting the better of Barbary Coast pirates. Thus, Americans did not define their identity merely in opposition to Europe; they also forged it through the active (and most often violent) relations they maintained with nations that belonged to other civilizations.

Making the United States Respected Abroad: Gouverneur Morris and George Washington

Gouverneur Morris in Great Britain

At the time when John Adams was the minister plenipotentiary in London, after the revolution, his mission was to establish a treaty of commerce with Great Britain; but that plan never materialized. Surmising that the icy welcome given to the diplomat had probably had its cause in the mediocre image of the Confederation, George Washington decided to take up the fight again in October 1789. He wrote Gouverneur Morris to entrust him with an unofficial diplomatic mission. In January 1790 he sent him his credentials, stating that Morris was to "discover the sentiments" of the British government on the following topics:

1. Their detention of the Western posts contrary to the treaty of peace.
2. Indemnification for the negroes carried off against the stipulations of the same treaty.
3. A Treaty for the regulation of commerce between the two countries.
4. The exchange of a minister.[3]

The order of priorities was perfectly clear: six years after the peace treaty had been signed, the United States had to secure first and foremost the surrender of northwestern posts and a compensation for stolen slaves. At stake was the honor of the new government, "our national honor."[4] Indeed, Morris saw and carried out his mission under the light of nationalism. On March 29, 1790, he met for the first time with the Duke of Leeds, then secretary for foreign affairs, in which position the duke was to be replaced the following year by Lord Grenville. As soon as the western posts and the compensation for stolen slaves were mentioned, the Duke of Leeds tried to dodge the issue; but Morris was not intimidated: "He changed the conversation, which I bring back, and which he changes again."[5] In late April George Washington's envoy managed to get another interview, this time with Pitt and the Duke of Leeds, during which he discussed the western posts. Far from accepting their evasive answers, Morris did not hesitate to drive the British ministers into a corner.

As he explained to George Washington, Morris "thought it best to heap coals of fire in their heads, and thereby either bring them into our views or put them most eminently in the wrong."[6]

In the end Morris understood that the only reason the British kept up a dialogue with him during the spring and summer of 1790 was that they did not want to add to the number of their enemies in the event of a war with Spain over the Nootka Sound affair (see chapter 7).[7] For Morris, these negotiations ought to be a lesson in national independence, even if they failed. Only by maintaining a tough attitude and a strong government could the United States achieve respectability abroad.[8] Nothing less than an education of his fellow citizens in civic values was in order, for while foreign countries did not respect America because they "[did] not yet know America," the fact remained that "perhaps America [did] not yet know herself."[9] In the language of the time, this meant that the American national character—American identity—was not yet sufficiently defined, either in reference to other nations or for American citizens themselves. Thus, Morris's adventures in Great Britain led him to reflect upon American identity: if it was poorly perceived abroad, perhaps that was because it had not yet taken shape within the nation itself.

Washington and Jefferson took Morris at his word. In two messages to Congress on February 14, 1791, they vented their indignation at seeing that U.S. honor was being trampled upon by the former enemy, whose behavior they criticized: "they [the British] declare without scruple that they do not mean to fulfill what remains of the treaty of peace to be fulfilled on their part."[10] Such patriotic indignation, emanating from the highest realms of government, symbolized the official determination of the country's leaders to have the United States respected. At the time, however, Hamilton was more interested in seeking out Britain's favor, and he clearly had a hand in the ensuing rumors that went around Philadelphia, according to which the failure of the negotiations with Britain had to be imputed to Morris's toughness and lack of flexibility (i.e., lack of diplomacy, in Hamilton's eyes). Thus, the secretary of the treasury's attitude was tantamount to a disavowal of the firmness of Washington, Morris, and Jefferson. In the former special envoy's opinion, Hamilton's reasoning was odd, as can be gleaned from his ironic comments in a letter to his business partner, Robert Morris: "I will suppose it to be a very good reason to be given to America for not conferring a favor on her, that the man sent to ask it was disagreeable, no matter from what cause—but I trust that they will never avow to the British nation a disposition to make sacrifice of their interests to please a pleasant fellow."[11]

In fact, the reason why the British did not yield to Gouverneur Morris's toughness was not that they thought it undiplomatic; rather, they knew there existed, within Washington's administration, an "English party" with a decisive influence. Morris, otherwise a social and political conservative, was not won over to the ideas of Hamilton's party on that score; he held that in order for America to make itself respected and achieve its ends in its relations with the great powers, it had to rely on determination, and not on friendly behavior: "If you mean to make a good treaty with Britain, support your pretensions with spirit, and they will respect you for it."[12]

George Washington:
From the Proclamation of Neutrality to the Farewell Address

In 1791, however, the nation was not yet caught up in the political disputes that were to pit supporters of France against supporters of Great Britain after 1793. Americans did not yet know who they were; but at the same time their political life did not yet revolve around a debate that seems to have been largely borrowed from Europe. With the spread of war on the European continent in 1793, however, the intellectual colonialism that seemed to take over the political life of the new republic could only reinforce the doubts of Morris and of those who shared his views. Where, in that debate, was American identity to be found? If one had to be either pro-French or pro-British, where was there room to be an American? It was the search for such a national feeling, as the only means of uniting the nation, that pushed George Washington to exclaim in irritation: "In a word, I want an American character . . . never forget that we are Americans."[13]

For a national feeling to arise, there had to exist a national ideology distinguishing America from the Old Continent. George Washington went a long way toward building up such an ideology in both the proclamation of neutrality of April 1793 and his Farewell Address of September 19, 1796. The first elements of this nationalist doctrine were articulated on April 22, 1793, when the president proclaimed U.S. neutrality. All of Europe was ablaze, but in the president's words, "the duty and interest of the United States require that they should with sincerity and good faith adopt and pursue a conduct friendly and impartial towards the belligerent powers."[14] This declaration was somewhat hasty, as France had not asked her ally to enter the war. The chief goal of the declaration was to clearly set off American affairs from those of Europe, and thus to assert American identity as being different. That difference was not only geographical, but moral as well: in contrast to war-torn Europe, America symbolized peace and a desire for neutrality.

Washington's declaration was criticized by many pro-French Republicans, and in response, he received in the ensuing months many messages of support, which he answered by stressing the peaceful character and moral superiority of the United States. Through these exchanges of addresses and responses, Washington was able to create the image of a president who was close to his fellow citizens and who kept up a dialogue with them—in short, the image of a "Father of the Nation." To the people of Salem he asserted: "In making this declaration, I was persuaded that I spoke the wishes of my countrymen."[15] By making a formal occasion out of this foreign affairs decision, Washington came off as a figure who was more than a president: he was the symbol of the nation, which spoke through his mouth. He was not formulating a nationalist ideology; rather, the nation was speaking through him. Washington thus killed two birds with one stone: he articulated a foreign policy doctrine and also fashioned one of the earliest versions of a national political myth (i.e., America as neutral and peaceful, different from warlike Europe), the unifying function of which is obvious.

To be sure, defining the new nation in terms of an opposition to Europe was not an entirely novel gesture in America: indeed, this idea was a secularized transposition of the intellectual heritage of New England millenialist Puritans. In the seventeenth century, the Puritans could not have imagined that the colonies might one day resemble the Europe they had left because they wanted to build a better world.[16] Even before the Declaration of Independence, the idea of American difference had become one of the essential ingredients of the early republic's foreign policy, with Thomas Paine warning Americans against political relations with Europe. The first American diplomats to be sent to Europe after 1776 had quickly realized that America was a mere pawn on the diplomatic chessboard, and that Europeans, as masters of the game, intended to move it about according to their every whim.[17] They had concluded that American independence would have to be defined in essentially negative terms, as an absence of political relations with Europe. In *The Federalist* no. 11, Alexander Hamilton himself had linked national greatness to a separation from Europe.[18]

In that sense, Washington was not saying anything new, and yet it was the nation's first president who, in his Farewell Address, gave—with Hamilton's help—official and solemn expression to the doctrine of the necessary isolation of America. By linking isolation to the messianic calling of the United States, he exalted national feeling just as he was defining it.[19] In his speech, after thanking his fellow citizens for their support through his two presidential terms, Washington could not refrain from voicing "some sentiments" at the thought of the "danger" awaiting them. Fearing that division might be sown among Americans, he exhorted his fellow citizens to strengthen their love for the union, that is to say, for both the country and the federal institutions. Ignoring "local discriminations," Washington cautioned that: "The name of American . . . must exalt the just pride of patriotism, more than any appellation derived from local discriminations."

Regionalism, however, did not constitute in the president's eyes the chief obstacle to American national feeling and love for the Union. The real challenge to a feeling of unity was none other than "the spirit of party." Party spirit, as George Washington perceived it from 1793 to 1796, was especially detrimental to the rise of national feeling, because it allowed foreign nations to influence American politics (of course, what Washington had in mind here was the alleged French influence on the Republican Party). The true patriot, for Washington, was the American who understood that America and Europe belonged to two different spheres. The vocabulary he used underscored the difference, the distance or the peculiarity of America, whose identity became apparent through comparison with Europe: "Europe has a set of primary interests, which to us have none, or a very remote relation. . . . Our detached and distant situation invites and enables us to pursue a different course. . . . Why forego the advantages of so peculiar a situation?" Washington did not merely posit the difference between New and Old Worlds; he enriched this opposition by recourse to a moral hierarchy between the two spheres. Since he characterized Europe by "Ambition, Rivalship, Interest, Humour or Caprice," it could logically be inferred that the United States was destined to be the country of self-denial, equality, detachment, and stability. In that sense, Washington remained true to the ideas of the American Revolution, which pitted a pure, virtuous America against a corrupt, degenerate Europe.[20]

Going back to the theme of neutrality, Washington did not conceal that it was in the nature of Europe to be "engaged in frequent controversies, the causes of which are essentially foreign to our concerns."[21] It followed that America, by its very nature, could not be as bellicose as Europe. Historian Gilbert Chinard has gone so far as to point out, in Washington's Farewell Address, the "mystique of Americanism,"[22] as an illustration of which he quotes the following passage: "It will be worthy of a free, enlightened, and, at no distant period, a great Nation, to give to mankind the magnanimous and too novel example of a People always guided by an exalted justice and benevolence."[23]

Evidently, Washington's Farewell Address laid the foundations of isolationism.[24] The geographical isolation of America from Europe also implied a moral difference: because it was better than Europe, and although it was far away and isolated, America found itself paradoxically invested with a universal mission. By the example it set, the United States was supposed to contribute to the progress of humankind, though without meddling in European affairs. Insofar as the Farewell Address defined American national identity on the basis of the peculiarity of the United States, its moral superiority and universal mission, this document went beyond the exposition of a doctrine in foreign policy; it was also a nationalist credo, whose function was to make it possible for all Americans to commune in the patriotic worship of their nation, presented as being different, better, and exemplary. Even though the Farewell Address also read as a Federalist pamphlet that implied that Republicans were bad Americans, the nationalist dimension clearly set the tone. In fact, the last paragraph combined both aspects of nationalism. Washington here expressed his love for a land where after several generations had passed, the people had become rooted: "Actuated by that fervent love towards it [my country], which is so natural to a Man, who views in it the native soil of himself and his progenitors for several generations." He also expressed, however, his attachment to the country's institutions and values, which, for its citizens, were all the more precious since they had recently fought to obtain them: "I anticipate with pleasing expectation that retreat, in which I promise myself to realize, without alloy, the sweet enjoyment of partaking, in the midst of my fellow citizens, the benign influence of good laws under a free government, the ever favourite object of my heart, and the happy reward, as I trust, of our mutual cares, labours and dangers."[25] To shape American national identity, Washington formulated foreign policy principles that presented America as different and better. Such an identity, however, could not truly exist until it found a way to assert itself on the international stage. It was John Adams who, during the XYZ crisis, obtained this recognition and who pushed citizens to approve the definition of the nation that was being set forth through the foreign policy of the federal government.

John Adams and the XYZ Affair

As late as September 1796, it was still possible, despite Federalist attacks, to display pro-French leanings. But Pierre-Auguste Adet's blunders around the time of the 1796 elections played into the hands of the Federalist executive leaders. President Adams was then able to use the crisis between the United States and France to build up the nascent American patriotism, of for the benefit of both his party and himself. At the time of the inauguration, John Adams was already well aware that the poor relations between France and the United States were to be one of the hot issues on his administration's agenda, and on March 7, 1797, that is, three days after the inauguration, he learned that the Directory had refused to receive Charles Cotesworth Pinckney, who had come to replace James Monroe. In addition to this, the disclosure of increased French depredations on the American merchant marine led the new president to convene an extraordinary session of Congress in May.[26] He opened the session on May 16 with a message, the wording of which was designed to inflame his fellow citizens. After recounting Pinckney's misfortunes, he subtly introduced the topic of American sovereignty being trampled upon: "The refusal on the part of France to receive our minister is then the denial of a right; but the refusal to receive him until we have acceded to their demands, without discussion and without investigation, is to treat us neither as allies, nor as friends, or as a sovereign state." The dissent between France and the United States was not only a matter of politics or diplomacy. As Adams explained, everything about France's attitude proved that it did not consider the United States to be a full-fledged nation. He made the following conclusions: "Such attempts ought to be repelled with a decision which shall convince France, and the world, that we are not a degraded people, humiliated under a colonial spirit of fear and sense of inferiority; fitted to be the miserable instruments of foremost influence; and regardless of national honor, character, and interest."[27]

There was only a thin line separating the statements of Gouverneur Morris in 1790 from those of John Adams. Both were nationalists, and both thought that the United States still needed to prove itself on the international stage—in short, that the United States did not yet exist. In Adams's view, the crisis with France was a test for the new nation. It was up to the United States to show, by a tough stance, that it could make itself respected, and Adams would be the one to guide the United States in this undertaking. Adams would thus become the symbol of national independence and restored unity, and by the same token he would establish his party as the protector of national independence and glory. The vividness of his wording reflected a desire to stir up his fellow citizens' pride in order to rally them to his cause. Two words—"people" and "colonial"—were especially aimed at linking the Franco-American crisis to the revolutionary one, thus fusing the two causes and their issues, and reviving in 1797 the patriotism of 1776. France was another England; American citizens were called upon to unite against it as they had done before against England.

Nevertheless, although John Adams adopted an aggressive tone in this speech, he and the rest of his cabinet had already resolved to send a conciliatory mission to France, one that would be composed of John Marshall, Elbridge Gerry, and Charles Cotesworth Pinckney.[28] In the way of military measures, the special session of Congress merely planned a "slight improvement in land defenses," reserved the necessary funds "to complete, equip, and man three frigates already under construction," and authorized "the use of revenue cutters for naval purposes." Instead of uniting the members of Congress around national measures, the debates of the extraordinary session actually had a divisive effect.[29] The only tangible result of Adams's management of the crisis was a rise in xenophobia, which made life more and more difficult for French residents in the United States. Adet did not realize the truth of his words when, speaking of the Republicans, he exclaimed on November 19, 1796, in Philadelphia: "Everyone senses that the Directory has thought over [the issue before refusing to receive Pinckney]; but not all are equally satisfied to see Americans spoken to the way that they would only like to speak to other peoples. There may be here, among certain patriots, love of liberty; but there is even more vanity."[30] Indeed, the French attitude had hurt American "vanity," that is, American national feeling, even among the supposedly pro-French Republicans, and Adams had only needed to exploit and cultivate that reaction. That in the end was precisely what he had wanted, since his goal seems to have been first and foremost to muster up a flurry of national unity around his policies.

On March 4, 1798, Secretary of State Timothy Pickering received the XYZ dispatches from special envoys John Marshall, Elbridge Gerry, and Charles Cotesworth Pinckney, in which they related their Parisian misfortunes.

Unsure of congressional support, the president still did not request a declaration of war and merely ordered merchant ships to be armed. The Republicans rejected any war measures and supported an amendment by John Allen, who was a Federalist representative from Connecticut; this amendment required that the notorious dispatches be remitted to Congress. Adams was overjoyed: he knew that in obeying that injunction, he would unleash a hurricane of patriotism and xenophobia, the intensity of which would far surpass the first wave of 1797.[31] Once made public, the dispatches were published in their entirety in the Federalist newspapers.[32] In addition, Congressmen were given many copies that were published with an eye to feeding the Federalist nationalist propaganda. As a result of Talleyrand's brash diplomacy, the account of the American trio's adventures in Paris could only set all American hearts aflame and turn any remaining reluctant citizens into fiery patriots. The bribe that the French minister for external relations had demanded was explicitly depicted as an insult to American sovereignty.[33] Such was the import of John Marshall's diary entry for November 4, which echoed Adams's message of May 19, 1797: "It appears to me that for three envoys extraordinary to be kept in Paris thirty days without being received can only be designed to degrade and humiliate their country."

The envoys' firm attitude in the face of French corruption was summarized by Charles Cotesworth Pinckney's exclamation of October 27: "No, no, not a sixpence." Such toughness was admirable because it was truly courageous. Indeed, Pinckney's "No!" did not in the least worry the banker Hottinguer, one of Talleyrand's secret messengers, who was confident enough in the power of the Directory to answer with a threat of reprisals against the United States. According to Marshall, Hottinguer intimated that no one in Europe had been capable of resisting France: "He stated that Hamburg and other states of Europe were obliged to buy a peace and that it would be equally for our interest to do so."[34]

Corruption, then, was not exclusively French: it extended to all those countries that accepted French rule. The fact that the three envoys fell prey to French abuse, threats, and contempt was turned into a symbol of American virtue and served to restate the superiority and the peculiarity of the new nation. Marshall aptly summarized the meaning of his charge when he told Pinckney that upon coming home to America, he was happy to say farewell forever to Europe and its "crimes"—specifying that he only had in mind Europe's "political crimes."[35] This rejection of Europe was a way of asserting American identity.

After the XYZ dispatches were published, Federalist papers started filling up with addresses in support of the president, followed by Adams's answers, thus feeding patriotic enthusiasm. The general emphasis of these columns was the opposition between the "corrupt stratagems" of the French and the "firm and dignified resistance" advised by the president "for the preservation of our national honor and rights."[36] The words "independence," "honor," "sovereignty," "patriotism," and "unanimity" recurred in most articles. Patriotic songs exalted the superiority of the new nation, the sole country capable of resisting French arrogance:

> But tho' Holland, Rome, Naples and Switzerland bend
> Americans will their freedom defend.[37]

As the *Boston Columbian Centinel* of May 9, 1798, trumpeted, America was not only more prosperous than Europe; it was also more courageous. The two primary ingredients of American nationalism, namely, economic greatness and moral superiority, were thus tangibly linked. The partisan aim of this propaganda campaign was clear: Adams's conservative supporters sought to use the patriotic fever as a means of silencing the Republicans. This is illustrated in the following excerpt from the Address by the Grand Jurors of the Country of Plymouth, where a link was established between the threat to national honor and the peril for social order: "In such a crisis, when all that is dear and valuable to Freemen, when liberty and independence, National honor, social order, and public safety appear to be in danger—a danger which union alone, under the blessing of heaven, can repel: we think it not improper . . . to express to you our grateful acknowledgements for the firmness and discretion with which you have encountered such new and peculiar difficulties."[38] Indeed, although Adams camouflaged his language, he did not hide the fact that he hoped the patriotic rallying of a large part of the population in support of his ideas would eliminate Republican opposition: "Providence may indeed intend us a favor above our wishes, and a blessing beyond our foresight, in the extinction of an influence, which might soon have become more fatal than war."[39]

Clearly, through his answers to the addresses, Adams was preparing public opinion for the laws of June and July 1798.[40] A large part of public opinion followed suit, and as a result, the *Aurora* and other Republican newspapers went through a difficult time.[41] The majority in the House of Representatives switched from Republican to Federalist.[42] The times called for *union sacrée* under the Federalist banner and the president's patronage. Indeed, through his answers to the addresses, Adams embodied the nation, and thereby gained popular support; and he used this newly crafted persona of "Father of the Nation" to further the political agenda of the conservatives. In fact, the bravest among the Republicans were quick to grasp the president's goal. Although Adams appealed to the "spirit of '76" to rally all citizens around himself, not even the Federalist newspapers of Massachusetts could avoid mentioning the existence of a political opposition that refused to join in the patriotic fervor kindled by Adams and that sometimes went so far as to surreptitiously ridicule the president. On August 11, an indignant reader of the *Boston Columbian Centinel* reported: "The members from these towns [Cambridge, Roxbury, Dedham,

Dorchester, etc.] in the General Court, voted against the Address to the President . . . . We hear that on the road to Providence, there are several poles hoisted, stuck at the top with the American cockade, and tar and feathers below. The men (brutes rather) who could do this, were certainly born to be slaves, or to be hanged."[43] Nevertheless, this was a time of xenophobia, suppression of all opposition, and departure of French residents. In April 1798 a French dancing master named Dupont felt compelled to place an announcement in the *Boston Columbian Centinel* disavowing any intention to leave Boston—presumably his departure had been announced unbeknownst to him.[44] Moreau de Saint-Méry opted to head to France with his entire family, and he wrote in his diary on July 14: "Antagonism against the French increased daily."[45] Yet, unlike members of his cabinet, who, in making Marshall and Pinckney national heroes, were only trying to smash the opposition, the president sincerely hoped to weld together a nation that until then had only made news in Europe through its internal dissents. Thus, from the summer of 1798 on, Adams embarked upon a clearly national policy from which the partisan aspects gradually vanished.

On June 18, 1798, John Marshall returned from France and confided to the president that he did not think the Directory wanted war.[46] On October 1, Elbridge Gerry returned to the United States fully convinced that Talleyrand now wanted peace.[47] As is evident from his correspondence with the French minister from March to July 1798, the publication of the XYZ dispatches in the American press and the ensuing patriotic hurricane had persuaded Talleyrand that he had gone too far. In his letters to Gerry, Talleyrand claimed he had acted in good faith in the XYZ affair, and insisted above all that he sought negotiation and rapprochement with the United States. Gerry had stayed behind in Paris after the other Americans had left, and once Talleyrand realized that Gerry refused to open official negotiations without formal orders to do so, he intimated that the American envoy could at least convey French intentions to the U.S. government.[48] After Gerry arrived in the United States, he was granted a meeting with Adams, much to the surprise of hard-line Federalists such as Timothy Pickering, Oliver Wolcott, and Alexander Hamilton, who either regarded Gerry as a traitor or refused to take Talleyrand's overtures seriously.[49] Was it because they regarded these gestures simply as more tricks, as did William Vans Murray, the American minister in the Netherlands? Vans Murray indeed received, in July, the first diplomatic advances from Pichon, the secretary for American affairs whom Talleyrand had sent to The Hague with the special purpose of seeking a conference with the American minister.[50] In the end, however, Vans Murray let himself be convinced by the French diplomat and decided to forward word of Talleyrand's overtures. On July 31, 1798, the Directory annulled all commissions for Caribbean privateers and abrogated the rule of using the muster, which had served as a pretense for seizing American ships during the quasi war.[51] In his correspondence with Vans Murray from Berlin,

John Quincy Adams foresaw his father's future policy even before he learned of this news—the first tangible sign of a Franco-American rapprochement: "Everything possible to avoid a war. We shall always be ready, therefore, to negotiate, but God forbid that we should relax one particle of our defensive exertions while we treat."[52]

In the answers he had written to the addresses in the spring, John Adams did not recommend a declaration of war, but only a firm attitude in response to French insults. His answers echoed the tone of the addresses themselves, which were written more in support of the president than in support of war. By the fall of 1798 John Adams had received the dispatches from Talleyrand, Gerry, Vans Murray, and his son John Quincy Adams, and he was aware that the privateering war in the Caribbean was slowing down. It is likely that he then opted definitively for peace, even though he already knew that ultra-Federalists, including members of his own cabinet as well as Hamilton, would view this choice as the death blow to their dreams of political and military domination. Talleyrand then took a decisive step when he stated in a letter to Pichon that a new American envoy would be welcome in Paris, and this letter was transmitted to Vans Murray. Adams was thus comforted in his views and encouraged to make steps toward peace. Indeed, Talleyrand's letter stated that any minister the United States would send would be treated with all the respect due to a representative of a free, independent, and powerful nation.[53]

In late February 1799 Adams posted Vans Murray as special envoy to Paris, which the ultra-Federalists perceived as a coup by the president within the party.[54] One senses, for example, the mounting anger in the letters of Fisher Ames, a conservative politician and pamphleteer from Massachusetts. Ames was unable to fathom the meaning of the measure. On February 27 he was still able to write that Adams's patriotism was "undoubted," but on March 12 he gave his anger free rein in a passage that deserves to be quoted, for it shows that what the ultra-Federalists meant by patriotism was "public fervor" for war. Such an agenda was incompatible with Adams's intention to raise patriotic "virtue" among his countrymen without dragging them into a costly war. As Ames wrote:

> But the thing was so totally contrary to his conduct, his speeches, and the expectations of all men, that reasons, though sought for, could not be found, and must therefore be imagined; and when that failed, they must be referred further on the mysteries of state locked up in his cabinet. That even that plea, so paramount to all others, fails in this instance, because negotiation can be vindicated only as the means to an end—peace with France; the end being a bad one, all means are unwise and indefensible. . . . France is neither loved nor trusted. . . . War is desired for its own sake, as it should be. . . . We begin to feel a little patriotism, and the capture of the *Insurgente* cherishes it.[55]

When he realized that American public opinion did not find his militarism palatable, Ames displayed contempt for the "Dutch taste" of his fellow citizens, who let their love of money dissuade them from "fighting for some years, building great ships and spending millions." He bitterly concluded: "our citizens are rather democrats than republicans," meaning that they lacked the manliness of the implied republican model, namely, the Roman citizen, that is, a soldier-citizen.[56]

Adams's motivations in agreeing to negotiate with France reveal not only a good assessment of the diplomatic situation, but also a thorough knowledge of the national character that he was trying to strengthen through the Franco-American crisis. Americans did not care to go to war in the traditional European context, as was shown by their lukewarm response to Hamilton's provisional army.[57] Furthermore, their attraction to "virtue" was a far cry from the manly enthusiasm evoked by Ames, for it could not be separated from the irresistible appeal of personal gain. Yet they wanted to emerge victorious from the crisis and assert their moral superiority over corrupt Europe. To see France making entreaties to the United States flattered the nascent American national pride, while staying out of combat left American purses intact and brought calm to domestic politics. The measures that Adams took formed a national policy because they brought together most of the nation's citizens and gave the entire country the impression that its honor was not only saved, but was made even greater through weathering the crisis. Adams thus left to his successor a country at peace, one that was prosperous, and above all, a "great country." Such at least was the evaluation that Abigail Adams gave of her husband's administration after he was defeated in the 1800 election: "Peace with France,—a revenue increased beyond any former years,—our prospects brightening upon every side."[58]

Through his careful and pragmatic management of the Franco-American crisis, as well as his ability to withstand the pressures of party politics, Adams had therefore succeeded in showing Americans a way to merge wealth and glory through a policy of peace and firmness. Thenceforth Europe would know America because America knew itself. Through the XYZ crisis, the United States was able to assert its identity and to have it acknowledged by a great power (France), thanks to a wave of patriotism that bound the nation together. Although Adams lost to Jefferson in 1800, he seemed more popular then than he had been previously, as historian Stephen G. Kurtz observes in his detailed study of this election and the Adams presidency.[59] According to Kurtz, the outgoing president's popularity can be explained by the fact that voters were satisfied with his policies.[60] Adams had managed to build national unity around the issue of defending U.S. sovereignty, thus paving the way for Jefferson's famous 1801 inaugural speech quip, "We are all Republicans, we are all Federalists."[61] Indeed, Jefferson showed his approval of his predecessor's policies by ratifying the Mortefontaine Convention, which Adams's envoys had negotiated with France.[62]

On March 2, 1800, Oliver Ellsworth and William R. Davie had in fact come to Paris in order to conduct negotiations along with Vans Murray. As a result of these negotiations, a convention was signed on September 30, settling the points of contention that had arisen between the two countries after Jay's Treaty and the quasi war. Among other things, the Mortefontaine Convention confirmed the end of the 1778 treaties between France and the United States (the Treaty of Amity and Commerce and the Treaty of Alliance). It was up to Jefferson to see the final ratifications through, and although one would have expected him to be unhappy with this part of the document, such was not the case. The new president's conduct was directly inspired by the cardinal principle of foreign policy that he himself had formulated in his inaugural address: "peace, commerce, and honest friendship with all nations, entangling alliances with none."[63] This principle ensured continuity between George Washington, John Adams, and himself. Political isolationism had been recommended by the first president and had been applied by the second, who had managed not to give in to French "colonialism" without trying to please the British; it was also in Jefferson's credo. The same isolationism was now part and parcel of the ideological apparatus of all Americans, Republican and Federalist, and even of women, or at least those women in the social elite who, although unable to vote, were still moved by a love for their country. As an example, it is worth quoting the following statement of patriotism, which appeared in the last pages of Mercy Otis Warren's *History of the Rise, Progress, and Termination of the American Revolution,* published in 1805:

> It will be the wisdom, and probably the future effort of the American government, forever to maintain with unshaken magnanimity, the present neutral position of the United States. The hand of nature has displayed its magnificence in this quarter of the globe, in the astonishing rivers, lakes, and mountains, replete with the richest minerals. . . . America may with propriety be styled a land of promise. . . . The western wilds, which for ages have been little known, may arrive to that stage of improvement and perfection, beyond which the limits of human genius cannot reach.[64]

In linking neutrality with westward expansion, Mercy Otis Warren revealed the true implications of the opposition between Europe and America. Americans defined themselves by turning their backs on Europe: America was virtuous while Europe was corrupt; Europe was old and America was the land of promise. This polarization, however, was not merely rhetorical; it coincided with reality. Americans needed to be neutral and to stay away from the diplomatic and military games of Europe; indeed, they could not fight on two fronts at once—in the East and in the West—and the stakes were much higher for them in the battle in the West.

Bandits and Barbarians

Peaceful Expansion and the Indians

In its relations with the Indians as well, the United States had to assert its specific identity, in other words its moral superiority, but in a different way. Or at least that was what Secretary of War Henry Knox thought when he summed up, on December 29, 1794, the official policy of George Washington's administration with respect to the other nations living on American territory: "As we are more powerful, and more enlightened than they are, there is responsibility of national character, that we should treat them with kindness, and even liberality." Knox explained that this "national character" had until then hardly shown such a disposition. Far from differing from other colonizing countries by humane treatment of the natives, the United States (and the thirteen colonies before it) had surpassed everyone in cruelty. Knox seemed to define his country more as a colonizing country than as a young decolonized nation, and he had no mercy for his predecessors. He mused: "[I]t is a melancholy reflection, that our modes of population have been more destructive to the Indian natives than the conduct of the conquerors of Mexico and Peru." And he added: "A future historian may mark the causes of this destruction of the human race in sable colours." Fortunately, he went on to explain, the Indian policy of George Washington's administration had managed to reverse this disastrous trend, and its concern for justice would "reflect permanent honor upon the national character."[65] Even in its Indian policy, America was better than Europe had been, and its principles were different and more faithful to the generous spirit of the Enlightenment. Where one might have expected to find America's disgrace, one found its superiority instead.

Underlying such noble principles, one finds an agenda of "peaceful expansion,"[66] which was described in reports by Knox dated June 15 and July 7, 1789.[67] The two directions of this program were peace and civilization, and they were linked. Knox's basic premise was that as the progression of white settlement meant the depletion of game, the Indians would always be willing to sell their land. Once new borders were established, the process would be repeated: game would disappear, the Indians would no longer be able to hunt, they would have to sell, and so on. The goal, however, was not to exterminate the Indians, only to civilize them. This would reveal the superiority of American colonization, which would inspire the admiration of "every philosophic and humane mind."[68] The disappearance of native habitats and cultures that resulted from white settlement was thus presented as progress and evolution of human societies, and not destruction; it was therefore self-legitimizing.[69] Thus George Washington could, in all sincerity, declare the specificity and the superiority of the American plan for colonization in the following draft for a speech in Congress (April 1789): "We shou'd not, in imitation of some nations which have been celebrated for a false kind of patriotism, wish to aggrandize our own Republic at the expense of freedom and happiness of the rest of mankind."[70]

Was Washington officially renouncing here a policy of conquest?[71] That is not likely; rather, he suggested that the way to American expansion was through peace and progress, thus differentiating it from other types of colonization. The American president did emphasize this topic when addressing Indian chiefs. To Cornplanter and the other chiefs of the Seneca nation, who, quite realistically, were wondering whether they would be allowed even to practice farming on the land left to them, the president optimistically responded: "The United States will be happy in affording you every assistance in the only business which will add to your numbers and happiness." He added: "You may, when you return from this city to your own country, mention to your nation my desire to promote their prosperity, by teaching them the use of domestic animals, and the manner that the white people plough and raise so much corn."[72] What the administration wanted was to promote the well-being of the Indians: "Humanity and good policy must make it the wish of every good citizen of the United States, that Husbandry, and consequently civilization should be introduced among the Indians."[73]

The official policy of George Washington and Henry Knox toward the Indian nations clearly shows that their isolationist doctrine was exclusively directed toward Europe. The indigenous nations of the American continent lay outside of the scope of the rule that the first president spelled out in his Farewell Address: "The great rule of conduct for us in regard to foreign nations is, in extending our commercial relations, to have with them as little political connection as possible. So far as we have already formed engagements, let them be fulfilled with perfect good faith. Here let us stop."[74]

While it was seeking to sever its political connections with Europe, the United States, as a colonizing power on the American continent, was trying to increase such connections with the Indian nations. The Native Americans were informed that "the United States are desirous not only of a general peace with all the Indian tribes, but of being their friends and protectors."[75] From January 1, 1789, to December 17, 1801, the federal government signed no fewer than eighteen treaties with the Indian nations residing on its territory; half of these included provisions for establishing "perpetual peace," which clearly indicates that the United States did not shrink from making long-term diplomatic commitments when it was in its best interest to do so.[76]

It may seem out of place to use the word "diplomacy" here, since it applies by definition to relations between states. Yet, on the contrary, not to use it would amount to stripping the Indian nations of their dignity and commit them to oblivion. We are indeed dealing with diplomacy, since negotiations were conducted and treaties were signed between the federal government and the Indian nations, as was the case with other foreign nations. But it would be naive to deny that such relations took place within a colonial framework, in which the United States always managed in the end to impose their demands, despite Indian resistence.[77] Although Americans mistrusted European diplomacy and found their mistrust justified in 1798 by Talleyrand's attitude during the XYZ affair, they nevertheless waged a broad diplomatic campaign during George Washington's first presidency. That campaign was specifically directed at the Indian nations.

In his first report on the Indians, Knox explained that the United States would achieve through diplomacy better relations, and at lower cost, with the Indian nations than they would through war; moreover, he pointed out that the Indians could avail themselves of fourteen thousand warriors in the Southwest and five thousand in the Northwest.[78] Knox knew that the new republic had no army to speak of, despite Jefferson's oft-repeated claim that each pioneer was a potential soldier; he did not volunteer this information without considering that it was a decisive argument. George Washington agreed with his secretary of war: from 1790 to 1792 Philadelphia hosted many international summit meetings between the United States and the Indian nations. In the spring of 1790 the Creek chief Alexander McGillivray was invited to New York, and he went during the summer. Americans were not above the unethical methods of European diplomats, as is shown by the fact that they introduced secret clauses into the treaty they signed with McGillivray and promised to pay him a yearly sum of twelve hundred dollars in an attempt to lure him away from the Spanish. In December 1791 a group of Cherokees who were dissatisfied with the Treaty of Holston, which had been signed in July of that same year, came to Philadelphia and obtained additional advantages after a meeting with the administration.[79] It is tempting to think, as historian Katharine C. Turner has suggested, that the true agenda of these summits was not so much the petty details of the transactions with tribes, as the necessity of impressing upon Native Americans the sheer power of the whites and the vanity of resisting them;[80] but that would actually amount to misjudging their true diplomatic import. The real reason why George Washington so much wanted to befriend the tribes of the Southwest was that he feared more trouble in establishing peace in the Northwest and that he was trying to avoid a global conflict. In June 1791 the chiefs of the Six Nations of Iroquois were invited to Philadelphia because George Washington wanted to convince them to plead with the hostile nations of the Northwest (Miamis, Shawnees, and others). As it happened, fifty Iroquois chiefs arrived in Philadelphia on March 14 for a seven-week stay of uninterrupted festivities and discussions. After they left, the next to come to the negotiation table was Joseph Brant, the famous and powerful Mohawk chief.

Like the other chiefs, he agreed to plead the cause of peace with the hostile Indians.[81] That these visits were important in George Washington's eyes is illustrated by a letter he wrote to Gouverneur Morris on June 21, 1792, not long after Joseph Brant had left:

> In the course of last winter I had some of the chiefs of the Cherokees in this City, and in the spring I obtained (with some difficulty indeed) a full representation of the Six Nations to come hither. I have sent all of them away well satisfied; and fully convinced of the justice and good dispositions of this government towards the Indian nations, *generally.* The latter, that is, the Six Nations, who before, appeared to be divided, and distracted in *their* Councils, have given strong assurance of their friendship; and have resolved to send a deputation of their tribes to the hostile Indians with an Account of *all* that has passed; . . . With difficulty still greater, I have brought the celebrated Captn. Joseph Brant to this City, with a view to impress him also with the equitable intentions of this government towards all the Nations of this colour.[82]

The American government also tried to enlist the help of the peaceful tribes of the Southwest against the hostile tribes, and in February 1792 asked the Choctaws and the Chickasaws to join up with the American troops in their fight against the northwestern Indians; they would take part in General Wayne's expedition.[83] The U.S. government also invited the chiefs of these nations to come to Philadelphia after the next campaign for appropriate thanks and celebrations. Meanwhile, similar invitations were also sent to tribes that were generally hostile, such as the Chickamaugas, who represented the five lower cities of the Cherokees.[84]

The Indian Wars and the Creation of the American Army

Nevertheless, as we saw in chapter 1, the frontier of the Federalist era was clearly not marked by "peaceful expansion"; from north to south, it was the stage for continuous westward movement, sporadic fighting, and massacres. About the situation in the South, Reginald Horsman rightly considers that, despite its noble principles, the federal government did not improve much on the Indian policy of the Confederation.[85] In fact, the administration contradicted itself even more flagrantly in the Northwest, since in going to war against the hostile nations, it relinquished all pacifist pretenses and actually created the first American army. The "peaceful expansion" policy of George Washington and Henry Knox was doomed to failure, for it embodied solely the white point of view, without taking into account the Native American bond to their land and their culture.[86] For Washington and Knox, the western frontier was destined by definition to be ever shifting. The statesmen could not have imagined that the Native Americans might not sell the greater part of their land or refuse to "civilize." Furthermore, neither Washington nor Knox was ready to do what was necessary for the peace policy they advocated. When, for instance, George Washington installed William Blount as governor of the territory south of the Ohio River, the president must have known that he was committing the future of U.S.–Indian relations in that area to a merciless speculator. He was thereby annulling another official principle of his administration, according to which "the Indians, being the prior occupants, possess the right of the soil," and such right "cannot be taken from them unless by their free consent, or by the right of conquest in case of a just war."[87] In fact, George Washington needed to secure for the new administration the support of great local figures such as Blount, even at the risk of their openly trampling upon official policies. Indeed, Blount clearly did not expect "free consent" from the Indians (which was unlikely); instead he used strong-arm tactics to achieve his ends, as is apparent from the account given by chief Bloody Fellow, a Cherokee who had understood from Blount that it was better to strike a deal with him than to leave his people defenseless:

> When I found Governor Blount wanted to purchase our lands, I told him that I love my lands, and would not part with them; that I came there not to treat of selling land, but on public business of friendship between the white and red people. . . . We remained seven days at the place of treaty on this business, and Governor Blount still urging us to sell our lands, the thoughts of which made tears to come into my eyes daily.
>
> On the seventh day, finding Governor Blount still urging the sale of lands, I told him I was desirous of going to General Washington and Congress, to see whether I could not obtain better satisfaction; to which Governor Blount replied, that he was fully authorized for the purpose, therefore, it would be unnecessary for the Indians to go.
>
> I however persevered in my wishes to go to Philadelphia; when Governor Blount asked me whether I had money to defray the expenses of my journey; this struck me forcibly, and reflecting that our people, young and old, were in his power, I then told him that, if he would not demand so much land of us, we would give him a small piece, without any consideration whatever, if he would let us and our children return to our country in peace and safety.[88]

Washington and Knox had to reckon not only with the corrupt representatives they sent to the frontier, but also with the states and their elected officials, as well as with pioneers, whose expansionism stood in the way of peace.[89] George Washington himself explained that the reason why his "peaceful expansion" policy was failing, or could not be implemented, was that the pioneers were an obstacle.[90] These pioneers, however, were also citizens of the United States. No matter how much or how often George Washington called for punishment of those who infringed on Native American lands (as per the Trade and Intercourse Acts of 1790, 1793, and 1796) or assured Native Americans that they would only have to deal with the federal government,[91] he could not possibly have given preference to Native Americans over his own citizens without jeopardizing the Union itself. George Washington's line of reasoning was that if the peace policy of the federal government failed, even at the hands of the pioneers, war would break out and the Native Americans would be punished.[92]

Thus, Washington and Knox decided to protect the frontier populations against the Native Americans, but without initially acknowledging that their retaliation operations (which they termed punitive "expeditions") in fact constituted episodes of actual war.[93] The distinction between war and the defense of law and order was indeed not very clear in the minds of the American leaders. In 1790, in his second inaugural address, George Washington referred to the hostile Native Americans of the area around the Wabash and Maumee Rivers as "certain banditti of Indians from the North West side of the Ohio."[94] Likewise, the Creeks who supported the Chickamaugas in their constant raids against land-hungry pioneers of the Cumberland area were described by Knox, in 1792, as "banditti."[95] For the Native Americans, this was clearly war, but the federal administration was hesitant. This hesitation reflected the ambiguous status of Native Americans: were they actual foreign nations or were they protectorates? George Washington put the question to the Senate in connection with the Treaty of Fort Harmar: were the treaties signed with Native Americans applicable without ratification by a two-thirds majority of the Senate? Were they essentially different from treaties concluded with European nations?[96]

According to Charles Carroll, a senator from Maryland, the difference was clear: since the treaties with Native Americans, unlike those signed between "civilized" European nations, had never been formally ratified by either side, no official ratification of the treaty signed at Fort Harmar in 1789 between the United States and the Wyandot, Delaware, Ottawa, Chippewa, Pattiwatima, and Sac nations was advisable or necessary.[97] Yet the Senate eventually decided to ratify this treaty in the same fashion as it did treaties binding the United States toward foreign nations; this precedent was never to be called into question throughout the era of Indian treaties, that is, until 1871.[98] At the same time, however, the colonialist argument that allowed Charles Carroll to draw a line between two kinds of diplomatic partners, one "civilized" and the other (implicitly) "savage," underlay the entire U.S. Indian policy from then on. The bottom line was that Indian nations were not recognized as equal nations. By casting doubt on the legitimacy of the treaties that embodied Native American resistance, Carroll meant to preserve at home and abroad the pacifist identity and moral superiority that the United States had claimed for itself.

Despite the fiction of an official peace policy and a refusal to call a war a war, the fact remains that from 1789 to 1794 the secretary of war was mainly busy with Indian affairs. Peaceful expansion, if it came to be, could only take place after Native American resistance had been forcefully brought down, or so Jefferson thought when he assessed the situation in 1791: "As to myself, I hope we shall give the Indians a thorough drubbing this summer, and I should think it better afterwards to take up the plan of liberal and repeated presents to them."[99]

After Saint-Clair's bloody defeat in November 1791, the army was reorganized. Regular soldiers in good number (Congress approved five thousand men), less dependence on the state militias, and a new commander—everything was done to transform the unruly and disorderly Saint-Clair battalion into "the efficient military machine that eventually smashed the Indian confederacy in the Northwest."[100] After Wayne's victory in August 1794, the army was essentially kept as a series of garrisons housed in forts along the frontier, thus symbolizing the true nature of U.S.–Native American relations, that is, a permanent state of war.[101] "National character" was to develop through military—and therefore violent—confrontation with the "savage," through conquest rather than through the generous donation of superior knowledge and technology. The elite were unanimous on this score, and Jefferson, who upheld the expansionist plans of the pioneers and local leaders, understood that in order to preserve the nation's unity and to develop its own identity, it was necessary to support popular expansionism—that is, expansionism that was anything but peaceful.

Pirates in the Mediterranean and the Birth of the American Navy

The United States was also to show its military ability and its warlike spirit outside of North America. Winning its independence meant that the United States had lost the protection formerly afforded by the British navy against Barbary Coast pirates in the Mediterranean. Americans were now prevented from reaching Mediterranean markets, except at the risk of having their ships confiscated and their teams sold as slaves. In Morocco, Algeria, Tunisia, and Libya, where the tutelage of the Ottoman Empire no longer carried much weight, leaders encouraged piracy, which was a reliable source of revenue and an excuse not to take care of their country's economy or of its modernization and development. Through piracy, which they firmly controlled, the pashas collected ransom for prisoners, took in plunder, and signed treaties worth their while, whereby they pledged not to attack ships from a given power in exchange for large sums of money. Because they were richer, the great powers—such as France, England, and Spain—suffered less from Barbary Coast raiders than did other European countries.[102]

The first American merchant ships were captured by Algerian pirates at the end of the War of Independence.[103] During his embassy term in France, Jefferson had tried to negotiate the release of the American captives in Algiers, but to no avail.[104] The new secretary of state had learned his lesson, and upon his return home he changed strategies; he described his new doctrine in two reports to Congress on December 28, 1790. In the first, which was devoted to American commerce in the Mediterranean, the secretary of state considered three ways of settling the crisis. The first way was to pay ransom for the prisoners, but such an option, he explained, was at odds with the overriding goal of putting an end to all piracy. The second option was to "buy peace" by paying a large sum to the leaders of the countries involved, an idea that repelled Jefferson in that it would amount to aligning the United States with the corrupt methods of Europe: "For this we have the example of rich, powerful Nations, in this instance counting their Interest more than their Honor." The third solution was the one Jefferson favored. Far from expressing a pacifist credo, his plan was based on the Mosaic "eye for an eye" (*lex talionis*): "to repel force by force" and, for once, an alliance with smaller European nations. In the second report, which dealt with the issue of captives, Jefferson took up the same ideas, suggesting that in the event of hostilities, Barbary Coast prisoners could be traded for American slaves, at a rate of five to one.[105]

This tough option was not chosen by Congress, whose primary goal was to secure revenue for the new government before spending it, and who therefore opted to "buy peace" or to pay ransom. In the fall of 1793, however, even before negotiations had had a chance to start, Algiers signed a cease-fire with Portugal, opening the Atlantic to Algerian pirates, and more Americans were captured.[106] Now even the Atlantic was unsafe for U.S. ships. Jefferson's ideas came back to the fore, and on March 10, 1794, the Senate passed "An Act to Provide a Naval Armament," which called for six frigates to be built; these were to be the embryo of an American navy.[107] But before construction of the frigates had even begun, the dey of Algiers suddenly expressed a wish to open negotiations. A treaty was not signed until September 5, 1795, but the talks were followed by two other treaties, one with Tripoli and the other with Tunis. In spite of these treaties, George Washington insisted that the construction of three frigates be carried out, contrary to the pacifist stipulations of the 1794 act, which called for this construction to be interrupted if the conflict stopped.[108] These frigates marked the beginning of the history of the American navy and naval power, even before the Department of the Navy was created in 1798, at the time of the XYZ crisis. By 1801, when hostilities broke out again with Algiers, the American navy had the experience of the quasi war years, during which U.S. ships, along with the powerful British navy, inspected French government privateers and frigates and escorted American merchant ships to their destinations.[109] What is significant in the American reaction toward the North African countries is that military action was promptly considered and untempered by any pacifist undertones. When a riposte seemed feasible to the Americans, and when it seemed justified by the defense of economic interests, they proved willing to wage war.

In the 1790s some Federalist leaders developed the idea of isolationism in order to build up a "national character," which they found deficient. Having severed its political ties to Europe, the United States asserted its moral superiority by staying clear of the quarrels that seemed peculiar to the corrupt Old Continent. This isolationist theme was skillfully used by Adams in 1798, and it effectively marshaled a large portion of the country into a nationalist élan. Although the Republicans at first regarded this agenda as a mere partisan maneuver, they were eventually won over to this unifying ideological construction after 1801, when Jefferson took office. It should be noted that the isolationist idea only applied to Europe; and if one takes into account the economic dimension, it was far from being just. Indeed, the United States dealt at the same time with many other nations, which resided on territory over which the United States claimed sovereignty, although it acknowledged these nations' property rights. These nations were unfortunately not "civilized" in American eyes. In relations with them, U.S. leaders also spoke of virtue, justice, and humanity. But the "superior" civilization they intended to bring to Native Americans amounted to continuous warfare as well as constant pressure and destruction. Virtue and neutrality applied to Europe, while corruption and belligerence were used with Native Americans and any "less civilized" people that might stand in the way. This formidable ambiguity was the cornerstone of American identity. It was only with one country that Jefferson's America found itself at a loss over what stance to take, even though it had intended to expand relations with that country. Indeed, in dealing with Haiti, the United States came to choose silence over the assertion of its identity, whether by a display of neutrality or force.

PART 3

Implementing Foreign Policy Goals: Ambitions and Ambiguities

CHAPTER 6

The United States and Haiti: Rejecting the Other American Republic

On February 28, 1806, Thomas Jefferson signed a law completely prohibiting trade with Haiti, the "Act to suspend the commercial intercourse between the United States and certain parts of the island of St. Domingo." This measure reflected a radical change in approach in American policy toward the former French colony, insofar as American merchants had always kept up commercial relations with the richest of the Caribbean islands, even at the height of the revolutionary wars, the quasi war with France, and the wars between Saint-Domingue and its former parent country. To be sure, by 1806 Saint-Domingue, which was now Haiti, had been torn apart and ruined by seventeen years of war and civil wars, and the island was no longer quite as necessary to the American export and reexport trade as it had been. By the same token, however, since 1804 it had become the second American nation to be decolonized, after the United States. For Jefferson's government, interrupting commercial relations with Haiti was indeed the only way to avoid facing certain undesirable consequences of the American Revolution, and especially the problem posed by the incompatibility of slavery and freedom, a problem that the Haitian Revolution once again brought to the fore.

Much more so than the Federalists—who harbored counterrevolutionary views despite their claims on the revolutionary heritage—the Republicans had tried since 1789 to appropriate the revolutionary and authentically democratic heritage of the Revolution of 1776. They did not clearly realize, however, that in so doing they were becoming entangled in its ambiguities. The American Revolution had indeed left unanswered many questions that it had raised, such as the problem that the concepts "liberty," "equality," "inalienable rights," and their universal scope posed for American society. These concepts were written into the Declaration of Independence, but how could they be construed as the foundations of the true American institutions and values if they only applied to whites in a society that upheld slavery? Such was the question that the leaders of the Republican Party should have pondered in the 1790s, when the rebellion of the black slaves of Saint-Domingue gave it a new urgency. Although they supported the French Revolution, the Republicans in fact chose to ignore the problem of slavery in their own country and refused to consider the Haitian slave revolt to be a true manifestation of the same revolutionary spirit that had arisen in 1776 in the United States and then in 1789 in France.

Although until 1804 it might have been possible to entirely ignore the ideological challenge that the Haitian Revolution posed for Americans, this was no longer an option after that date. Once Dessalines had proclaimed Haitian independence, the mere fact of keeping up commercial relations with Haiti would have implied recognition of a "negro government."[1] By implication, recognition of a government that was made up of former slaves would have forced the leaders of the Republican Party to admit that their own society, which they held up as a model in contrast to Europe, was not as democratic as they claimed, since 20 percent of its population was made up of black slaves. By choosing to reject the Haitian Revolution, American leaders thus implicitly limited the universality of their own revolution: the American Revolution had only applied to whites, and such would be the case for many years to come.

It may be tempting to view the severing of ties with Saint-Domingue, whose trade had been so avidly coveted by Americans, as foreshadowing the oppositions that were soon to divide the United States into hostile regions (the abolitionist North versus the slaveholding South). But that would be going too far. To be sure, the Haitian Revolution had a major impact on the development of a proslavery ideology in the South; at the time, however, not just the South but the whole country benefited from slavery and was imbued with a kind of self-satisfaction about it, and the desire for prosperity was more widespread than the religion of freedom. These basic facts should not be overshadowed by the Federalist protests of 1806. The policy that American leaders conducted toward the new Caribbean republic was indeed the expression of a national will, and not the product of exclusively southern and proslavery inclinations.

The United States and the Insurrection of Saint-Domingue (1789–1793)

Most recent historians consider that the American Revolution involved a careful examination of colonial society, including the institution of slavery. Among the hopes cherished by Americans during the revolutionary years, one of the most fervent was to do away with slavery.[2] The ideology of equal rights, which was the basis for the ideals of the new republic, implied universal recognition of these rights, meaning that they should be extended to the slaves. British despotism could not be rejected without also rejecting the very peculiar American despotism that was the core of relations between masters and slaves. As

Jefferson and several other Founding Fathers felt, American citizens could not be democrats among themselves and despots toward their slaves. In 1780, at the height of the American Revolution, Jefferson wrote: "And with what execration should the statesman be loaded, who permitting one half the citizens thus to trample on the rights of the other, transforms those into despots, and these into enemies."[3]

Such indignation clearly reveals that Jefferson was aware of the political nature of relations between masters and slaves: the new nation's democratic character would be threatened if one admitted a dual political life, granting democracy to some, and imposing despotism on others. According to Jefferson, the ongoing American Revolution was to put an end to the odious "commerce" between masters and slaves and bring about the emancipation of the latter: "I think a change already perceptible, since the origin of the present revolution. The spirit of the master is abating, that of the slave rising from the dust, his condition mollifying, the way I hope preparing, under the auspices of heaven, for a total emancipation, and that this is disposed, in the order of events, to be with the consent of the masters, rather than by their extirpation."[4]

Nonetheless, in 1787 the Philadelphia Constitutional Convention made no steps toward organizing gradual emancipation of the slaves; instead, it essentially sought to create a compromise whereby each state would be free to settle the issue as it wished.[5] As Jacques Thibau has observed, the text of the federal Constitution does not use the words "slavery" or "slave trade," and yet the problem of slavery is nevertheless touched upon, albeit in essentially indirect terms. Slavery is indeed acknowledged in Article I, section 2, which in computing the respective weight of each state at the House of Representatives, takes into account "three fifths of all other persons" in addition to "the whole Number of free Persons." Section 9 of the same article prevented the federal government from outlawing the slave trade before 1808, the trade itself being described as "the migration or importation of such Persons as any of the States now existing shall think proper to admit." Article IV also allowed the owners of fugitive slaves to reclaim them in nonslave states. Rather than striking a compromise between North and South, the Constitution, as the founding legal document, in fact established slavery at the very heart of national institutions.[6]

In the beginning of George Washington's presidency, this topic was not on the agenda, unlike Indian affairs, the economy, or foreign relations; in fact, it seemed to have vanished from the immediate concerns of American leaders and the American elite in general. Meanwhile, in France the issue of slavery, because it was linked to the rights of man, was one of the great issues dividing the Constituent Assembly: on one side were the Friends of the Blacks (with Condorcet as their most famous representative), and on the other was the Club Massiac, which defended the interests of the big landowners of Saint-Domingue and therefore upheld slavery. As soon as the Revolution was announced, Saint-Domingue, which was a great source of wealth for the French economy,[7] fell prey to rivalries between local interest groups: royalists, prorevolutionaries, independence fighters, and so on. In order to preserve French control over the largest of the Caribbean islands, which was farmed by 500,000 slaves,[8] the members of the Constituent Assembly showed consideration for those who held the keys to its economic power (i.e., the great planters) and paid little attention to the demands of the Friends of the Blacks and to the free mulattos who were asking for equal political rights. Only after the torture of Ogé, a young mulatto who had tried to rouse his brothers to fight for equal rights, did the Assembly wake up to the issue, but then all it did was decree equal political rights for free mulattos on May 15, 1791,[9] and black slavery was not called into question. What followed may have been a consequence or a mere coincidence. In Saint-Domingue, on the night of August 22, 1791, a slave insurrection broke out in the rich northern plain, soon to overtake and inflame the whole island.

Insofar as the issue of slavery was no longer a crucial one in the United States, and as the French Revolution only marginally incorporated it into the revolutionary debate, it is not surprising that George Washington's government saw the insurrection only as one more slave rebellion, of the kind that was so common in slaveholding societies. In Jamaica, another large island of the Caribbean where insurrections were especially frequent, authorities had even had to sign an agreement with the fugitive blacks who had escaped to the mountains.[10] In the United States, there were 750,000 blacks in 1790, which was a lesser proportion of the population than in the Caribbean islands (South Carolina was the only state with a "black majority,"[11] whereas these Caribbean islands had a ratio of one white to eight or nine blacks). Nevertheless, rebellions, and especially localized outbursts of violence, were not unknown in the United States.[12] Americans, furthermore, were so eager to gain entry into the Saint-Domingue market that they chose to regard this revolt, which actually increased the island's political and social disorganization, as an opening in the wall of French mercantilism. Whereas the United States had immediately acknowledged the French Revolution as the heir to their own revolutionary principles, they could not or would not give similar acknowledgment to the uprising of the Saint-Domingue slaves. In 1780 Jefferson had realized that the American Revolution contained the promise of freedom for black slaves, but in 1791 he did not understand that Boukman, the first leader of the black insurrection, and his followers were turning this promise into reality.

There were, however, observers at that time who were able to perceive the revolutionary dimension of the slave revolt in Saint-Domingue. A relevant testimony is that of the British historian and counterrevolutionary thinker, Bryan Edwards, himself a slave owner, who passed through Saint-Domingue at the beginning of the slave revolt in 1791. For Edwards, this revolt was undoubtedly the product of Enlightenment philosophy, rather than the mere result of hardship and misery:

> These reflections necessarily arise from the circumstance which is incontrovertibly proved in the following pages, namely, that the rebellion of negroes in St. Domingo, and the insurrection of the mulattoes . . . had one and the same origin. It was not the strong and irrepressible impulse of human nature, groaning under oppression, that excited either of these classes to plunge their daggers into the bosoms of unoffending women and helpless infants. They were driven into these excesses—reluctantly driven by the vile machinations of men calling themselves philosophers . . . whose pretences to philanthropy were as gross a mockery of human reason, as their conduct was an outrage on all the feelings of our nature, and the ties which hold society together.[13]

However extreme and clearly counterrevolutionary these remarks were, they prove that it was possible for contemporary observers to draw a link between the Saint-Domingue slave revolt of 1791 and the revolutionary spirit that had come of age in 1776 in the United States and in 1789 in France. Although there were in fact a few isolated voices in the United States to make that link, the majority of the political establishment still refused to identify the insurrection as a sister revolution.[14]

In fact, American leaders did more than merely deny that dimension to the insurrection that tore apart Saint-Domingue; they even contributed to the attempted repression of the rebellion by lending funds to the Saint-Domingue colonists from 1791 on, for an amount that by 1793 totaled $726,000.[15] Initially the French minister plenipotentiary, Jean-Baptiste Ternant, had been wary of the delegates from the Saint-Domingue Assembly, in view of their royalist and secessionist tendencies. As he was faced, however, with an emergency situation, and unable to secure sufficient help from Paris, he eventually accepted American aid, which George Washington was more than happy to volunteer, as shown in this letter of September 24:

> I have not delayed a moment since the receipt of your communications of the 22nd instant, in dispatching orders to the Secretary of the Treasury to furnish the money, and to the Secretary of War to deliver the Arms and Ammunition, which you have applied to me for. Sincerely regretting, as I do, the cause which has given rise to this application; I am happy in the opportunity of testifying how well disposed the United States are to render every aid in their power to our good friends and Allies the French to quell "the alarming insurrection of the negroes in Hispaniola" and of the ready disposition to effect it, of the Executive authority thereof.[16]

The American government, then, was ready to help the Saint-Domingue planters in their actions against the rebel slaves. Did this show of solidarity with the masters of Saint-Domingue prove that the American leaders had renounced their ideals, or instead, that they had misunderstood the true scope of the Saint-Domingue insurrection, not realizing that it forecast an actual revolution—that it marked the end of the American Revolution?

U.S. Dealings with the Free Blacks

In 1791 the leaders of the French Revolution had not seen fit to grant freedom to the slaves in the colonies; thus, America and France set similar bounds to the socially acceptable scope of liberty and equality. Such behavior overlooked the military power of the black rebels, which Sonthonax, the Convention's envoy, had to call to the rescue once he was deadlocked by royalist forces, that is, Spanish and British. In the summer of 1793, in order to procure the aid of the black rebels, Sonthonax gave them their freedom, a decision that was made official by a decree of August 29, 1793: "The Republic desires liberty and equality among all men whatever their color; kings are only happy in the midst of slaves. The Republic adopts you among her children."[17] The Convention had no choice but to ratify this decision, which it did on February 4, 1794. As David Brion Davis and other historians have noted, blacks mainly freed themselves.[18] In the United States, such a decision, made as it was by the "sister republic" in the name of revolutionary principles, should have had an impact, at least with the Republicans, if not with the Federalists. In fact, by comparison with other issues of the day, it received little comment from the leaders of either major party; and in Congress debates on slavery became less and less heated.[19]

Such a weak reaction, especially on the part of the pro-French Republicans, did not in fact reflect a lack of enthusiasm for the French Revolution. On the contrary, as historian Alfred Hunt has explained, the Republicans managed to dissociate the issue of slave emancipation from the French Revolution, and to remain "pro-French and anti-Black."[20] After 1791 and again after 1793, a number of refugees from Saint-Domingue, including both white royalists and revolutionary mulattos, headed for the southeastern U.S. coast (especially Norfolk and Portsmouth in Virginia, Charleston in South Carolina, and New Orleans in Louisiana); as a result of this influx, American newspapers were filled with grueling details of racial massacres, and feelings of insecurity grew in the South.[21] These areas, however, remained firmly Republican and friendly toward France throughout the period. Thus, while the slave revolt in Saint-Domingue seems to have strengthened the racial prejudices of white southerners and their fears as landowners, it did not jeopardize, threaten, or shake the dual nature of their political structure. In these southerners' view, the precarious balance they achieved between their democratic principles and their despotic behavior toward the slaves was not called into question by the emancipation of Saint-Domingue slaves. In the end, slavery consolidated, rather than threatened, the social consensus in the South, and perhaps even in the United States as a whole, for the institution of slavery limited the number of poor freemen, and thus enabled whites to have more common interests—property in particular—than they had topics of disagreement.[22]

In South Carolina, a state with a black majority, small Republican planters joined with big Federalist planters to pass a ban on importing slaves in 1792; the measure, which was dictated by fears that the rebellion would spread, was renewed year after year.[23] The same planters, however, continued actively supporting the French Revolution until 1797; they toned down such support during the quasi war, but reaffirmed it in 1800, as if saying that France and its principles had nothing to do with the events in the great Caribbean island. Americans had thus managed initially to ignore the political consequences that the slave revolt in Haiti had on American society.

After 1793 Americans no longer took part in attempts at repressing the insurrection; instead, they merely took advantage of it to pursue their own goals in the area, the chief one being to obtain a trade monopoly on Saint-Domingue and not let the British occupy the vacancy left by revolutionary France. Despite the capture of ships by the British navy as well as by French privateers, in 1793 American merchants started providing arms and supplies to the various opponents of the wars and civil strife that tore apart the island.[24] At the height of the quasi war with France in 1799 and 1800, Adams opposed the loyalist mulatto Rigaud and took the side of Toussaint-Louverture, one of the former leaders of the insurrection, who had gradually assumed power over the island and was guiding it toward independence. Adams's support took the form of delivering supplies to Toussaint and launching the American navy against Rigaud's positions.[25] It was indeed an American navy ship, the *Experiment,* that captured Rigaud and handed him over to the British.[26] As a result of these maneuvers, the island's trade did in fact fall to the Americans, who immediately launched a commercial takeover on the Spanish portion of Saint-Domingue even before Toussaint set about military conquest.[27]

Relations with Saint-Domingue could not, however, be solely commercial. In the absence of official French representatives, the mere fact of dealing with Toussaint, who was leader of the island, more or less amounted to acknowledging the independence of that nation of former slaves. Federalist leaders, such as Secretary of State Timothy Pickering, Secretary of Treasury Oliver Wolcott, or John Adams, all came from northern or central states; they had little sympathy for southern politicians, and little respect for slavery. Yet, however eager they were at the time to improve the lot of their merchants and shipowners, they were not prepared to deal with former slaves on equal footing. The Federalists and ultra-Federalists were almost unanimously opposed to recognizing the independence of Saint-Domingue,[28] even though independence was a fact, and France could not possibly do anything about it. As a result, when it came to signing a commercial treaty with Toussaint-Louverture, the United States let the British make an official commitment, and did not sign it themselves. In dealing with Toussaint and his delegates, President Adams, just like Lord Grenville, was only trying to annoy France and promote the growth of American trade, not to encourage the development of a new nation.[29]

Once in office in 1801, Jefferson did not put an end to the privileged commercial relations between the United States and Saint-Domingue, even though a reconciliation had occurred between France and the United States after the Mortefontaine Convention. Louis-André Pichon, the newly nominated chargé d'affaires in Washington, D.C., understood from his first interviews with members of Jefferson's cabinet that above all the United States wanted to preserve their commercial relations with Saint-Domingue, be it at the cost of acknowledging Toussaint's de facto authority over the island: "When I hinted at these questions, I was told that only commerce was envisioned in Saint-Domingue, and that one had to take things as they came and thus to consider Toussaint as having full authority over the island."[30]

In order not to antagonize Toussaint, the American leaders took special care when choosing a new consul, Tobias Lear, who replaced Dr. Stevens. They stated that they would not quarrel with the black leader, although they also claimed that they wanted France to get back its colony.[31] The moderate American attitude toward Toussaint—whom France considered to be a mere rebel—ended up annoying even the chargé d'affaires, who was normally pro-American. Pichon thought that the United States would let France take back Saint-Domingue, but not without misgivings. In his opinion, the bottom line was that American leaders wanted France to maintain order and security on the island, thus preventing the blacks from propagating their subversive ideas, while enabling the Americans to keep their trade monopoly:

> Everything I have related about the conduct of the government with respect to Saint-Domingue testifies that we shall find willing partners to bring down the colony. But we should have no illusions. Only the fright that a black government arouses dictates these inclinations. From the questions I am asked, and from the insinuations I perceive, I can see clearly that such an arrangement is desired [by the United States] as would leave America with free and indefinite access to this possession, which is for this country a source of wealth.[32]

The American leaders did not actually confide to Pichon their fears about this island, which was now governed by former slaves; it was Pichon who drew these conclusions. At any rate, even if the American leaders were at one point in a position to pledge help to France, they ceased to do so as soon as they found out that it had just acquired Louisiana. At the same time, foreseeing the impending landing of General Leclerc's troops on Saint-Domingue, Toussaint officially declared that he would count on American aid in the event of an attack by France.[33]

As a matter of fact, suppressing the Saint-Domingue rebellion was a less pressing concern for Americans than expanding their trade in an area that they coveted. Meanwhile, Bonaparte wanted to reestablish the mitigated exclusive in those colonies he had been able to get back for France at the Amiens negotiations.[34] As a result, General Leclerc's arrival in Saint-Domingue in February 1802 revived tensions between France and the United States: the French general restricted access to the island's ports for foreign ships, impounded goods aboard American ships, set prices for such goods but only paid a fourth of the price up front, and finally sent Tobias Lear back to Washington, D.C.[35] After Leclerc's death on November 2, 1802, and the failure of his expedition (18,000 soldiers out of his force of 28,000 died), his successor General Rochambeau used similarly hostile—if not more aggressive—methods against American merchants: "About the middle of the month, General Rochambeau, as he was hard-pressed for money, raised a mandatory loan among French and American merchants of the Cape . . . , and since several of those who were taxed the highest refused to pay up, they were threatened with being deported to France and having their property sold off. In the end, four or five of them were imprisoned along with some Frenchmen, and all paid their way out of prison."[36]

Little by little, however, the French forces lost control over the situation, and the American merchants took up their trade with the vacated parts of the island, which was now under the rule of Dessalines, successor to Toussaint.[37] Despite criticism from Pichon, Madison saw no reason to step in and put an end to a trade that was unlawful from the French point of view, even though the de facto consequence of that trade was to encourage the rebels. Indeed, if the American president were to ban such trade, the British, as foes of France, would step right in. Whether the Americans furnished them with supplies or not, the rebels would not starve.[38] Such an attitude, however, was not acceptable from a supposedly friendly country, and Pichon reacted angrily: "Commerce with the rebels of that colony assumed . . . in the course of March [1804] a shape and public character that appeared to me to offend too openly the dignity and rights of France for me not to make a forceful claim without waiting for orders from the government. Not only has this commerce gone on publicly, . . . but also several of these ships have been armed openly in order to protect this unlawful commerce against our privateers."[39]

For the first time in these dispatches, Madison was forced to confess, despite his support of American merchants, that the whole affair was troubling in view of its multiple internal implications, and he wished that there be as little debate as possible about it.[40] As Alfred Hunt has explained, Americans initially gave precedence to their diplomatic and commercial concerns over their racial antipathies toward the black rebels, and it was only after the massacres of whites by Dessalines that slave owners such as Thomas Jefferson began to turn against Saint-Domingue.[41]

Between 1791 and 1804 the American political elite saw the slave rebellion as a mere localized insurrection, and not as the revolution it really was—one that was heir to their own revolution, albeit with a degree of critical distance. After 1793 the leaders of the early republic dismissed the issue: it was up to France to deal with the political problem that the slave rebellion raised. Meanwhile, the American leaders were only trying to pursue peaceful commercial relations with whoever was willing to pay; the insurrection could by no means have repercussions on the ideology of the new nation, and in no way did it reveal its contradictions. On that count, the Republicans in particular proved to be strikingly inconsistent: most of them supported the French Revolution through 1799, but it never dawned on them that the actions of the black rebels might be construed as a direct consequence of their own revolutionary ideology.

The Threat of Contagion

Never in the course of the many interviews between Madison and Pichon from 1800 to 1804 did the word "slavery" come up. That in itself is not surprising, insofar as even official documents such as the Constitution did not mention "slaves" but rather "other persons." "Other persons," however, were also not mentioned in the conversations between the secretary of state and the French chargé d'affaires. Only in 1804, after Dessalines had declared the independence of Haiti, and Rochambeau and his troops had vacated the island (in late November 1803), did James Madison admit that the unlawful commerce with Saint-Domingue involved some drawbacks that were linked to the domestic problems of the new republic. Until then, the "commercial" argument had served as a screen to hide the actual questions that the Saint-Domingue rebellion posed for American society. The nation's elite did not want to consider the fact that the Haitian Revolution actually called their own slave system into question. North and South were unanimous in this attitude, which could in fact be justified, if need be, in terms of international law: since France continued to assert its sovereignty over the island, it was up to the French to settle the problem. After 1804, however, Dessalines's declaration of independence destroyed the awkward argumentation and brought to light the embarrassment and uneasiness of the United States.

The Americans were gradually forced to admit that the insurrection of the Saint-Domingue slaves was not a peripheral problem, and that it concerned them as much as it did France, if not more. By proclaiming the independence of the second decolonized nation in the Americas, Dessalines explicitly linked the founding of Haiti to that of the United States. Since the freedom of Haitian blacks derived from the same universal principles as that of Americans to the north, it heralded freedom for black American slaves in the near future. The birth of Haiti forced American leaders to revive ideals that they had lost or cast aside, and it called upon them to choose once and for all the real political structure of their society: was it to be a true democracy, or, as Jefferson had feared in 1780, a despotic regime in democratic clothing?

This dilemma was all the more bitter, and its resolution all the more pressing, since the Haitian Revolution's message of universal liberty had already reached the slave populations in the United States. Since 1791 a wave of rebellions and insurrections had been rolling through the southern states, reaching a climax in 1800 with the conspiracy of Gabriel, in Richmond, Virginia.[42] If we are to believe the account that historian Joseph Cephas Carroll gave of this conspiracy, the black slaves—unlike their masters—had not dissociated the goal of emancipation from the revolutionary principles of freedom. In the democratic petitions of southern Republicans, the slaves found an incentive to rebellion: Gabriel had every reason to believe in success, since, because of the election, the doctrines of equality and liberty resounded in every valley and on every mountain.[43] For James Monroe, who was governor of Virginia at the time of the conspiracy, it was beyond doubt that the cause of the conspiracy lay in the slaves' growing desire for freedom: "It is our duty on this occasion to remark that the publick danger proceeding from this description of persons is daily increasing. A variety of causes contribute to produce this effect, among which may be enumerated the contrast in the condition of the free negroes and slaves, the growing sentiment of liberty existing in the minds of the latter, and the inadequacy of the existing patrol laws."[44]

To prevent the contagion of revolutionary ideas, an act was passed by Congress in 1803 restricting the entry of blacks coming from Saint-Domingue, which was similar to other acts previously passed in the southern states.[45] From that moment, which more or less coincided with the final victory of the black revolutionaries over the French army in Saint-Domingue, the question of slavery started to reappear in American political discourse. The Haitian Revolution, however, had changed the nature of the debate: it was no longer a matter of calling for the abolition of slavery in the name of liberty; slavery was now viewed as a threat to social order, to be contained as best one could, in view of the destructive potential against white property that the civil war in Saint-Domingue had revealed. Whether Republican or Federalist, whether for or against slavery, American politicians used Haiti as an illustration of their arguments, always for the same purpose of protecting social order and property.

In 1803 South Carolina decided to take up the slave trade again until 1808. A heated debate took place in the Senate in 1804: those opposed to increasing slavery tried to impose a tax of ten dollars per imported slave, as a means of curbing or preventing that trade. David Bard, a representative from Pennsylvania, stated that the importation of slaves into the United States should be terminated, for "to import slaves is to import enemies into our countries." This congressman began with an allusion to hair-raising accounts of the horrors of civil and racial war in Saint-Domingue, which his audience had been able to read in their newspapers since 1791: "Gentlemen tell us, though I can hardly think them serious, that the people of this description can never systematize a rebellion. I will not mention facts, it is sufficient to say that experience speaks a different language." Having thus given a factual basis to his remarks, he was able to go on with his depiction of the threat that slavery constituted: "Their circumstances, their barbarism, their reflections, their hopes and fears render them an enemy of the worst description."[46] Representative Bard did not, however, want to base his rejection of slavery on the sole fear of insurrection. He therefore changed his tactics and resorted to a less impassioned argument, pointing out the ideological inconsistency of the American stance on slavery. How can "Americans boast of being the most enlightened people in the world," he asked, if they "hold a million of men in the most degraded slavery?" His conclusion was obvious: "[I]f then, we hold a consistency of character in any estimation, we will give every discouragement in our power to the importation of slaves."[47] Yet his speech did not culminate in a call for emancipating American blacks. In banning the importation of slaves, Bard wanted above all to ward off the possibility of an insurrection, not to improve American society. The only message that came across from his speech was his opening imprecation that the slaves were the "natural enemies" of Americans. His incomplete reasoning betrayed a primal fear, which Federalists and Republicans shared, as is evident from remarks by other senators.

For example, John Smith, a Republican senator from New York State, warned fellow senators about the nefarious consequences of increasing the number of slaves: "Will you increase their number, and lay the necessary foundation for the horrors of another St. Domingo?"[48] Samuel White, a Federalist senator from Delaware, echoed this warning when he said that it was the duty of the Senate to prevent by all means "the horrid evil of slavery and thereby avoid the fate of St. Domingo."[49] Likewise, Jesse Franklin, a Republican senator from North Carolina, declared: "We must make laws against slavery, unless we mean to aid the destruction of our southern states, by laying the foundation for another St. Domingo."[50] For these orators who opposed the expansion of slavery, the true concern was not a magnanimous desire to emancipate the slaves, but the fear of jeopardizing the social order. In their eyes, the Haitian Revolution stood for barbarism and not a struggle for freedom; this was the sole reason why they opposed any further increase in the number of slaves. There was no indication that for them the Haitian Revolution represented the latest episode in the revolutionary era in America, or was a sequel to the American Revolution. Their attitude was almost wholly reactionary: it was aimed primarily at checking the growing threat that slavery constituted for their property and safety.[51]

When the discourse did not center on the fear of insurgent blacks, the reasoning was inconsistent, as was the case with the few speakers who actually recognized the dignity of the former slaves' fight for freedom. After the Louisiana Purchase in 1803, Congress had to organize the new territories. Speaking in this context, John George Jackson, a Republican representative from Virginia, was one of those who thought that the people of Louisiana could govern themselves perfectly well, and did not need to be submitted to a period of disenfranchisement in order to test whether they were fit for democracy: "Allow, for the sake of argument, that the people are slaves. This does not prove that they are not fit subjects of a free government. Look at the ensanguined plains of St. Domingo." Jackson considered the struggles of the slaves in the former French colony as a symbol of liberty: "[T]he oppressed have broken their chains and renounced their long lost rights. . . . There, notwithstanding the great debasement of the human character, the sacred fire of liberty is not extinguished. Wherever it exists, sooner or later, it bursts forth into an irresistible flame and consumes everything opposed to it."[52] But there was a paradox: when Jackson invoked the spirit of liberty and used the example of the struggles of the Saint-Domingue blacks, his point was to demand full political rights for the inhabitants of Louisiana, a number of whom were in fact slave owners. This brand of despotism, however, was not criticized by John George Jackson.

Furthermore, from that moment on it seemed impossible for American leaders to talk about Haitian freedom; to mention or acknowledge it would amount to declaring that their own system was shaken. So they kept silent, and no direct reference to Haiti is to be found in their writings.[53] Only James Monroe, in his London isolation, actually mentioned the unmentionable, though without realizing it. On May 6, 1804, he wrote Madison:

> I have seen a proclamation of the negro government in St. Domingo, offering a reward of 40 dollars to the commanders of our vessels, for everyone of its blacks now in the United States, whom they may bring back to the island. This is probably a measure of policy, intended to increase their strength, to enable them to make a better resistance thereafter. It may be otherwise, and in any event may escape the attention of the French government. If you are formally applied to, it is much to be wished, that such a course be taken as to show, we have no interest in the measure and give it no sanction.[54]

This letter contrasts with the official silence of the administration with regard to Haiti, and by the same token underscores how much this silence concealed.

The first sentence is actually tantamount to a recognition of the black republic, insofar as Monroe analyzes that "proclamation of the negro government in St. Domingo" in the same manner he would have the proclamation of any European nation. Although the former governor of Virginia had suppressed Gabriel's Conspiracy in 1800, he now not only seemed to accept the fact of a "negro government in St. Domingo," but he obviously assumed that the American government shared that premise. Hence his advice "If you are formally applied to . . . ," meaning that if the French government requested an explanation, Jefferson's government was to say that it knew nothing of the matter (as though the American government might helped the black "resistance"). Monroe's atypical attitude here can be ascribed to his being far away and to the many purely European problems that he was dealing with then.

In the United States, meanwhile, Jefferson's and Madison's silence on Haiti revealed their confusion over what their attitude should be with respect to the new republic, whose freedom was the fruit of the only successful slave rebellion recorded in history, as Robert Debs Heinl Jr. and Nancy Gordon Heinl have observed.[55] In 1804 the American government could no longer claim that the Saint-Domingue rebellion was the mere domestic problem of a foreign nation, or that it could avoid dealing with it in the hope that the slaves' enterprise would fail. The slaves had won, the rebellion had turned into a successful revolution, the hordes of savages had formed a "government" (as Monroe himself noted), and the government looked a lot like a white one. Haiti was not simply a community of fugitive as the United States had hoped it would become. As it was ostracized by the colonial nations of Europe, Haiti had no choice but to turn to the United States, which was now the only other revolutionary nation, since France was ruled by a dictator, in order to secure aid, advice, and a degree of economic cooperation. Indeed it did turn to the United States: at the end of 1803 Dessalines sent Bunel, Toussaint's former emissary, to plead the cause of Haiti in Washington, D.C., in order to revive the privileged commercial links that had been established between the rebel island and the United States before Leclerc's expedition. The details of the outcome of that negotiation are not known; but at any rate, it was not successful.[56]

Insofar as the United States was the only nation that remained in contact with the "black government," and although such contact had taken the form of commercial relations that the government preferred to ignore officially, the position of Americans as slave owners or members of a slaveholding society was indeed becoming untenable. By keeping its ambiguous attitude over the years, the American government had executed a brilliant ruling class maneuver, as David Barry Gaspar puts it;[57] it had managed to preserve the interests of both the merchant class and the planter class, while at the same time maintaining its status as a symbol of democracy for the rest of the world. But now that they were pressed by Haiti, Americans would soon have to choose between remaining faithful to their avowed ideals and preserving their social order. On March 28, 1804, the newspaper *Aurora,* which was close to the administration, described the ambiguities of the official U.S. position. The newspaper greeted Haiti's independence warmly: "On this subject we presume there are few who entertain dissimilar sentiments; the right to proclaim independence was unquestionably inherent in the people of that island." But the article ended on a dark and mysterious note: "However, as respects the relative situations of the United States and St. Domingo, the late occurrence in the latter will make it necessary for us to follow a delicate and circumspect line of conduct, for reasons too obvious for elucidation."[58] This was a reference to the massacre of whites in Aux Cayes, which the newspaper had reported on March 18, 1804. A prelude to the systematic massacring of the whites remaining on the island in 1805, this event nourished the growing fears of Americans over the spread of the black revolution, and their final refusal to recognize Haiti or to have any dealings with it.

Censorship, Cotton, and the 1806 Act

What kind of solution the American leaders were about to come up with can be gleaned from the coverage that the *Richmond Enquirer* gave on July 23, 1805, of the first Haitian Constitution. On May 20, 1805, Dessalines had ratified that document, the preamble of which contained a declaration about the equality of all men modeled after the French declaration of the Rights of Man of October 2, 1789.[59] The natural right to equality was stated again in Article 3. What is surprising for a Republican newspaper[60] is that certain articles of the Haitian Constitution were omitted. The presentation given by the *Richmond Enquirer* can be usefully compared with those given by the *Raleigh Register and North Carolina Gazette* (another southern Republican newspaper)[61] of July 29, 1805, and by the *Aurora* (a Republican newspaper from Philadelphia) of July 17, 1805. The constitutional articles omitted in the *Richmond Enquirer* (3, 2, and 12) concerned equality (Article 3), the abolition of slavery (Article 2), and the ban on former masters coming back to the island (Article 12: "No white man of whatsoever nation he may be, shall put his foot on this territory with the title of master or proprietor, neither shall he in future acquire any propriety therein"). Further on, among the general principles of the constitution, one also notices the omission of Article 13, which decreed that former masters would not be compensated. No explanation was given by the newspaper for the missing articles, which were left in blank.

All three newspapers had, however, procured the text of the constitution in the same way: by reproducing the text published in the *Mercantile Advertiser.* Why, then, did only the *Richmond Enquirer* publish it in a truncated version?

All three newspapers were Republican and faithful to the administration. Was there a risk that the readers of one newspaper might be more shocked than the others by the publication of the document in its entirety? Such would appear to be the case, as the wave of insurrections since 1791 had mostly struck Virginia, and in 1805 the population of Richmond was barely recovering from the shock caused by the disclosure of the Gabriel's Conspiracy. In contrast, the *Aurora,* although a Republican paper, was published in Pennsylvania, where slavery had just been abolished; thus, publishing the Haitian Constitution there would not hurt local sensibilities.

One thing is certain: all the articles omitted in the *Richmond Enquirer* dealt with the implications of the American and French Revolutions for slavery and equality. How could the American republic, founded as it was on liberty and slavery, have recognized a "black government" that affirmed the incompatibility of liberty and slavery? Dealing with Dessalines and the Haitian leaders amounted to admitting that American society was not only a symbol of liberty for the world, but also a symbol of oppression. Haiti's independence threatened the ideological foundations of the American republic and jeopardized the socioeconomic balance that was a basic ingredient of the nation's ideological cohesion. The constitution of Haiti clearly showed that, while inspired by the same principles as the American and French Revolutions, the Haitian Revolution had also been a class war, resulting finally in an upheaval of the social order, as white landowners lost control over their property.[62] The Haitian Constitution attacked the basic principles of American society: liberty proved incompatible with a particular conception of property, namely the property of slaves. Once independence had been proclaimed and the constitution ratified, the Haitian Revolution was no longer a distant threat.

In censoring the most controversial articles of the Haitian Constitution, the editor of the *Richmond Enquirer,* Thomas Ritchie, was obeying the instinct of self-preservation. His attitude went beyond mere silence: he introduced censorship of the principle of liberty in the country of civil liberties, which Republicans themselves had eagerly defended six years earlier at the time of the Sedition Act. In North Carolina Joseph Gales Jr., editor of the *Raleigh Register,* was soon to follow suit and conform to the mounting pressure for censorship, by discontinuing publication of any pro-abolition writing. Suppressing information in that manner was aimed at preventing its circulation among the population, both white—to protect it—and black—not to encourage it. Haiti itself gradually came to be viewed as a subversive island in ideological as well as political terms.

As Rayford W. Logan has noted, the shock of seeing former slaves setting up a nation may be compared to the effect that the 1917 Russian revolution had upon capitalist countries.[63] But because it was novel and unexpected, this shock was not felt by American leaders until some time later. It is easy to understand that there existed a certain amount of ideological confusion in the Republican camp, as is illustrated by James Monroe's remark and the eulogy of the Haitian Revolution delivered by John George Jackson in the early months of 1804. After the Republicans had fought the Federalists for ten years in order to preserve the democratic heritage of the American Revolution and to support the French Revolution, many of them probably had a hard time accepting the fact that their commitment to the rights of man was not universal and that its international dimension only applied to whites. The Haitian Revolution forced the Republicans to a painful realization, in foreign affairs as well, of the ambiguities of their own system. That is the reason why, until June 1804, the most experienced politicians, such as Thomas Jefferson, only considered Haiti in terms of commercial expansion, and refused to weigh the consequences of continuing relations with the black nation.[64]

In June 1804 the American government finally made a first move when it lent an ear to Pichon's complaints about the smuggling of goods into Haiti.[65] In November Jefferson requested a bill on that topic in his annual address: "While noticing the irregularities committed on the ocean by others, those on our own part should not be omitted or left unprovided for. Complaints have been received that persons residing within the U.S. have taken on themselves to arm merchant vessels and to force a commerce into certain ports and countries in defiance of the laws of these countries."[66] It is striking that Jefferson did not use the word "France"—probably not to offend the sensibilities of those members of Congress who would have resented being given orders by a great power—but he also avoided the words "Haiti" and "Saint-Domingue." The latter omission is more remarkable; had Jefferson only wanted to ingratiate himself with France, as he has been accused of, he would have used the term "Saint-Domingue," which clearly indicated that the United States still considered the island a French possession. It is likely that the vague phrasing of the passage not only reflected Jefferson's concerns regarding European affairs, but also that it marked, more fundamentally, the beginning of a new attitude toward the black nation on the part of the American government. It would seem that the president of the United States could not utter the name "Haiti," as though not uttering that name sufficed to wipe the island off the map of the world. On October 3, 1805, Congress passed an act aiming at curbing departures of merchant ships for Haiti, as it had been requested to do.[67] This did not prevent American merchants from continuing to supply arms, ammunition, and black recruits to Dessalines, and the French government made an official protest. As the United States was then trying to gain the favor of France in view of a projected purchase of the Floridas,[68] Congress enacted a complete ban on trade with Haiti on February 28, 1806.[69] As Rayford W. Logan has explained, a purely diplomatic interpretation cannot account for the "indecent" haste with which the bill was passed, and there is little doubt that banning commerce with Haiti was intended to appease France and to alleviate fears of the consequences that an independent Haiti would have on slavery in the United States.[70]

If one examines Jefferson's attitude toward Great Britain and France from 1803 on, it appears that the president trusted neither nation, and that he hoped to capitalize on their European quarrels in order to take hold of more territory on the American continent.[71] It is therefore improbable that he would have yielded something valuable in return for mere promises; indeed, after 1806 France did not help the United States obtain the Floridas any more actively than it had before. That means that by 1806 Jefferson had come to the conclusion that the trade with Haiti was no longer valuable enough, and that it hampered more than it consolidated the ideological unity on which the American nation rested.

The wars had indeed impoverished Haiti and dismantled its economic structure: by 1804 the island's sugar output had dropped to 23,800 quintals, from 81,700 in 1791. The coffee production had fallen by half. What money would have been available to the Haitian leaders to go on buying American products indefinitely?[72] Besides, by 1805 American exports to Haiti made up no more than a mere 4 percent of the country's total exports.[73] Northeastern merchants, whom Jefferson had long been protecting against France, could not fault him for taking a measure that hurt them little and that at the same time protected a sector of the American economy that was on the rise, thanks to the recent Louisiana Purchase: cotton growing. Since 1791 Eli Whitney's invention of the cotton gin had given new strength to the languishing farming industry of the southern states. From a total of 945 quintals in 1791, cotton exports had risen to 104,555 quintals in 1800 and 201,915 in 1805.[74] Such a massive increase would have been inconceivable without the labor of slaves in growing numbers, who were becoming more and more profitable for their owners. More than ever before, the quest for prosperity was proving incompatible with the propagation of the ideals of liberty, especially in the South. It was thus incompatible, on the international front, with a liberal attitude toward Haiti. The 1806 act that suspended commercial relations between the United States and Haiti was therefore a political decision, dictated by the belated realization on the part of American leaders of what the Haitian Revolution meant for American society and economy. It was their response to the challenge that Haiti posed for a country that already depicted itself as the haven of freedom. That act was the concrete manifestation of an important turn in the foreign policy of the United States toward the former French colony. It also indicated a shift in the direction of the American government's policy of expansion, in the sense that the commercial drive for Haiti was officially abandoned and that westward expansion (with the increase of cotton production as a corollary) became foremost among the long-term goals for the American economy.

Masters and Slaves: What Was at Issue in the 1806 Debate

By 1806 embarrassment and silence no longer fit the bill; what came instead was an unqualified rejection of the new nation. By refusing to recognize Haiti's independence and by depicting the former slaves as mere rebels, the new French ambassador to the United States, General Turreau, set the tone for the Republican stance during the congressional debates over this measure. For the French ambassador, the Haitian leaders were only "rebels," and he depicted them in racist and degrading terms.[75] This was the discourse of a colonial power about its rebellious former colony, and yet it was nonetheless taken up with great enthusiasm by General James Jackson, a Republican senator from Georgia. For General Jackson, the Haitians constituted a "horde" that "it must . . . become the interest of every nation having colonies in the West Indies, to extirpate and ship off to some other place."[76] After much hesitation, the Republicans now became the advocates of colonial nations, and resolutely sided with imperial France. Expressing support for General Ferrand, who was entrenched in the former Spanish part of Saint-Domingue, General Jackson declared that it was neither possible to recognize Haiti nor to trade with it: "As to the total separation of the self-created emperor [Dessalines] and nation of Haiti, and its independence on the parent country, under which gentlemen declared our right of trade founded on the laws of nation—the late attack on that general by the emperor proved it did not exist." Of course, one cannot overlook the unconscious irony of the use—by a Republican—of the phrase "self-created," which George Washington had used in 1794 to deny the legitimacy of the democratic-republican societies that supported the Republican Party. Jackson, however, did not merely renounce the Republicans' past; he clearly announced the choice the American nation had made. Between liberty for all and despotism of some over others, it chose the second option: "The separation was not such as to warrant the arguments used for a right to trade—it would be a fatal argument used against us as respected our southern states by other powers."[77]

Indeed, the obvious topic of the 1806 debate was neither the rights of neutral countries nor smuggling; what was at stake was the nature and the security of American society. When introducing his bill on December 20, 1805, Dr. George Logan, a senator from Pennsylvania, put the matter in very clear terms: "While we are anxious to have our natural rights respected, is it honorable to violate the rights of a friendly power with whom we are at peace? or is it sound policy to cherish the black population of St. Domingo whilst we have a similar population in our Southern States, in which should an insurrection take place, the government of the United States is bound to render effectual aid to our fellow-citizens in that part of the Union."[78] In recognizing Haiti, the United States would have run the risk of having France, or any other nation, recognize any group of rebel black slaves on American soil as an independent nation, and thus of jeopardizing the country's security and unity. As James Jackson explained: "On the same grounds, a group of runaways and outcasts from South Carolina and Georgia, to the amount of some hundreds now collected on or near Okafaunucau swamp in Georgia, might be termed an independent society; or if an insurrection took place in those States, the rebellious horde on creating an emperor, be supplied with arms and ammunition as a separate and independent nation."[79] What Jackson voiced here was a perfectly fine analysis of the new situation that resulted for the United States from the existence of a black nation in the Caribbean. Haiti was no longer a nightmare or a threat; it was a model for political upheaval and revolutionary change that could very well be applied to the United States. The Haitian Revolution meant that a slave rebellion could truly be victorious. Slaves could seize power and keep it. Keeping power meant more than a mere withdrawal from slave society, as had been the case with the fugitive slaves in Jamaica in the early eighteenth century. It entailed the destruction of a social system based on slavery and its replacement by something else—namely, a true nation—equipped with real armies and real presidents, and determined to get rid of former masters. When the Haitian leaders adroitly claimed to be the logical heirs to the principles of the French and American Revolutions, and when they repeated these principles in their public proclamations (liberty, equality, and natural rights), they could hardly be construed as fugitives or as rebels. One could not destroy them openly without tearing the fabric of American society and bringing to light one of its fundamental ambiguities.

As a consequence of the Republicans' anti-Haitian stance, the Federalists were able to make a strong ideological comeback. Samuel White, a senator from Delaware, reminded his colleagues that like the American Revolution, the Haitian Revolution had been a colonial war of independence: "The people of St. Domingo, as did the people of these States under other circumstances, declared themselves free and independent, determined to take their stand among the nations of the world."[80] This adept reference to the spirit of 1776 and to the Declaration of Independence was well suited to the Federalist strategy of the early 1800s. As historian Linda K. Kerber has explained, it was not the successes or the principles of the Jeffersonians that made an impression upon the Federalists; rather, it was their failures and contradictions.[81] In an effort to draw attention to the inconsistency of the Republicans' domestic policies (more democracy) with their foreign policies (no recognition of the black republic), Samuel White elaborated on his comparison of the United States and Haiti in 1804. His speech, however, sounds more like that of a devil's advocate than that of a sincere partisan of the rights of man. At one point, he extolled the bravery of the Haitian troops: "after a war of so many years with France, we see them not only yet independent, but having actually besieged the only French force in the country." But White's praises were to sound hollow later on when, carried away by his hatred for Napoleonic France, he twice lapsed into racist remarks. In the first of these, he said: "Then, sir, such is the ground we now occupy among nations, that the mandate of a French officer, besieged in the West Indies by a rabble of starving negroes, is a requisition too imperious for us to resist." And then: "General Ferrand might have been serious in writing such a proclamation or decree, expecting it to have some operation on the feeling and the fear of the ignorant blacks of St. Domingo, but he certainly . . . could never have been crazy enough, for a moment to suppose, that any citizen of the United States, arrived at years of maturity, or rather discretion, would be serious in reading it."[82]

In 1806 the Federalists had lost a lot of support on account of their aristocratic tendencies, but they were not yet political abolitionists.[83] They simply were waging a battle from behind. Their discourse about respecting Haiti's independence was primarily rhetorical and was aimed at attacking the Republicans rather than supporting Haiti. As a matter of fact, the Federalist anger soon faded, and when an act was passed in 1808 that definitively outlawed the slave trade, the nation's elite could feel that the slavery issue had been settled for good. Slavery, according to Winthrop Jordan, was no longer a divisive issue in the union.[84]

The Haitian Revolution could have rekindled the debate on slavery in the United States and thereby brought the American Revolution to its fulfillment through the emancipation of the "other persons," but this did not occur. At first the United States helped France and the planters; then they were satisfied with capitalizing on the events in Saint-Domingue to further their commercial interests in the area. The shortcomings of such a blind attitude were brought to light by Haiti's Declaration of Independence in 1804. By rejecting the second decolonized nation of the continent, American leaders opted for maintaining the status quo of slavery, and in this they were followed by the entire elite, Republican as well as Federalist. The 1806 act that banned trade with Haiti, while overtly defined as a token of solidarity with other colonial nations, was meant to crush Haiti, to silence it, and even to negate its existence. The titling of the act even avoided mentioning Saint-Domingue or Haiti; the black nation was referred to as the "part of the island of St. Domingo, not in possession, and under the acknowledged government of France."[85] The writing of the act introduced even more confusion, insofar as the lawmakers were trying to show that the law did not apply to the Spanish part of Saint-Domingue, which at that time was in French hands: "That all commercial intercourse between any person or persons resident within the United States, and any person or persons resident within any part of the island of St. Domingo, not in possession, and under the acknowledged government of France, shall be, and is thereby prohibited."[86] That part of the island that was still under Ferrand's control was, conversely, "in possession, and under the acknowledged government of France": the whole point of this long and awkward circumlocution was to avoid naming Haiti and referring to the actual political situation on the island. In keeping with the contradictory nature of their society, American leaders passed a law that upheld that contradiction and prevented the example of Haiti from spreading over their territory. To combat Haiti, they chose silence, not force or violence. The silence of the United States was more than indifference: it signified a rejection of the new nation and everything it stood for, a kind of political censoring of the new nation. Furthermore, by closing off Haiti to American trade at a time when cotton farming was on the rise, the leaders of the early republic demonstrated their desire for continental economic expansion. In that sense, one might think that they were already acting as southerners, were it not for the consensus that seemed to set in across the nation at that time in favor of the "peculiar institution."

CHAPTER 7

The Louisiana Purchase: American Expansion and Its Problems from 1803 to 1812

Much was said and written, at the time, concerning the policy of adding the vast regions of Louisiana, to the already immense, and but half-tenanted territories of the United States. . . . It soon became apparent, to the meanest capacity, that, . . . the measure had made us the masters of a belt of fertile country. . . . It gave us the sole command of the great thoroughfare of the interior, and placed the countless tribes of savages . . . entirely within our controul; . . . it opened a thousand avenues to the inland trade, and to the waters of the Pacific.[1]

James Fenimore Cooper was an apt observer of his fellow countrymen and their political mores; it was not without reason that he set the plot of his romance, *The Prairie,* in the wild expanse of Louisiana, a few months after Jefferson's envoys had taken possession of the area. The first lines of the book, where Cooper described the many positive aspects of the purchase—territorial, economic, commercial, and geopolitical—sized up the extent of the upheaval the purchase of Louisiana implied for the United States. The year 1801, with the election of Jefferson, may have signaled a political revolution in the United States, as the Republicans finally did away with the Federalists and their excessive nostalgia for a hierarchical society, but it was 1803 that heralded the continental turn of the ambitious new nation. By suddenly doubling the territorial area of their country, American leaders could now identify with and invest their energies in a territorial and scientific conquest, which allowed them to give free rein to the missionary calling of their nation and to distance themselves from European turmoil. Among other aspects, the opening of the West gave Jefferson an opportunity to realize his dream as a man of the Enlightenment and the ideology of progress. The expeditions he launched into the West—those of Lewis and Clark, William Dunbar, and Zebulon Pike—were true scientific voyages with an encyclopedic aim. Because they captured the nation's imagination, they gave U.S. citizens a chance to appropriate the North American continent on the level of emotion and myth. Neither the military intent nor the commercial and political goals of these expeditions were lost on the Spanish, who were attentive and critical witnesses of this expansionist wave. There were victims, too: Native Americans, who were slowly pushed back to the Mississippi; the Louisiana French, whose cultural individuality was not recognized; and the Spanish from both old and new continents. Through these unfortunate partners of the United States, we can gain insight into a nation that found its meaning in an irresistible drive to conquer, wherein it wholeheartedly imposed its civilization without any desire for "exchange" with the other.[2]

The Sale of Louisiana to the United States

The Rebirth of French Colonial Policy

On October 1, 1800, General Berthier signed the Treaty of San Ildefonso, whereby Spain retroceded Louisiana to France. In compensation for territorial losses Spain had incurred by helping France, Louisiana had been ceded to Spain in November 1762, at the end of the Seven Years' War, which the North American colonists called the French and Indian War.[3] Like other colonies that France had lost in the eighteenth century, Louisiana had vanished from the immediate concerns of the French. A policy of conquest had actually been officially rejected by the Constituent Assembly in May 1790. Although the first plans for revolutionary expansion were debated by the Convention in 1792 and 1793, they aimed primarily at annexing neighboring territories, in accordance with the principle of conquering France's natural borders.[4]

Still, French leaders soon turned their thoughts again to the colonies they had lost. As Michael Garnier has written, "everyone threw in his two-cents' worth against the *ancien régime* for having so cheerfully discarded the riches of Louisiana and its 'souls' in 1763."[5] Louisiana, then, was still part of French colonial memory, or at least of that of the ruling elite. Fleeing the Terror, Talleyrand had come to Philadelphia, where he became friends with the colonist Moreau de Saint-Méry, who was prevented from going home by the continuing rebellion of the blacks in Saint-Domingue. In the evenings at Moreau's, the exiles entertained the dream of settling down in Louisiana, as indeed many planters who had fled from Saint-Domingue were in the process of doing.[6] In fact, Talleyrand was already speculating on western land.[7]

After the end of the Terror, Talleyrand returned to France and became the minister of external relations on July 15, 1797. For him, as well as for the victorious and arrogant Directory as a whole, Louisiana and the colonies were once again a priority.[8] In the negotiations that led to the Peace of Basle in 1795, all the French were able to obtain from King Charles IV was the Spanish part of Saint-Domingue, but what they really wanted was Louisiana. When Franco-American political relations deteriorated, after Jay's Treaty was signed, the French diplomats in Philadelphia shed all scruples. In 1795 a wary French republic asked Pierre-Auguste Adet "to convey to the government every piece of intelligence that he can procure on the states extending to the west and Louisiana, as well as on the disposition of their inhabitants."[9]

The spirit of the westward journey that Adet sent General Collot on in March 1796 was in fact quite different from that of Michaux's trip in 1793. The issue at stake was no longer to help the western pioneers to "liberate" the Spanish provinces, but instead to reconnoiter territory that was hopefully one day to become French. An expert mapmaker, Collot gathered information at every stage of a peregrination that took him from Philadelphia to Pittsburgh, then down the Ohio and the Mississippi all the way to New Orleans. What caught his attention was the strategic points, that is, the future strongholds "that could prevent American troops from going down the Ohio" once France again took possession of Louisiana.[10] Meanwhile, the philosopher Volney, friend to both Jefferson and Talleyrand, also undertook in the same year a great western journey in the direction of Upper Louisiana; not too keen on the idea of Louisiana being reunited with France, he came back "convinced that it was a fanciful and dangerous plan."[11] There was thus no consensus on this plan.

American Worries

The renewed colonial policy of France explains why when during the Consulate it finally wrested Louisiana from Spain, it kept the news of this retrocession a secret for as long as possible, in order not to scare the United States. Still, the news spread quickly: on March 29, 1801, Rufus King informed Madison about it, and Jefferson echoed the rumor on May 26 in a letter to Monroe.[12] The French chargé d'affaires, Pichon, soon became aware of the American leaders' bitter feelings,[13] and they eventually vented their concerns to him. What worried them was that having France as a neighbor in New Orleans and Louisiana involved radically different consequences from having Spain in that position. With regard to the Spanish, Madison said that "it was a peace-loving government, and it always grew tired of fighting soon enough to let one have one's way." Pichon denied the retrocession and feigned surprise: why, even if the news were true, would there be a difference between Spain and France?[14] There was indeed a difference, which explained why American leaders were worried: unlike Spain, France was a strong country bent on conquest, and it could only be an obstacle in the way of U.S. westward expansion, if it did not actually become a rival of the new republic on the North American continent.[15] The immediate reaction of American leaders upon learning about the retrocession of Louisiana revealed their long-term plans for expansion, which the French apparently expected given the fact that they kept the news a secret. As Jefferson confided to James Monroe: "However our present interests may restrain us within our own limits, it is impossible not to look forward to distant times, when our rapid multiplication will expand itself beyond these limits, and cover the whole northern, if not the southern continent, with a people speaking the same language, governed in similar forms and by similar laws."[16] To Pichon, too, he remarked that "the U.S. would possess Louisiana by the sheer force of circumstances."[17]

By the force of circumstances, what Jefferson meant was the irresistible drive of the pioneers, which he counted on to nibble away at the declining empire of Spain, and which he knew could not operate in a peaceful way if France took possession of Louisiana. However vague and hazy they appeared then, the president's plans for expansion were quite real, and they would be jeopardized if France took Spain's place. As Jefferson explained to the minister plenipotentiary in Paris, Robert R. Livingston, in reference to New Orleans: "Spain might have retained it [New Orleans] quietly for years. Her pacific dispositions, her feeble state, would induce her to increase our facilities there, so that her possession of the place would be hardly felt by us, and it would not perhaps be very long before some circumstance might arise which might make the cession of it to us the price of something more worth to her. Not so can it ever be in the hands of France."[18] That the retrocession of Louisiana was of paramount importance to France became even clearer to Jefferson after January 1802, when General Leclerc and his troops landed in Saint-Domingue. Until then, the threat of having France as a neighbor had been merely hypothetical, but that changed with the landing of French troops in an area in which the United States had a commercial interest. Jefferson may have thought that the First Consul and the Minister of External Relations would promote a symbiosis between Saint-Domingue and Louisiana, of the kind that had once existed between the American colonies and the British West Indies. At any rate, the analysis of Barbé-Marbois, by then minister of the treasury, went along these lines: "[Napoleon's plan] consisted first of subduing the rebel colony by sending there a considerable force. . . . Once the rebels were brought down, a portion of the army was to be transferred to Louisiana. . . . Louisiana was destined to provide the other colony with supplies, cattle, and wood."[19]

Whether Jefferson believed in this theory or not, French military operations in Saint-Domingue could only be a cause for concern for American leaders. As Leclerc scored victory after victory over the Saint-Domingue rebel troops in the spring of 1802, American leaders were now faced not only with the problem of future American expansion; they were also concerned about the immediate security of the current national borders in the presence of a future, very powerful neighbor. The chief worry was the New Orleans depot, which the United States had won over in 1795 at the end of an exhausting negotiating process with Spain, and through which all goods from the western states had to pass. These western states had been enjoying an economic boom since 1795, and they had always faithfully voted for the Jeffersonian Republicans.

While Robert Livingston, the American minister in Paris, was trying in vain to secure information about the retrocession of Louisiana, Jefferson thought it proper to speak his mind to Pierre Samuel Dupont de Nemours, who was about to go back to France, in order for Dupont to explain the American position to the First Consul. He formally requested that France refrain from occupying New Orleans if it did not want to run the risk of having the United States side with Great Britain in a renewed war against France: "There is on the globe one single spot, the possessor of which is our natural and habitual enemy. It is New Orleans, through which the produce of 3/8ths of our territory must pass to market. . . . The day that France takes possession of New Orleans fixes the sentence which is to restrain her forever within her low water-mark. It seals the union of two nations who in conjunction can maintain exclusive possession of the ocean. From that moment we must marry ourselves to the British fleet and nation."[20] Dupont explained to Jefferson that his warlike tone could only antagonize Bonaparte. The threats of a military alliance gave way to a diplomatic solution, namely, the purchase of New Orleans and the Floridas, an option that Jefferson had been considering. This solution would at least guarantee an outlet to the sea for westerners in the event that expansion to Louisiana should prove impossible.[21]

While the precise extent of the territory covered by the retrocession was still unclear, in early May 1802 Madison asked Livingston to try to buy New Orleans and the Floridas. The French fleet that General Victor was to lead to Louisiana had not yet left Holland, and Madison even considered the possibility that the arrangement between Spain and France would in fact not go through. Charles Pinckney, the American minister in Madrid, was then ordered to ask Spain for New Orleans and the Floridas. In October 1802 the secretary of state once again asked Livingston to try to secure these territories for the United States.[22] While the French troops in Saint-Domingue were falling victim to yellow fever and the unflinching resistance of the blacks, American leaders grew more and more confident that peaceful negotiations would allow them to achieve their goals.[23] All of a sudden, on October 29, 1802, they received a dispatch from William Charles Coles Claiborne, the governor of the Territory of Mississippi, notifying them that what they had dreaded the most had just occurred. As historian Henry Adams was to explain later, "the Spanish Intendant, Don Juan Morales, had forbidden the Americans to deposit their merchandise at New Orleans, as they had a right to do so under the treaty of 1795."[24]

The Closing of the New Orleans Depot and Its Political Consequences

Pinckney's Treaty did in fact include an article conferring to the Spanish a right to deny American commerce and navigation the use of the port of New Orleans. But the same article also bound Spain to provide the Americans, in that event, with an equivalent facility, which Morales did not do.[25] The decision was therefore received as a deliberate affront. The aggressive conduct of General Leclerc toward American merchants in Saint-Domingue and the hostile stance that France was thought to be taking toward Americans were added ingredients to feed the wrath of the westerners. If Morales acted the way he did, they reasoned, it might have been upon orders from France, which was bent upon impeding the development of its young neighbor.[26] As Jefferson observed: "The agitation of the public mind . . . is extreme. In the western country it is natural and grounded on honest motives." Madison concurred—"The Mississippi is to them everything"—and he quoted the ever increasing numbers of western exports: "The produce exported through that channel last year amounted to $11,622 from the District of Kentucky and Mississippi only, and will probably be fifty per cent more this year."[27]

Meanwhile, the Federalist wrath, which was less predictable, caught the government unawares. The Federalist diehards, who had little sympathy for France, saw an opportunity to win the favor of the predominantly Republican West and waged a large-scale campaign to support war against France and invasion of the coveted territories. The legislatures of the western states were venting their discontent in addresses they sent to Washington, D.C., which entitled the Federalists to speak on behalf of the whole nation. Their argument no longer centered on the country's security, but on its honor, its greatness, and its future.

For the Federalist *New York Evening Post,* the government's inertia would compel westerners to take New Orleans on their own, which could only result in the dismantling of the American "empire."[28] From January 24 to 28, 1803, the same paper published a report of a "Memorial on the war in St. Domingue and cession of the Mississippi to France, drawn up by a French councillor of state." Whether this document was authentic or not, it was especially well suited for stirring up the flame of American patriotism, since it depicted in the most derogatory fashion American institutions and national character. For the councilor of state, France was to assume exclusive navigation rights over the river. The editorialist who commented on this "Memorial" concluded: "[I]t belongs of *right* to the United States to regulate the future destiny of *North America.* The country is *ours;* ours is the right to its rivers and to all the sources of future opulence, power and happiness, which lay scattered at our feet."[29]

According to this view, the United States and France—both of them powerful and ambitious nations—could not possibly have equal status on the American continent. The former had a "right" to expansion, and the latter did not. The debate was being moved, then, from the field of diplomacy to that of ideology: on the North American continent, the new nation's status was special, and privileged over other nations, and it was here that its exceptional destiny should be fulfilled. In the view of the above-quoted journalist, French presence in New Orleans would not only be a hindrance to the economic growth of the western states and territories; it would also put an end to the development of one of the most "promising" nations on earth. As for the *Charleston Courier*, another Federalist newspaper, its editorialist could not find enough words of praise for the future of this nation of promise: "The mind of man can scarcely prescribe bounds to the probable greatness, and glories of a vast nation, extending from the Atlantic to the Pacific Ocean. . . ."[30] As can be seen here, this kind of nationalistic lyricism drew its epic force from a vision of the nation's continental expansion.

The Federalists also praised national union and greatness in Congress, where they called for forceful measures with respect to France. In the Senate, Gouverneur Morris urged the invasion of Florida and New Orleans in the name of "national honor," once again resorting to the nationalist rhetoric he had inaugurated ten years earlier against Great Britain. To display strength, he explained, was to defend one's honor and thus the country's independence. Negotiating with Bonaparte without having anything to offer in return would be demonstrating exceptional naiveté. The United States had no other choice but "manly resistance or vile submission."[31]

While the uncompromising measures that Gouverneur Morris advocated were supported only by a minority, his appeal to consolidating national union through the conquest of New Orleans reflected the opinion of all Americans. As Pichon observed, the United States was more united than ever before: "It is a mistake . . . to think that these [western] states have a desire or an interest to separate from the seaward parts of the Federation."[32]

The states of the Atlantic seaboard in fact supported their western neighbors through their representatives and senators in Congress. The country's future was what united the nation, and this future was symbolized by the right to deposit goods at New Orleans. What was at stake was not only present prosperity, but also a great destiny. This was the reason why the difference between Gouverneur Morris and Thomas Jefferson was not one of essence, but of tactics. Whereas Morris advocated rushing into war even before hostilities had broken out again on the European continent, Jefferson preferred to delay entering the war until England once again was mistress of the seas.[33] It was especially important to the American government to avoid frustrating westerners, and to follow a policy that was to their taste.[34] In the end, westerners were the vanguard of American expansion, and they made up the popular army Jefferson was counting on: "Although I am not sanguine in obtaining a cession of New Orleans for money, yet I am confident in the policy of putting off the day of contention for it, till we are stronger in ourselves and stronger in allies, but especially till we shall have planted such a population on the Mississippi as will be able to do their own business, without the necessity of marching men from the shores of the Atlantic 1,500 or 2,000 miles thither, to perish by fatigue and change of climate."[35]

After the commotion that winter over the prospect of the French returning to the American continent, Jefferson invoked the legitimate anger of westerners when he asked Monroe to go to France as envoy extraordinary. Monroe's mission was to inform the French government about the state of mind of the western population, and to purchase New Orleans and the Floridas.[36] Monroe, who, according to Pichon, enjoyed "great popularity among the western people," left for Paris on March 8, 1803.[37] His departure was depicted as a final attempt at negotiation, and appeased the political fever. In the spring of 1803 the *Tennessee Gazette* showed total confidence in the government's measures and reprinted the official protests to Intendant Morales by the Spanish minister plenipotentiary Carlo Martinez de Yrujo.[38] But this was the eve of combat. The noble cause of expansion, which was crucial to the growth of the early republic, kept the nation on the alert, as Pichon noted: "As for the national mind, . . . it is preparing more and more for any event. Lately a great dinner was given in Natchez where the governor of the Mississippi Territory, Mr. Claiborne, was present. Among other remarkable toasts, the following two were proposed: 'free navigation on the Mississippi or war'—'may Mr. Monroe's mission succeed in full, or fail in full.'"[39]

The Louisiana Purchase

Back in Paris, the news was not good: the Saint-Domingue expedition had failed; General Leclerc's death was announced on January 7, 1803; and the prospect of renewed hostilities with Great Britain was looming large. These developments gradually forced Bonaparte and Talleyrand to revise their plans for colonial expansion. Following the advice of Barbé-Marbois, the First Consul resolved to sell Louisiana rather than letting it fall into British hands.[40] On April 11 an offer to that effect was transmitted to Livingston. The next day Monroe arrived in Paris with the same orders that the American minister had: to buy New Orleans and the Floridas. What the French proposed to the two diplomats did not match their instructions, and yet they did not hesitate, since it was a desire for expansion, as much as a concern for security, that had led their government to send them both to Paris. How could they refuse to discuss an offer to double the U.S. national territory? On May 2 the treaty was finally signed.

For the measly sum of sixty million francs, the United States had just purchased a huge chunk of territory with a diverse population, one whose geography and precise borders were poorly known. Chance would have it that events and political decisions gave the Americans exactly what they wanted, which they would not have dared to take for themselves. All the letters and debates that led up to this purchase reflected an expansionist discourse, in which the nation identified itself with a glorious future. Yet that discourse was still shaky and halfhearted; reading some of their statements, one might think that the American leaders only wanted to buy Florida and New Orleans. But their reluctance to have the French for neighbors clearly meant that they intended to settle the whole continent. As Jefferson had written Monroe on November 24, 1801, "it is impossible not to look forward to distant times," when the United States would "cover the whole northern, if not the southern continent."[41]

This expansionist discourse was often more clearly enunciated by the opposition than by the administration itself, since the opposition did not have the constraints of a governing party, whereas the administration had to tone down any warlike attitudes out of consideration for powerful and widely feared France. The Louisiana Purchase was Bonaparte's way of giving Americans the means to realize their dreams for expansion.

Now that the dream was coming true, the continental dimension of the American nation came to the forefront in editorial comments: it was no longer simply a particular feature of the early republic's future; it was also the visible sign of its exceptional and exemplary mission. As Aristides explained in his column ("Reflections on Political Economy and the Prospect before Us. Addressed to the Citizens of the Western Country"), which was reproduced in the *Tennessee Gazette:* "In addition to these felicities (uncommon prosperity, liberty, national honor, economy, simplicity, and private virtue) the late cession of Louisiana comes at the most propitious juncture to expand the horizon of our views, and to prompt the wisdom of the nation to the exercise of all those energies which may give to America a character more elevated than that of any other, in either ancient or modern times."[42]

In his address to Congress on October 17, 1803, Jefferson elaborated on the meaning of that expansion of the national territory. The acquisition of Louisiana promised "an ample provision for our posterity" and guaranteed beyond the Mississippi "a wide spread for the blessings of freedom and equal laws."[43] The mission of the United States acquired a political meaning: the expansion of the republic meant the expansion of the rule of liberty, a value that the United States was now alone in defending, since the French Republic had turned into a dictatorship.

Exploration Expeditions

National Rivalries Over Much Sought-After Territory: The Northwest

In the words of Barbé-Marbois, "They had hardly taken possession of Louisiana before they sent out exploring expeditions in all directions to inspect these western regions, which geographers still designate by the names of unknown countries and wild deserts."[44] This account is somewhat erroneous: preparation for exploration expeditions had started long before Louisiana was acquired, and therefore was not a result of it, although it is true that the purchase facilitated these journeys considerably.

As we have seen, in 1793 Jefferson had contemplated a continental expedition. It would have been launched under the aegis of the American Philosophical Society, which was ready to subsidize botanist André Michaux in this undertaking, but then interest for this kind of journey had subsided. In January 1802 another member of the American Philosophical Society, Caspar Wistar, mentioned to Jefferson that a book had just been published in London that ought to be of special interest to Americans. The book was entitled *Voyages from Montreal on the River St. Laurence, through the Continent of North America, to the Frozen and Pacific Oceans,* and it was the work of Sir Alexander McKenzie, a British explorer and the first European to have led an expedition across the North American continent. Although it was a scientific voyage, McKenzie's epic was also a journey with an expansionist aim, during which the author had taken note of propitious areas for British colonization and ways of reaching them. Its avowed goal, indeed, was to make it possible for Great Britain to get a monopoly on the fur trade in the interior of the continent and on the Northwestern Coast.[45]

According to historian Donald Jackson, McKenzie's program was in fact the starting point of an international competition over the control of the Pacific Northwest, and Jefferson was not long in putting the United States into the race.[46] In the summer of 1802 the president ordered McKenzie's book.[47] It would seem that the closing of the New Orleans depot played a role in his decision to set up a transcontinental exploration expedition; at any rate, in early December he started to organize what was to become the Lewis and Clark expedition, and he communicated this plan to various people. If the measures taken by Intendant Morales were any indication of future French behavior in Louisiana, it would perhaps be sound policy to preempt the French before they too joined the race for the Northwest. This, at least, was the analysis given of Jefferson's plan by the British minister plenipotentiary in Washington, D.C.

Albert Gallatin, then secretary of the treasury, seemed to think that such an expedition would allow the United States to take control of the Northwest before Great Britain did. What he had in mind was the imminent renewal of hostilities, which the British might use as a good excuse to march from Canada to French Louisiana and, in the process, to take over the Northwest. The important thing was not to waste time, for, according to Gallatin, it was clear that "the future destinies of the Mississippi country are of vast importance to the United States, it being perhaps the only large tract of country, and certainly the first which lying out of the boundaries of the Union will be settled by the people of the United States."[48] Although Gallatin did not conceal the expansionist, commercial, and military aim of the journey, the U.S. president acted otherwise. To the British and Spanish ministers plenipotentiary, he merely described the planned journey as a scientific and even "literary" exploration, which was meant to crown a successful administration; as Edward Thornton explained:

> The president has for some years past had it in view to set on foot an expedition entirely of a scientific nature for exploring the Western Continent of America by the route of the Great River Missouri, and for tracing the proximity of the sources of this river to the streams, which fall on the other side into the Pacific Ocean. He supposes this to be the most natural and direct water-communication between the two Oceans, and he is ambitious in his character of a man of letters and of science, of distinguishing his Presidency by a discovery, now the only one left to his enterprize. . . . [49]

Nonetheless, the idea that this was a purely scientific expedition did not convince the Spanish minister Yrujo, who clearly explained the geopolitical consequences of such a venture to his government.[50]

In Congress the expedition was described from yet another angle: the journey was meant to foster relations between the western Native American tribes and the U.S. government. The exploring venture was being turned into a journey of commercial canvassing, and its true goal, that is, to reach the Pacific Ocean by following McKenzie's example, was at first only mentioned in passing: "An intelligent officer with ten or twelve chosen men, fit for the enterprize and willing to undertake it, taken from our posts, where they may be spared without inconvenience, might explore the whole line, even to the Western ocean. . . ." Only at the end of this confidential message did Jefferson unambiguously describe the scientific purport of the journey: "While other civilized nations have encountered great expense to enlarge the boundaries of knowledge, by undertaking voyages of discovery, and for other literary purposes, in various parts and directions, our nation seems to owe to the same object, as well as to its own interest, to explore this, the only line of easy communication across the continent. . . ."[51] In Jefferson's presentation, this voyage was to allow the United States to take its place among "civilized" nations, and the appropriation passed by Congress was meant to further the development of knowledge. It was in the name of scientific progress that Meriwether Lewis, the man chosen to head the expedition, was to lead his companions through the wild expanses west of the Mississippi. The 1803 expedition was conceived in the spirit of the Enlightenment: Jefferson would rank with Louis XVI and George III among the great patrons of science and progress, while Lewis and his adjunct William Clark (who was Jefferson's secretary at the time) would be the Bougainville and the Cook of the North American West. Why, then, could Jefferson not announce such a grand goal more openly? Donald Jackson's surprise is legitimate: why did the American president give priority to commercial justifications in his message to Congress?[52] The answer is to be found in Barbé-Marbois's history: "To explore [these territories], to cross them, was in a way to acquire sovereignty over them."[53]

Since 1790 and the Nootka Sound affair, the doctrine of sovereignty through prior discovery was no longer valid, and the Northwest was indeed an unclaimed area. The Spanish, however, did not acknowledge this, and Jefferson was trying to divert their attention by clouding the issue. The diplomatic conflict between Great Britain and Spain over Nootka Sound on the Northwestern Coast had in fact led to important developments as to the meaning and modes of conquering North American territories that were as yet "unoccupied" ("unoccupied," that is, by people other than Native Americans). Since the 1750s the Spanish had started to feel the threat of Russian expansionism on their northwestern frontier. The lucrative fur trade emboldened the Russians, who kept enlarging their hunting domain, from Siberia to the Aleutian Islands and eventually to Alaska.[54] Since the Spanish laid claim to the whole of the Pacific Coast of North America, which they called "California," they decided, at the behest of the energetic José de Gàlvez, Inspector of New Spain, to organize explorations in order to counter that threat. The first of these expeditions was launched in 1769; it reached San Diego, then San Francisco and Monterey. The first two missions were created in San Diego and Monterey.[55]

In 1774 the Perez expedition discovered the Nootka Sound harbor on what is today Vancouver Island. In 1775 the Hereta-Bogota expedition discovered the mouth of the Columbia River and made four official land claims, one of them on the 57th parallel north. Although the Spanish were secretive about these journeys, news of their activities spread. When James Cook reconnoitered the area, he made only one land claim at 61°30' N, which was in observance of Spanish claims. The Spanish authorities were reassured by this and they mistakenly considered that such costly voyages could be discontinued and their rights over these lands be preserved without occupying them. In addition, as Warren L. Cook observed, the silence of the Spanish over their expeditions resulted in weakening their claims based on prior discovery.[56] The principle of "prior discovery" meant that the "discoverers" of a piece of land could lay claim to it and maintain sovereignty over it even without occupying it. In an era of heightened commercial competition, however, such a principle was no longer tenable, as the Spanish were to learn at their own expense.

Starting in 1783 British and American ships searched the Northwestern Coast for precious furs. This is the true context of the famed Nootka Sound affair mentioned earlier. In 1788 a British sailor named John Meares, whose ship, however, flew a Portuguese flag, settled at Nootka Sound, a small bay located on the Pacific coast of Vancouver Island, later abandoned by both countries. There he made a temporary camp, allegedly after having bought the land from the chief of the Native American tribe who lived in the area and was the origin of its name. In the spring of 1789 one of Meares's partners, James Colnett, came back to Nootka, this time flying a British flag, only to run into an official Spanish party and have the latter discover that the British did not carry Spanish licenses to land on that coast. The ships were seized and the sailors were jailed.[57] For William Pitt, the British prime minister, this crisis was a boon: in this year, 1790, he had the upper hand, since Spain could not resort to the Family Pact and call on France for help; so he could demand the abolition of the principle of prior discovery and the substitution of the principle of occupation.[58] In the Anglo-Spanish Convention of October 1790, the Spanish did not actually cede anything more than Nootka Sound; but they did give up their claims to any territories they did not occupy, which applied mostly to the Northwestern Coast.[59] What Pitt may not have realized is that his new principle would benefit others, and in the first place American sailors. As soon as the 1790 crisis was over, an American captain named Kendrick bought a tract of land in the vicinity of Nootka Sound and then entrusted the property titles to the American Consul in Canton, thus putting the first American landmark on this coast,[60] to be backed up in 1811 by a commercial outpost in Astoria.

By 1803 California had been developed by the Spanish: from San Francisco to San Diego there were eighteen missions, where 13,500 Indians lived. The civil sector had not expanded as much, with Hispanic residents numbering no more than about 1,800 and no new establishments created north of San Francisco, despite new scientific and military expeditions. Spain had still not given up on the rest of the Northwestern Coast, the lands in the interior, New Mexico, Texas, and the West. To the Spanish, these sparsely populated areas (such as Texas, with only four thousand residents), where they did not control the activities of Native American tribes, were to serve as buffer zones between the British, the Americans, and the mines of Mexico.[61] Before 1803 the Spanish themselves had supported attempts at exploring the course of the Missouri (from 1794 to 1797) in order to establish good relations with the northwestern tribes, but no tangible results ensued.[62] After the sale of Louisiana, their determination was strengthened: they would not let the Americans through.[63] At the end of 1802, Yrujo tried to talk Jefferson out of his plan.[64] The president was aware that he was sending explorers across territory that was claimed by Spain; he nevertheless decided to defy Spanish power. In his instructions to Lewis, he did not conceal the fact that after giving notice of the planned voyage to the representatives of France, Spain, and Great Britain, only France and Great Britain had extended him passports for the expedition. Yet Jefferson had decided to go ahead regardless, since two pages further in the instructions, he envisioned his secretary arriving on the Pacific shore, which the latter could not possibly reach without crossing the Spanish-claimed Northwest.[65]

Jefferson's confidence was due in Part to Pitt. The Lewis and Clark expedition was clearly presented as a voyage of exploration destined to reconnoiter unoccupied areas, as opposed to regions that were not claimed by any country at all. From then on, a given territory would belong to whomever first set up trade posts there, gave names to the rivers and mountains, and was able to keep up occupation by maintaining a presence of commercial agents, trappers, and pioneers. Such was now the price for sovereignty over disputed territories. It was up to the Spanish to draw the right conclusions and join the race for fur and outposts if they were capable of it, or so Jefferson seemed to think when launching this expedition. The secrecy he maintained about it was one of his weapons in this battle for a continent.

American Expeditions from 1803 On

The two expedition leaders, Meriwether Lewis and William Clark, were both career soldiers, which inevitably underscored the strategic aspect of their voyage across the continent. A mere soldier, however, could not be in charge of an expedition that was also claimed for scientific progress. The kind of man Jefferson had in mind to head the expedition was both a master and lover of nature: he should be brave and healthy, that is, fit for life outdoors; he should be familiar with the "Indian character"; and he should also be an expert in astronomy and the natural sciences.[66] Since no such man could be found in the United States, Captain Lewis would do the job—he knew American nature and forests well, but he would have to undergo, from March to June 1803, intensive training in the natural sciences. For that purpose, Jefferson sent Lewis to Philadelphia, to be instructed by eminent members of the American Philosophical Society.[67] After this "training period," he should be able to follow his instructions and bring back valuable information to Jefferson as concerned geography (about the Missouri, the Rockies, and the Northwest), ethnology and diplomacy (about various Native American tribes), botany, biology, mineralogy, the climate, and the economy.[68] Lewis left Philadelphia at the beginning of the summer of 1803; he did not come back to St. Louis until September 23, 1806.

In the meantime, the excitement over the Louisiana Purchase had led Jefferson to launch a series of trans-Mississippian expeditions, the goal being reconnaissance of the other rivers of Louisiana (the Platte, the Arkansas, and the Red Rivers) and more detailed maps of the territory. Jefferson imparted his project to William Dunbar on April 15, 1804.[69] Dunbar had become a regular correspondent of Jefferson's in 1802 and 1803, when Jefferson was concerned about Louisiana and its borders. Dunbar was a prosperous planter in Natchez, and a valuable source of information for the president. He was fond of the sciences, and he had helped the Spanish draw the demarcation line between the United States and Florida in 1798. In addition to his mathematic and scientific knowledge, Dunbar was deeply interested in Native American languages and the geog-

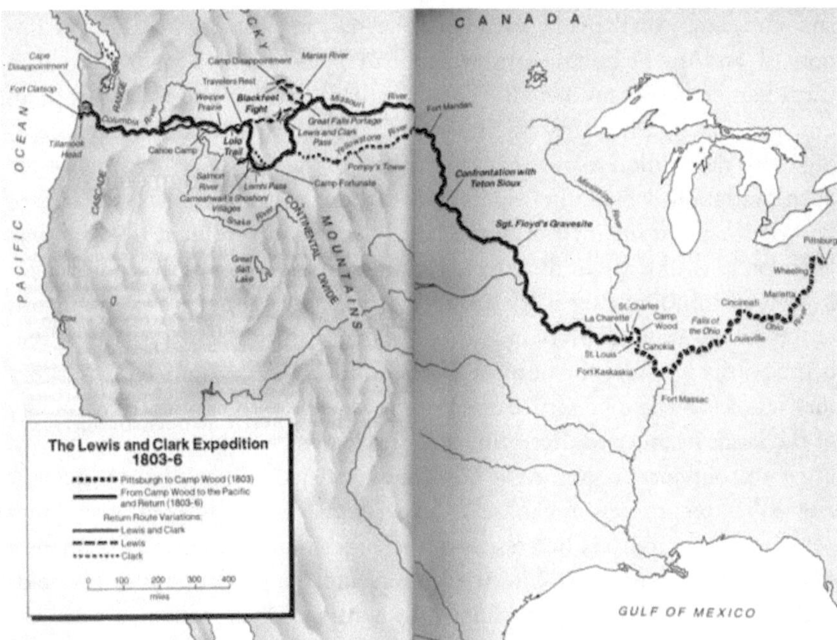

The Lewis and Clark Expedition 1803–1806 (David Lavender, *The Way to the Western Sea,* p. xiv–xv)

raphy of the area. An expert planter, he also displayed mechanical ingenuity to improve the methods of cotton-growing, inventing the square cotton bale as well as the technique of extracting cottonseed oil.[70] His eclectic character and the range of his skills made him just the kind of man Jefferson liked, and the president entrusted him with the organization of an expedition to the Arkansas and Red Rivers, which would be funded by the three thousand dollars Congress had just approved for this purpose. Dunbar and chemist Dr. Hunter eventually left on October 16, 1804. They did not, however, go to the Arkansas River, because a schism in the Osage tribe had made navigation of the river unsafe;[71] instead, they set out for the Washita River, with orders to go up it.

Dunbar's was a small expedition, but a serious one scientifically, as is shown by his diary. Besides Dunbar and Dr. Hunter, the party counted some soldiers but no officers, which Dunbar regretted in a rare expression of personal feeling, for the soldiers sometimes lacked proper discipline. On the whole, however, the diary was a simple and rather dry account of the team's observations. Each day, Dunbar carefully recorded the temperature and geographical position, and described the landscapes he discovered. For a modern-day reader, this somewhat tiring routine is relieved by the intrusion of fancy into the discourse of science. Always one to search for explanatory theories, Dunbar put science and pure fantasy on the same level. Once, he most seriously reported the description of an American unicorn, which had been mentioned to him by a Canadian he had encountered: "The Canadian pretends also to have seen an unicorn; the single horn he says rises out of the forehead and curls back, according to his description so as to convey the idea of the fossil Cornu Ammonis."[72] Such hesitations were quite widespread at the time, and reflected the lack of knowledge about the interior of the North American continent (for example, Jefferson himself thought there were volcanoes at the center of the continent).[73] In spite of this, Dunbar's diary was that of a scientist and not of a conqueror; or rather, it was both. Dunbar indeed sometimes uttered remarks that betrayed the fact that the purpose of his journey was to reconnoiter territory that was destined to be settled soon thereafter. Often he assessed the quality of the land, in order to determine whether it was farmable or not. One day, in a lyrical outburst, he even evoked the future settlement and welfare of a colonist established on prosperous banks: "In a year or two he arrives at a state of independence, he purchases horses, cows and other domestic animals, perhaps a slave also who shares with him the labours and the productions of his fields and the adjoining forests. How happy the contrast, when we compare the fortune of the new settler in the U.S. with the misery of the half starving, oppressed and degraded Peasant of Europe!!"[74] In such a visionary moment is revealed the whole ambivalence of the notion of progress as Americans perceived it at this time. A demanding and passionate scientist, Dunbar was also an expansionist who was convinced that this expansion meant real progress for humankind. He did not, however, care about Native Americans, whose lands would be taken away, nor about the black slave, whose fate would not be improved along with his master's fortune. Although cheap land in the United States spared the farmer the fate of the European peasant, and thus the United States was the favored environment for the happiness of mankind, such happiness appeared to be less universal in scope than the advocates of American expansion would have liked.

Only on April 16, 1806, did the expedition for the Red River leave Fort Adams, near Natchez; it started as a failure, however.[75] The Spanish had never been fooled by the dual goal of these American voyages, and they had indeed started to react to this wave of expeditions, which they considered to be threats. On March 12, 1805, Secretary of State Madison received an official brief of protest against the expedition, sent by the Spanish; meanwhile, between 1804 and 1806 Spain ordered four expeditions out of Santa Fe, with the charge of intercepting the Lewis and Clark team. These expeditions failed, but they were indicative of Spanish determination. Since 1805 the Spanish had been justifiably worried by the dubious activities of former vice president Aaron Burr in the lower Mississippi valley, as well as the support he enjoyed locally and the silence the administration kept about this; indeed, they regarded this conspirator as the vanguard of a conquest movement that was aimed at Mexico and supported by Jefferson.[76] Since they knew the goal as well as the route of the Red River expedition, the Spanish were able to interrupt its progress at a distance of 635 miles from the mouth of the river, and they forced the expedition back on July 29.[77]

Yet on July 15, 1806, another expedition was under way, sponsored by General Wilkinson, governor of the Louisiana Territory; it left St. Louis to explore the heads of the Red and Arkansas Rivers. Its leader was Zebulon Montgomery Pike, a lieutenant in the U.S. Army and an experienced explorer. Having decided to approach the Rocky Mountains, Pike and his team got lost and ended up on the banks of the Rio Grande, an unchallenged possession of Spain. His party was arrested in February 1807 by a Spanish patrol, and Pike regained American territory in June. Whether Pike got lost on purpose is a matter of discussion among historians.[78] At any rate, the most important expedition, and the one that Jefferson had planned, designed, and launched, that is, the Lewis and Clark expedition, came back to the United States without difficulty, loaded with Indian objects and valuable scientific observations. The triumphal welcome it received was in keeping with the feats it had achieved.

A Continental Vision of the Nation

Originally a state secret, the Lewis and Clark expedition had metamorphosed into a national epic. The whole scientific community, at home and abroad, had taken a passionate interest in the voyage; some scientists were sorry not to have been part of it, such as naturalist Constantin Samuel Rafinesque; others, such as Volney, compared the success of the expedition to the greatest events in history.[79] The press kept the public interested by printing accounts of the publications of other expeditions, such as that of William Dunbar in 1804 or the New World voyages of naturalist Alexander von Humboldt.[80] Lengthy articles reported on the return of explorers in glowing terms, bringing to today's mind the enthusiasm that surrounded the first transatlantic flights, as, for example, in the case of Dunbar's and Dr. Hunter's return to New Orleans after their trip on the Washita River.[81] Behind this passion for scientific discovery one clearly senses national pride and patriotism, rooted in love for the land. The various stages of the Lewis and Clark expedition also fed the public's curiosity. One of these episodes was the arrival in Washington, D.C., of an Osage delegation, which Lewis and Clark had sent there upon taking possession of Upper Louisiana, while they were wintering in Wood River, near St. Louis, and before they got ready to go up the Missouri.[82] These Native Americans visited Jefferson during the summer of 1804; they were depicted as exceptional beings—exceptional because they were American: "They are of a gigantic stature, being all [the men] above six feet in height, and well proportioned."[83]

A newspaper correspondent noted that they were also more intelligent than any other people, before concluding: "Buffon can produce no fat Englishman or meagre Frenchman superior to these people."[84] The American native was superior to the European. In discovering the continent, its wonders, its secrets, and its riches, Americans also appropriated it and grew attached to it. Through the conquest of the continent, they built a national identity, based on their opposition to Europe. That, however, would have been a merely negative construction if Americans had not added enormous pride and love for their country, the wild expanses of which continually amazed them.[85] Thus, the expeditions helped Americans appropriate the continent on an emotional level; they allowed the United States to assert sovereignty over the territories it had just acquired (the Osages now came to Washington, D.C., to meet their new "father," who would exact complete allegiance from them); the expeditions also amounted to appropriating territory that had not yet been officially acquired, such as the Northwest and soon perhaps the Southwest. In the words of one *Enquirer* editorialist: "We live on a continent where we may be said to constitute the only nation."[86] Failing to mention the numerous Native American nations who lived in the West, this editorialist suggested that the trip of a handful of Americans had been enough to establish the sovereignty of the new nation over territory that was occupied by others, although not by European nations. Hardly had the continent been explored by Lewis and Clark when it was already becoming the property of the American nation.

The interest of Americans for the continent was, then, nurtured by the publication of exploration accounts, and the fact that they were of national importance was underscored by the president's active support. In February 1806 Jefferson published a "Message from the President" that included a letter written by Lewis before leaving the Mandan village, as well as geographical accounts by Dunbar.[87] The president also oversaw the publication of the travel notes taken by Zebulon Pike in 1805 during an expedition on the Mississippi.[88] The welcome Jefferson gave Lewis and Clark was a measure of his satisfaction. Before he even saw them again, Jefferson praised them in his sixth annual address to Congress, on December 2, 1806.[89] Meriwether Lewis was made governor of Louisiana, and William Clark the superintendent of Indian affairs in the same area. Thus it was that both remained in the region that had made them famous.

The two explorers took hold of the popular imagination. For the people of Fincastle, Lewis and Clark attained superhuman stature and the aura of mythical heroes: "You have navigated bold and unknown rivers, traversed mountains, which had never been impressed with the footsteps of civilized man, and surmounted every obstacle which climate, Nature, or ferocious Savages could throw in your way. You have the further satisfaction to reflect that you have extended the knowledge of the geography of your country; in other respects enriched Science; and opened to the United States a source of inexhaustible wealth."[90] A popular myth called for a popular literature. The notebooks of the two explorers, compiled by Nicholas Biddle, appeared in 1814 in a form that emphasized the exploration process rather than its scientific content.[91] Culturally and emotionally, the Northwest now belonged to Americans. By crossing the continent Lewis and Clark had improved the geographical knowledge of "their country," as the people of Fincastle said. Jefferson also commended "the additions he [Lewis] brings to our knowledge of the geography and natural history of our country." The language of the statesman echoed that of the citizens; both said that the American nation and the North American continent were already one.[92]

Barbé-Marbois described this process in the following terms: "Conquerors expand their states through war: their reigns are marked by the blood of men and the desolation of the countries they subjugate. What they leave behind is nothing but the memory of disaster. The republic of the United States enlarges its borders by sending surveyors and men of science distances of 1,500 leagues. It sets unimpeded the limits of its peaceful conquests and ensures through good laws the durable happiness of the communities who settle in them."[93] This idyllic picture, however, needs qualification. As far as the Northwest was concerned, the "peaceful conquests" of the United States were nonetheless conquests, not mere reconnaissance of "unoccupied" or previously acquired territory. As for the territories that were declared to be American—legally or illegally—the happiness that was available for those communities already settled in these areas, such as the many Native American tribes or the French-speaking community of Louisiana, was a function of their ability to adjust to a strictly defined *pax americana:* were they to rebel, the threshold of tolerance would soon be reached. Nevertheless, it cannot be denied that the Lewis and Clark expedition, while being an expansionist undertaking, had an international scientific dimension. Was it botany or diplomacy? Americans did not choose one or the other; as children of the Enlightenment, they made their own cocktail.

Expansion's Rejects

The Expansionist Passion: Negotiating Over West Florida

The Louisiana Purchase whetted the American appetite for land and strengthened their national feeling. For their unfortunate partners—Native Americans, Spaniards, and the French of Louisiana—American methods smacked more of greed and intolerance than pacifism and benevolence. No sooner had the treaty been signed, whereby the French sold Louisiana to the United States, that American leaders set out to investigate the exact boundaries of the territory they had just acquired. Indeed, the wording of the treaty signed with France, which quoted that of the Treaty of San Ildefonso of 1800, was quite hazy about the exact position of the eastern and western borders of Louisiana: "His Catholic Majesty promises and engages on his part, to cede to the French Republic . . . the colony or province of Louisiana, with the same extent that it now has in the hands of Spain, and that it had when France possessed it, and such as it should be after the treaties subsequently entered into between Spain and other States."[94] Louisiana, as it had been when a French possession until 1763, did encompass the whole Ohio valley and extended eastward to the Perdido River. Then, however, upon the negotiations that ended the Seven Years' War, France had ceded to Spain only the west bank of the Mississippi plus New Orleans; the Floridas fell to Great Britain (West Florida, which spread from the Apalachicola River to the Mississippi, and East Florida, which corresponded roughly to Florida as we know it today).[95] Since East Florida had never belonged to France, the United States could not claim it openly in 1803. West Florida, on the other hand, was more uncertain, since it had been part of French Louisiana until 1763. Was it, or was it not, included in those possessions that were returned to France by Spain, and then turned over to the United States?

Had the obscurity in the wording of the treaty been deliberate on the part of the First Consul, as Barbé-Marbois claimed?[96] Or, on the contrary, was it obvious that West Florida was part of the 1800 retrocession and, consequently, of the 1803 treaty, as Livingston claimed shortly after the treaty was signed?[97] Historians remain divided on this issue: admirers of Jefferson and Madison, such as Irving Brant, have felt that Livingston was right,[98] while more critical observers of the American president, such as Henry Adams, have considered that this line of reasoning was simply an additional weapon in a war of conquest.[99] What is important for the present study is not to arbitrate between Spain and the United States on this count, but to observe the passion with which the president and the secretary of state, both southerners and slave owners, strained to wring out of Spain "very satisfactory" borders for the Louisiana territory.[100]

During the summer of 1803 Jefferson wrote a long historical account, entitled "An Examination into the Boundaries of Louisiana," which allowed him to conclude that West Florida belonged indeed to the United States.[101] Since Madison and Jefferson had not given up on acquiring the whole of Florida, they proposed sending to Madrid a special mission led by James Monroe, for the purpose of purchasing East Florida, while at the same time obtaining a recognition of American sovereignty over West Florida.[102] Confident that the Spanish Empire was about to collapse, the American leaders thought a diplomatic mission should suffice. If they did not obtain what they wanted through diplomacy, they would take it anyway. As Madison said, "We are the less disposed also to make sacrifices to obtain the Floridas, because their posi-

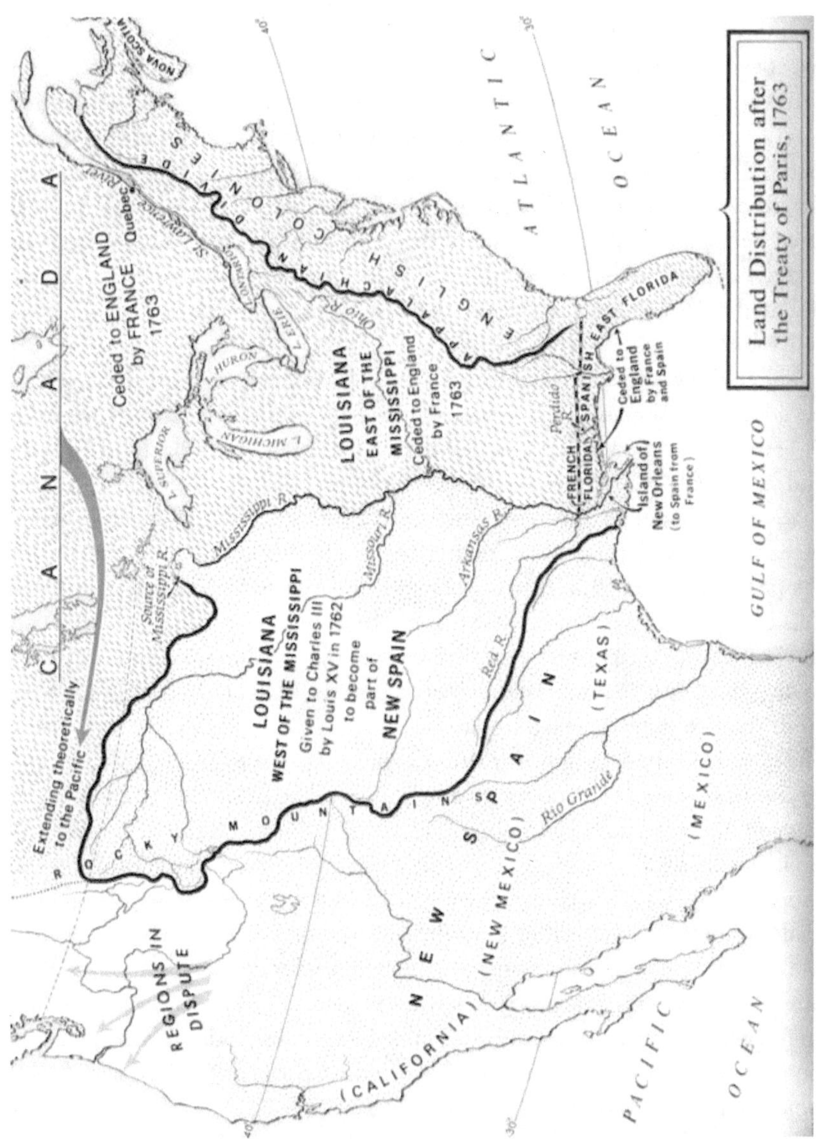

Louisiana and the Treaty of Paris in 1783 (Marshall Sprague, *So Beautiful a Land: Louisiana and the Purchase,* p. 182)

tion and the manifest course of events guarantee an early and reasonable acquisition of them."[103]

As it turned out, this American contribution to the carving up of the Spanish Empire was not as trouble-free as it seemed. Spain had never given its consent to France for the sale of Louisiana to a third country; it vented its anger through its minister in Washington when Congress started to legislate over West Florida in November 1803.[104] Indeed, Congress resorted to a legal and fiscal pretense (protecting the United States from smuggling) to pass a bill that included the area around Mobile into the Mississippi district (this was called the "Mobile Act").[105] This amounted to annexing the area, and it could not fail to rouse Spain, or for that matter France, which did not want to be accused by Spain of endorsing these encroachments. When power was transferred between France and the United States, on December 20, 1803, in New Orleans, Prefect Laussat declared to Wilkinson and Claiborne that Louisiana did not extend all the way to Mobile.[106]

Jefferson was forced to temper his enthusiasm, and he tried to correct the negative impression the Mobile Act had made. In his annual address of November 8, 1804, he declared that the goal of the act had been misunderstood by Spain, and he added: "Candid explanations were immediately given and assurances that, reserving our claims in that quarter as a subject of discussion and arrangement with Spain, no act was meditated, in the meantime, inconsistent with the peace and friendship existing between the two nations."[107] As for the borders of Louisiana west of the Mississippi, the United States also tried to extend the boundaries of its purchase as far as possible. If Monroe could find a way to negotiate with Spain, his orders were to assert the claims of the United States all the way to the Rio Bravo (today the Rio Grande)—in other words, over all of Texas.[108] As the U.S. government was pressing him to go to Spain, Monroe ignored Talleyrand's uncooperative attitude, and he finally left to carry out his mission in December 1804, shortly before the French minister of external relations openly disavowed American attempts at obtaining West Florida.[109] Thus supported by France, Spain was now able to counter American wishes and forestall any negotiation, and as a result, Monroe had to leave Madrid again in May 1805. The responsibility for the failure of these negotiations did not, therefore, lie solely with France, as has been claimed.[110] They failed also because Spain, when given a chance, did everything in its power to slow American expansion, the inevitable advance of which it sensed through the Lewis and Clark expedition and the activities of Aaron Burr.

As in 1803, Jefferson first considered an alliance with Great Britain in order to be able to occupy the Floridas and the area corresponding to the state of Texas today. Once again, however, he preferred to resort to diplomacy—this time in France, where Talleyrand now intimated that he would support the United States.[111] In a confidential message to Congress dated December 6, 1805, Jefferson played two hands: while announcing that France was willing to help the United States, he did not rule out the option of obtaining the territories by force.[112] Jefferson had in fact already made up his mind: in order to overcome Spanish opposition, he wanted to buy Florida through the mediation of France. When, however, the American president was finally able to give the minister plenipotentiary Armstrong authorization to negotiate the purchase, it turned out that Napoleon no longer needed money.[113] This little flurry of diplomatic activity continued until 1809, with France alternately offering and refusing to help.

Although the details of this maneuvering may seem of little interest, they must not be neglected. Because of the determination of American leaders to obtain Florida—and even, possibly, Texas—the foreign policy efforts of the United States were concentrated on very specific geopolitical goals, which led the new nation away from the generous ideals it wanted its mission in the world to be associated with. In order to secure Florida, Jefferson's government was willing to help Napoleon trample Spain. Through the contempt he showed this oppressed nation and its representatives, Jefferson imitated French behavior toward Spain. He wrote James Bowdoin, the minister plenipotentiary in Spain: "We expect therefore from the friendship of the Emperor that he will either compel Spain to do us justice, or abandon her to us. We ask one month to be in possession of the city of Mexico." In moments of impatience, Jefferson betrayed even more ambitious objectives, similar to those of Aaron Burr, whose activities he had just condemned: "Our southern defensive force can take the Floridas, volunteers for a Mexican army will flock to our standard, and rich [rewards] . . . will be offered to our privateers in the plunder of their commerce and coasts. Probably Cuba will add itself to our confederation."[114]

Nevertheless, in order to obtain Florida, Jefferson needed to avoid offending the old colonial nation of Spain too much. In December 1805 Jefferson and Madison met with Francisco de Miranda, the Venezuelan revolutionary who had proved himself in the armies of the French Revolution. It is known that on this occasion Miranda confided his plans for an expedition to the secretary of state. Yet in February 1806, when the general left New York for Caracas, the American administration failed to show solidarity with the South American revolutionary, and actually took action against those who had made his departure possible.[115] To spread "the blessings of freedom and equal laws" was an objective the United States wanted to implement first and foremost on territories that belonged to them. Insofar as the only links that the United States had with Spanish America were of a commercial nature, the 1807 embargo was to further accentuate the redirection of American efforts to the interior of the continent. Only in 1810, at the beginning of Madison's administration, did the United States become seriously interested in Latin America and support revolutionary movements there; even then, the amount of help the North Americans extended to South Americans should not be overestimated.[116]

At any rate, in September 1810 the war with France put Spain in a critical situation, and this created an opportunity for a group of Americans residing in West Florida to put into practice the kind of popular expansionism that Jefferson had so often predicted. Having formed a convention, they proclaimed the independence of the state of West Florida on September 26, and asked to join the American republic. On October 27, 1810, the new president, James Madison, who had in fact had a hand in these proceedings, extended U.S. authority over that area, alleging that West Florida belonged to the United States by virtue of the Louisiana Purchase, and provisionally integrating it into the Orleans Territory. In December of that year, the territory was occupied in part by American troops.[117] The following year, Madison had Congress authorize him to take possession of East Florida if a foreign power tried to appropriate it.[118] Lastly, in March 1812, on the eve of the war with England, a group of "patriots" occupied the island of Amelia in East Florida, although they were unable to take the capital, St. Augustine. It was perfectly clear, however, that Florida was bound to be occupied by American troops some time soon—to be determined by the international situation and the boldness of the frontier citizens.

Indian Policy

Besides the Spanish, another group fell victim to the great movement of expansion: Native Americans. Yet of all the presidents of the eighteenth and nineteenth centuries, it was probably Jefferson who was the most sincerely interested in Native American cultures. He asked not only Lewis and Clark, but other explorers as well, to record Indian vocabulary and to observe Indian customs. This was already archaeological work of sorts, for the president did not doubt that Native American civilization was doomed by the inexorable and beneficial advance of American civilization. Far from being acknowledged and accepted, the Native American cultural identity was bound to disappear: Native Americans had to adopt the way of life of the white settlers, that is, if they wanted to join in the general march of progress. As Jefferson blandly put it to the Seneca chief Handsome Lake: "a little land, well-stocked . . . will yield more than a great deal without stock or improvement."[119] Once they became true farmers, Native Americans would in addition be able to sell their surplus of land and consequently buy more farming tools. All's well that ends well—since through the same deal the pioneers would be satisfied by the sale of former Native American hunting grounds. Like Henry Knox, Jefferson thought expansion should be peaceful and did not envision the possibility that Native Americans might refuse to go along with that scheme. His good intentions, however, were tainted with what historian Reginald Horsman calls "ambivalence."[120] Was it out of a desire to see their situation improve that Jefferson wanted Native Americans to become farmers, or was it merely a way to obtain more land from them? The following letter by Jefferson, dated February 16, 1803, would seem to favor the second analysis: "Among the Indians two objects are principally kept in view[:] 1. the preservation of peace 2. the obtaining lands. Towards the latter object we consider the taking the Indians to agriculture as the principal means from which we can expect such effect in future. When they shall cultivate small plots of earth . . . they will sell from time to time to help out their personal labour in stocking their farms. . . ."[121] And yet his interlocutor, Handsome Lake, had come for the very purpose of asking him that Native Americans not be forced into selling their lands unless they wanted to. The tribes from the old Northwest, that is, east of the Mississippi, were generally dissatisfied with the land sales Governor William Henry Harrison pushed them into.[122] The chiefs of the Six Nations of New York State requested that their remaining lands be made nontransferable, a request that Jefferson politely, but firmly, refused.[123]

Native Americans, however, decided that they would not disappear without putting up a fight. Their resistance took the form of a great political and religious movement aimed at pan-Indian unity. Among the Senecas, the prophet Handsome Lake had become disgusted at the shameful state that alcohol reduced his compatriots to; he preached temperance and the return to past customs, which was essentially a means of countering the influence of land buyers who often relied on alcohol to persuade the Native Americans to sell.[124] With the northwestern tribes, it was Tenskwatawa, the Shawnee prophet, who spread the good word and tried to accomplish a regeneration of Native American culture. His brother Tecumseh gave this religious movement a political dimension by attempting to unite all the tribes east of the Mississippi, from the Northwest to the Southwest, in this effort to restore the old culture.[125] The actions of the two brothers started to bear fruit in 1805, and one can sense Jefferson's irritation at this in his second inaugural address. As a man of progress and the Enlightenment, he resented the success of these "prophets" with theories he viewed as reactionary. In Jefferson's view, the Native Americans were driven out by the inexorable stream of American expansion, and since hunting was no longer open to them, they had been provided with all the necessary implements for agriculture. These measures were dictated by the "humanity" and generosity of the American leaders. And yet, as Jefferson deplored, some conservative Indians let themselves be misled by their priests. In terms that recall his attacks upon the Federalists at the outset of the French Revolution, Jefferson denounced the obscurantist spirit that influenced the Native Americans, and concluded with these words: "in short, my friends, among them is seen the action and counteraction of good sense and bigotry; they, too, have their anti-philosophers, who find an interest in keeping things in their present state. . . ."[126] In sum, whoever would not follow the road to progress as Jefferson saw it was automatically considered a victim of fanaticism and reactionary views. By no means could the American president admit the possibility that Native Americans might follow a road to development other than the one he had sketched out: "civilization" through education, agriculture, and Christianization.

The French-Speaking Population of Louisiana

The cultural difference of the Louisiana French-speaking population who had just been integrated into the Union was not recognized any more than that of Native Americans. Since the birth of the United States, the American citizen had implicitly been defined by his conformity to certain criteria, namely, that he be white, a Protestant, and an English speaker.[127] In *The Federalist* no. 2, John Jay defined the American people as "a people descended from the same ancestors, speaking the same language, professing the same religion, attached to the same principles of government, very similar in their manners and customs."[128] The French-speaking population of Louisiana, needless to say, did not exactly fit that description. Like Native Americans, the Creoles were characterized in American eyes by their "ignorance." On September 29, 1803, William Charles Cole Claiborne, the governor of the Mississippi Territory, wrote to Jefferson that "until a knowledge of the American Constitutions, laws, language and customs, is more generally diffused, a state government in Louisiana would not be managed with discretion." For the planter William Dunbar, the ignorance and prejudices of the Louisiana people were an important fact to be conveyed to the administration.[129] In January 1804 Claiborne, who by now was governor of New Orleans, once again stressed the expensive tastes and lack of education of the Louisianans, and their ensuing inability to take part in the civic life of a republic that was founded on virtue.[130] It is difficult to see what Claiborne could have based such a harsh judgement on when he did not speak French and could therefore not evaluate his new constituents very well. At any rate, since he thought the Louisianans were strongly attached to France, he decided to Americanize them as quickly as possible.[131]

Article III of the Franco-American treaty of 1803 stipulated that the inhabitants of Louisiana be "incorporated in the Union of the United States, and admitted as soon as possible, according to the principles of the Federal constitution, to the enjoyment of all the rights, advantages and immunities of citizens of the United States."[132] Jefferson thought, however, that a transitional period was in order. Already on July 11, 1803, he told Horatio Gates that in his view, the newly acquired territory would not have a separate administration, and the New Orleans area would instead be annexed to the Mississippi Territory. Furthermore, Jefferson went on, American laws should be introduced among its population, and for this to occur a sufficient number of Americans must be incorporated into it so that they could take control of the legislature and government.[133]

The point was that such responsibilities could not be entrusted to the "Creoles" of Louisiana: their superior numbers had to be neutralized by a massive influx of American immigrants. Then, the more recent arrivals could in a perfectly legal way take control of an American-style government. Congress indeed went along with Jefferson's ideas: while passing the territorial act of March 26, 1804, it denied Louisianans the right to elect their representatives to the legislature. The Louisianans, who so far had basically accepted American domination without protest, balked at this treatment, which so clearly made them second-class citizens. Jean-Etienne Boré, mayor of New Orleans, had already written Jefferson to ask that French be kept as the official language;[134] in the spring of 1804 Louisianans organized meetings, drafted statements that they themselves took to Congress, and resigned from official positions they held. Their reaction caused a bit of a stir, and in 1805 the provisions of the first territorial act were softened, so as to allow Louisianans to elect one delegate per district to a general assembly.[135]

The Louisiana Purchase doubled the area of the United States and thus considerably reinforced feelings of national unity and identity. Indeed, the western expeditions lay the foundations of a national myth—that of the conquest of the West—which was rooted in a love for the virgin land and a great pride in discovery. American expansion became the basic ingredient of the national feeling, in which everyone consciously partook in the greatness of the nation and forged a patriotic bond based on a love for the American land. Yet with all its emphasis on progress, expansion was not free of ambiguities. Its very success encouraged attitudes of intolerance toward those who were left out or those who did not agree with it. The strength of the United States scorned the weakness of Spain, and while an interest in Native American cultures continued to exist thanks to Jefferson and other enlightened minds, the military power of the tribes was no longer an object of fear, and it now went without saying that they would have to cede their lands whenever asked to do so. On that score, the threatening tone of John Quincy Adams was quite revealing: "But what's the right of a huntsman to the forest of a thousand miles over which he has deliberately ranged in quest of prey? Shall the liberal bounties of Providence to the race of man be monopolized by one of ten thousand for whom they were created?"[136] For Jefferson, American expansion could not be turned down by those it encompassed, since it was a popular, democratic kind of expansion that brought political liberty along with the progress of civilization. Yet at the same time Jefferson felt that American civilization was a superior one: it had to be deserved and its purity preserved. Louisianans learned this unpleasant lesson when their customs and language were openly criticized, and when they were deemed unfit for democracy. The paternalistic advice that Jefferson extended to Native American chiefs was a far cry from the cautious negotiations that George Washington had conducted with them a decade earlier. In the span of ten years or so, the American nation had grown stronger and more confident: this was no longer a time for fearing Indian attacks, but for visions of a grand continental future.

CHAPTER 8

From Tripoli Harbor to the 1812 Declaration of War: Identity and Recognition

Once he was elected president, Thomas Jefferson could finally put into practice the ideas he had defended in 1790 concerning the North African regencies. He found the prevailing tribute system humiliating, and he decided to discontinue it, ordering the American navy, which had proven itself against the French during the quasi war, to use force to settle relations with the North African countries. As it turned out, the American navy effectively protected the new nation's trade in 1801 and 1802.[1] But at the end of 1803 the famous *Philadelphia* episode occurred: this ship, which was one of the most handsome frigates of the American fleet, ran aground in the Tripoli harbor; its crew was captured, and a few days later, the *Philadelphia* was refloated by the Tripolitans, who proudly took possession of the ship. It was then that one of the heroic deeds in the history of the American navy took place: a group of Americans, led by Lieutenant Stephen Decatur, managed to recapture the frigate in the very harbor of Tripoli, right under the guards' nose; as they could not bring it back, they burned it, without losing a single man. After a four-year blockade and an attempted coup plotted by the former American consul in Tunis, William Eaton, the pasha of Tripoli finally gave in: in 1805, the United States obtained a treaty in which there was no mention of tribute.[2] Thus, the United States paved the way for "gunboat diplomacy" in relations with these small countries, a policy that France was to imitate successfully from 1830 on.[3]

American newspapers printed in detail the news of the loss of the *Philadelphia* and the account of Decatur's bold raid.[4] When word got out about the loss of the frigate, the Republican *Aurora,* which supported the government, appealed to the national feeling of Americans: "The loss of this vessel is unquestionably a real calamity, and we are fully confident there is not a man in the union . . . who does not sensibly feel for the situation of his fellow-citizens [the imprisoned sailors]." When Decatur's action became known, the newspaper insisted on its significance: "The importance of this bold and intrepid enterprise to the commerce of America must be acknowledged very great; but what affords the highest satisfaction is, that we have lost in this action, not a single officer or private."[5] According to the *Aurora,* this show of American bravery turned Tripoli into "a scene of terror and confusion" and demonstrated the superiority of the new nation over the Barbary Coast regencies; the newspaper added that it filled other countries' navies with admiration.[6] Admiral Nelson praised Decatur's raid as "the most bold and daring act of the age." The burning of the *Philadelphia* was celebrated in engravings, which helped create a naval tradition in the American imagination.[7] The various components of a mature nationalism now fell into place; this was truly a "secondary national feeling,"[8] which was soon to help America acquire full status as a nation on the international scene, through the use of military force if necessary. In 1807, when the confrontation with England took a dramatic turn, Americans would call up the spirit of Decatur and his superior, Preble: "The Navy—May our Commodores be Prebles—and our Captains Decaturs."[9]

In 1804, however, Decatur's feat flattered American pride, but it did not cause loud displays of patriotism. When the *Philadelphia* was captured, there were no crowds marching down the streets; when Decatur's raid was announced, the newspapers did not fill up with emotional addresses from citizens; and in the spring of 1804 Stephen Decatur was not acclaimed as a national hero. The greatness of the nation, its identity, and its status among the nations of the world did not depend on that faraway episode. In 1804 American citizens identified more with the conquest of the continent than with military deeds, however brilliant, that were accomplished in theaters of operation traditionally reserved for European powers.

After the war with Tripoli was over, Jefferson considerably reduced the force of the American navy, replacing the frigates that were capable of carrying war far and wide with strictly defensive gunboats—mere "toys"[10] about fifty feet long and armed with only one cannon. American neutrality and pacifism with regard to Europe were supposed to allow the United States to develop within its own sphere. Jefferson's decisions echoed the isolationist principles he had articulated in his 1801 inaugural address; they also reflected the president's mistrust of professional armies, which went back to the revolutionary years, and his preference for militias and such popular armies. That suspicion was typical of most men of his generation, and was apparent in the Constitution, especially in Article I, Section 8, which made Congress responsible for revising the sums appropriated for the army every other year, as well as in the Second and Third Amendments, which gave special rights to the soldier-citizen and institutionalized the distrust of a professional army. Jefferson's own feelings in the matter, however, were reinforced by Napoleon's accession to power in France: the prospect of the republic being overthrown by a military dictator was exactly what he wanted to avoid in America.[11]

Still, continental expansion and economic prosperity were not yet sufficient to give shape to American identity. Before setting out for the riches of the West, the American nation needed to have its new identity recognized by the former parent country. While the American public had been relatively unmoved by the performance of its navy in Tripoli harbor in 1803, it was a different story in 1807 after another frigate, the *Chesapeake*, fell prey to an attack by a British warship, the *Leopard*. Although it was shocking between two countries at peace—several American sailors were killed—the attack was not without some justification. Indeed, the commander of the British ship was trying to recover some deserters who had boarded the *Chesapeake* during a stopover in the United States. Enjoined to return the men, who claimed to be American citizens, the *Chesapeake*'s commander chose an armed confrontation over a humiliating submission. It was perfectly logical, then, that American public opinion would go wild over the event. In seeking to capture American citizens, the British navy displayed contempt for American citizenship. Wasn't England attempting to blacken something that, since 1798 and even more so since 1803, had become a symbol of American power abroad? In this case, the issue was not minor: even though the new nation was rich and ambitious, and even though it had already wrought out the main features of its identity, it could not reach maturity without obtaining recognition from the great power from which it had wrested its independence.

"War in Disguise" and the Rise of American Nationalism

In the course of the summer of 1805, the British navy seized a number of American merchant ships. An action of that dimension had not been seen since the 1793 Orders in Council, when the British had intended to break up U.S. commerce with France and its colonies on the basis of the Rule of 1756. At the time, in January 1794, more flexible orders had been forwarded to British navy officers, instructing them to seize only ships that carried goods originating in the French Caribbean and going directly from there to Europe.[12] During the discussion of Jay's Treaty, the U.S. Senate had refused to ratify Article XII, which would have limited American commerce to the British West Indies. After the treaty was ratified, the 1794 ordinance was put back in effect in 1798.[13]

It was this ordinance that allowed the United States to take over and turn to their profit the trade of the European nations, by substituting for the national freighters. U.S. ships could not make a straight run to Europe from the French or Spanish colonies, but they could stop over in the United States, unload, reload, and start again, which did not bother them or take them out of their way very much. In fact, when stopping over at an American port instead of unloading their cargo, the captains of U.S. ships soon adopted the simpler procedure of destroying their former documents, getting new ones, and paying minimal fees. This practice of the "broken voyage" was also made legal in 1800 by the decision of a British judge, Sir William Scott.[14] Although it was temporarily stopped by the Peace of Amiens, the reexport trade continued to develop unfettered from 1800 to 1805, growing from forty million to sixty million dollars.[15]

In 1805, however, the British navy suddenly went back to seizing American ships that were engaged in the reexport trade, marking the end of this period of "indulgence," as James Stephen—one of its fiercest critics—called it.[16] On May 22, 1805, Judge Grant ruled in the case of the *Essex* that he could not find the slightest evidence of the merchandise being actually imported into the United States. Insofar as the fees paid upon unloading in the United States had been refunded (a practice that had become frequent), and as both ship and cargo had remained the same, the judge found that the voyage had not actually been broken, and therefore the procedure was a fraud, consisting of fake importation into the United States and real, direct importation from one colony to its parent country, the latter being an enemy of England. As a result, it was now up to ship captains to prove that their voyage had effectively been broken, and from this point on the reexport trade was to be a risky business.

This action, which shook the foundations of U.S. economic growth in the postrevolutionary period, had been preceded in the early 1800s by a gradual cooling of Anglo-American relations. In 1803, upon assuming his position in Washington, D.C., the new British ambassador, Anthony Merry, had been unable to adapt to the informal atmosphere of American political life. What was even worse, he had made contact with opponents of the Republican government, such as Aaron Burr and pro-secession Federalists, and this certainly did not ingratiate him with the president and his secretary of state.[17]

In March 1804 James Monroe, who had taken Rufus King's place in London in 1803, had started to complain about the unfriendly attitude of the British officials he was dealing with, and more generally of British political circles; this attitude he assigned to "ancient feelings excited at present by light causes."[18] These "light causes" were none other than the quarrels over etiquette that Anthony Merry had picked against Jefferson in Washington; but the "ancient feelings" referred to the alleged bitterness of the former colonizing power toward the United States. Monroe thought it was also possible that the British had taken offense at the Louisiana Purchase and the restoration of Franco-American relations. The fundamental reason for British hostility, he believed, was jealousy: "Many circumstances have tended to convince me that they entertain very false impressions with respect to our growth and that they view the rapid advancement we have made and are making with no very favorable eye.

They seem to consider our prosperity not simply as a reproach to them, but as impairing or detracting from theirs."[19] Monroe seemed also to think that the British sought to humiliate the United States and to treat them as a second-class power: "In respect to the ministers of other powers we appear to hold the lowest grade; in a diplomatick dinner at Lord Hawkesbury's precedence was given, and apparently by design, to all the other ministers, and on more occasions than one to the minister of Portugal, evidently by design."[20]

In Monroe's view, the former mother country was now trying to smother the nation it had given birth to. The issue of American sovereignty, and Great Britain's respect of it, had come to the fore of U.S. current affairs in course of the summer of 1804. Captain Bradley, aboard the British warship *Cambrian,* had inspected a number of American commercial ships in American waters to see if there were any of His Majesty's subjects among the sailors. Bradley had made several American sailors come on board his ship in order to enlist them for the British Crown.[21] As Jefferson had observed at the time, that kind of action threatened U.S. independence and sovereignty: "We cannot be respected by France as a neutral nation, nor by the world ourselves as an independent one, if we do not take effectual measures to support, at every risk, our authority in our own harbors."[22] But since at that time Jefferson was almost exclusively preoccupied with obtaining the Floridas, he paid little attention to the deterioration of relations between the United States and Great Britain. He chose instead to take an optimistic view of the situation—rather unjustifiably so—as when he heard about Pitt's new cabinet in Great Britain: "The new administration in England is entirely cordial. There has never been a time when our flag was so little molested by them in the European seas, or irregularities there so readily and respectfully corrected. As the officers here [of the *Cambrian*] began their insults before the change [of cabinets], it is a proof it did not proceed from that change."[23] Even in his annual message of November 1804, Jefferson reaffirmed his trust in the British government: "[E]ven within our harbors and jurisdiction, infringements on the authority of the laws have been committed which have called for serious attention. The friendly conduct of the governments from whose officers and subjects these acts have proceeded, in other respects and in places more under their observation and control, gives us confidence that our representations on this subject will have been properly regarded."[24] At the same time, Monroe also showed renewed confidence in the British attitude regarding the American reexport trade.[25]

Going back now to Judge Grant's ruling of 1805, one can better understand American leaders' surprise over that decision and the wave of seizures of U.S. ships that it triggered. Americans felt that their confidence had been betrayed, as the British government had not informed them of the decision. In addition, they found that this struck at the foundations of more than ten years of prosperity: upon the news of the seizings, insurance rates for American ships quadrupled.[26] The American leaders had not wanted, or been able, to prevent this turnabout; they found it all the more disquieting, since it was accompanied by the publication of a polemical work, more than two hundred pages long, and significantly entitled—probably at the behest of the Pitt cabinet—*War in Disguise; or, The Frauds of the Neutral Flags.*[27] The author, James Stephen, called for the enforcement of the Rule of 1756, which had not been applied since 1794, and an end to the policy of indulgence toward neutral countries, whom he described as Napoleon's hidden accomplices. Stephen proposed to show: " . . . in the encroachments and frauds of the neutral flags, a nursery, a refuge of the confederated navies; as well as the secret conduits of a large part of those imperial resources, the pernicious application of which to the restitution of his marine, the Usurper has lately boasted. I propose to show in them his best hopes in a naval war; as well as channels of a revenue, which sustains the ambition of France, and prolongs the miseries of Europe."[28] The book was supposed to be aimed at all neutral powers, but this posture soon revealed its true colors, as Stephen could not refrain from admitting that his attacks were mainly targeted at one neutral power, the United States, for having exploited its neutrality the most: "A new power had now arisen on the western shore of the Atlantic, whose position, and maritime spirit, were calculated to give new and vast importance to every question of neutral rights; especially in the American seas. The merchants of the United States, were the first, and by far the most enterprising adventurers in the new field that was opened to neutrals in the Antilles, and the ports of the French islands were speedily crowded with their vessels."[29]

As is indicated by Monroe's dispatches of 1804, Americans were not willing to excuse a libel such as *War in Disguise* or the *Essex* ruling as resulting from Great Britain's military troubles in 1805; they opted instead to interpret these events as signs of the former parent country's jealousy. And indeed, in the years leading up to the War of 1812, there undoubtedly existed in Great Britain a form of resentment toward the former colonies.[30] Still, the modern-day reader senses real distress in *War in Disguise.* When hostilities broke out again in 1803, the war between the British and the French was now total war, and in relations with the United States, Great Britain could no longer afford the conciliatory attitude that it had espoused since 1794. The year 1805 especially was a turning point in military operations: Nelson destroyed the French fleet at Trafalgar, but in December Napoleon defeated the Russians and Austrians at Austerlitz. Thus, England ruled over the seas, and France over the continent.

Americans, however, were too focused on their own prosperity to take into account the new situation in Great Britain, which reflected increasing danger. Eager to have the former parent country recognize their new strength, they discerned only envy and resentment in the ideas of James Stephen and the British cabinet. For Monroe, British jealousy called for a firm American reaction: "I decided at once to push the business here in a manner to let the government see that we were not afraid of it."[31] In other words, it was time for the United States to show the former parent country that it was worthy of respect as a nation. U.S. honor was at stake, and also the future of the form of government which it had chosen after the Revolution, which it had identified itself with, and which now made up one of its most distinctive features in a world of monarchies and dictatorships. Continuing the debate Madison had opened in *The Federalist* no. 10, Monroe reckoned that a republic could and ought to show its resolution: "In all doubtful cases a bold and manly council ought to be preferred. It rallies the nation round us; keeps up its spirits; and proves at home and abroad that republicanism is not incompatible with decision."[32]

This new spirit of decision quickly manifested itself in Madison's *Examination of the British Doctrine . . .*, in which he countered Stephen's arguments.[33] Meanwhile, in London Monroe had to face a series of laws and decrees aimed at putting the Caribbean trade under the control of the British navy. He asked that the *Essex* ruling of May 22 be repealed, since as he told the Secretary of Foreign Affairs Lord Mulgrave, he regarded that decision as a hostile act. Having failed in that request, he commented: "Nothing is more true than that no accommodation will ever be granted us . . . which they can avoid."[34] His pessimism mounted when he found out that Captain Bradley, who had perpetrated the violation of American sovereignty in 1804, had been promoted, not punished as Jefferson assumed:

> It appeared also by your letters . . . that the President expected that this government would make such an example of the officers who had most signalized themselves, by their misconduct, as would serve as a warning to the commanders of the vessels, who may hereafter seek shelter or hospitality in our ports. This has not been done. On the contrary, I was informed . . . that Captain Bradley of the *Cambrian*, whose conduct had been most offensive, had been promoted immediately on his return to the command of a ship of the line. By that measure which prejudged the case the government seems to have adopted those acts of its officers as its own, and even to announce to all others that the commission of like aggressions within our jurisdiction would pave the way to their preferment.[35]

At the same time, however, Jefferson was considering an alliance with Great Britain, which would allow the United States to obtain the Floridas in return for taking part in the hostilities. On October 11, 1805, he wrote: "The only questions which press on the Executive for decision are whether we shall enter into a provisional alliance with England to come into force only in the event that *during the present war* we become engaged in war *with France*."[36] But in his annual message of December 3, 1805, the American president took exception to the new British stance on the reexport trade,[37] albeit only after harshly criticizing Spanish privateers, whom he deemed more dangerous. In sum, a defensive kind of American nationalism clearly emerged after 1804; it was directed at the former colonizing power, which was perceived as hostile and bent on humiliating the new nation by denying its strength and prosperity. Insofar as the people were not yet really mobilized, this feeling was primarily expressed by American leaders, although they had to tone it down because of other more pressing foreign policy affairs.

The Monroe-Pinkney Treaty and the Revival of the Idea of Economic Retaliation

As we saw with the *Cambrian* episode of 1804, the *Essex* ruling, with its consequences for the American reexport trade, was not the only matter that poisoned Anglo-American relations after 1805: another issue was the impressment of American sailors by the British navy. Since the onset of the revolutionary wars, Great Britain had lost a large part of its roster to American ships—the owners offered higher wages and better working conditions—and also to the U.S. Navy, which needed more personnel to keep up with expansion.[38] British sailors who landed in an American port when their ships put in would go and enroll on American ships. From the British wartime point of view, this constituted desertion and was not in any way compensated by American citizenship, which lenient naturalization laws made easy. In 1805, according to historian Bradford Perkins, more than half of the eleven thousand naturalized Americans who served in the American navy had been born in England.[39]

As a result, the British navy had started back in the 1790s to search American ships for British subjects who should have been in combat. Such actions always constituted serious violations of American sovereignty: whether the abducted sailors had been born in Great Britain or the United States, they were, in any case, American citizens, and the American government owed them protection on that count. For the new nation, accepting the impressment of sailors amounted to admitting that it had no means of protecting its citizens and that it was still a second-class nation, bending under the yoke of the former parent country. The impressment of American sailors had thus become a major bone of contention between the two countries. When in London between 1796 and 1801, as the American minister plenipotentiary, Rufus King had devoted part of his time to this problem;[40] similarly, James Monroe had not failed to raise the issue upon arriving in London.

In December 1803 Monroe transmitted a memorandum on this topic to the British government, which he expected to answer promptly.[41] In 1804 he broached the topic again, this time in connection with a planned treaty, since Jay's Treaty was no longer valid (Jay's Treaty had been set to expire two years after a peace agreement was signed between France and England).[42] While British leaders seemed to want to renew the treaty, they clearly did not want to hear about the impressment issue. After returning from Spain in the summer of 1805, Monroe had to deal first and foremost with the new British doctrine that Judge Grant's decision symbolized. In late 1805 new hope arose in the American diplomat's heart: British military ambitions on the European continent were crushed at Austerlitz, and Charles Fox, a pacifist and moderate politician who had supported the cause of American independence during the Revolution, replaced Pitt as head of the British government. As Monroe observed: "[T]he prospect of a fortunate termination of the business is now as favorable as it can possibly be; . . . the crisis is essentially past: the ministry has completely failed in all its operations on the continent. The allies have been defeated, the coalition broken and the ministry itself subjected to the same fate. A new ministry is forming, the chief character of which is understood to be favorably disposed to the United States. . . ."[43] Jefferson was of the same mind, except that he also counted on the new American spirit of determination: "With England I flatter myself our difficulties will be dissipated by the disasters of her allies, the change of her ministry, and the measures which Congress are likely to adopt to furnish motives for her becoming just to us."[44]

Congress did in fact react to British abuses by passing in the spring of 1806 a bill banning importation of British products. In view of the British cabinet's favorable dispositions, this act was not immediately enforced, but it was typical of the kind of retaliation measures the Republicans wanted to use. Eager to resist Great Britain but without going to war, they wanted to put into practice the kind of economic retaliation that Madison had set forth in 1789, 1790, and 1794. The *Aurora* had not called for war after Judge Grant's ruling in 1805; instead, it had given an optimistic presentation of all the other prospects for retaliation that the new nation had. In the October 16 issue, an "American gentleman" supposedly writing from England advocated "non-intercourse," that is, the absence of trade relations: "We can certainly fight England better without guns, than any other nation can with, and perhaps we shall never have so good an opportunity as the present. It is acknowledged here by all parties, that their manufactoreries would be ruined, should such a thing take place in America; and if the English did not give up their pretensions thus to restrict us, in three months, I would be willing to forfeit all I have, the fourth month. . . ."[45] In the same issue, an editorialist also pleaded in favor of economic retaliation and listed measures such as sequestration, non-importation, confiscation, and embargo as being more "rational" for the United States than traditional war: "Our mode of warfare, therefore, by calling in *sequestration, non-importation,* and in the dernier resort, confiscation as allies, is the most rational. . . . We cannot meet her in a line of battle at sea—for her fleets cover it; we must therefore make war where we can, sequester, first; and if that does not procure justice, embargo; if that fails, *confiscate*. . . ."[46]

Great Britain was mistress of the seas: it would therefore have been irrational to confront her on her own territory. Meanwhile, if the United States waged economic war, it could defeat Great Britain in a few months' time. Such optimism and confidence in a favorable outcome of the conflict had been absent from the congressional debates back in 1789–94, when Madison had propounded similar ideas. In 1804 Madison's ideas rallied many hopeful supporters, because the economic context of the new nation had evolved dramatically. The Republicans now felt they could rely on their country's unequalled expansion and prosperity, and they no longer shied away from implementing ideas that had seemed dangerous to Congress ten years earlier, at a time when America was chiefly seeking to establish its economic development. In addition, the isolation of Great Britain and the state of wartime Europe were winning arguments: the Americans knew they were the principal buyers of British textile products and the suppliers of most of Manchester's cotton.[47] As the "American gentleman" explained, Great Britain was vulnerable to an economic war waged by the United States.

On April 25, 1806, the *Leander,* an British frigate that blocked the New York harbor and inspected every American ship in search of British sailors, shot at an American merchant ship and killed one crew member by the name of John Pierce. The New York crowds broke out into a violent reaction, as the *Aurora* reported: "This murderous act produced the utmost sensation in New York, and we hope it will excite equal sensation and abhorrence everywhere else. Immediately after the body of Mr. Pierce was landed, we learn that the populace carried it through the principal streets of the city, as a spectacle and as an evidence of British honor, justice, humanity and respect for America. . . ."[48] In spite of his trust in Charles Fox, Jefferson wished on this occasion, as George Washington had in 1794, to manifest the anger of the American people and the determination of their leaders by sending a special envoy to London. Thus, William Pinkney joined James Monroe; both were officially required to conclude a commercial treaty to replace Jay's Treaty and to settle the issues arising from infringements on the rights of neutrals and British violations of American sovereignty. Charles Fox had already shown his conciliatory attitude: in May he had imposed by an Order in Council a blockade that amounted to restoring the American reexport trade with all its former advantages.

In the instructions Madison drafted for Monroe and Pinkney, two demands formed a nonnegotiable core, to be obtained at all costs: the end of the impressment of American sailors by the British navy, and the lifting of barriers to the reexport trade.[49] On the strictly commercial items, the negotiations that continued into the fall of 1806 yielded some worthwhile concessions for the United States. According to the assessment by historian Donald Hickey:

> All in all, the terms of the Monroe-Pinkney Treaty were quite favorable to the U.S., especially compared to those of the Jay Treaty. The U.S. gave up the right of commercial retaliation and the doctrine of free ships-free goods. It accepted greater restrictions on its trade with India. . . . In exchange the U.S. received almost all the privileges and guarantees of the Jay Treaty and much more. The reexport trade was guaranteed, the nation's territorial waters were extended, a narrow definition of contraband was established, a more favorable structure of commercial duties was secured. . . . [50]

The treaty was signed on December 31, 1806. Although Monroe had always pressed for a firm stance, he admitted his satisfaction, even without a settlement on the impressment issue. Yet as soon as Jefferson received the treaty and realized that it contained nothing about this issue, he dismissed it without even forwarding it to the Senate. For Donald Hickey, in hindsight this decision was unquestionably a mistake. In Hickey's view, there was another option besides those mentioned by Republican pamphleteers (submission, commercial sanctions, or war); in particular, the Monroe-Pinkney Treaty offered accommodation as an alternative.[51] This treaty was indeed a compromise, as its authors readily acknowledged: " . . . as you readily believe [I have] done everything in my power to bring the negotiation to a satisfactory conclusion. I think it will be concluded in six weeks from this time, and on terms that our government and country will approve, not on every point, or such as they may desire, or perhaps expect; but on such as will essentially improve our situation, on several of the first importance, and injure it in none."[52] The fact that it was a compromise was precisely what made the treaty unacceptable in the eyes of the American president, who even refused to submit it to the Senate. In the letter, it may have offered greater commercial advantages than Jay's Treaty of 1794, but as Bradford Perkins has pointed out, in spirit it more clearly implied American inferiority.[53] In refusing to include a ban on the impressment of sailors in the treaty, Great Britain demonstrated, in American eyes, that it did not fully recognize the sovereignty of the new nation. Commercial advantages mattered little in the end: by 1806 the American republic was no longer the small peripheral power in quest of concessions that it had been in 1794; rather, it was the second trading nation in the world.[54] What really mattered in the treaty, then, was not trade but the impressment of sailors; U.S. greatness and honor depended on it.

Americans felt that the hostile attitude of the British navy and government since 1805 proved that the former colonizing power did not accord the United States its true value. Instead, through a policy of smothering the U.S. economy and through isolated acts of humiliation that mounted to trampling on U.S. sovereignty, Great Britain seemed to avoid acknowledging the spectacular growth of the United States. Thus, there was nothing surprising about Jefferson's rejection of the treaty in 1807, an action that signaled first and foremost a desire for recognition. The United States wanted to be regarded as an independent nation and to be treated by Great Britain with all the respect due to a great power that actually held the keys to the British economy, but the British accorded second place to those demands, after the necessities of war with France. Whereas the Republican leaders wanted to be considered equals, they felt that they were regarded as impatient children who could easily be tamed. At the beginning of the crisis in 1805, a correspondent for the *Charleston City Gazette* had quite eloquently summed up the issue that this crisis represented for American nationalism: " . . . are some people impressed with such a reverential awe for England, that they will look up trembling to that country as children do their parents, kissing the hand that strikes, the rod which castigates them? Away, away with such notions . . . arouse, O my countrymen, be yourselves, be Americans! Do not suffer any power on earth to trample upon you with impunity—You have broken the leading strings which shackled your infancy; you are come to manhood, and I hope that you can cope with any one who dares to be your enemy."[55]

Jefferson did not have to regret rejecting the Monroe-Pinkney Treaty, for the changes in the international situation were soon to make it irrelevant. Indeed, shortly before the treaty was to be signed in December 1806, the news of the Berlin Decree wreaked havoc among the British cabinet, which was now deprived of the moderating influence of Charles Fox, who had died in September. According to the decree, all British goods found on the territory of France or its allies were to be confiscated, and all ships from neutral or belligerent countries trading with Great Britain or its colonies were to be seized. Great Britain had then retorted with a series of Orders in Council that were promulgated in November 1807, under which any ship carrying merchandise to or from a port under French authority would be good for the taking, unless it first stopped over in Great Britain to pay customs duties. This constituted a blockade of all of Europe, and it amounted to forbidding the United States to trade with any country except Great Britain, whereas the Fox blockade of May 1806 had only been strictly applied to the coast stretching from the mouth of the Seine to Ostende.[56] In the beginning of 1808 Napoleon's "continental system" applied to all of Europe with the exception of Sweden and Turkey. The result was that neutral American commerce was caught between the British maritime blockade and the French continental one.[57]

The Failure of the Embargo

Americans had already felt considerable irritation over these measures as well as the increasing impressments aboard their merchant ships. Then in June 1807 came news that was to create an uproar throughout the nation: one of the frigates of the American navy, the *Chesapeake,* had been attacked by a British warship, the *Leopard,* because it refused to surrender three sailors suspected of being British deserters. According to the account given in the *Aurora,* the *Leopard* kept shooting until the *Chesapeake* could no longer sustain the enemy fire and lowered its flag.[58] The attack violated American sovereignty by hitting one of its most conspicuous symbols, namely, the navy, toward which the British frigate seemed not to have shown the least bit of consideration. The whole nation was therefore humiliated; furthermore, this was an act of war between two countries at peace, aimed at implementing the principle of impressment, which the United States had officially condemned as undermining its own sovereignty.

From north to south, the American people were in a rage. Even the Federalist newspapers echoed the numerous patriotic resolutions that were passed by citizens' assemblies in Norfolk, Baltimore, Philadelphia, New York, and so on.[59] The addresses sent by citizens denounced the action of the *Leopard* and expressed their readiness to take up arms, or at any rate to "cooperate with the government in any measures which they may adopt, whether of vengeance or retaliation."[60] Since the news spread around the time of the Fourth of July celebrations, the traditional toasts made reference to the event, expressing confidence in the American navy and support for the president. As the citizens of Groton, Massachusetts, put it to the president, "in repelling foreign insult, may he find us all united."[61] In an outburst of patriotism strengthened by hostility toward Great Britain, the nation was indeed united in support of its president; it kept a lid on political dissent, much to the satisfaction of the progovernment *Aurora:* "We congratulate the country upon the propitious fact, that in every quarter and amongst all classes of Americans, the utmost abhorrence of the late indignity to the nation is manifested. . . ." Similarly, one of the editorialists of the *Boston Colombian Centinel,* an opposition newspaper, declared his solidarity with the patriotic demonstrations, while hinting that he would still disapprove of every one of the executive's decisions.[62] Such unanimity was not limited to the East Coast, which was more quickly informed of that outrage; as soon as the news reached towns in the West, they too followed suit with patriotic resolutions.[63] In fact, the West and the South eventually proved the most willing to support a forceful reaction of the government.[64]

It remained to be decided what the right attitude should be after such an affront. The first impulse of the *Aurora's* editorialists was to recommend non-intercourse, which they had been advocating for several years, and which was the favored choice of Republican leaders: "Nothing will bring the British to a sense of their condition, nothing will rescue the American people from disgrace and plunder—*but a total suspension of intercourse.* In three or six months we can reduce them to terms—the provocation we have had and the honor of the nation demand it—the state of Europe will render it doubly efficacious."[65] As the last sentence indicates, the confidence that pervaded these comments was justified by the military situation in Europe, where, in the spring of 1807, the allies of Great Britain were losing ground to Napoleon's forces. On July 7, 1807, at the very moment when the American nation was raging over the abuses of the British navy, France and Russia signed a peace treaty, and on July 9, Prussia in turn came to terms with Napoleon.[66] But whereas the whole nation was behind Jefferson, urging him to avenge the national honor that Great Britain had trampled upon so often, he felt it was enough to publish a proclamation, dated July 2, 1807, whereby he demanded compensation from Great Britain.[67] Although Jefferson also thought that non-intercourse would be the best way of striking Great Britain, he preferred to let Congress take that decision, which meant delaying it until the fall. This wait-and-see strategy was also intended to give American ships time to reach their home ports, which actually meant no time was being lost: "It gives us at the same time an opportunity of getting home our vessels, our property and our seamen—the only means of carrying on the kind of war we should attempt."[68]

Jefferson had no doubt that congressmen, when they met, would favor non-intercourse over war.[69] On July 3, the *Aurora* in turn expressed its trust in measures of commercial retaliation:

> *War* we do not apprehend—there may be some hostilities committed by ships, and depredations may increase, but *we have the power to command peace, and on our own terms.* . . .
>
> A *suspension of intercourse* will convert the whole West India interest in England, which is stronger than any other, into active enemies of the present ministry—it will throw upon the parishes of England, tens of thousands of paupers, in addition to the present member. . . . The cessation of imports from America, of cotton, flour, rice, etc., will give a shock to the government, that it will with difficulty sustain; and the cessation of exports to this country, the medium of the greatest part of British trade in manufactures, will place every class in England, in the same bankrupt and wretched condition.[70]

While Jefferson and the *Aurora*'s editors could serenely envision a war of commercial retaliation, the same was not true for the majority of Americans. The surge in patriotism that had arisen among the American people after the attack on the *Chesapeake* translated into warlike passion, not into that noble spirit of republican self-denial that was a condition of non-intercourse, as envisioned by Jefferson. On July 10, 1807, he wrote that the country had not known such excitement since the Battle of Lexington, and on July 17 he used that comparison once again.[71] The *Aurora* acknowledged the situation when it wrote: "Everything around us breathes the spirit of war. The volunteer corps are parading in the morning and evening. The young are animated by the highest sensations of military ardour, and the old heroes of the war are seen shedding tears of joy at the revived spirit of the American Revolution."[72]

Jefferson realized that the situation was now ripe for the United States, as a united nation, to initiate hostilities against Great Britain without delay: "They have often enough, God knows, given us cause of war before; but it has been on points which would not have united the nation. But now they have touched a chord which vibrates in every heart." Before taking action, however, he had to wait for an answer from the British, whatever it might be, and hope that, in the meantime, public opinion remained pro-war.[73] The problem was that this kind of enthusiasm could not last for long without something to feed the fire. Waiting for three months would surely weaken the resolve of American citizens. By July 20, the *Aurora* felt the need to exhort its readers not to forget the abuse the nation had suffered and not to be satisfied merely with the withdrawal of British ships out of American waters: "We have repeatedly called upon the public not to relax into supineness, and false confidence in the apparent retreat of the British commodore from his first insolent ground."[74]

When writing his July 2 proclamation, Jefferson apparently did not expect that the popular outcry would, only a few days later, demand more aggressive retaliation measures than those he had in mind. The American people and their president reacted in entirely different ways: for the people of Norfolk or Groton, the president must avenge the honor of the nation forcefully and speedily; for Jefferson, the right course of action consisted in planning a form of response, that is, non-intercourse, that would suit the situation of the country and the republican faith of its citizens. Unlike John Adams in 1798, Jefferson did not know how to utilize the anger and indignant patriotism of his fellow countrymen in such a way as to have an impact on Great Britain, without at the same time leading the country into a useless war; as a matter of fact, he did not see a way to reconcile his strategy with the anger of the citizens: "[T]he present ministry, perhaps no ministry which can now be formed, will not in my opinion give us the necessary assurance, respecting our flag. In that case, it must bring on a war soon, and if so, it can never be in a better time. I look to this, therefore, as most probably now to take place, although I do most sincerely wish that a just and sufficient security may be given us, and such an interruption of our prosperity avoided."[75] Although at the peak of popular anger Jefferson did toy with the idea of a war with Great Britain, and although he hoped that the patriotic fervor of citizens would last, he ultimately was really opposed to war. As soon as the popular fervor abated, he was again able to explain the reasons behind his nonaggressive attitude. In his view, the United States could not go to war until its prosperity was definitively established through removal of the national debt: "[T]ime may produce peace in Europe that removes the ground of difference with England until another European war, and that may find our revenues liberated by the discharge of our national debt, our wealth, numbers increasing, our friendship and our enmity more important to every nation."[76] According to the views of the U.S. president, then, the greatness of the new nation would make itself felt through its wealth and its strength, and it would be recognized by Great Britain and other nations without blood being shed; Jefferson presumed—wrongly, as we shall see—that the nation shared these views.[77] It would seem, then, that in Jefferson's opinion, the reason why the popular fury had abated was that the American population had rallied to the judiciousness of his economic and nonaggressive war plan.

As a result, when the American leaders finally found out that the British government refused, as had been expected, to forbid the impressment of sailors and intended to separate that issue from the *Chesapeake* affair, Jefferson and Congress logically opted to respond by setting up an embargo.[78] It is hard, however, not to think that such a measure was regarded by American patriots as a real retreat, as compared to what had been considered at the peak of the crisis in July 1807. Back then the *Aurora* had written: "The crisis has, in fact, arrived, when England must either peacefully accede to the demands . . . or engage in a war . . . there is no other alternative: on our part, we cannot recede, we cannot abandon the high and just ground we have taken, without becoming the scorn of mankind."[79] The embargo meant that the Republican leaders could implement the policy of commercial retaliation they had been dreaming of since 1789. In theory, conditions were favorable: England was isolated both militarily and economically, and the United States had just enjoyed over ten years of prosperity, with the sole interruption of the Peace of Amiens. An embargo should then make it possible for the United States to defeat Great Britain, without investing in costly military preparations and without really putting its prosperity at risk, since the embargo was supposed to be short-lived. It was also supposed to have the added advantage of boosting American industry, which until then had been neglected in favor of trade, and thus of producing a better overall balance of the American economy. In the words of historian John R. Nelson Jr., "as the policy's failure to coerce England became evident, its salutary impact on manufacturing became its principal justification."[80]

The embargo could not have been a popular policy. For it to bear fruit, it needed the support of the whole nation; and already back in July 1807, the consensus had been in favor not of an embargo, but of a declaration of war. After that date, in the absence of further sensational attacks by the British navy, popular enthusiasm had waned. In addition, not all of the American leaders actually agreed to defend a measure that Treasury Secretary Gallatin called "a doubtful policy, and hastily adopted."[81] In fact, the optimistic mood of late June 1807, when the *Aurora*'s editorialists predicted an immediate collapse of the British economy upon implementing non-intercourse, quickly yielded to real disillusion. On May 2, 1808, the Spaniards rose up against Napoleon, and South American markets opened up to British trade. Hope was rekindled among the British business community, which had feared the worst from the continental blockade.[82] British exports grew from 37 million pounds in 1808 to 47 million in 1809, even without the United States, which until then had made up a third of the British export market.[83] The embargo on American products might have been disastrous for the British textile industry, if it were not for the fact that sizeable stocks had been piled up the previous year. Also, the British managed against all odds to supply their Caribbean islands,[84] and British planters, whose support the Americans had counted on, were actually delighted to be rid of the competition of French and Spanish colonial products, which formerly had been transported by the American merchant marine.

Although in Great Britain the poorest were hurt by the rise in the price of wheat, and although textile workers suffered from unemployment and misery, the protests of these groups were never enough to shake the national union that the continental blockade created in the country. As Bradford Perkins observed, "the miseries of a disenfranchised and inarticulate proletariat could not be expected to sway the policy of the cabinet."[85] The embargo, which was supposed to last only a few months, became a problem and a seeming dead end, which Americans were compelled to get used to. In New England the economic situation immediately took an unexpected turn: for unemployed sailors, the embargo did not mean a republican sacrifice, but the loss of a job, with no alternative prospect. By January 7, 1808, William Bentley, a Republican minister from Salem, Massachusetts, wrote in his diary: "A procession of mariners and persons without employment from the embargo, paraded the streets of Boston with a flag halfmast, to excite alarm, and not without encouragement from our internal enemies."[86] In his eagerness to support Jefferson against the embargo's enemies, William Bentley later on avoided dwelling on the topic. In September 1808 he stated that he had not noticed an increase in the number of paupers, but in fact, Salem was badly hurt by the embargo, and by early 1809, 15 percent of the inhabitants were reduced to begging.[87] Beginning in the spring of 1808, the anger of sailors, shipowners, and merchants from the northeastern states enabled those whom William Bentley called the "internal enemies," that is, the Federalists, to regain a real audience and win back their dominant position in New England.[88] In the mid-Atlantic states, the rise of manufacturing predated the embargo and did not stop, which helped keep down discontent. In the southern states, cotton prices dropped, but that trend had started in 1805,[89] and so these states continued to support the government. The crisis was perhaps more taxing for New England merchants, who suddenly went from unequalled prosperity to poverty, than it was for southern farmers and planters, who had seen prices decline for three years and were less hard-hit. It is also possible that the traditionally Republican loyalties of southern citizens played a significant role in their attitudes.

The western pioneers also suffered from the economic backlash of the embargo, since their merchandise could no longer be exported. Far from protesting, however, they vigorously supported government decisions; indeed, they felt even more bitter about insults to American sovereignty since these insults went along with renewed military aid from Great Britain to the northwestern Indians. There had been skirmishes between the pioneers and the Shawnee Indians since 1803.[90] In the spring of 1808 the British had initiated new contacts with Tecumseh and his brother Tenskwatawa.[91] In September 1809 William Henry Harrison, the governor of the Indiana Territory, purchased huge areas of land in the Wabash valley, which was the last area with a large amount of game, and prepared for military occupation. Since Tecumseh opposed such sales, Harrison thus indirectly strengthened the chief's influence with the majority of northwestern tribes. For westerners, the enemy was clearly England.

Once it became clear that the embargo did not produce the desired effect, and that the administration was nevertheless going to keep enforcing it, northeastern discontent changed into a rebellion against an economic policy that drove the area into misery without offering measures of compensation. Violations of the embargo became common: on the Canadian border, violent confrontations pitted smugglers against customs officers; in certain ports, ships laden with contraband goods sailed off in contempt of injunctions from government officials.[92] By August 6, 1808, Albert Gallatin, who was in charge of enforcing the embargo, wrote in unambiguous terms: "I deeply regret to see my incessant efforts in every direction to carry the law into effect defeated in so many quarters, that we will probably produce, at least on the British, but an inconsiderable effect by a measure which at the same time threatens the Republican interest. For there is almost an equal chance that if propositions from Great Britain or other events do not put into our power to raise the embargo before the 1st of October, we will lose the presidential election."[93] The embargo was an unpopular measure that alienated much of the nation from the government; despite the support of the South and the West, these ill feelings must have spread beyond the mere Northeast, since Gallatin envisioned a Republican defeat in the 1808 presidential election, which was a national contest.[94] The secretary of the treasury cautioned that if the embargo had to be prolonged, "arbitrary" measures would be needed; as a bona fide Republican who had fought against the 1798 laws, Gallatin felt such powers were dangerous. The embargo had failed to mobilize American patriotism: "the people, being distracted by the complexity of the subject, orders of council, decrees, embargoes, and wanting a single object which might rouse their patriotism and unite their passions and affections, selfishness has assumed the reins in several quarters, and the people are now there altogether against the law."[95]

Toward the end of 1808, Jefferson thus found it necessary to propose a bill reinforcing the embargo, which was passed in early 1809. This act was aimed at the state of insurrection on the Canadian border. It enabled the Federalists to point out once again the inconsistency of the Republicans—as democrats who smothered liberty. It was now the Federalists' turn to don the garment of democratic principles. Equating the smugglers of 1808 with the insurgents of 1776 and Thomas Jefferson with George III, they claimed the revolutionary heritage for a New England turned Federalist once again: "Gentlemen have said much about insurrection and rebellion; and in language not very conciliatory, pointed their allusions to the people of New England. Other rulers pronounced them rebels, more than thirty years ago: while many then unborn now wish to cover themselves with their mantle, and to share the honors of the patriots of 1776."[96] A political insurrection, however, was not at hand, despite the Federalists' dreams; instead, what was happening then in New England was, justifiably, economic unrest, which revealed not a divided nation, but above all the failure of the embargo policy and its planners. By trying to impose a measure that had failed to excite enthusiasm, and which proved to be disastrous, Jefferson had severely jeopardized the credibility of a government that in principle was founded on popular sovereignty. The Federalists' success only confirmed the loss of faith.

The embargo had been designed at a moment when the United States was carried away by economic prosperity and thought it possible to bring Great Britain to terms in a few months' time; it was therefore proving to be a bitter failure. The executive had stubbornly kept enforcing a measure that was clearly unpopular, and as a result, had impoverished the nation that should, in the leaders' view, have rallied around their determination. The reason behind the failure of the embargo was not merely that Great Britain had put up an exceptional resistance; it was also that Jefferson and the American people had in fact interpreted the meaning of this confrontation with Great Britain in completely opposite ways. In Norfolk or New York, when citizens had learned of the *Leopard's* conduct, they had quickly reached the conclusion that such an outrage was tantamount to a declaration of war, and that it called for an appropriate response, that is, a military one. Americans were ready to go to war against Great Britain so as to sever, once and for all, the postcolonial links that still bound them to their former parent country. For all their economic power, they had not yet achieved the recognition they felt they deserved.

Moving Toward the War of 1812: Reflections and Interpretations

Between 1809 and 1811 diplomatic relations between the United States and Great Britain deteriorated slowly but surely. In March 1809 the government substituted for the decidedly unpopular embargo a policy that was supposed to be more effective: the Non-Intercourse Act, which allowed commercial relations with all countries except France and Great Britain.[97] In July of the same year, the rejection of the Erskine Agreement dashed the last hopes for an

Anglo-American reconciliation. David M. Erskine, the British minister plenipotentiary who was fairly favorable to the United States, had hoped to use the lifting of the embargo as an occasion to settle the differences of opinion between the two countries. Eager to strike an agreement at all costs, he had deviated from Canning's orders, much to the latter's dismay; the agreement had therefore been rejected, and Erskine was recalled.[98]

Along with the rejection of the Erskine Agreement came the announcement of new Orders in Council, which were no more favorable to American commerce than the previous ones had been. New modes of economic coercion were then undertaken by Congress. Nathaniel Macon's Bill No. 2, introduced on May 1, 1810, lifted restrictions on American trade with Europe but also stipulated that if one of the warring parties repealed its decrees against American trade, the United States would take up non-intercourse measures against the other unless it followed suit. France, however, far from taking the bait and repealing its decrees, confiscated with the Rambouillet decree ten million francs worth of American property.[99]

It seemed that the United States was facing the two warring nations alone, and that it could bring neither one to terms with the kind of measures that the Republicans had favored since 1789. The first one to give up on this war of attrition was the American minister plenipotentiary in Great Britain, William Pinkney, who left London on February 28, 1811. Signs of the hostilities to come were already accumulating in the United States. In 1810 the new Congress was elected; although its first session would not open until October 1811, its makeup revealed the voters' desire for change, since more than half of the former Congress was voted out, and many of the newcomers were very young and pro-war: they were nicknamed the "war hawks."

The first naval confrontation took place on May 16, 1811, when the American frigate *President* attacked the British ship *Little Belt*, resulting in nine dead and twenty-three injured. Whether this attack was justified is not at all clear, but Americans saw the fight as revenge for the *Chesapeake* incident, and they rejoiced over it.[100] Paradoxically, at this very moment the controversy over the *Chesapeake* was extinguished, as the new British minister, Augustus Foster, came over with an offer for a settlement that James Monroe, as the new secretary of state, accepted. What Foster did not offer, however, was the repeal of the Orders in Council, which alone could have truly satisfied American leaders.[101]

Meanwhile in the Northwest, in the fall of 1811, Tecumseh left his home, Prophet's Town at the fork of the Tippecanoe and Wabash Rivers, to join up with the tribes of the old Southwest, whom he guaranteed British aid in the event of war against the United States. William Henry Harrison took advantage of Tecumseh's absence to attack Prophet's Town on November 7, 1811, which earned him the nickname of Tippecanoe, and which—if one is to believe Henry Adams—touched off the War of 1812.[102]

While the battle had in fact already started, the new Congress set about preparing for war. Casting off the Jeffersonian tradition and ideology, which were ostensibly pro-peace, the young Congressmen set up an army of 35,000 men (instead of the existing 10,000), but they did not manage to get a respectable navy created. On June 18, 1812, war was declared.[103] This declaration of war came in the wake of five years of diplomatic tensions between the United States and Great Britain, punctuated by waves of popular anger and fruitless diplomatic missions. Ironically, it was pronounced at the very moment when Great Britain finally yielded to American pressure, since on June 16, 1812, the Orders in Council had been suspended.

In Great Britain, the optimism of 1807 had receded in the face of an economic crisis, and the manufacturing interests had rallied to the cause of the Whig opposition in its attacks on the Tory government. The year 1810 had witnessed consistent deterioration of the British economy. Massive imports of grain, required to fend off the prospect of a food shortage, had caused rising prices, which brought on unrest among the working class population; to make matters worse, a financial crisis had set in, and export attempts to South America had failed. The drop in British exports had been accentuated by Napoleon's tightened surveillance of the European coasts. Therefore, in 1812 recovery was not in sight,[104] which explains why the decrees were repealed—as a means to improve England's relations with its one remaining viable economic partner.

In an expression of his anti-Republican bias, Henry Adams depicted the declaration of war not only as a partisan decision, but also as a sectional one. He observed that while declarations of war are usually manifestations of national union, and often sanctioned by at least part of the opposition, such was not the case with the War of 1812, which was declared solely by southern and western Republicans. According to Adams, the War of 1812 distinguished the United States as perhaps the first country to throw itself into a war that it dreaded in the hope that war itself would create the spirit of war.[105] It is true that many American citizens—most of them Federalists—did oppose the war, but even so-called wars of national union never get the approval of the entire population, despite what Henry Adams claimed. As J. C. A. Stagg aptly remarked, in the ultrapartisan political context of the early republic, war could only rouse the hostility of the party not in power.[106] In point of fact, although the Federalists' opposition to the War of 1812 benefited them throughout the conflict in their northeastern stronghold, in the end it proved fatal to them as a party. From December 15, 1814, to January 5, 1815, delegates from the state assemblies of Massachusetts, Connecticut, and Rhode Island, joined by a few more from Vermont and New Hampshire (who, however, had not been officially commissioned by their state assemblies), gathered in a convention in Hartford, Connecticut. This convention was meeting to protest the war, but public opinion saw it as a separatist congress, traitor to the nation, and once the war was over and an honorable peace secured, the Hartford convention discredited the Federalist Party forever.[107]

Like Henry Adams, Donald R. Hickey considers that the War of 1812 was an unpopular one, but his argument is no more convincing than that of his illustrious elder as concerns the southern, central, and western regions. Although he also claims that the causes of the war are shrouded in mystery, he mentions the following causes: an expansionist drive (which explains the attempts at invading Canada and the final occupation of West Florida, with both occurring during the war), the Orders in Council and the impressment issue,[108] and ideological factors, such as a will to establish the prestige of the republic and defend the honor and sovereignty of the nation.[109] The last aspect is neglected in Hickey's book, even though he agrees that the war could have been avoided if the real, nonideological factors opposing the two countries had alone been taken into account by diplomats and politicians.

It is clear, however, that the ideological factors played an essential role in the stages leading up to the war, as shown first of all by the selection of Great Britain as the enemy, when France was being just as hostile to the United States, and later by the image of the war in American collective memory, which has generally viewed it as the "Second War of Independence." Thus, it cannot be ignored that there existed in 1812, latent in the hearts of a large section of the American population, a patriotic fervor that was hostile to England and that pushed for war. No better evidence of that feeling is to be found than the waves of popular anger that followed the attacks on the *Chesapeake* and the *Leander*. From November 1811 to June 1812, the war hawks strove to rekindle this warlike ardor, which they knew existed among the population. As historian Steven Watts has clearly explained, the rising postrevolutionary generation saw the prospect of a war as a means of regenerating and redefining America. In that generation of new Republicans, young writers, ministers, or politicians sought to break out of the mold their fathers had forced upon them in order to recreate America.[110]

The nationalist drive was the means that would enable them to reach their goals: by extolling America versus the former parent country, the young Republicans were the political heirs to George Washington, Gouverneur Morris, and John Adams, and provided a tangible answer to the quest for identity of their countrymen. Through military actions, America was in fact going to give visible proof of its ability to exist and to assert itself in the face of the nations of a world at war. Whatever its outcome, the war was thus supposed to enable Americans to define themselves against others and then, once their identity and sovereignty were recognized, to devote their energies to themselves.

The War of 1812 was not a great military success, as will be shown in the summary of operations that follows. General Hull's attempted invasion of Canada ended on August 16, 1812, with the British troops taking over Detroit and the Americans surrendering. Other western posts such as Fort Dearborn (Chicago) later fell to the British, in episodes that betrayed the incompetence of several American field officers. Conversely, the small American navy immediately scored a number of brilliant successes: on July 18, 1812, the frigate *Constitution* managed to outdistance four British frigates that were chasing it; on August 19, it shattered the vessel *Guerrière;* on August 25, the frigate *United States* destroyed the British ship *Macedonian.* In spite of these isolated feats, however, the British navy had no trouble, from late December 1812 on, in bringing the United States under the grips of a blockade that became tighter and tighter, and in launching deadly raids onto the coast, as in the pillaging of Hampton on the James River. It was only the American privateers that managed to cause constant concern for the British navy, by seizing numerous merchant ships.

As events unfolded, the incompetence of some American leaders became blatant: on December 3, the secretary of war, William Eustis, had to resign, to be followed by the secretary of the navy, Paul Hamilton, on December 29. In the West, a similar overhaul was taking place: following the assignment of William Henry Harrison as head of the army of the Northwest, the British offensive was stopped on August 1, 1813, at Fort Stephenson. On September 10, the American fleet, under the orders of the young officer Olivier Hazard Perry, thrashed the British fleet on Lake Erie. This victory was soon followed by that of the Thames battle (on October 5, 1813), which saw the death of Tecumseh, Harrison's archenemy. These successes were followed, however, by the failure at the end of the year of a new plan for the invasion of Canada, carried out by the famously inefficient General Wilkinson.

The year 1814 first saw a British fleet penetrate into the Chesapeake Bay, and then a troop landed on August 18. After quickly eliminating their opponents, the British walked into a desolate Washington, D.C., where they burned down public monuments (on August 24 and 25, 1814). A few weeks later, Baltimore was besieged (on September 13 and 14) but not taken, a failure that inspired Francis Scott Key to write the American national anthem.

Although shaken by the burning of Washington, D.C., American patriotism was to be rejuvenated by good news: on March 27, 1814, Andrew Jackson earned a decisive victory against the Creeks, who could have allied with the British had they landed; on September 11, at the battle of Lake Champlain, the British suffered a setback in their attempted invasion of the Northwest; and on September 12, Jackson forced the British out of Mobile. The news of these successes enabled the American negotiators not to yield to British demands. Jackson also won the last battle of the war at New Orleans on January 8, 1815, two weeks after peace had been signed at Ghent on December 24, 1814.[111]

The Americans had suffered smashing defeats, and highly symbolic ones in terms of national identity, such as the burning of their new capital,

Washington, D.C.; yet of the war they only remembered their victories, such as the 1815 Battle of New Orleans. In 1815 a national cult was to build up around that battle and its winner, Andrew Jackson; this proved that a conflict with Great Britain could fulfill American nationalism, and it answered American citizens' wish for recognition. As long as they did not obtain that recognition, which alone would loosen their ties to Europe and avenge their national honor, Americans could not confidently set out to conquer the continent. In fact, how could the West be conquered as long as Great Britain supplied the Indians with arms and food, thus perpetuating a threat on the frontier? The War of 1812 also put an end to these alliances that imperiled American expansion. By 1813 William Henry Harrison had reached his goal in the Northwest, with the Indian defeat at the Battle of the Thames, where Tecumseh died; in the Southwest, Andrew Jackson's victory over the Red Sticks (hostile Creeks) at the Battle of Horseshoe Bend put him in a position to dictate, in August 1814, the terms of a merciless treaty that dispossessed all the Creeks, friends or foes.

Contrary to the war hawks, who in 1811 had supported the logic of recognition through confrontation, Jefferson—though he sometimes considered going to war against Great Britain—had favored the logic of recognition through continental development and isolation until his exit from power in 1809; in that scheme of things, relations with Europe, whether with Great Britain or any other country, already played a minimal role. In October 1808, at the time when he was strengthening the embargo despite popular opposition, he wrote about South America: "We consider their interests and ours as the same, and that the object of both must be to exclude all European influence from this hemisphere."[112]

Jefferson knew that the commercial prosperity the United States enjoyed could not last forever: it depended on the continuation of hostilities in Europe and the good will of Great Britain, mistress of the seas, as had been proved by the Orders in Council of 1807. Since 1789 he had always been of the opinion that the United States must draw maximum benefit from European crises so as to solve the public debt and lay the foundations for American prosperity by developing commercial relations with Europe. He also knew, however, that the nation's economic development would have to rely on more diverse resources, including manufacturing and farming. The Louisiana Purchase, by doubling the area of American territory, was evidence that a great domestic market, that is, a great continental market, could and must be created. The breaking of commercial ties with Saint-Domingue in 1806 showed that foreign trade was no longer the capital objective of American development. The embargo was therefore to be, according to Jefferson, the first vigorous step in the transition of the American economy. Had it succeeded, it would have brought the new nation the added advantage of reconciling its economic development and the recognition by other nations of both its status as a great power and its exceptional character. To defeat the former parent country by the sheer virtue of stoic courage and republican unanimity was a typically Jeffersonian project.

By electing young representatives who were ready to declare war, American citizens demonstrated that the classical republican virtues of self-denial and sacrifice were no longer relevant for them. They might be ready to take up the big continental challenge, but they would first avenge their national honor in a more traditional and less stoic fashion than that recommended by Jefferson and the Republican old guard.[113] Only the War of 1812 could bring the new nation the recognition it sought before setting out to conquer the great domestic market that the American continent was to become.[114] As noted above, the war was actually to be the means for Americans to assert openly a global continental ambition, from Canada to Florida, and this time with arms rather than scientific expeditions. The American complex as an "inferior nation" was erased by the Peace of Ghent, which reestablished the territorial status quo ante between Great Britain and the United States in North America, and which the U.S. Senate ratified on February 16, 1815. From then on, Americans did not have any more accounts to settle with their former parent country, and they could now turn their energies toward fulfilling their "manifest destiny."

Conclusion

1789–1812: A Period of Transition and Transformation of the American Nation and American Nationalism

In 1790, when George Washington received the Native American chief Cornplanter, the president was cautious to avoid using a tone of superiority or aggressiveness. Instead, he resorted to very diplomatic language; as a veteran soldier, who had had many chances to witness Native American bravery on the battlefield, he paid them the respect due formidable adversaries. Since the beginning of his term, he had in fact tried above all to prevent a generalized breakout of hostilities. It would take him a full four years and several true disasters before the victory of Wayne in 1794 to redress the situation on the frontier. In contrast, when Jefferson talked to Handsome Lake in 1802 to advise him to give up hunting and take up farming, his self-assured tone betrayed paternalism: the American president did not for a moment doubt that he was right. In offering Native Americans the means to attain "civilization," he believed that he was leading them on the way to progress and Enlightenment and did not envision the possibility that his interlocutors might have valid reasons for turning him down.

The two presidents did, however, share the same optimistic vision of their country's future, and the same belief in the disappearance of the Native American way of life, but they could not use the same language, for they were faced with different realities. In 1790 the new republic was a fragile one, and its borders, far from being impenetrable, were threatened. In 1802 in contrast, the United States was a prosperous country, which was openly trying to expand by purchasing West Florida and the New Orleans island. From 1789 to 1803 there was a shift in mentality that followed the country's evolution. Driven by a faith in their nation's future, Americans saw their dream gradually come true. Jefferson's dominating triumphalism succeeded Washington's justifiable anxiety. As he was faced with Native American and foreign threats, as well as local secessionist attempts and partisan divisions, Washington could not have displayed the kind of serenity that characterized Jefferson. Jefferson was the great unifier of a nation that was now rich and virtually free from foreign and domestic dangers, and whose diplomatic endeavors were soon to be rewarded by the Louisiana Purchase.

In 1812, when Madison and Congress declared war on Great Britain despite the former parent country's unquestioned supremacy on the seas, they gave new evidence of American confidence in the country's strength. Donald R. Hickey has called that conflict a "forgotten war," and its causes "obscure," for in 1812 the United States was no more driven into war with Great Britain than it might have been in 1807—hence Hickey's irritation, which echoes that of Henry Adams: the war could have been avoided and it brought nothing. But these conventional judgments about the outbreak and consequences of an unconventional war tend to mask the real issue. The War of 1812 occurred at a time when national feeling reached maturity, that is, when it acquired its "secondary" dimension: the army and navy of a country that was now organized were entrusted with the heavy responsibility of defending national honor. The congressmen from the West and South who advocated an uncompromising attitude toward Great Britain in 1811 had been born during or after the War of Independence, and unlike the revolutionary generation that was still in office, never had had to break ties with the former parent country. They naturally placed their trust in a government and nation with which they fully identified. They no longer tried, as the revolutionary generation had done, to build the nation around its institutions; they believed in their nation's greatness, without any doubts or second thoughts.

In this connection, it is perhaps in order to go back over the definition of eighteenth-century American nationalism that was given in the beginning of this book. There nationalism was presented not only as an overriding commitment "to preserving independence, maintaining full sovereignty" or to "extolling national feeling," but also as a specific attempt at elaborating a national character and building up patriotic feeling. By 1812 American nationalism was undergoing a change in its very nature. Starting with the Jefferson presidency, the American leaders no longer complained, as George Washington once had, about the absence of an "American character"; the nation's patriotic feeling no longer had to be stirred up by deft political maneuvers, as in the time of John Adams; it spontaneously expressed itself on the street and in the newspapers when national pride was threatened by attacks from abroad. The point was no longer to create but merely to consolidate national feeling. The War of 1812 was the endpoint of this nationalist process; its goal was to uphold full American sovereignty over the seas and in the West, and it resulted in uplifting American national feeling for years to come.

The same period also witnessed the formation process of a national culture, which was destined to give American nationalism a historical and cultural dimension that had theretofore been little developed. Knowing that the United States did not possess a specific cultural background except that of its former parent country, the revolutionary generation had wanted to elaborate nationalism first on the basis of the institutions that had been chosen by the representatives of the states at the Philadelphia convention. By the turn of the century, that peculiarity of American nationalism, that is, its lack of grounding in a common past and heritage, was beginning to fade.

Historical works such as David Ramsay's *History of the American Revolution* (1789) and Mercy Otis Warren's *History of the Rise, Progress and Termination of the American Revolution* (1805) fabricated the official memory of a nation that, according to these authors, had been chosen by Providence. Ramsay also wrote a *Life of George Washington,* published in 1809, which contributed to creating a pantheon of the nation's great men. A pioneer in his field, the patriotic schoolteacher Noah Webster published in 1787 his *American Spelling Book* with a view to teaching school children the American language and its peculiar spelling; this book was to enjoy great success until the mid-nineteenth century. With Charles Brockden Brown, the republic found its first truly American professional man of letters, who published his six major novels between 1797 and 1801, before going on to a commercial career. This was only a beginning, though, for painters especially could not yet find in America the kind of market and patronage that existed in an organized fashion in Europe; the first half of the nineteenth century would witness the real blossoming of American nationalism in painting (with the Hudson River School) and in literature (with James Fenimore Cooper).

The Nationalist Ferment: A Test of the Interactions between Foreign and Domestic Policies

From 1789 to 1812 foreign policy fostered the growth of American nationalism. The wars of the Revolution, and then of the Empire, translated into opportunities that the United States managed to make the most of: owing to generalized war in Europe after 1793, the early republic was able to build up a prosperous economy on the basis of the phenomenal growth of its foreign trade; in addition, the renewal of hostilities in 1803 compelled Napoleon to sell Louisiana, which Americans had counted on making their own, without hoping to obtain it quite so easily. These events brought Americans together around two goals that were to serve as common denominators at least until the end of the nineteenth century: economic expansion and territorial expansion.

While U.S. foreign policy thus facilitated the growth of American nationalism as a defining and unifying factor, it also brought to light the modes of exclusion that were practiced by the nation within itself. Indeed, the agonies Republican leaders experienced about the right attitude to take toward Haiti underscored the growing commitment of southerners to the institution of slavery and the uneasiness of American society as a whole in confronting that issue. Similarly, the rather contemptuous way in which the Louisiana Creoles were treated by their new American authorities from 1803 on clearly indicates that the American expansionist drive went hand in hand with a feeling of superiority, excluding from democracy all those that were not deemed worthy of it because they did not quite conform to the national mold. The American citizen was to be white, English-speaking, and Protestant.

This triumphant nationalism, which extolled national values, influenced foreign policy in turn: thus, Madison's annexation of West Florida clearly derived from a lack of respect on the part of the United States for certain foreign nations, perhaps because they were weak, but also because they belonged to another culture. Analyzing American nationalism from 1789 to 1812 through the lens of foreign policy leads one to highlight its unifying power, which enabled a community of men and women to define and unite itself within the modern framework of the nation-state. This analysis also highlights its capacity for exclusion, which proved cruel to those, whether inside or outside, who did not bend to the chosen criteria for union, or who opposed the citizens' common objectives.

One of the intentions of this study was to avoid neglecting those groups that are too often forgotten by the history of international relations of this period, namely, Native Americans and black slaves. Hopefully, the voices of these outcasts of the political and social system of the time have been made audible, while the dual face of nationalism—union and exclusion—was constantly kept in view. The term "exclusion," however, calls for qualification as far as the Native Americans are concerned. In the United States of today, the descendants of the first dwellers of the American continent lead for the most part precarious and miserable lives on reservations that are riddled with poverty, alcoholism, and crime, and thus fully justify the notions of "outcasts" and "exclusion," as also do the blacks of the inner-city ghettoes; such was not the case, however, in 1812.

At the time, Native Americans, like the black slaves, were kept out of the political and social life of the nation by the very text of the Constitution, which did not regard them as citizens. But unlike the slaves, who were excluded against their will, Native Americans demanded autonomous sovereignty on their lands, and the Supreme Court had not yet ruled, as it would in 1831, that they were "domestic, dependent nations." Those who led a free life, such as Tecumseh and his people, as well as the tribes of the West, did not seek integration into the world of whites, but instead tried at all costs to preserve their independence.

Indeed, Native Americans were oppressed and excluded whenever the numerical predominance of the whites in their area forced them to accept the life of the reservation and the ensuing procession of painful or impossible adjustments.

Between 1789 and 1812, such was the case especially with the Iroquois, who were defeated during the War of Independence, and had to try to adjust to the life of the reservation during the first decades of the early republic. But as long as they could resist the inroads of pioneers, Native Americans remained above all members of independent, proud nations, whose struggle should be acknowledged in its dignity. After Tecumseh's death, armed resistance became an impossibility east of the Mississippi, but it was to continue in the West throughout the century. American popular expansionism always had to reckon with the fierce resistance of the native nations; this democratic expansionism could only develop with the help of violence and colonialism, thus perhaps laying the foundations of future characteristic features of American foreign policy.

The Origins and Foundations of American Foreign Policy

Although any investigation into the origins is by necessity grounded in a reflection on the present, this study of the origins of American foreign policy has constantly tried to fend off the temptations of presentism and anachronism, which would lead one to read the past as a mere source of the mistakes or the successes of the present. This accounts for the special importance that has been given here to the weakness of the American government at the beginning of the period under review, or to the succession of military defeats in the West up to 1794, or again to the surprise of the Louisiana Purchase, until then a mere dream of American leaders. Still, this study would not be complete if it did not highlight the foundations that the American republic's first quarter century laid for future policies.

As we saw, foreign policy allowed Americans to gather around common objectives. The popular expansionism that Jefferson formulated in countless letters and official papers, and that his successor Madison enacted in Florida, or again, the doctrine of isolation that was elaborated by Washington and Jefferson may rightly be considered as the main principles underlying all the doctrines and practices of American foreign policy down to the end of the nineteenth century. These two principles anticipated, and then in the mid-nineteenth century, informed the doctrine of "manifest destiny," whereby the feeling of a democratic superiority took shape, to serve as justification for every violation of international law and the rights of peoples, and to bar interference from other great powers.

Away from such haughty and boastful proclamations, the hesitating way in which the recognition of Haiti was refused in 1806 foreshadowed the U.S. withdrawal out of an expansion zone that had nonetheless been considered, but a few years before, a "natural" one: in the opinion of the American leaders, the social organization of the United States would have been threatened had American diplomacy ventured the least official action toward that other new republic. Once the Civil War was over, and the slavery question settled, the United States was soon to become interested again in its close Caribbean neighbors, under the guidance of President Andrew Johnson's secretary of state, William H. Seward.

In 1812 white American men were enjoying the blessings of a unity that was based on prosperity, but social, racial, and economic tensions could rise up again and tear apart the national fabric. It would be a long time, however, before those tensions actually broke off the impulse that the Louisiana Purchase gave to the conquest of the continent. In the beginning of the nineteenth century, American nationalism definitely found its real meaning, as well as its apotheosis, in the conquest of American space, which was acted out in the name of progress and the moral superiority of the United States, and in the accompanying economic expansion. Before embarking on that great westward expansion, American citizens were ready to stand the ultimate test of recognition—war—which was to prove to the world, as well as to themselves, that the United States was a great power, able to compete with France and Great Britain.

Notes

Notes to Introduction

1. In *Les Mythes fondateurs de la nation américaine. Essai sur le discours idéologique aux Etats-Unis à l'époque de l'indépendance (1763–1800)* (Paris, 1976, 1992), 11, Elise Marienstras declares that "nationalism has been discredited once and for all," but she adds that it is not clear whether one can "reduce all cases to the Western model, the one that was established in the nineteenth century." In his article "Logiques de la nation," published in Gil Delannoi and Pierre-André Taguieff, *Théories du nationalisme. Nation, nationalité, ethnicité* (Paris, 1991), 29, Alain Renaut speaks of "the frightening phenomenon of nationalism—which has played a powerful destabilizing role in Europe and the rest of the world in the twentieth century, to the point of becoming a feature of one of the most tragic episodes of our recent history." For a similar viewpoint on the part of an American scholar, see Geoff Eley, "Nationalism and Social History," *Social History* 6 (January 1981), 85.

2. Eley, "Nationalism and Social History," 86.

3. *Le Monde Diplomatique,* September 1991, 7; Ibid., August 1991, 1.

4. Gérard Malkassian, "Diaspora et question nationale," *Le Messager Européen* 5 (1991), 58.

5. Ibid., 49, 58, 61.

6. Pierre-André Taguieff, "Le nationalisme des nationalistes. Un problème pour l'histoire des idées politiques en France," in *Théories du nationalisme,* 47–48, 61, 58. For an example of an antinationalist definition of nationalism, see Maurice Agulhon, "Aspects du nationalisme français," *Raison Présente,* 103, 1992, 59–62.

7. Gil Delannoi, "La théorie de la nation et ses ambivalences," in *Théories du nationalisme,* 14; Taguieff, "Le nationalisme des nationalistes," 110; Marienstras, *Les Mythes fondateurs,* 12.

8. Robert Darnton, *The Great Cat Massacre and Other Episodes in French Cultural History* (New York, 1984, 1985), 4.

9. American nationalism has been the topic of far fewer books than, for example, French nationalism. A probable explanation for this is that American nationalism is

generally perceived as less of a cause of international conflicts. For a contrasting study of European nationalism and American nationalism, see the work of journalist William Pfaff, *The Wrath of Nations: Civilization and the Furies of Nationalism* (New York, 1993). Among recent historical works on American nationalism and its origins, one may mention Wilbur Zelinsky, *Nation into State: The Shifting Symbolic Foundations of American Nationalism* (Chapel Hill, N.C., 1988), which analyzes the transformations of nationalism as a civic religion throughout the history of the United States; and David Waldstreicher, *In the Midst of Perpetual Fetes: The Making of American Nationalism, 1776–1820* (Chapel Hill, N.C., 1997), which emphasizes American civic practices, rather than political discourses and the cult of institutions, as the primary constituents of American nationalism.

10. Taguieff, "Le nationalisme des nationalistes," 63.

11. Eric J. Hobsbawm, *Nations and Nationalism Since 1780: Programme, Myth, Reality* (Cambridge, 1990), 18.

12. Historian Merrill Jensen, in *The New Nation: A History of the United States During the Confederation, 1781–1789* (New York, 1950), saw those "nationalists" primarily as an elite that was frightened by democracy. In contrast, Edward Millican, in his book *One United People: The Federalist Papers and the National Idea* (Lexington, Mass., 1990), analyses their main theoretical text, the *Federalist Papers,* as a protonationalist document, because it emphasizes the new nation's cultural homogeneity and its need for centralized institutions.

13. As quoted in Taguieff, "Le nationalisme des nationalistes," 60; see John J. Breuilly, *Nationalism and the State* (Manchester, 1982, 1985), 3.

14. Raoul Girardet, ed., *Le Nationalisme Français* (Paris, 1983), 9.

15. See David Hackett Fischer, *Albion's Seed: Four British Folkways in America* (New York, 1989), and for debates on this book, *William and Mary Quarterly,* 3d series, vol. 47, no. 2, April 1991, 224–60.

16. Jack P. Greene, *Pursuits of Happiness: The Social Development of Early Modern British Colonies and the Formation of American Culture* (Chapel Hill, N.C., 1988), 170; according to Greene, the main colonial areas were distinguished by clear cultural and socioeconomic features, but their diversity should not be overestimated.

17. Marienstras, *Nous, le peuple: Les origines du Nationalisme américain* (Paris, 1988), 13.

18. Marienstras, *Les Mythes fondateurs,* 14. In the same book, 16, Marienstras offers the view of a "two-tiered conception of the nation": "on the one hand, the nation results from a consensus of individuals who share the same will to found a political community (nation as artefact); on the other hand, such a consensus is made possible by a preexisting community of fact" (organic nation).

19. Marienstras, *Nous, le peuple,* 8.

20. According to Otto Bauer's definition, as quoted by Marienstras in her presentation of the idea of nation, in *Les Mythes fondateurs,* 7–20.

21. Marienstras, *Nous, le peuple:* see chapters 19 to 21, 357–418.

22. Ibid., 363.

23. For a more detailed elaboration of this idea, see Hobsbawm, *Nations and Nationalism,* 10.

24. Ernst Gellner, "Nationalism and the two forms of cohesion in complex societies," in *Culture, Identity and Politics* (Cambridge, 1987), 13–16.

25. Sean Wilentz, *Chants Democratic: New York City and the Rise of the American Working Class, 1788–1850* (New York, 1984), 4–5. The same thesis is developed by Joyce Appleby, *Capitalism and a New Social Order: The Republican Vision of the 1790s* (New York, 1984).

26. To quote Richard D. Brown in *Knowledge Is Power: The Diffusion of Information in Early America, 1700–1865* (New York, 1989), 13, "by the early decades of the nineteenth century virtually all the northern white population was literate."

27. Frank Luther Mott, *American Journalism: A History of Newspapers in the United States Through 250 Years, 1690 to 1940* (New York, 1942), 159, 161. Postal rates were high at the time, which explains why only a minority of Americans regularly exchanged private correspondence. In 1793, however, Congress decided by means of the Post Act to stimulate the postal distribution of newspapers by granting discount rates to publishers; see Allan R. Pred, *Urban Growth and the Circulation of Information: The United States System of Cities, 1790–1840* (Cambridge, Mass., 1973), 61, 81–82.

28. See Mona Ozouf, "Le concept d'opinion publique du XVIIIe siècle," in *L'Homme régénéré. Essais sur la Révolution française* (Paris, 1989), 25. In the eighteenth century, according to Ozouf, French intellectuals considered that in France, public opinion was still in infancy, for lack of institutional channels and because of the traditional weakness of public political life. Ozouf contrasts this situation with that of England, where "public opinion" or "the opinion of the public" had had a real status since 1730. In view of her analyses and those of Roger Chartier, in *Les Origines culturelles de la Révolution française* (Paris, 1990), 41, 52, it appears that public opinion meant at that time an opinion that was well informed and able to express itself in writing. Those who could not read or write were de facto excluded from this realm, and therefore popular opinion was distinct from public opinion. It follows from this that the United States was a relatively privileged country at the time, since the high rate of literacy produced a broader public opinion (in the eighteenth-century sense) than in Europe.

29. Christophe Jaffrelot, "Les Modèles explicatifs de l'origine des nations et du nationalisme. Revue critique," in *Théories du Nationalisme,* 143. Jaffrelot borrows the concept of "imagined community" from Benedict Anderson, *Imagined Communities: Reflections on the Origin and Spread of Nationalism* (London: Verso, 1991).

30. Marienstras, *Les Mythes fondateurs,* 23.

31. This distinction is borrowed from Marienstras, *Nous, le peuple,* 95.

32. See Marienstras, *Les Mythes fondateurs,* 13. For a discussion of the notion of colonial identity in America, and its relationship to the processes of independence, see Nicholas

Canny and Anthony Pagden, eds., *Colonial Identity in the Atlantic World, 1500–1800* (Princeton, N.J., 1987).

33. See L. S. Kaplan, *Colonies into Nation: American Diplomacy, 1763–1801* (New York, 1972), and James Trapier Lowe, *Our Colonial Heritage: Diplomatic and Military* (Lanham, Md., 1987).

34. Allan R. Pred, *Urban Growth and the Circulation of Information,* 22, explains that even after the War of Independence, news from Europe continued to reach the United States faster than news from one state reached another state; hence this predominance of foreign news, which ceased only after the War of 1812.

35. Comte de Garden, *Traité Complet de Diplomatie* (Paris: Librairie de Treuttel et Würtz, 1833), vol. I, 1–2.

36. Walter La Feber, "Liberty and Power: U.S. Diplomatic History, 1750–1945," in *The New American History,* ed. Eric Foner (Philadelphia, Pa., 1990), 274.

37. Richard W. Van Alstyne, *Empire and Independence: The International History of the American Revolution* (New York, 1965), vii.

38. Charles S. Maier, "Marking Time: The Historiography of International Relations," in *The Past Before Us: Contemporary Historical Writing in the United States,* ed. Michael Kammen (Ithaca, N.Y., 1980), 355. In France, meanwhile, Jean-Baptiste Duroselle and Pierre Renouvin had set a new trend as early as 1964, in defining their conception of the history of international relations in their *Introduction à l'histoire des Relations Internationales* (Paris, 1964, 1970). While granting that "government policies are 'at the core of international relations,'" these authors maintained that the study of policies "is far from being enough to produce the necessary explanations," and should be complemented with a grasp of "the influences on the course of such policies," including "geographical conditions, economic and financial interests, deep forces" (1–2).

39. Thomas G. Paterson, "Introduction," in "Explaining the History of American Foreign Relations," *Journal of American History* 77(1) (June 1990), 93.

40. Ibid., 96.

41. Lucien Febvre, as quoted by Jacques Le Goff, in "L'histoire nouvelle," *La Nouvelle Histoire* (Paris, 1978, 1988), 41–42.

42. See Charles R. Lilley and Michael H. Hunt, "On Social History, the State, and Foreign Relations: Commentary on 'The Cosmopolitan Connection,'" *Diplomatic History* 11 (1987), 250.

43. The best work on this topic remains Ray W. Irwin, *The Diplomatic Relations of the United States with the Barbary Powers, 1776–1816* (Chapel Hill, N.C., 1931); see Reginald Horsman, "Bibliographical Essay," in *The Diplomacy of the New Republic, 1776–1815,* The American History Series (Arlington Heights, Ill., 1985).

44. Lowe, *Our Colonial Heritage,* 169: "It was for our own empire building in the first place that we wanted written (not verbal) treaties with the Indians who could not read and write."

45. James H. Merrell, *The Indians' New World: Catawbas and Their Neighbours from European Contact through the Era of Removal* (Chapel Hill, N.C., 1989), 204–5.

46. Akira Iriye, "Culture," *Journal of American History,* 77(1) (June 1990), 100.

47. Ibid., 101.

48. Michael H. Hunt, "Ideology," *Journal of American History,* 77(1) (June 1990), 108.

49. Clifford Geertz, "Ideology as a Cultural System," in *Ideology and Discontent,* ed. David A. Apter (London, 1964), 48–53.

50. Marienstras, *Nous, le peuple,* 7.

51. Pierre Nora, *Les lieux de mémoire: La République* (Paris, 1984), viii.

52. George Burdeau, *Le Libéralisme* (Paris, 1979), 7, explains that "although in reference to a doctrine the term 'libéralisme' appeared for the first time only in 1823 in Claude Boiste's lexicon, the trend of thought it referred to existed before that date." About the difference between economic and political liberalism, Burdeau adds that "although the two currents may be separated intellectually, historically they are inseparable, in so far as political liberalism only established itself in order to safeguard economic liberalism. It follows that, if political liberalism consists in the control of power by the governed, this control is primarily established in favor of property" (74).

53. In this book, the term "expansion" is not used in sole reference to territorial growth. Instead, borrowing Marc Egnal's definition, I consider expansionism as "a fervent belief in America's potential for greatness." Marc Egnal, *A Mighty Empire: The Origins of the American Revolution* (Ithaca, N.Y., 1988), 6–7.

54. In his book *The Opening of American Society* (New York, 1984), 133, Robert H. Wiebe writes: "eighteenth-century gentlemen commonly used the term 'empire,' denoting an extensive country and a diverse population."

Notes to Chapter 1

1. The papers in question are nos. 3, 4, 11, and 15 of the *Federalist Papers,* pamphlets that were published during the winter of 1787–88 by John Jay, Alexander Hamilton, and James Madison as a means of supporting the ratification of the 1787 Constitution, and were subsequently collected into a book. The edition used here is *The Federalist or the New Constitution, Papers by Alexander Hamilton, James Madison, John Jay* (New York: Heritage Press, 1945).

2. *The Federalist* no. 15, *op. cit.,* 90–91.

3. The title of John Fiske's book, *The Critical Period of American History, 1783–1789* (Boston, Mass., 1888), was for a long time a mandatory quote for the historians who followed his theses. See Samuel Flagg Bemis, *Jay's Treaty* (New Haven, Conn., 1923, 1962), 1. On the contrary, Merrill Jensen tries to do justice to the period of the Articles of Confederation in *The New Nation* (xiii).

4. Samuel Flagg Bemis, ed., *The American Secretaries of State and Their Diplomacy* (New York, 1927–29, 10 vols.), vol. 1, 228. See Article VII of the Definitive Treaty of Peace Between Great Britain and the United States, signed at Paris, September 3,

1783, in *Treaties and Conventions Concluded Between the United States of America and Other Powers Since July 4, 1776* (Washington, D.C.: Government Printing Office, 1889), 378.

5. Jensen, *The New Nation,* 169, 174.

6. See Denis Lacorne, "Une présidence hamiltonienne: la politique étrangère de Ronald Reagan," *Revue Française de Science Politique,* 39, 4, 1989, 540–41. Lacorne draws a comparison between the America of 1787 and the United States of the late Carter years : "[T]wo centuries later, the same humiliations, the same feeling of decline, the same inferiority complex . . . America is weakened from within by the 'Vietnam syndrome,' the aftermath of Watergate, and an economic crisis that hits American consumers hard. The time has come to improve the image of the United States, and to give new vigor to a weakened executive branch."

7. Forrest McDonald, *E Pluribus Unum: The Formation of the American Republic, 1776–1790* (Indianapolis, 1979), 257.

8. It is worth recalling that, in this particular context, the term "nationalist" applied to those who, at the Philadelphia Convention, wanted to replace the *federal* government with a *national* one, i.e., a strong executive branch endowed with specific powers.

9. Bemis, *The American Secretaries of State,* vol. 1, 226, 261, 268; Wiley Sword, *President Washington's Indian War: The Struggle for the Old Northwest, 1790–1795* (Norman, Okla., 1985), 79, 81.

10. *The Federalist* no. 23, *op. cit.*

11. Gregory H. Nobles, "Breaking into the Backcountry: New Approaches to the Early American Frontier, 1750–1800," *William and Mary Quarterly,* 3d series, 46(4) (1989), 642. Francis Jennings, *The Ambiguous Iroquois Empire* (New York, 1984), 59.

12. Frederick Jackson Turner, "The Significance of the Frontier in American History," in *The Frontier in American History* (Tucson, Ariz., 1920, 1986), 3.

13. Richard Van Alstyne, *The Rising American Empire* (New York, 1974), 67.

14. Wiley Sword, *President Washington's Indian War,* 12, 13, 15. Bemis, *Jay's Treaty,* 2.

15. See Article IV of the Definitive Treaty of Peace Between Great Britain and the United States, signed at Paris, September 3, 1783: "It is agreed that creditors on either side shall meet with no lawful impediment to the recovery of the full value, in sterling money, of all *bona fide* debts heretofore contracted" (*Treaties and Conventions,* 377).

16. Richard B. Morris, *The Peacemakers: The Great Powers and American Independence* (New York, 1965), 220–38.

17. Article II of the Definitive Treaty of Peace Between Great Britain and the United States, signed at Paris, September 3, 1783: "South, by a line to be drawn due east from the determination of the line last mentioned, in the latitude of thirty-one degrees north of the equator, to the middle of the river Apalachicola . . . ; thence along the middle thereof to its junction with the Flint river; thence strait to the head of St. Mary's River; and thence down along the middle of St. Mary's River to the Atlantic Ocean" (*Treaties and Conventions,* 377). In Article V of the Treaty of Peace and Amity Between

Great Britain and Spain, also signed September 3, 1783, Great Britain granted Spain full property of both East and West Floridas (M. de Martens, *Recueil des Principaux Traités* [Göttingen, 1791–1801, 11 vols.], vol. 2, 487). In 1764 Great Britain had set the administrative boundary of West Florida at latitude 32°28'. After reoccupying this area during the war, Spain could legitimately claim that boundary as the true one. See F. E. Chadwick, *The Relations of the United States and Spain* (New York, 1909), 29; and Samuel Flagg Bemis, *The Diplomacy of the American Revolution* (New York, 1935), 101.

18. Bemis, *The American Secretaries of State,* vol. 1, 234. Article VIII of the 1783 peace treaty between Great Britain and the United States : "The navigation of the river Mississippi, from its source to the ocean, shall for ever remain free and open to the subjects of Great Britain, and the citizens of the United States" (*Treaties and Conventions,* 378).

19. Reginald Horsman, *The Frontier in the Formative Years, 1783–1815* (New York, 1970), 15.

20. Chadwick, *The Relations of the United States and Spain,* 30–34.

21. Ibid., 15.

22. Sword, *President Washington's Indian War,* 5 ; Wilcomb E. Washburn, *The Indian in America* (New York, 1975), 152, 154, 155.

23. James H. O'Donnell III, *Southern Indians in the American Revolution* (Knoxville, Tenn., 1973), vii.

24. Elise Marienstras, *La résistance indienne aux Etats-Unis du XVIe au XXe siècle* (Paris, 1980), 81.

25. Richard White, *The Middle Ground: Indians, Empires, and Republics in the Great Lakes Region, 1650–1815* (New York, 1991), 351, 407.

26. Washburn, *The Indian in America,* 157; Sword, *President Washington's Indian War,* 17, 18.

27. Dorothy V. Jones, *License for Empire: Colonialism by Treaty in Early America* (Chicago, 1982), 150.

28. Charles J. Kappler, ed., *Indian Affairs,* Laws and Treaties (Washington, D.C., 1903), vol. 2, 2–13.

29. Horsman, *The Frontier,* 9, 10–11.

30. Jones, *License for Empire,* 151–56.

31. Bemis, *Jay's Treaty,* 23, and the chapter "The Anglo-American Frontier."

32. R. S. Cotterill, *The Southern Indians: The Story of the Civilized Tribes Before Removal* (Norman, Okla., 1954), 69.

33. White, *The Middle Ground,* 418–19 ; Sword, *President Washington's Indian War,* 69–78.

34. White, *The Middle Ground,* 446–47.

35. Bemis, *Jay's Treaty,* 19, 20, 21, 23.

36. Although Col. Beckwith was a British intelligence agent, many political figures met with him in the open, meaning that his status was semiofficial. Jefferson always

refused to enter into official contact with him; see Dumas Malone, *Jefferson and the Rights of Man* (Boston, Mass., 1951), 273.

37. White, *The Middle Ground,* 114, 404, 410, 453, 463–64. On the role of gifts in relations with the southwestern Indians, see O'Donnell, *Southern Indians in the American Revolution,* 5.

38. Lord Dorchester was Governor General of Canada and therefore represented the British government on the American continent.

39. Thomas Jefferson, *The Writings of Thomas Jefferson,* ed. Paul Leicester Ford (Washington, D.C., 1892–99, 10 vols.), vol. 5, 321 (Thomas Jefferson to the President of the United States, April 17, 1791), 323 (Thomas Jefferson to the President of the United States, April 24, 1791).

40. Bemis, *The American Secretaries of State,* vol. 2, 30.

41. Bemis, *Jay's Treaty,* 160, 165, 168, 181.

42. Jefferson, *The Writings,* Ford ed., vol. 5, 450 (Thomas Jefferson to the American Minister in France, Philadelphia, March 10, 1792); Bemis, *Jay's Treaty,* 168–75, 182.

43. Sword, *President Washington's Indian War,* 229–31, 245–47.

44. White, *The Middle Ground,* 464–65.

45. Ibid., 258–60, 261, 262.

46. Ibid., 298.

47. The same treaty acknowledged the situation in the field and announced British withdrawal from the northwest posts. See Article II of the Treaty of Amity, Commerce and Navigation Between Great Britain and the United States signed at London, November 19, 1794: "His Majesty will withdraw all His Troops and Garrisons from all Posts and Places within the Boundary Lines assigned by the Treaty of Peace to the United States. This Evacuation shall take place on or before the first Day of June 1796" (Clive Parry, ed., *The Consolidated Treaty Series* [Dobbs Ferry, N.Y.: Oceana Publications, 1969], vol. 52 [1793–95], 246).

48. Floridablanca was Spain's minister of foreign affairs until 1789. Details of his plan can be found in Arthur Preston Whitaker, *The Spanish-American Frontier, 1783–1795* (Boston, Mass., 1927), 35.

49. Thomas P. Abernethy, *The South in the New Nation* (Baton Rouge, La., 1951), 95; Cotterill, *The Southern Indians,* 76, 81, 85, 86. For the text of this treaty, see Kappler, *Indian Affairs,* vol. 2, 19–22.

50. Horsman, *The Frontier,* 17.

51. Jefferson, *The Writings,* Ford ed., vol. 5, 216–17 (Thomas Jefferson to the American Chargé d'affaires in Spain, August 2, 1790); 219–20 (Thomas Jefferson to the American chargé d'affaires in Paris, August 10, 1790).

52. Thomas Jefferson was the instigator of William Short's memoir; see Jefferson, *The Writings,* Ford ed., vol. 5, 304 (March 19, 1791).

53. See *Diplomatic and Consular Instructions of the Department of State* (M 28, Roll no. 1), folio 99, Thomas Jefferson to William Carmichael, November 6, 1791;

American State Papers, Foreign Relations, vol. 1, 251 (The Secretary of State to the President, December 22, 1791), 257 (The Secretary of State to William Carmichael and William Short, April 24, 1792). In contrast to this, Whitaker argues in *The Spanish-American Frontier,* 149–50, that Jefferson was actually in no hurry to conclude a treaty and sought ways to delay the negotiation.

54. *American State Papers, Foreign Relations,* vol. 1, 261 (William Carmichael and William Short to the Secretary of State, April 18, 1793).

55. Cotterill, *The Southern Indians,* 98, 100.

56. *Diplomatic and Consular Instructions of the State Department* (M 28, Roll no. 2), folios 200 to 202 (the Secretary of State to William Short and William Carmichael, October 14, 1792).

57. Ibid., folios 313 and 314 (the Secretary of State to William Short and William Carmichael, June 30, 1793); Cotterill, *The Southern Indians,* 104.

58. Favorite of the queen of Spain Maria-Louisa, Manuel Godoy was made Duke of La Alcudia on November 14, 1792. The former prime minister, Floridablanca, had been sent off in February 1792. See Jacques Chastenet, *Manuel Godoy et l'Espagne de Goya* (Paris, 1961).

59. *American State Papers, Foreign Relations,* vol. 1, 441 (Sirs Carmichael and Short to the Secretary of State, January 7, 1794).

60. *Despatches of American Ministers to Spain* (M 31, Roll no. 2), despatch no. 139, folio 169, January 21, 1794.

61. Ibid., despatch no. 185, folio 390, December 12, 1794.

62. Ibid., despatch no. 186, folio 419, December 29, 1794.

63. Treaty of Friendship, Limits and Navigation Between Spain and the United States, signed at San Lorenzo el Real, October 27, 1795, Article II: " . . . The southern boundary of the United States, which divides their territory from the Spanish colonies of East and West Florida, shall be designated by a line beginning on the River Mississippi, at the northernmost part of the thirty-first degree of latitude north of the equator, . . ."; Article IV: " . . . His Catholic Majesty has likewise agreed that the navigation of the said river, in its whole breadth from its source to the ocean, shall be free only to its subjects and the citizens of the United States . . ."; Article V: "The two high contracting parties shall, by all the means in their power, maintain peace and harmony among the several Indian nations who inhabit the country adjacent. . . . And the bet[t]er to obtain this effect, both parties oblige themselves expressly to restrain by force all hostilities on the part of the Indian nations living within their boundaries . . ." (*Treaties and Conventions,* 1007–8).

64. Cotterill, *The Southern Indians,* 107, 114.

65. Samuel Flagg Bemis, *Pinckney's Treaty: America's Advantage from Europe's Distress, 1783–1800* (New Haven, Conn., 1926, 1960), 313.

66. Arthur Preston Whitaker, *The Mississippi Question, 1795–1803: A Study in Trade, Politics, and Diplomacy* (New York, 1934), 78.

67. William G. McLoughlin, *Cherokee Renascence in the New Republic* (Princeton, N.J., 1986), 33, 46–92.

68. Neal R. Price, *The New England States: People, Politics and Power in the Six New England States* (New York, 1976), 241.

69. Bemis, *Pinckney's Treaty,* 101, 109, 110, 121.

70. Abernethy, *The South in the New Nation,* 126.

71. Ibid., 49, 51, 53, 54.

72. Bemis, *Pinckney's Treaty,* 128, 129.

73. Ibid., 60–64.

74. Ibid., 81.

75. Thomas Robson Hay and Morris-Robert Werner, *The Admirable Trumpeter* (Garden City, N.Y., 1941), 135; *Correspondance Politique* Etats-Unis, vol. 37, folio 99; Abernethy, *The South in the New Nation,* 109–26.

76. *Dictionary of American Biography,* vol. 2, 390, 391.

77. Translation from the French original quoted in Frederick J. Turner, "Documents on the Blount Conspiracy, 1795–1797," *American Historical Review* 10(2) (1905), 574–606 (the quote appears on 585).

78. Isabel Thompson, "The Blount Conspiracy," *East Tennessee Historical Society Publications,* 2, 1930, 14.

79. Frederick J. Turner, "Documents on the Blount Conspiracy," 588–89 (Liston to Grenville, March 16, 1797, and May 10, 1797).

80. *Despatches from U.S. Ministers to Great-Britain* (M30, Roll no. 4), despatches no. 45 (August 28, 1797), no. 51 (October 31, 1797), and no. 57 (December 10, 1797).

81. Abernethy, *The South in the New Nation,* 176.

82. *Dictionary of American Biography,* vol. 20, 222–26.

83. Thompson, "The Blount Conspiracy," 14, 15. On the impeachment procedure, see Buckner F. Melton, *The First Impeachment, The Constitution's Framers and the case of Senator William Blount* (Macon, Ga.: Mercer University Press, 1998).

Notes to Chapter 2

1. Frederick W. Marks III, *Independence on Trial: Foreign Affairs and the Making of the Constitution* (Wilmington, Del., 1973, 1986), 205.

2. The intellectual history of republicanism in the United States has been the topic of many publications in the past thirty years. I have used the following books: Bernard Bailyn, *The Ideological Origins of the American Revolution* (Cambridge, Mass., 1967); Gordon S. Wood, *The Creation of the American Republic, 1776–1787* (New York, 1972); Lance Banning, *The Jeffersonian Persuasion: Evolution of a Party Ideology* (Ithaca, N.Y., 1978); Drew McCoy, *The Elusive Republic: Political Economy in Jeffersonian America* (New York, 1980, 1982). I also used the following articles: Gordon S. Wood, "Interests and Disinterestedness," in *Beyond Confederation: Origins of the Constitution and American National Identity,* ed. Richard Beeman (Chapel Hill, N.C., 1987); Robert E. Shalhope, "Toward a Republican Synthesis: The Emergence of an Understanding of Republicanism in American

Historiography," *William and Mary Quarterly,* 3d series, 29(1) (1972); Lance Banning, "Jeffersonian Ideology Revisited: Liberal and Classical Ideas in the New American Republic," *William and Mary Quarterly,* 3d series, 43(1) (1986). In stressing the consensus that existed among the revolutionaries, the "republican" interpretation of the American Revolution has tended to obscure ideological and social divisions between the inhabitants of the thirteen colonies in 1776. See Colin Gordon, "Crafting a Usable Past: Consensus, Ideology and Historians of the American Revolution," *William and Mary Quarterly,* 3d series, 46(4) (1989). The "consensus" interpretation of the American Revolution should therefore be taken with a grain of salt, especially given the alternative vision that lays the stress rather on the divisions among revolutionaries: see Alfred F. Young, ed., *The American Revolution: Explorations in the History of American Radicalism* (DeKalb, Ill., 1976).

3. Wood, *The Creation of the American Republic,* 393–411.

4. *The Federalist,* no. 10, *op. cit.,* 55.

5. Ibid., 55, 58.

6. Ibid., 61.

7. Wood, *The Creation of the American Republic,* 603–15; Denis Lacorne, *L'Invention de la République. Le modèle américain* (Paris, 1991), 139, 141.

8. *The Federalist,* no. 10, *op. cit.,* 62.

9. Here is Madison's view of how partisan divisions would be eliminated at the national level: "The federal Constitution forms a happy combination in this respect; the great and aggregate interests being referred to the national, the local and the particular to the State legislatures" (ibid., 61).

10. John C. Miller, *Alexander Hamilton, Portrait in Paradox* (New York, 1959), 221.

11. For Mary P. Ryan, who did a quantitative analysis of congressional votes between 1789 and 1796, the division of Congress into two stable blocks clearly emerged through the votes of the first Congress. Although Ryan puts forth no particular argument to account for the rise of parties, her study shows that the most partisan votes occurred in matters of foreign policy (Mary P. Ryan, "Party Formation in the United States Congress. 1789 to 1796: A Quantitative Analysis," *William and Mary Quarterly,* 3d series, 28[4] [1971], 531, 539, 540, 542). In *The Origins of the American Party System* (New York, 1961), Joseph Charles established a direct link between the birth of political parties and foreign policy debates (84, 97, 99), although he qualified that view by stressing that at that time foreign policy events were also domestic events (137), which shows that it is difficult to separate them from one another.

12. Charles, *The Origins of the American Party System,* 13.

13. Gilbert Chinard, *Honest John Adams* (Boston, Mass., 1933), 198–99, 215–17.

14. Miller, *Alexander Hamilton,* 222–24.

15. George Washington, *The Writings of George Washington,* ed. John C. Fitzpatrick (Washington, D.C., 1931–44, 39 vols.), vol. 31, 102. See also Jefferson, *The Writings,* Ford ed., vol. 5, 238.

16. Jefferson, *The Writings,* Ford ed., vol. 5, 239 ("Opinion on Course of the United States toward Great Britain and Spain," August 28, 1790).

17. See Alexander Hamilton, *The Works of Alexander Hamilton,* ed. Henry Cabot Lodge (New York, 1885–86, 9 vols.), vol. 4, 313–42. In his response to George Washington, Hamilton explained that in view of its less than friendly conduct with the United States, Spain could hardly expect gestures of good will on the part of the United States.

18. Bemis, *Jay's Treaty,* 71–73.

19. Such is the thesis that is carefully developed by Julian P. Boyd in *Number 7: Alexander Hamilton's Secret Attempts to Control American Foreign Policy* (Princeton, N.J., 1964), where Boyd, despite an excessive anti-Hamiltonian bias, describes the secret diplomacy of the secretary of the treasury. John C. Miller, *The Federalist Era, 1789–1801* (London, 1961), expresses similar views on Hamilton's influence in foreign policy, and states that Hamilton vied with Jefferson to define U.S. foreign policy and behaved as a prime minister (84).

20. Gouverneur Morris, a true patrician who had been a member of the Continental Congress and the Constitutional Convention, sailed for Europe as an agent to merchant Robert Morris. See Jared Sparks, *The Life of Gouverneur Morris* (Boston, Mass., 1832, 2 vols.), vol. 1, 308; *Dictionary of American Biography,* vol. 13, 209–12.

21. Boyd, *Number 7,* 24. Boyd quotes "Beckwith's report of conversations," which is mentioned in the correspondence from Lord Dorchester to Lord Grenville dated October 25, 1789.

22. Ibid., 31.

23. Ibid., 31, 32, 33. Boyd quotes "Beckwith's report of conversations," which is mentioned in the correspondence from Lord Dorchester to Lord Grenville dated May 27, 1790.

24. Jefferson, *The Writings,* Ford ed., vol. 5, 221–30. The secret letters were addressed to secret agent David Humphreys (August 11, 1790), to Gouverneur Morris (August 12, 1790), and to William Carmichael (August 22, 1790). See chapter 1.

25. Boyd, *Number 7,* 73.

26. Ibid., 74–75.

27. For the text of the presidential message, see George Washington, *The Writings of George Washington,* ed. Worthington Chauncey Ford (New York, 1889–93, 14 vols.), vol. 12, 1–4.

28. Jefferson, *The Papers of Thomas Jefferson,* ed. Julian P. Boyd, vol. 18, 99.

29. Ibid., 220ff. For the Navigation Acts, see G. M. Trevelyan, *A Shortened History of England* (1942; Harmondsworth, 1979), 309.

30. See *The Writings of Thomas Jefferson,* ed. H. A. Washington (Washington, D.C., 1853–54, 9 vols.), vol. 7, 519–26, 532–38, 538–55.

31. *American State Papers, Foreign Relations,* vol. 1, 121. See also Jefferson, *The Papers,* Boyd ed., vol. 18, 232.

32. Jefferson, *The Papers,* Boyd ed., vol. 18, 233.

33. Ibid., 221ff.

34. Ibid., 237.

35. When he was the American minister in France, Jefferson had obtained easy terms for the importation of American tobacco as well as whale and fish oils into France. These terms were granted by France only to the United States, which thus enjoyed a favored status as compared to other nations. In return, the French now expected a favor from the United States, specifically an exemption from the consequences of the new American laws on customs and tonnage duties; the French also claimed that these laws were in violation of the spirit of the 1778 treaty. See Malone, *Jefferson and the Rights of Man,* 328; Jefferson, *The Papers,* Boyd ed., vol. 18, 558–59.

36. Jefferson, *The Papers,* Boyd ed., vol. 18, 545, 565.

37. Ibid., 544–55.

38. Jefferson, *The Writings,* Ford ed., vol. 5, 282 (Thomas Jefferson to Nicholas Lewis, February 9, 1791).

39. Ibid., 326 (Thomas Jefferson to Thomas Mann Randolph, May 1, 1791).

40. Charles A. Beard, *Economic Origins of Jeffersonian Democracy* (New York, 1929), 399.

41. John R. Nelson Jr., *Liberty and Property: Political Economy and Policymaking in the New Nation, 1789–1812* (Baltimore, Md., 1987), 90–99.

42. David Brion Davis, *Revolutions: Reflections on American Equality and Foreign Liberations* (Cambridge, Mass., 1990), 30–31.

43. *Pennsylvania Gazette,* October 14, 1789; see also the *Gazette of the United States,* December 16 and 23, 1789.

44. Richard Buel Jr., *Securing the Revolution: Ideology in American Politics, 1789–1815* (Ithaca, N.Y., 1972), 37, 39, 40.

45. Davis, *Revolutions,* 37.

46. Thomas Paine, *The Rights of Man,* in *Common Sense, The Rights of Man and other Essential Writings of Thomas Paine,* introduction by Sydney Hook (New York, 1969), 121.

47. Philippe Raynaud, "Révolution américaine," in *Dictionnaire critique de la Révolution française,* ed. François Furet and Mona Ozouf (Paris, 1988), 860.

48. Jefferson, *The Writings,* Ford ed., vol. 6, 147.

49. Ibid., 151 (Thomas Jefferson to the American minister in France, December 30, 1792).

50. Ibid., 329 (Thomas Jefferson to the President of the United States, Philadelphia, May 8, 1791). See also Malone, *Jefferson and the Rights of Man,* 357, 358.

51. Jefferson, *The Writings,* Ford ed., vol. 5, 355 (Thomas Jefferson to John Adams, July 17, 1791).

52. John Adams, *The Works of John Adams,* ed. Charles Francis Adams (Boston, Mass., 1850–56, 10 vols.), vol. 6, 399.

53. Jefferson, *The Writings,* Washington ed., vol. 7, 258.

54. Ibid., 209.

55. Buel, *Securing the Revolution,* 38.

56. Washington, *The Writings,* Fitzpatrick ed., vol. 32, 54.

57. Gouverneur Morris, *The Diary and Letters of Gouverneur Morris,* ed. Anne Cary Morris (New York, 1888, 2 vols.), vol. 2, 36–37.

58. Jefferson, *The Writings,* Washington ed., vol. 3, 257–58 (Letter to George Washington, May 8, 1791).

59. For George Washington's questions and the answers of the cabinet, see "Cabinet Opinion on Proclamation and French Minister," in Jefferson, *The Writings,* Ford ed., vol. 6, 217.

60. *American State Papers, Foreign Relations,* vol. 1, 140.

61. Jefferson, *The Writings,* Ford ed., vol. 6, 149 (Thomas Jefferson to the American minister in France, December 30, 1792). Jefferson's opinion was in keeping with Emer de Vattel's in *Le Droit des Gens* (Paris, 1758, 1863), book 2, chapter 12, § 185: "the State and the Nation always remain the same, whatever changes are made in the form of government." For Vattel, as well as for Jefferson, sovereignty lay in the nation, not in the regime. Vattel's book, published in 1758, had considerably influenced Enlightenment thinking on international law.

62. Hamilton's preferred option would have been to refuse to recognize the French republic and to suspend, if not to annul, the existing treaties (see Miller, *Alexander Hamilton,* 369).

63. Alexander Hamilton, *The Works of Alexander Hamilton,* ed. John C. Hamilton (New York, 1859–61, 7 vols.), vol. 4, 382–90.

64. Jefferson, *The Writings,* Ford ed., vol. 6, 231 ("Opinion on French Treaties," April 28, 1793).

65. Vattel, *Le Droit des Gens,* book 2, chapter 12, § 197.

66. Jefferson, *The Writings,* Ford ed., vol. 6, 220 ("Opinion on French Treaties"); Jefferson thought Hamilton's reasoning was more ingenious than it was rigorous.

67. "Adresse des citoyens de Philadelphie au citoyen Genêt" [Address by the citizens of Philadelphia to Citizen Genêt], May 20, 1793 (supplement to the *Gazette de France Nationale,* July 17, 1793, *Correspondance Politique* Etats-Unis, vol. 37).

68. For the popular festivities that followed Genêt's arrival and the French republic's victories, see Merrill D. Peterson, *Thomas Jefferson and the New Nation: A Biography* (New York, 1970), 479. See also *Correspondance Politique* Etats-Unis, vol. 37, dispatch no. 2 from Genêt in Philadelphia, May 18, 1793: "My journey has been an uninterrupted succession of civic festivals, and my entrance into Philadelphia a triumph for liberty."

69. Jefferson wrote to James Monroe on May 5, 1793: "The war between France and England seems to be producing an effect not contemplated. All the old spirit of 1776 is rekindling" (Jefferson, *The Writings,* Ford ed., vol. 6, 238).

70. Eugene Perry Link, *Democratic-Republican Societies, 1790–1800* (New York, 1942), 21–35, 135.

71. Gordon S. Wood, *The Radicalism of the American Revolution* (New York, 1992), 96.

72. Jefferson, *The Writings,* Ford ed., vol. 6, 260. On May 19, 1793, Jefferson wrote

to Madison that although public opinion suspected that the president's aides would not receive Genêt, the citizens decided to receive him themselves.

73. Ibid., vol. 5, 282. On February 9, 1791, Jefferson had made this clear to Nicholas Lewis: "Government being founded on opinion, the opinion of the public, even when it is wrong, ought to be respected to a certain degree."

74. Jefferson, *The Writings,* Ford ed., vol. 6, 251 (Thomas Jefferson to James Madison, May 12, 1793).

75. Ibid., 260 (Thomas Jefferson to James Madison, May 19, 1793). In fact, Genêt's instructions, which had been drafted before the proclamation of neutrality, contained a striking contradiction: the goal was to secure aid from the United States, while at the same time strictly respecting American neutrality. They could almost be compared to "the vicious kind of orders that incite an agent to go and raise hell without making waves," according to Jean-Jacques Jusserand, "La Jeunesse du Citoyen Genêt," *Revue d'Histoire Diplomatique* 44 (3) (1930), 239. Genêt's interpretation of his orders, however, was especially extreme.

76. Jefferson, *The Writings,* Ford ed., vol. 6, 233. In his "Opinion on French Treaties," Jefferson merely doubted that this provision could be invoked, without being sure that it would not be. This is the reason why he sounded relieved when he found that Genêt did not intend to use the clause of mutual guarantee of the Treaty of Alliance Between France and the United States signed at Paris, February 6, 1778. Under Article XI, this provision read: "The two parties guarantee mutually from the present time and forever against all other powers, to wit: the United States to His Most Christian Majesty, the present possessions of the Crown of France in America, as well as those which it may acquire by the future treaty of peace . . ." (*Treaties and Conventions,* 309).

77. Jefferson, *The Writings,* Ford ed., vol. 6, 233 ("Opinion on French Treaties"). See Article XXII of the Treaty of Amity and Commerce Between France and the United States signed at Paris, February 6, 1778: "It shall not be lawful for any foreign privateers, not belonging to subjects of the Most Christian King nor citizens of the said United States, who have Commissions from any other Prince or State in enmity with either nation, to fit their ships in the ports of either the one or the other of the aforesaid parties, to sell what they have taken, or in any other manner whatsoever to exchange their ships, merchandises or any other lading; neither shall they be allowed even to purchase victuals, except such as shall be necessary for their going to the next port of that Prince or State from which they have commissions" (*Treaties and Conventions,* 303).

78. Worth mentioning here is the former hero of the War of Independence, George Rogers Clark, who from Louisville wrote to the Committee of Public Safety (see chapter 4). In South Carolina Governor William Moultrie himself also directly appealed to the Committee of Public Safety. See Rachel Klein, *Unification of a Slave State: The Rise of the Planter Class in the South Carolina Backcountry, 1760–1808* (Chapel Hill, N.C., 1990), 207.

79. See *Correspondance Politique* Etats-Unis, vol. 36, dispatch no. 1, folio 217. For Jefferson's version of Genêt's activities, see Bemis, *The American Secretaries of State,* vol. 2, 78–81,

and Jefferson's letter asking for the French minister to be recalled (*The Writings,* Ford ed., vol. 6, 371–93, Thomas Jefferson to the American minister in France, August 16, 1793).

80. Jefferson, *The Writings,* Ford ed., vol. 6, 282.

81. *Correspondance Politique* Etats-Unis, vol. 36, "Supplement to Instructions," folios 496, 497. Genêt's instructions, however, seemed to call upon him to prevent the outfitting of English privateers, rather than to assist French ones. Thus it was "particularly enjoined to Citizen Genêt to insist rigorously on the execution of articles 17, 21 and 22 of the 1778 treaty and to prevent, in American ports, any outfitting of privateers except for the benefit of the French Nation, as well as any entry of prizes other than those made by the vessels of the [French] Republic." This proves that Genêt's interpretation of his instructions was excessive.

82. Jefferson, *The Writings,* Ford ed., vol. 6, 294 (Thomas Jefferson to the French minister, June 11, 1793); 307 (Thomas Jefferson to the French minister, June 17, 1793).

83. For a detailed account of this episode, see Peterson, *Jefferson and the New Nation,* 498–500.

84. Thomas Jefferson used the phrase "fair neutrality" in a letter to James Monroe on May 5, 1793, and spoke of "English neutrality" in a letter to James Madison on May 12, 1793 (*The Writings,* Ford ed., vol. 6, 239 and 251).

85. Ibid., 361 (Thomas Jefferson to James Madison, August 3, 1793).

86. Ibid., 391; 398 (Thomas Jefferson to James Madison, August 25, 1793).

87. Link, *Democratic-Republican Societies,* 151.

88. *American State Papers, Foreign Relations,* vol. 1, 300–4.

Notes to Chapter 3

1. Buel, *Securing the Revolution,* ix.

2. In *The Jeffersonian Republicans: The Formation of Party Organization, 1789–1801* (Chapel Hill, N.C., 1957), 256, Noble E. Cunningham Jr., has shown that the development of political life in the United States between 1790 and 1815 arose out of divisions in Congress and then spread to the states. Richard Hofstadter, in *The Idea of a Party System: The Rise of Legitimate Opposition in the United States, 1780–1840* (Berkeley, Calif., 1969), 75, has explained that the structures of American society were highly conducive to the development of a moderate political life. His arguments are: land ownership was widespread; most landowners benefited from a generous system of franchise, which led to a large number of voters; this large voting public was used to taking part in public life.

3. Banning, *The Jeffersonian Persuasion,* 285.

4. Hofstadter, *The Idea of a Party System,* viii, ix, xii, 4, 6, 8, 39.

5. Ibid., 86.

6. John C. Miller has observed, in *The Federalist Era,* 138, that in December 1793, when George Washington communicated Genêt's correspondence to Congress, he did not extend his criticism to the French government, and, over Hamilton's objections,

included in his message a full account of British as well as French depredations of American commerce.

7. *Correspondance Politique* Etats-Unis, vol. 36, folio 494.

8. Treaty of Amity and Commerce Between France and the United States, signed at Paris, February 6, 1778, Article XXIII: "and it is hereby stipulated that free ships shall also give a freedom to goods, and that everything shall be deemed to be free and exempt which shall be found on board the ships belonging to the subjects of either the confederates, although the whole lading or any part thereof should appertain to the enemies of either, contraband goods being always excepted" (*Treaties and Conventions,* 303).

9. Bemis, *Jay's Treaty,* 152.

10. Ibid., 156–58.

11. Ibid., 158.

12. In 1784 and 1785 France had opened five Caribbean ports, including Saint-Domingue, to American trade. In 1793 all French ports were opened to Americans. See John H. Coatsworth, "American Trade with European Colonies in the Caribbean and South America, 1790–1812," *William and Mary Quarterly,* 3d series, 24(2) (1967), 245–50.

13. Bemis, *Jay's Treaty,* 159–60.

14. "Discours de Lord Dorchester aux Indiens des Sept Villages du Bas Canada" [Speech by Lord Dorchester to the Indians of the Seven Villages of Lower Canada], February 10, 1794, St. Louis, *Correspondance Politique* Etats-Unis, vol. 40, folio 80.

15. John Jay, *The Correspondence and Public Papers of John Jay, 1794–1826,* ed. Henry P. Johnston (New York, 1890–93, 4 vols.), vol. 4: John Jay to Mrs. Jay, April 10, 1794, 2–3. The letters of Edmund Randolph to John Jay and James Monroe during the summer of 1794 are also quite revealing. On July 30, 1794, for example, Edmund Randolph wrote to John Jay: "there is great reason to apprehend that British troops will be found mixed with the Savages who are prepared to meet General Wayne." See also his letters to Jay of August 18 and September 12, 1794, as well as his letter to James Monroe of September 25, 1794. All of these letters by Randolph appear in *Diplomatic and Consular Instructions of the State Department,* Roll 2 (August 22, 1793–June 1, 1795), 118, 134, 167, 185.

16. Kaplan, *Colonies into Nation,* 235.

17. As Edmund Randolph explained to Gouverneur Morris on April 29, 1794: "It is now nearly a fortnight, since Mr. Jay was nominated as Envoy Extraordinary to London. . . . The irritation, which appears in all classes of people, renders it probable, that if he fails in his errand, the United States will risque all the consequences of strong measures" (*Diplomatic and Consular Instructions of the State Department,* Roll 2, 72).

18. Bemis, *Jay's Treaty,* 210.

19. The two conditions were the following: no treaty should be signed that would be contrary to U.S. commitments toward France; nor should there be a treaty of commerce that would not allow American ships entry into ports of the British Caribbean. Both of these requirements, as well as the nineteen recommendations, are found in

Bemis, *Jay's Treaty,* 212–15. For the text of the instructions, see Jay, *Correspondence and Public Papers,* Johnston ed., vol. 4, 10–21.

20. Bemis, *Jay's Treaty,* 212.

21. Ibid., 217.

22. In *The Federalist Era,* 164, John C. Miller claims that Jay arrived in London at a bad time if he intended to obtain advantages from the British government. This is highly debatable, as the French were then scoring a number of military victories, as Bemis makes clear in *Jay's Treaty,* 221; see also Michael Glover, *The Napoleonic Wars* (New York, 1978), 28–38.

23. Jay, *Correspondence and Public Papers,* vol. 4, 28–29 (John Jay to Edmund Randolph, June 23, 1794), 30 (John Jay to Alexander Hamilton, July 11, 1794). These letters reveal that the close relationship between Jay and Hamilton led the envoy to confide more about his negotiations to Hamilton than to the secretary of state. Jay thus wrote to Hamilton: "On Monday next I am to dine with the Lord Chancellor, and on next Friday with Mr. Pitt. I mention these facts to explain what I mean by favourable appearances. I think it best that they should remain unmentioned for the present, and they make no part of my communications to Mr. Randolph, or others."

24. Bemis, *Jay's Treaty,* 243–50.

25. Kaplan, *Colonies into Nation,* 241–42.

26. Bemis, *Jay's Treaty,* 268–69.

27. Article XVII of Jay's Treaty violated the rule that "free ships shall also give a freedom to goods," which had been spelled out in Article XXIII of the Franco-American Treaty of Amity and Commerce (quoted above, note 8); to that extent, Americans were going back on the principles they had defended along with the French until that time. Here is the text of Article XVII of the Treaty of Amity, Commerce and Navigation Between Great Britain and the United States, signed at London, November 19, 1794: "It is agreed that, in all Cases where Vessels shall be captured or detained on just suspicion of having on board Enemy's property or of carrying to the Enemy, any of the articles which are Contraband of war; the said Vessel shall be brought to the nearest or most convenient Port, and if any property of an Enemy, should be found on board such Vessel, that part only which belongs to the Enemy shall be made prize, and the Vessel shall be at liberty to proceed with the remainder without any Impediment" (Parry, *The Consolidated Treaty Series,* vol. 52 [1793–1795, 1969], 258). In addition, Article XXV allowed privateers, warships, and prizes of the other country entry into the contracting country's ports: "It shall be lawful for the Ships of war and Privateers belonging to the said Parties respectively to carry whithersoever they please the Ships and Goods taken from their Enemies without being obliged to pay any Fee to the Officers of the Admiralty, or to any Judges whatever; . . . Nothing in this Treaty contained shall however be construed or operate contrary to former and existing Public Treaties with other Sovereigns or States" (ibid., 262). Despite its last provision, this article contradicted Article XXII of the Franco-American Treaty of Amity and Commerce (quoted above, chapter 2, note 77). At a time when France was at war against Great Britain, it is hard to understand

how Jay could include this article in his treaty without realizing that it was likely to cause immediate tensions between France and the United States.

28. Klein, *Unification of a Slave State,* 219.

29. Thomas P. Slaughter, *The Whiskey Rebellion: Frontier Epilogue to the American Revolution* (New York, 1986), 206–7.

30. Sharon V. Salinger, "Artisans, Journeymen, and the Transformation of Labor in Late Eighteenth-Century Philadelphia," *William and Mary Quarterly,* 3d series, 40(1) (1983); James P. Walsh, "'Mechanics and Citizens': The Connecticut Artisan Protest of 1792," *William and Mary Quarterly,* 3d series, 42(1) (1985).

31. Alan Taylor, *Liberty Men and Great Proprietors: The Revolutionary Settlement on the Maine Frontier, 1760–1820* (Chapel Hill, N.C., 1990), 4.

32. Link, *Democratic-Republican Societies,* 67.

33. Ibid., 78–89.

34. Washington, *The Writings,* Fitzpatrick ed., vol. 33, 457.

35. Ibid., 475–76 (George Washington to Governor Henry Lee, private letter, August 26, 1794).

36. Slaughter, *The Whiskey Rebellion,* 205–21.

37. Washington, *The Writings,* Fitzpatrick ed., vol. 34, 29.

38. Slaughter, *The Whiskey Rebellion,* 165.

39. Steven Watts, *The Republic Reborn: War and the Making of Liberal America, 1790–1820* (Baltimore, Md., 1987), 46, 47.

40. Wilentz, *Chants Democratic,* 73–76.

41. Klein, *Unification of a Slave State,* 164.

42. Slaughter, *The Whiskey Rebellion,* 221.

43. The September 13, 1795, issue of the French newspaper *Le Moniteur Universel* (vol. 25, no. 357) reported on a meeting of citizens who were displeased with Jay's Treaty, in Charleston on July 18: "Chief Justice Rose . . . said that this was called a treaty of amity and commerce and so forth, but that this was in fact a humble acknowledgement of the fact that the United States was dependent on His British Majesty, and a relinquishment of its rights and privileges, which for the future it pledged to enjoy only as much as the gracious favor of the King of England would suffer it to."

44. Edmund Randolph to James Monroe, July 14, 1795, in *Diplomatic and Consular Instructions of the Department of State,* Roll 3 (June 5, 1795–January 21, 1797).

45. Dispatch no. 10 of 10 brumaire an 3 (October 31, 1794) in *Correspondance Politique* Etats-Unis, vol. 42, folios 125–26. In this dispatch Joseph Fauchet mentioned dispatches nos. 6 and 3, where he had reportedly recounted other interviews with the American secretary of state. Although dispatch no. 6 is written in code and is thus unintelligible, dispatch no. 3 of 16 prairial an 2 (June 4, 1794) contained lengthy disclosures by Randolph on American political life. The secretary of state depicted George Washington as a man surrounded by advisors (Alexander Hamilton in particular) who "mislead [him] about the true mind of the people." Randolph also confided to Fauchet about "the internal divisions that secretly undermined the United States" (*Correspondance Politique* Etats-

Unis, vol. 41, folios 157, 158). As Fauchet himself remarked in this dispatch: "This Mr. Randolph is undoubtedly a fine man, and a strong supporter of our revolution, but I believe him to be of a weak character. He is easily moved into confiding his secret" (folios 159, 160). Randolph obviously lacked the prudence and discretion required of a career statesman; his dismissal was much more understandable than the recall of Monroe.

46. Bemis, *The American Secretaries of State,* vol. 2, 151–53.

47. Cunningham, *The Jeffersonian Republicans,* 70–85.

48. James Monroe, *The Writings of James Monroe,* ed. Stanislaus Murray Hamilton (New York, 1898–1903, 7 vols.), vol. 2, 8.

49. Ibid., 4: "If we may judge from what has been at different times uttered by Mr. Fauchet, he will represent the existence of two parties here irreconcilable to each other. One Republican, and friendly to the French Revolution; the other monarchical, aristocratic, Britannic, and anti-Gallican. . . . If this intelligence be used, in order to inspire a distrust of our good will to France, you will industriously obviate such an effect."

50. Ibid., 34, 195 (letters to Edmund Randolph, August 25, 1794, and February 12, 1795), 13–15 (Address to the National Convention). Soon after he arrived in Paris on August 2, 1794, James Monroe sensed the defiant attitude of the Committee of Public Safety toward him. On August 15, he managed to be received by the Convention, to which he delivered a speech extolling the friendship between the two nations, and transmitted a letter in the same spirit from the House of Representatives; all this was done on Randolph's instructions.

51. When Monroe arrived in Paris, many American vessels were held up at Bordeaux, while others had been arraigned in violation of the rule "free ships make free goods." Monroe quickly managed to improve trade relations between France and the United States; see his December 2, 1794, letter to Edmund Randolph, in Monroe, *The Writings,* vol. 2, 140.

52. Edmund Randolph to Colonel Monroe, March 8, 1795, in *Diplomatic and Consular Instructions of the Department of State,* Roll 2 (August 22, 1793–June 1, 1795), 330.

53. Monroe, *The Writings,* vol. 2, 169 (James Monroe to Edmund Randolph, January 13, 1795).

54. Ibid., 159, 154 (James Monroe to Edmund Randolph, private letter, December 18, 1794; James Monroe to James Madison, December 18, 1794).

55. Ibid., 181 (James Monroe to John Jay, January 17, 1795); 229–30 (James Monroe to the Secretary of State, March 17, 1795). See also the "Answer of the President of the Executive Directory to Monroe's Farewell Address," March 2, 1797, in *American State Papers, Foreign Relations,* vol. 2, 747.

56. *Le Moniteur Universel,* 6 ventôse an 4 (February 25, 1796), vol. 127, no. 166.

57. Timothy Pickering to James Monroe, September 12, 1795, and November 23, 1795, in *Diplomatic and Consular Instructions of the Department of State,* Roll 3, 55–66, 89.

58. Monroe, *The Writings,* vol. 3 (49 for Monroe's letter to the secretary of state of August 4, 1796). The French had chosen Mangourit for a special mission to the United States.

Since Mangourit, as the French consul in Charleston in 1793, had drawn attention for his zealous support of Genêt, Monroe dissuaded the French leaders from sending him, on the assumption that his arrival would be regarded as a provocation by the Federalists.

59. Marshall Smelser, "The Federalist Period As an Age of Passion," *American Quarterly* 10(4) (1958). Other historians have investigated the meaning of the political violence of the 1790s; see an excellent synthesis by John R. Howe, "Republican Thought and the Political Violence of the 1790s," *American Quarterly* 19(2) (1967).

60. *Gazette of the United States,* November 2 and 24, 1796; *Minerva,* November 16, 1796.

61. *Aurora,* November 2, 3, and 30, 1796; *National Gazette,* November 8, 1796.

62. John Adams, *The Works,* vol. 8, 534.

63. During his stay in Berlin, the young Adams translated the work of the counterrevolutionary thinker (and himself the translator of Edmund Burke) Friedrich von Gentz, *The Origin and Principles of the American Revolution, compared with the Origin and Principles of the French Revolution,* in which Gentz demonstrated that the two revolutions did not partake of the same spirit.

64. John Quincy Adams, *The Writings of John Quincy Adams,* ed. Worthington Chauncey Ford (New York, 1913–17, 7 vols.), vol. 2, 67 (December 30, 1796), 82 (January 14, 1797), 245 (January 27, 1798), 300 (June 7, 1798).

65. Raoul Girardet, "La Conspiration," in *Mythes et Mythologies Politiques* (Paris, 1986), 25–62. Richard Hofstadter, in *The Paranoid Style in American Politics and Other Essays* (New York, 1963), describes the conspiracy narrative as a constant feature of American political life.

66. David Osgood, *Some facts evincive of the atheistical, anarchical, and in other respects, immoral principles of the French Republicans* (Boston, Mass., May 9, 1798), 10; see also Jedidiah Morse, *The Present Situation of the Nations of the World contrasted with our own* (Boston, Mass., February 19, 1795), 12–14.

67. *A Defence of the Constitutions of Government of the United States of America* was written in 1786 and 1787 while John Adams was in England. See Chinard, *Honest John Adams,* 203–11.

68. John Quincy Adams, *The Writings,* vol. 2, 82.

69. Genêt's instructions did not plan for him to act in a subversive way, as he started doing in May 1793. Far from being ordered to raise civil war in the United States, he was required to adopt "a frank and loyal conduct as to the common interests [of the two countries], but a measured and circumspect one in internal matters" ("Instructions de Genêt," *Correspondance Politique* Etats-Unis, vol. 36, folios 484–99).

70. "Rapport de Fauchet sur les Etats-Unis," in *Correspondance Politique* Etats-Unis, vol. 44, folio 487.

71. Stephen G. Kurtz, *The Presidency of John Adams: The Collapse of Federalism, 1795–1800* (Philadelphia, Pa., 1957), 45.

72. Cunningham, *The Jeffersonian Republicans,* 83; Kurtz, *The Presidency of John Adams,* 54, 56, 57.

73. *Correspondance Politique* Etats-Unis, vol. 46, dispatch no. 24, folio 32, Philadelphia, 21 prairial an 4 (June 9, 1796).

74. Ibid., dispatch no. 36, folio 199, Boston, 3 vendémiaire an 5 (September 24, 1796).

75. Ibid. According to Stephen G. Kurtz, *The Presidency of John Adams,* 143, this letter is one of the few documents that prove the connection between the French minister and Republican leaders, and there is no evidence that the leaders of the party approved of Adet's actions.

76. *Aurora,* October 31, 1796.

77. *Aurora,* November 18, 1796.

78. A letter published in the November 9, 1796, issue of the *Aurora* suggested that, instead of the "ambiguous" name of "Republicans," the name "Democrats" be applied to the Jeffersonians, to make it clear that only Jefferson's supporters, and not Adams's, were on the side of the people and of government by the people. It was this democratic aspect of their political commitment that the founders of the democratic-republican societies had intended to underscore.

79. "Arrêté du Directoire exécutif, concernant la navigation des navires neutres chargés de marchandises appartenant aux ennemis de la République" [Order of the Executive Directory regarding the navigation of neutral ships laden with goods belonging to enemies of the Republic], in *Lois, Décrets, Ordonnances, Règlements et Avis du Conseil d'Etat,* tome 9, ed. J. B. Duvergier (Paris, 1825), 358–61.

80. Jean Martin, *L'Empire Renaissant 1789–1871* (Paris, 1987), 42.

81. Alexander De Conde, *The Quasi-War: The Politics and Diplomacy of the Undeclared War with France, 1797–1801* (New York, 1966), 9.

82. Ibid., 17–23.

83. Kaplan, *Colonies into Nation,* 267.

84. John Marshall, *Journal of General Marshall at Paris* (1797–1798) (manuscript, Library of Congress). On October 30, 1797, Talleyrand's envoys said to John Marshall: "Perhaps said he you believe that in venturing and exposing to your countrymen the unseasonableness of the demands of this government you will unite them in their resistance to those demands. You are mistaken. You ought to know that the diplomatic skills of France and the means she possesses in your country are sufficient to enable her with the French party in America to throw the blame which will attend the rupture of the negociation on the Federalists as you term yourselves but on the British party as France terms them."

85. Ibid., October 14, 1797.

86. Ibid., October 17, 1797.

87. James Morton Smith, *Freedom's Fetters: The Alien and Sedition Laws of American Civil Liberties* (New York, 1956), 7.

88. John C. Miller, *Crisis in Freedom: The Alien and Sedition Acts* (Boston, Mass., 1951), 23.

89. Smith, *Freedom's Fetters,* 21.

90. Bradford Perkins, *The First Rapprochement: England and the United States, 1795–1805* (Philadelphia, Pa., 1955), 95.

91. Rufus King to the Secretary of State, dispatch no. 79, June 15, 1798, in *Despatches from U.S. Ministers to Great-Britain,* vol. 5.

92. Ibid., dispatches Nos. 62 and 64, Rufus King to the Secretary of State, January 14, 1798 and February 7, 1798.

93. Perkins, *The First Rapprochement,* 98.

94. Miller, in *Crisis in Freedom,* tends to favor the first hypothesis, while Richard Hofstadter, in *The Idea of a Party System,* defends the second one, and James Morton Smith, in *Freedom's Fetters,* the third.

95. Thomas M. Ray, "'Not One Cent for Tribute': The Public Addresses and American Popular Reaction to the XYZ Affair, 1798–1799," *Journal of the Early Republic 3(4)* (winter 1983), 389–412.

96. *The Public Statutes at Large of the United States of America, 1789–1891,* ed. R. Peters (Washington, D.C., 1875–91, 27 vols.), vol. 1, 566–72, 577–78, 596–97.

97. Miller, *Crisis in Freedom,* 50.

98. Frances Sergeant Childs, *French Refugee Life in the United States, 1790–1800: An American Chapter of the French Revolution* (Philadelphia, Pa., 1940, 1978), 188. The émigrés were a mixed group, combining aristocrats who had fled the French Revolution, Saint-Domingue planters who had been dispossessed in the 1791 insurrection or the 1793 capture of Cap Français, and moderates who were trying to escape the Jacobin Terror, such as Talleyrand. Although this population had a strong conservative component, the Federalists disliked the émigrés' internal political quarrels as well as the presence among them of individuals close to the French government (see Childs, *French Refugee Life,* 10, 11, 15, 23, 82,177, 185, 189, 190).

99. Miller, *Crisis in Freedom,* 47.

100. Smith, *Freedom's Fetters,* 22–34, 63–93.

101. Michael Durey, "Thomas Paine's Apostles: Radical Emigrés and the Triumph of Jeffersonian Republicanism," *William and Mary Quarterly,* 3d series, 44(4) (1987).

102. Ibid., 683.

103. Miller, *Crisis in Freedom,* 51. The Act Respecting Alien Enemies only applied in time of war. Even if war broke out, it would be between France and the United States, and English or Irish émigrés would be safe under that act.

104. *Public Statutes at Large,* vol. 1, 571.

105. Ibid., 596.

106. Smith, *Freedom's Fetters,* 83–84.

107. Ibid., 148–49.

108. Cunningham, *The Jeffersonian Republicans,* 116–43.

109. Jefferson, *The Writings,* Ford ed., vol. 7, 289–309.

110. Cunningham, *The Jeffersonian Republicans,* 175–210. See also *Dictionary of American Biography,* vol. 1, ed. Allen Johnson, 463; vol. 5, ed. Allen Johnson and Dumas Malone, 467; vol. 11, ed. Dumas Malone, 533.

111. Miller, *Crisis in Freedom,* 193, 221.

112. Michael H. Hunt, *Ideology and U.S. Foreign Policy* (New Haven, Conn., 1987), 96.

Notes to Chapter 4

1. Appleby, *Capitalism and a New Social Order,* 84.

2. Harold Underwood Faulkner, *Histoire économique des Etats-Unis d'Amérique des Origines jusqu'à nos jours* (Paris, 1958, 2 vols.), vol. 1, 76, 112; McCoy, *The Elusive Republic,* 83–85.

3. John C. Miller, *Origins of the American Revolution* (Boston, Mass., 1943), 482.

4. Paine, *Common Sense,* 40.

5. *Journals of the Continental Congress,* 1774–89 (Washington, D.C.), vol. 5, 768–79. Thomas Paine and the 1776 plan are also quoted by Merrill D. Peterson in "Thomas Jefferson and Commercial Policy: 1783–1793," *William and Mary Quarterly,* 3d series, 22(4) (1965), 588.

6. Vernon G. Setser, *The Commercial Reciprocity Policy of the United States: 1774–1809* (Philadelphia, Pa., 1937), 52.

7. Aside from opening five of its Caribbean ports in 1784 and 1785, as mentioned in the preceding chapter, France had granted the United States commercial advantages regarding imports of flour and other agricultural produce. See Coatsworth, "American Trade with European Colonies," 245, 247.

8. Setser, *Commercial Reciprocity Policy,* 98.

9. *The Federalist,* no. 11, *op. cit.,* 64.

10. Ibid., 66.

11. Setser, *Commercial Reciprocity Policy,* 105.

12. *Annals of Congress,* 1st session, 1st Congress, col. 209.

13. Ibid., col. 209/210.

14. Ibid., col. 214.

15. Ibid., col. 283, 286.

16. Ibid., col. 292, 244.

17. Ibid., col. 290, 292.

18. Ibid., col. 292, 289.

19. Peterson, "Thomas Jefferson and Commercial Policy," 592.

20. Setser, *Commercial Reciprocity Policy,* 83.

21. F. L. Nussbaum, "The French Colonial Arrêt of 1784," *South Atlantic Quarterly,* 27 (1928), 62–78.

22. F. L. Nussbaum, "The Revolutionary Vergennes and Lafayette v. the Farmers General," *Journal of Modern History* 3(4) (1931), 592–604; F. L. Nussbaum, "American Tobacco and French Politics," *Political Science Quarterly,* 40(1) (1925), 497–516.

23. Jefferson, *The Papers,* Boyd ed., vol. 16, 201 (William Short to John Jay, March

3, 1790); Jefferson, *The Writings,* Ford ed., vol. 5, 174 (Thomas Jefferson to Thomas Mann Randolph, May 30, 1790).

24. Jefferson, *The Writings,* Ford ed., vol. 5, 236 (Thomas Jefferson to William Short, August 26, 1790).

25. Jefferson, *The Papers,* Boyd ed., vol. 16, 33, 80, 87, 104, 220 (William Short to John Jay, December 15, 1789; January 2, 6, and 12, 1790; March 9, 1790).

26. Jefferson, *The Writings,* Ford ed., vol. 5, 234 (Thomas Jefferson to William Short, August 26, 1790).

27. Jefferson, *The Papers,* Boyd ed., vol. 16, 269–70 (William Short to John Jay, March 17, 1790); vol. 18, 15 (letter from William Short, November 6, 1790).

28. Ibid., vol. 16, 87 (letter from William Short, January 6, 1790).

29. Ibid., 220 (William Short to John Jay, March 9, 1790).

30. Ibid., vol. 18, 22 (letter from William Short, November 6, 1790).

31. Ibid., 16 (letter from William Short, November 6, 1790); 51 (letter from La Motte, November 9, 1790).

32. Jefferson, *The Writings,* Ford ed., vol. 5, 323 (Thomas Jefferson to the President of the United States, April 24, 1791).

33. Jacob M. Price, *France and the Chesapeake: A History of the French Tobacco Monopoly, 1674–1791, and of Its Relationships to the British and American Tobacco Trades* (Ann Arbor, Mich., 1973, 2 vols.), vol. 2, 787, 822, 832–33, 842.

34. Jefferson, *The Writings,* Ford ed., vol. 5, 346 (Thomas Jefferson to James Madison, June 28, 1791).

35. Jefferson, *The Papers,* Boyd ed., vol. 16, 444 (Thomas Jefferson to William Short, May 27, 1790).

36. Jefferson, *The Writings,* Ford ed., vol. 6, 131 (Thomas Jefferson to Gouverneur Morris, November 7, 1792).

37. Ibid., vol. 5, 420 (Thomas Jefferson to William Short, January 23, 1792); 428 (Thomas Jefferson to Gouverneur Morris, January 23, 1792).

38. Jefferson, *The Papers,* Boyd ed., vol. 16, 601 (Thomas Jefferson to Edward Rutledge, July 4, 1790).

39. *Annals of Congress,* 3d Congress, 1st session, col. 505, 506, 521–22. Congressmen thought first of defense measures, and then endorsed a peace mission.

40. Nelson, *Liberty and Property,* 53, 61.

41. William Appleman Williams, *The Contours of American History* (Cleveland, Ohio, 1961), 155.

42. *Annals of Congress,* 1st Congress, 1st session, col. 214, 253–54, 257.

43. Ibid., col. 245.

44. Ibid.

45. Ibid., col. 257, 246.

46. Ibid., col. 262–64.

47. Ibid., col. 244.

48. Hamilton, *The Works,* Lodge ed., vol. 3, 423–41.

49. McCoy, *The Elusive Republic,* 136; *Annals of Congress,* 3d Congress, 1st session, col. 208.

50. *Annals of Congress,* 3d Congress, 1st session, col. 201, 199.

51. Ibid., col. 227.

52. Ibid., cols. 262, 295, 415.

53. Douglas C. North, *The Economic Growth of the United States: 1790–1860* (1961; New York, 1966), 17. See the chart entitled "Growth of American Foreign Trade."

54. Jensen, *The New Nation,* 194–218.

55. Jefferson, *The Papers,* Boyd ed., vol. 16, 598 (Thomas Jefferson to Francis Eppes, July 4, 1790).

56. Jensen, *The New Nation,* 207; *Annals of Congress,* 1st Congress, 1st session, col. 246.

57. Stuart Bruchey, *The Wealth of the Nation: An Economic History of the United States* (New York, 1988), 27–28.

58. *Annals of Congress,* 3d Congress, 1st session, col. 356.

59. Watts, *The Republic Reborn,* 14, 68.

60. Nelson, *Liberty and Property,* 62.

61. Jefferson, *The Writings,* Ford ed., vol. 5, 364 (Thomas Jefferson to William Short, July 28, 1791).

62. Ibid., 174 (May 30, 1790).

63. Albert K. Weinberg, *Manifest Destiny: A Study of Nationalist Expansionism in American History* (Baltimore, Md., 1935), 14–15. Emer de Vattel opened the section of his book dealing with relations between nations (which today would be called international law) with these words: "Our maxims will seem quite strange to the politics of cabinet. . . . No matter, let us boldly propose what natural law prescribes to nations"; then he denounced colonial expansion: "These ambitious Europeans, who attacked the American nations and subjected them to their greedy domination, so as to civilize them, they said, and to have them instructed in the true religion; these usurpers, I say, based themselves on an equally unjust and ludicrous pretense" (*Le Droit des Gens,* book I, chapter 1, paragraphs 1 and 7). Rousseau, too, condemned the conquest in his *Extrait du Projet de Paix Perpétuelle de Monsieur de l'Abbé de Saint-Pierre:* "Though all the Kings have not yet overcome the folly of conquests, it seems at least that the wiser ones are beginning to perceive that they cost sometimes more than they are worth" (582).

64. Jefferson, *The Writings,* Ford ed., vol. 5, 1744.

65. Jefferson, *The Papers,* Boyd ed., vol. 16, 545 (Edward Rutledge to Thomas Jefferson, June 20, 1790).

66. Ibid., 20–21.

67. Rayford W. Logan, *The Diplomatic Relations of the United States with Haiti, 1776–1891* (Chapel Hill, N.C., 1941), 31; Jefferson, *The Papers,* Boyd ed., vol. 16, 557, and vol. 18, 22.

68. Coatsworth, "American Trade with European Colonies," 246.

69. Richard Van Alstyne, "The Significance of the Mississippi Valley in American

Diplomatic History: 1689–1890," *Mississippi Valley Historical Review,* 36(2) (September 1949), 229.

70. Walter La Feber, "Foreign Policies of a New Nation: Franklin, Madison, and the 'dream of a new land to fulfil with people in self-control' 1750–1804," in *From Colony to Empire: Essays in the History of American Foreign Relations,* ed. William A. Williams (New York, 1972), 14.

71. Van Alstyne, *The Rising American Empire,* 2.

72. Coatsworth, "American Trade with European Colonies," 243.

73. Ibid., 250–51.

74. Arthur P. Whitaker, *The United States and the Independence of Latin America, 1800–1830* (Baltimore, Md., 1941), 4; Coatsworth, "American Trade with European Colonies," 252.

75. Whitaker, *The United States and the Independence of Latin America,* 9–23, esp. 17; 25.

76. Mary Treudley, "The United States and Santo-Domingo: 1789–1866," *Journal of Race Development* 7 (1915–16), 95.

77. Van Alstyne, *The Rising American Empire,* 79.

78. Ibid., 74; Jefferson, *The Papers,* Boyd ed., vol. 16, 566 (D'Estaing to Washington, March 20, 1790).

79. John Breckinridge, Breckinridge Family Papers, Library of Congress, MS., vol. 10, December 13, 1793, quoted by Elise Marienstras, *Naissance de la République Fédérale 1783–1828* (Nancy, 1987), 122–23.

80. Jefferson, *The Writings,* Ford ed., vol. 5, 225.

81. Weinberg, *Manifest Destiny,* 25.

82. Jefferson, *The Writings,* Ford ed., vol. 5, 230 (Remarks on the navigation of the Mississippi for Mr. Carmichael, August 22, 1790).

83. Ibid., 226–27.

84. In *Empire of Liberty: The Statecraft of Thomas Jefferson* (New York, 1990), Robert W. Tucker and David C. Hendrickson also underscore Thomas Jefferson's opposition to traditional diplomacy and his alignment with the ideas of the philosophes (3–17). Seeking to reconcile this aspect of Jeffersonian politics with its expansionist dimension, they see it as a paradox of Jefferson's ideas—peaceful imperialism (3). In fact, although different from mercantilist expansionism, Jefferson's expansionism was nonetheless allied with force and the threat of war, as we have seen. There is no paradox between Jefferson's avowed "pacifism" and his expansionism, as we have just seen in the analysis of the New Orleans affair: indeed, the secretary of state said he would step in merely at the instigation of the people. Such expansionism is quite different from that of the great merchant empires, by virtue of its essentially democratic and popular nature, and not of its form, which remained altogether aggressive. Jefferson's expansionism was modern, not because it relied on a principle of peace, but because it claimed to be inspired by the will of the people.

85. N. S. Shaler, *Kentucky: A Pioneer Commonwealth* (Boston, Mass., 1884), 93, 108.

86. Ray Allen Billington, *Westward Expansion* (New York, 1949), 249.

87. Jefferson, *The Writings,* Ford ed., vol. 5, 298 (Thomas Jefferson to the American chargé d'affaires in Spain, March 12, 1791), 217 (August 2, 1790), and 481 (Report, March 1792).

88. Ibid., 217 (August 2, 1790).

89. Ibid., 219 (Thomas Jefferson to the American chargé d'affaires in France, August 10, 1790).

90. Ibid.

91. Ibid., 471 (Report on negotiations with Spain).

92. *Correspondance Politique* Etats-Unis, vol. 36, folio 490.

93. Ibid.

94. Billington, *Westward Expansion,* 239.

95. *Correspondance Politique* Etats-Unis, vol. 37, folio 99 (excerpt from letter written by General Clark to Citizen Genêt, at Louisville, near the Falls of the Ohio, February 2, 1793).

96. Jefferson, *The Writings,* Ford ed., vol. 6, 206 (March 23, 1793, draft of a letter to the American commissioners in Spain).

97. Ibid., vol. 5, 220 (Thomas Jefferson to the chargé d'affaires in France, August 10, 1790).

98. Gilbert Chinard, *Thomas Jefferson: The Apostle of Americanism* (Boston, Mass., 1939), 207.

99. Van Alstyne, *The Rising American Empire,* 79.

100. Jefferson, *The Writings,* Ford ed., vol. 1, 236 (July 5, 1793).

101. Ibid., vol. 6, 158–59; James P. Ronda, "Dreams and Discoveries: Exploring the American West, 1760–1815," *William and Mary Quarterly,* 3d series, 46(1) (1989), 156.

102. L. S. Kaplan, *Jefferson and France: An Essay on Politics and Political Ideas* (New Haven, Conn., 1967), 56.

103. Jacques Godechot, *La Grande Nation: l'expansion révolutionnaire de la France dans le monde* (Paris, 1956), 66–67. The case was different with the Directory (see chapter 7).

104. Ronda, "Dreams and Discoveries," 153.

105. Jefferson, *The Writings,* Ford ed., vol. 5, 36.

106. *The Federalist,* no. 11, *op. cit.,* 69–70.

107. *Despatches from United States Ministers to Great-Britain,* M30, Roll 5, despatch no. 64 (February 7, 1798).

108. Ibid., despatch no. 65 (February 26, 1798).

109. Ibid., despatch no. 71 (April 6, 1798); *The Life and Correspondence of Rufus King,* ed. Charles R. King (New York, 1894–1900, 6 vols.), vol. 2, 654–56.

110. King, *The Life and Correspondence,* vol. 2, 658 (Alexander Hamilton to Rufus King, August 22, 1798).

111. Ibid.

112. Ibid.; see also 659 (Alexander Hamilton to General Miranda, August 22, 1798).

113. Bryan Edwards, *An Historical Survey of the French Colony in the Island of Santo-Domingo* (London, 1797).

114. *Despatches of United States Ministers to Great-Britain,* M30, Roll 5, despatch no. 12 of December 11, 1798 (Rufus King to Henry Dundas, December 8, 1798); for the text of this convention, see ibid., despatch no. 11 (London, December 7, 1798). See Logan, *The Diplomatic Relations of the United States with Haiti,* 64–65.

115. *Despatches of United States Ministers to Great-Britain,* M30, Roll 5, despatch no. 12 of December 11, 1798 (Rufus King to Henry Dundas, December 8, 1798).

116. Logan, *The Diplomatic Relations of the United States with Haiti,* 73–75.

117. *Despatches of United States Ministers to Great-Britain* M 30, Roll 5, Henry Dundas to Rufus King, December 9, 1798, in despatch no. 12; see also despatch no. 17, January 10, 1799. See Mary Treudley, "The United States and Santo-Domingo," 137.

118. Jefferson, *The Writings,* Washington ed., vol. 8, 2.

119. James Henretta, *The Evolution of American Society: 1700–1815* (Lexington, Mass., 1973), 170; Linda K. Kerber, *Women of the Republic: Intellect and Ideology in Revolutionary America* (New York, 1980, 1986), 92.

Notes to Chapter 5

1. Moreau de Saint-Méry, *Moreau de St Mery's American Journey: 1793–1798,* ed. Kenneth Roberts, trans. Kenneth and Anna M. Roberts (New York, 1947), 269, 273.

2. Willi Paul Adams, ed., "Gouverneur Morris, 'An Address, circa 1800,'" *Amerikastudien/American Studies* 21 (1976), 332–34.

3. Jefferson, *The Papers,* Boyd ed., vol. 18, 301.

4. Morris, *The Diary and Letters,* vol. 1, 329.

5. Ibid., 311.

6. Ibid., 322.

7. Jefferson, *The Papers,* Boyd ed., vol. 18, 292, 295.

8. Ibid., 296.

9. Ibid., 297.

10. Ibid., 304, 305, 300.

11. Morris, *The Diary and Letters,* vol. 1, 488.

12. Ibid., 489.

13. Washington, *The Writings,* Fitzpatrick ed., vol. 33, 335.

14. Ibid., vol. 35, 154.

15. Ibid., vol. 32, 489, 490 (To the Freeholders and other inhabitants of Salem, Massachusetts, June 7, 1793; To the Mechanical Society of Baltimore, Philadelphia, June 7, 1793).

16. Felix Gilbert, *To the Farewell Address: Ideas of Early American Foreign Policy* (Princeton, N.J., 1961), 5.

17. Gilbert Chinard, *Les Origines Historiques de la doctrine de l'isolement aux Etats-Unis* (Paris, 1937), 234, 258, 259.

18. Gilbert, *To the Farewell Address,* 133.

19. Ibid., 115–47.

20. Bailyn, *The Ideological Origins of the American Revolution,* 86–87.

21. Washington, *The Writings,* Fitzpatrick ed., vol. 35, 218, 219, 220, 226, 234. All of the foregoing quotations from the Farewell Address are found in these pages.

22. Chinard, *Les Origines Historiques,* 286.

23. Washington, *The Writings,* Fitzpatrick ed., vol. 35, 231.

24. Dexter Perkins, *A History of the Monroe Doctrine* (Boston, Mass., 1963), 17.

25. Washington, *The Writings,* Fitzpatrick ed., vol. 35, 238.

26. De Conde, *The Quasi-War,* 16.

27. *American State Papers, Foreign Relations,* vol. 1, 40.

28. De Conde, *The Quasi-War,* 23–25.

29. Ibid., 31.

30. *Correspondance Politique* Etats-Unis, vol. 46, despatch no. 1 of 29 brumaire an 5 (November 20, 1796), folio 384.

31. De Conde, *The Quasi-War,* 67–71.

32. *Boston Columbian Centinel,* special issue of April 16, 1798, and *Gazette of the United States,* April 9, 1798.

33. *Gazette of the United States,* April 6, 1798.

34. *Journal of General Marshall at Paris,* November 4, October 27.

35. De Conde, *The Quasi-War,* 58.

36. *Boston Columbian Centinel,* May 5, 1798.

37. Ibid., July 7, 1798.

38. Ibid., May 23, 1798.

39. Ibid., May 26, 1798 ("Answer of the President to the Inhabitants of the city of Hartford").

40. Ibid.

41. De Conde, *The Quasi-War,* 79.

42. Kurtz, *The Presidency of John Adams,* 297.

43. *Boston Columbian Centinel,* August 11, 1798. As we have seen in chapter 3, however, the Republicans tried above all to keep the revolutionary heritage to themselves. Fisher Ames mentioned the erection of a liberty tree by the Republicans in December 1798. See Fisher Ames, *The Works of Fisher Ames,* ed. W. B. Allen (Indianapolis, 1983, 2 vols.), vol. 2, 1303.

44. *Boston Columbian Centinel,* April 1798.

45. Moreau de Saint-Méry, *American Journey,* 253.

46. De Conde, *The Quasi-War,* 95.

47. Ibid., 160.

48. *Despatches from U.S. Ministers to Great-Britain,* M30, Roll no. 5 (January 9–December 22, 1798), Letters from Talleyrand to Gerry, nos. 2, 3, 4, 5, 7, 8.

49. Ibid., despatch no. 95, Margate, September 3, 1798.

50. John Adams, *The Works,* vol. 8, 682 (William Vans Murray to John Adams, July 17, 1798).

51. Ibid., 684 (Talleyrand to Mr. Pichon, July 9, 1798); De Conde, *The Quasi-War,* 153.

52. John Quincy Adams, *The Writings,* vol. II, 347 (John Quincy Adams to William Vans Murray, August 11, 1798)

53. De Conde, *The Quasi-War,* 174.

54. Ames, *The Works,* vol. 2, 1318.

55. Ibid., 1309.

56. Ibid., 1314, 1324.

57. Richard H. Kohn, *Eagle and Sword: The Beginnings of the Military Establishment in America, 1783–1802* (New York, 1975), 248–49. During the 1798 session, when the Sedition Act and other exceptional measures were enacted, Congress had also passed legislation creating a Provisional Army, a New Army, and an Eventual Army. The New Army was to have been set up at once, but for lack of motivated recruits and in the absence of a declaration of war, Alexander Hamilton was unable to turn it into an efficient force. See also Allan Reed Millett and Peter Maslowski, *For the Common Defense: A Military History of the United States of America* (New York, 1984), 96–97.

58. Abigail Adams, *Letters of Mrs. Adams, the Wife of John Adams,* ed. Charles Francis Adams (Boston, Mass., 1841), 238.

59. Kurtz, *The Presidency of John Adams,* 406.

60. Ibid., 404.

61. Jefferson, *The Writings,* Washington ed., vol. 8, 2.

62. De Conde, *The Quasi-War,* 312–13.

63. Jefferson, *The Writings,* Washington, ed., vol. 8, 4.

64. Mercy Otis Warren, *History of the Rise, Progress, and Termination of the American Revolution* (Boston, Mass., 1805), 434.

65. *American State Papers, Indian Affairs,* vol. 1, 544, 543.

66. Reginald Horsman, *Expansion and American Indian Policy: 1783–1812* (East Lansing, Mich., 1969), 57.

67. *American State Papers, Indian Affairs,* vol. 1, 12–14, 52–54.

68. Henry Knox, *American State Papers, Indian Affairs,* vol. 1, 543; Reginald Horsman, *Expansion,* 57–58, 53.

69. Bernard W. Sheehan, *Seeds of Extinction: Jeffersonian Philanthropy and the American Indian* (New York, 1973, 1974), 325.

70. George Washington, *The Writings,* Fitzpatrick ed., vol. 30, 306–7.

71. Nelcya Delanoë, *L'Entaille Rouge: terres indiennes et démocratie américaine* (Paris, 1982), 47, stresses the fact that George Washington speculated on western lands and links the moderation of his ideas toward the Indians to his accession to the presidency.

72. *American State Papers, Indian Affairs,* vol. 1, 142 (December 29, 1790), 144 (January 19, 1791).

73. Ibid., 248; George Washington, *The Writings,* Fitzpatrick ed., vol. 31, 199.

74. Ibid., vol. 35, 233–34.

75. "Message from the President of the U.S. to the Delegation from the Five Nations of Indians in Philadelphia, 25th April, 1792," *American State Papers, Indian Affairs,* vol. 1, 231.

76. Ibid., lxxii, lxxiii.

77. F. P. Prucha, *The Great Father: The United States Government and the American Indians* (Lincoln, Nebr., 1984, 1986), 21, explains that although treaties signed with Native American tribes had the same legal status as those signed with foreign nations, the similarity should not be overstated; whether the tribes accepted this freely or were forced into it, they actually acknowledged in the treaties a degree of dependence on the United States and consequently a decrease in their sovereignty.

78. *American State Papers, Indian Affairs,* vol. 1, 13; see also George Washington's message to the Senate, in *The Writings,* Fitzpatrick ed., vol. 30, 385.

79. Horsman, *Expansion,* 72, 74.

80. Katharine C. Turner, *Red Men Calling on the Great White Father* (Norman, Okla., 1951), xiv.

81. Ibid., 5, 8, 16.

82. Washington, *The Writings,* Fitzpatrick ed., vol. 32, 62.

83. *American State Papers, Indian Affairs,* vol. 1, 248, 249, 488.

84. Ibid., 429.

85. Horsman, *Expansion,* 77, 76.

86. Ibid., 60.

87. *American State Papers, Indian Affairs,* vol. 1, 13.

88. Ibid., 204 (January 9, 1792).

89. Ibid., 411.

90. George Washington, *The Writings,* Fitzpatrick ed., vol. 31, 267, 273, 274; vol. 32, 338.

91. Ibid., vol. 33, 448; vol. 31, 99, 184.

92. Ibid., vol. 30, 431; vol. 32, 449; vol. 33, 188.

93. Ibid., vol. 33, 188; vol. 31, 166.

94. Ibid., vol. 31, 166.

95. James Paul Pate, *The Chickamauga, A Forgotten Segment of Indian Resistance on the Southern Frontier,* Ph.D. diss., Mississippi State University, 1969, 189; *American State Papers, Indian Affairs,* vol. 1, 262.

96. Washington, *The Writings,* Fitzpatrick ed., vol. 30, 406–7.

97. *American State Papers, Indian Affairs,* vol. 1, 59.

98. Prucha, *The Great Father,* 20.

99. Jefferson, *The Writings,* Ford ed., vol. 5, 321 (April 17, 1791).

100. Kohn, *Eagle and Sword,* 126, 125, 137.

101. Ibid., 186.

102. Irwin, *Diplomatic Relations,* 1–13. For the political and economic situation of the regencies at the end of the eighteenth century, see R. F. Nyrop, ed., *Algeria: A Country*

Study (Washington, D.C., 1979), 22–29, and *Libya: A Country Study* (Washington, D.C., 1979), 19–23.

103. A. B. C. Whipple, *To the Shores of Tripoli: The Birth of the U.S. Navy and Marines* (New York, 1991), 25–26.

104. Ibid., 37–45.

105. Jefferson, *The Papers,* Boyd ed., vol. 18, 423–25, 430–35.

106. Irwin, *Diplomatic Relations,* 55, 57–60.

107. Whipple, *To the Shores,* 43–44.

108. Dudley W. Knox, *A History of the United States Navy* (New York, 1936), 60. See also Whipple, *To the Shores,* 41–50.

109. Ulane Bonnel, *La France, les Etats-Unis et la guerre de course (1797–1815)* (Paris, 1961), 98.

Notes to Chapter 6

1. This expression was used by James Monroe in a letter to James Madison on May 6, 1804, in Monroe, *The Writings,* vol. 4, 185.

2. Among many specialized studies, special mention may be made of Winthrop Jordan, *White Over Black: American Attitudes Toward the Negro, 1550–1812* (New York, 1968, 1977), 34. This general thesis on slavery and the revolution has not yet been seriously challenged, although it is worth mentioning; for an opposing view, See Patricia Bradley, *Slavery, Propaganda, and the American Revolution* (Jackson: University Press of Mississippi, 1998).

3. Thomas Jefferson, *Notes on the State of Virginia,* ed. William Peden (1787; New York, 1982), 162–63.

4. Ibid., 162–63.

5. Jordan, *White Over Black,* 325.

6. Jacques Thibau, *Le Temps de Saint-Domingue: l'esclavage et la révolution française* (Paris, 1989), 189–90.

7. Ibid., 72: "Without its possessions in the Caribbean, France would not have balanced its trade and would have lost some of its wealth every year. Its foreign trade increased from 600 million pounds in 1750 to 1.153 billion in 1787. France was now on a par with the most commercially powerful country, England."

8. C. L. R. James, *The Black Jacobins: Toussaint Louverture and the San Domingo Revolution,* 2d ed. (New York, 1963), ix.

9. Ibid., 251–58.

10. Orlando Patterson, "The General Causes of Jamaican Slave Revolts," in *American Slavery: The Question of Resistance,* ed. John H. Bracey Jr., August Meier, and Elliott Rudwick (Belmont, Calif., 1971), 193–200.

11. Peter H. Wood, *Black Majority: Negroes in Colonial South Carolina from 1670 through the Stono Rebellion* (New York, 1974, 1975).

12. Jordan, *White Over Black,* 113.

13. Bryan Edwards, *Historical Survey,* xx. In *The Problem of Slavery in the Age of Revolution: 1770–1823* (Ithaca, N.Y., 1975), 185, David Brion Davis puts Bryan Edwards, Moreau de Saint-Méry, and Thomas Jefferson on the same level. But Bryan Edwards, like the Federalists whom Linda Kerber has analyzed, was on the margins of the dominant liberal ideology, and therefore in a better position to observe its contradictions.

14. Jordan, *White Over Black,* 378.

15. Timothy M. Mathewson, "George Washington's Policy Toward the Haitian Revolution," *Diplomatic History,* 3, no. 3 (1979), 321.

16. Washington, *The Writings,* Fitzpatrick ed., vol. 31, 375 (September 24, 1791).

17. Davis, *The Problem of Slavery,* 73–74, 148; Robert Debs Heinl Jr., and Nancy Gordon Heinl, *Written in Blood: The Story of the Haitian People, 1492–1971* (Boston, Mass., 1978), 60.

18. Davis, *The Problem of Slavery,* 148. See also Lucien Abénon, Jacques Cauna, and Liliane Chauleau, *La Révolution aux Caraïbes* (Paris, 1989), 95.

19. Jordan, *White Over Black,* 327.

20. Alfred N. Hunt, *Haiti's Influence on Antebellum America: Slumbering Volcano in the Caribbean* (Baton Rouge, La., 1988), 85.

21. Ibid., 2, 115.

22. This follows the argument presented by Edmund S. Morgan in *American Slavery, American Freedom: The Ordeal of Colonial Virginia* (New York, 1975). Of special relevance are the questions raised in the conclusion: Was America "Virginian"? Had Virginia continued importing white servants, would they have gone to the North after they were freed, thereby taking serious poverty there? Would northerners have been so prone to embrace ideas of equality if they had been surrounded by poor freemen (386–87)?

23. Klein, *The Unification of a Slave State,* 234–35. Throughout the South, laws were passed to forbid the landing of blacks coming from the French islands; see Michael Zuckerman, "The Power of Blackness: Thomas Jefferson and the Revolution in Saint-Domingue," in *Almost Chosen People: Oblique Biographies in the American Grain* (Berkeley, Calif., 1993).

24. Logan, *The Diplomatic Relations of the United States with Haiti,* 53, 61–63.

25. For a biography of Toussaint-Louverture, see Pierre Pluchon, *Toussaint Louverture* (Paris, 1989).

26. Logan, *The Diplomatic Relations of the United States with Haiti,* 103–9.

27. Ibid., 110–11.

28. Ibid., 89. This interpretation differs from that of Linda K. Kerber, *Federalists in Dissent: Imagery and Ideology in Jeffersonian America* (Ithaca, N.Y., 1970), who holds that the Federalists did not look unfavorably on the island's independence, and that once Thomas Jefferson came into office American policy toward Saint-Domingue radically changed (45–47). This interpretation is not confirmed by the study of diplomatic sources.

29. Ibid.

30. *Correspondance Politique,* Etats-Unis, vol. 53, folio 105.

31. Ibid., folio 170.

32. Ibid., folio 434.

33. Ibid., vol. 54, folios 66–67.

34. Jean Martin, "Colonies," in *Dictionnaire Napoléon,* ed. Jean Tulard (Paris, Fayard: 1989), 437–38.

35. *Correspondance Politique* Etats-Unis, vol. 54, folios 21, 254, 304. On the expedition's goals, see Yves Benot, *La démence coloniale sous Napoléon,* (Paris, 1992), 21, 22, 26, 57; and Henri Mézière, *Le général Leclerc (1772–1802) et l'expédition de Saint-Domingue* (Paris, 1990), 124.

36. *Correspondance Politique* Etats-Unis, vol. 55, folio 188.

37. Ibid., vol. 56, folios 56, 92, 95.

38. Ibid., folio 363.

39. Ibid., vol. 57, folio 59.

40. Ibid., folio 80.

41. Alfred N. Hunt, *Haiti's Influence,* 36.

42. Joseph Cephas Carroll, *Slave Insurrections in the United States, 1800–1865* (New York, 1938), 44–71.

43. Ibid., 50.

44. Monroe, *The Writings,* vol. 3, 329 (January 16, 1802).

45. Jordan, *White Over Black,* 382–83.

46. *Annals of Congress,* 8th Congress, 1st session, 995.

47. Ibid.

48. E. S. Brown, ed., "Documents. The Senate Debate on the Breckinridge Bill for the Government of Louisiana, 1804," *American Historical Review* 12(2) (1917), 347.

49. Ibid., 347.

50. Ibid., 354.

51. Davis, *The Problem of Slavery,* 149.

52. Ibid., 1070.

53. The only clues showing that Jefferson and Madison were interested in Haiti at this time are in the dispatches of Pichon, the chargé d'affaires in Washington, with whom the two men had long and stormy meetings. See, for a similar conclusion, Logan, *The Diplomatic Relations of the United States with Haiti,* 70, 154. The very fact that these dispatches are the main source of information on foreign policy in that period reveals the administration's increasing silence.

54. Monroe, *The Writings,* vol. 4, 185.

55. Heinl and Heinl, *Written in Blood,* 122.

56. Logan, *The Diplomatic Relations of the United States with Haiti,* 148–54.

57. David Barry Gaspar, *Bondmen and Rebels: A Study of Master-Slave Relations in Antigua with Implications for Colonial British America* (Baltimore, Md., 1985), 185.

58. *Aurora* (March 28, 1804): 182

59. Heinl and Heinl, *Written in Blood,* 134; M. Bouchary, ed., *La Déclaration des droits de l'Homme et du Citoyen et la Constitution de 1791* (Paris, 1946), 14, Articles I and II.

60. The *Richmond Enquirer* had been created at the behest of President Jefferson.

61. The *Raleigh Register and North Carolina Gazette* was published by Joseph Gales, who had been a popular figure with the workers of northern England and yet had had to leave for America. In 1799 he founded the *Raleigh Register,* a pro-Jeffersonian paper. For David Brion Davis, he was one of those men who had no qualms about the contradictions of American democracy; see *The Problem of Slavery,* 185.

62. Alfred N. Hunt, *Haiti's Influence,* 84–101.

63. Logan, *The Diplomatic Relations of the United States with Haiti,* 152–53.

64. Ibid., 156–57.

65. Ibid., 168.

66. Jefferson, *The Writings,* Ford ed., vol. 8, 325, 326.

67. Logan, *The Diplomatic Relations of the United States with Haiti,* 171.

68. Jefferson, *The Writings,* Ford ed., vol. 8, 423 (Thomas Jefferson to John Armstrong, February 14, 1806).

69. Logan, *The Diplomatic Relations of the United States with Haiti,* 171, 173, 174, 176–77.

70. Ibid., 179.

71. Jefferson, *The Writings,* Ford ed., vol. 8, 376 (Thomas Jefferson to James Madison, August 25, 1805). At that time, Jefferson wanted an alliance with Great Britain against France.

72. J. P. Parry, Philip Sherlock, and Anthony Maingot, *A Short History of the West Indies,* 4th ed. (New York, 1987), 146.

73. Logan, *The Diplomatic Relations of the United States with Haiti,* 180.

74. North, *The Economic Growth of the United States,* 231.

75. Letter from General Turreau to the Secretary of State, October 14, 1805, published in the *Richmond Enquirer* on January 21, 1806. The Senate debate was also published in the newspaper.

76. *Richmond Enquirer,* January 4, 1806.

77. Ibid., January 11, 1806.

78. Ibid., January 2, 1806.

79. Ibid., January 11, 1806.

80. *Annals of Congress,* 9th Congress, 1st session, 125.

81. Kerber, *Federalists in Dissent,* x.

82. *Annals of Congress,* 9th Congress, 1st session, 125, 132–33.

83. Kerber, *Federalists in Dissent,* 62.

84. Jordan, *White Over Black,* 331.

85. *The Public Statutes at Large,* vol. 2, 351.

86. Ibid.

Notes to Chapter 7

1. James Fenimore Cooper, *The Prairie* (1827; New York, 1964), 9.

2. Aimé Césaire, *Discours sur le Colonialisme* (Paris, 1950), 12.

3. Marshall Sprague, *So Vast, So Beautiful a Land: Louisiana and the Purchase* (Boston, Mass., 1974), 180.

4. Godechot, *La Grande Nation,* 62, 66, 72–73.

5. Michaël Garnier, "Louisiane," in *Dictionnaire Napoléon,* 1092, and *Histoire diplomatique de la France en Amérique du Nord (Louisiane), 1800–1803,* unpublished Ph.D. dissertation, EPHE, Université Paris 4, 1984, 48.

6. Moreau de Saint-Méry, *Voyage aux Etats-Unis d'Amérique: 1793–1798* ed. Stewart L. Mims (New Haven, Conn., 1913), 224. See Paul Lachance, "The 1809 Immigration of Saint-Domingue Refugees to New Orleans," *Louisiana History* 29(2) (1988), 109–41.

7. Gilbert Chinard, *Volney et l'Amérique, d'après des documents inédits et sa correspondance avec Jefferson* (Baltimore, Md., 1923), 43.

8. Ibid., 44.

9. *Correspondance Politique* Etats-Unis, vol. 46, folio 65, Philadelphia, 3 messidor an 4 (June 21, 1796).

10. Durand Echeverria, ed., "General Collot's Plan for a Reconnaissance of the Ohio and Mississippi Valleys, 1796," *William and Mary Quarterly,* 3d series, 9 (1952), 513–19.

11. Chinard, *Volney et l'Amérique,* 43–47, 63.

12. James Madison, *The Writings of James Madison,* ed. Gaillard Hunt (New York, 1900–1910, 9 vols.), vol. 6, 434; Jefferson, *The Writings,* Ford ed., vol. 8, 58.

13. *Correspondance Politique* Etats-Unis, vol. 53, folio 117, 11 floréal an 9 (May 1, 1801).

14. Ibid., folios 171–73, 1er thermidor an 9 (July 20, 1801).

15. Jefferson, *The Papers,* series 1, Manuscript Division, Library of Congress, vol. 28 (William Dunbar to Thomas Jefferson, Natchez, June 10, 1803).

16. Jefferson, *The Writings,* Ford ed., vol. 8, 105 (Thomas Jefferson to Robert R. Livingston, Washington, April 18, 1802).

17. *Correspondance Politique* Etats-Unis, vol. 53, folio 437, Georgetown, 12 frimaire an 10 (December 3, 1801).

18. Jefferson, *The Writings,* Ford ed., vol. 8, 145 (Thomas Jefferson to Robert R. Livingston, Washington, April 18, 1802).

19. François Barbé-Marbois, *The History of Louisiana, Particularly of the cession of that colony to the United States of America,* trans. from the French 1828 edition (Baton Rouge, La., 1977), 184–200. Barbé-Marbois makes an attractive case for linking the two projects within one inclusive American ambition, unlike recent works by French historians investigating Napoleon's colonial policy. Yves Bénot, *La démence coloniale sous Napoléon,* 102, does not elaborate on the idea of a link between the two expeditions; Pierre Pluchon, *Histoire de la colonisation française,* vol. 1 (Paris, 1991), 914, merely observes that "the sale of Louisiana . . . made official, without saying as much, the failure of the Saint-Domingue expedition"; Martin, in *L'Empire Renaissant,* 74, does not directly link the failure to reconquer Saint-Domingue to the sale of Louisiana. Louisiana was indeed part of Bonaparte's general plan to reconstitute the French Empire

as it had been until the various losses of the eighteenth century; but nothing seems to substantiate Barbé-Marbois's statements.

20. Jefferson, *The Writings,* Ford ed., vol. 8, 145 (Thomas Jefferson to Robert R. Livingston, Washington, April 18, 1802).

21. Jefferson, *The Papers,* series 1, vol. 26 (Pierre-Samuel Dupont de Nemours to Thomas Jefferson, April 30, 1802; Thomas Jefferson to Pierre-Samuel Dupont de Nemours, April 25, 1802).

22. Madison, *The Writings,* vol. 6, 452 (James Madison to Robert L. Livingston, May 1, 1802); 455 (James Madison to Charles Pinckney, May 11, 1802); 460 (James Madison to Charles Pinckney, October 15, 1802).

23. Jefferson, *The Writings,* Ford ed., vol. 8, 173 (Thomas Jefferson to Robert R. Livingston, October 10, 1802).

24. Henry Adams, *History of the United States of America During the Administrations of Thomas Jefferson* (New York, 1889–91, 1986), 282.

25. This is Article 22 of the Treaty of Friendship, Limits, and Navigation Between Spain and the United States, signed October 27, 1795: " . . . And in consequence of the stipulations contained in the IV article, His Catholic Majesty will permit the citizens of the United States, for the space of three years from this time, to deposit their merchandise and effects in the port of New Orleans, and to export them from thence without paying any other duty than a fair price for the hire of the stores; and His Majesty promises, either to continue this permission, if he finds during that time that it is not prejudicial to the interests of Spain, or if he should not agree to continue it there, he will assign to them on another part of the banks of Mississippi an equivalent establishment" (*Treaties and Conventions,* 1014).

26. *Correspondance Politique* Etats-Unis, vol. 54, folios 254, 411, and 412 (7 germinal an 10 [March 28, 1802] and 12 messidor an 10 [July 1, 1802]); vol. 55, folio 23 (24 vendémiaire an 11 [October 16, 1802]). In the latter dispatch, especially, Pichon wrote: "It is unquestionable . . . that this government is beginning not only to doubt our feelings of friendship, but even to suppose we have contrary ones."

27. Jefferson, *The Writings,* Ford ed., vol. 8, 190 (Thomas Jefferson to the special envoy in France, James Monroe, January 13, 1803); Madison, *The Writings,* vol. 6, 462 (James Madison to Charles Pinckney, November 27, 1802).

28. *New York Evening Post,* January 12, 1803.

29. Ibid., January 24–28, 1803.

30. *Charleston Courier,* January 15, 1803.

31. *Annals of the Congress of the United States,* 7th Congress, 2d session, 186, 204.

32. *Correspondance Politique* Etats-Unis, vol. 54, folio 412, le 18 messidor an 10 (July 7, 1802).

33. Jefferson, *The Writings,* Ford ed., vol. 8, 207 (Thomas Jefferson to Dupont de Nemours, February 1, 1803).

34. Madison, *The Writings,* vol. 7, 35 (James Madison to Charles Pinckney, March 8, 1803).

35. Jefferson, *The Writings,* Ford ed., vol. 8, 229 (Thomas Jefferson to John Bacon, April 30, 1803).

36. Ibid., 188 (Thomas Jefferson to James Monroe, January 10, 1803).

37. *Correspondance Politique* Etats-Unis, vol. 55, folio 186, 1er pluviôse an 11 (January 21, 1803).

38. *Tennessee Gazette,* January 29 and February 23, 1803.

39. *Correspondance Politique* Etats-Unis, vol. 55, folio 436: prairial an 11 (May–June 1803).

40. Barbé-Marbois, *History of Louisiana,* 261–77.

41. Jefferson, *The Writings,* Ford ed., vol. 8, 105.

42. "Reflections on Political Economy and the Prospect before Us. Addressed to the Citizens of the Western Country. No. 1," *Tennessee Gazette,* September 28, 1803 (from the *Kentucky Gazette*).

43. Jefferson, *The Papers,* series 1, vol. 29 (Message to the Senate and the House of Representatives, October 17, 1803).

44. Barbé-Marbois, *History of Louisiana,* 358.

45. Alexander McKenzie, *Voyages from Montreal on the River St Laurence, through the Continent of North America, to the Frozen and Pacific Oceans, in the Years 1789 and 1793* (London, 1801), 411.

46. Donald Jackson, *Thomas Jefferson and the Stony Mountains: Exploring the West from Monticello* (Urbana, Ill., 1987), 94–96.

47. Ibid., 124.

48. Donald Jackson, ed., *Letters of the Lewis and Clark Expedition, with Related Documents, 1783–1854* (Urbana, Ill., 1962), 32 (Albert Gallatin to Thomas Jefferson, March 13, 1803; also see Jefferson, *The Papers, op. cit.*).

49. Jackson, *Letters of the Lewis and Clark Expedition,* 26 (Edward Thornton to Lord Hawkesbury, March 9, 1803, Public Record Office).

50. Ibid., 5 (Carlo Martinez de Yrujo to Pedro Cevallos, December 2, 1802, Archivo Historica Nacional, Madrid).

51. Ibid., 12–13 ("Jefferson's Message to Congress," "Confidential," January 18, 1803).

52. Jackson, *Stony Mountains,* 128.

53. Barbé-Marbois, *History of Louisiana,* 358.

54. Warren L. Cook, *Flood Tide of Empire: Spain and the Pacific Northwest, 1543–1819* (New Haven, Conn., 1973), 41, 43, 47.

55. David J. Weber, *The Spanish Frontier in North America* (New Haven, Conn.: Yale University Press, 1992), 236–37.

56. Cook, *Flood Tide of Empire,* 55, 69–80, 85, 87, 100.

57. Ibid., 136–39, 146–99.

58. For a detailed analysis of this controversy from the viewpoint of French diplomacy, see the Ph.D. dissertation of Annick Foucrier, *La France, les Français et la Californie avant la ruée vers l'or (1786–1848),* Paris, E.H.E.S.S., 1991, especially chapter 10, 601–5.

59. Martens, *Traités,* Supplement 3.

60. Cook, *Flood Tide of Empire,* 323.

61. Weber, *The Spanish Frontier in North America,* 264–65, 288–89.

62. In 1794 the Missouri Company had been formed in Upper Louisiana for the purpose of going up the Missouri and reaching the Pacific, while trading with the Native American nations of the area. After several failed attempts, the Missouri Company had to give up these goals. See David Lavender, *The Way to the Western Sea: Lewis and Clark Across the Continent* (New York, 1988), 80–85.

63. Cook, *Flood Tide of Empire,* 427, 434, 437–41.

64. Jackson, *Stony Mountains,* 125.

65. Jefferson, *The Writings,* Ford ed., vol. 8, 194, 197 ("Instructions to Lewis"). Lewis and Clark would not need a Spanish passport, since they only crossed the Missouri after the transfer of sovereignty, in the spring of 1804. Then they dispensed with a passport of any kind to reach the Northwestern Coast, which was claimed by Spain.

66. Ibid., 197 (Thomas Jefferson to Caspar Wistar, February 28, 1803).

67. Joseph Kastner, *A Species of Eternity* (New York, 1977), 128.

68. Jefferson, *The Writings,* Ford ed., vol. 8, 195–99 ("Instructions to Lewis").

69. Jefferson, *The Papers,* series 1, vol. 30 (Thomas Jefferson to William Dunbar, April 15, 1804).

70. William Dunbar, *Life, Letters and Papers of William Dunbar, 1749–1810,* ed. Eron Dunbar Rowland (Jackson, Miss., 1930), 9–13.

71. Jackson, *Stony Mountains,* 225; Jackson, *Letters of the Lewis and Clark Expedition,* 200–201 (Thomas Jefferson to the Osages, July 16, 1804, Washington).

72. William Dunbar, *Documents Relating to the Purchase and Exploration of Louisiana* (Boston, Mass., 1904), 165.

73. Jefferson, *The Writings,* Ford ed., vol. 8, 196.

74. Dunbar, *Documents,* 13.

75. Jackson, *Stony Mountains,* 230.

76. Cook, *Flood Tide of Empire,* 460–86. Having not been renewed in his position as vice president in 1804, Aaron Burr had thereafter thrown himself into a conspiracy that was based in New Orleans. His plan apparently was to separate the western states from the Union, and/or to "liberate" Mexico; see Thomas P. Abernethy, *The Burr Conspiracy* (New York, 1954), 193. Abernethy seems to think that the Spanish believed for the longest time that Burr's sole goal was to divide the American republic. Yet Spanish concerns were made clear in October 1805, when soldiers coming from New Spain crossed the Sabine, which was the border between Texas and the United States. It is certain that by 1806 the Spanish were on their guard, for by then they had heard that an expedition was under way in Kentucky to attack Mexico. During the summer and fall of 1806, the Spanish were in a state of high military alert in West Florida and in Texas. See *Burr Conspiracy,* 32, 34, 51.

77. Jackson, *Stony Mountains,* 231, 232.

78. According to Jackson, Zebulon Pike had probably gotten lost (*Stony Mountains,* 253), but Cook reckons that the activities of Wilkinson, Pike's superior, were dubious at

best (*Flood Tide of Empire,* 486); this is consistent with Pike's orders, as cited by Abernethy, which clearly show that Pike was supposed to enter Spanish territory (*Burr Conspiracy,* 119).

79. Jackson, *Letters of the Lewis and Clark Expedition,* 217, 218 (Constantin Samuel Rafinesque to Thomas Jefferson, November 27, 1804, Colonial Williamsburg Library). Chinard, *Volney et l'Amérique,* 167 (Volney to Thomas Jefferson, May 7, 1804).

80. *Richmond Enquirer,* August 1 and September 29, 1804.

81. Ibid., February 14, 1805.

82. Lavender, *The Way to the Western Sea,* 76, 90–91, 101–2.

83. *Richmond Enquirer,* July 4, 1805. See also Marienstras, *Les Mythes fondateurs,* 184–208.

84. *Richmond Enquirer,* July 18, 1804.

85. Kastner, *A Species of Eternity,* 153.

86. *Richmond Enquirer,* May 17, 1805.

87. Thomas Jefferson, ed., *Message from the President of the United States, communicating Discoveries made in exploring the Missouri, Red River and Washita by Captains Lewis and Clark, Doctor Sibley and Mr. Dunbar . . . ,* Washington, 1806.

88. Jackson, *Stony Mountains,* 248.

89. Jefferson, *The Writings,* Ford ed., vol. 8, 492.

90. Jackson, *Letters of the Lewis and Clark Expedition,* 338 (Citizens of Fincastle to Lewis and Clark, January 8, 1807, Missouri Historical Society Library, St. Louis).

91. Nicholas Biddle, ed., *History of the expedition under the command of Captain Lewis and Clark, to the sources of the Missouri, thence across the Rocky Mountains and down the river Columbia to the Pacific Ocean* (Philadelphia, Pa., 1814).

92. Jackson, *Letters of the Lewis and Clark Expedition,* 361 (Jefferson to Jonathan Williams and Charles Willson Peale, January 12, 1807).

93. Barbé-Marbois, *History of Louisiana,* 359–60.

94. *Treaties and Conventions,* 331.

95. Sprague, *So vast, so beautiful a land,* 181–83 (including map on 182).

96. Barbé-Marbois, *History of Louisiana,* 286.

97. Jefferson, *The Papers,* series 1, vol. 28 (Robert R. Livingston to James Monroe, Paris, May 23, 1803).

98. Irving Brant, *James Madison: Secretary of State, 1800–1809* (Indianapolis, 1953), 149.

99. Henry Adams, *History of the United States of America During the Administrations of Thomas Jefferson,* 349–50.

100. Madison, *The Writings,* vol. 7, 170 (James Monroe to Robert R. Livingston).

101. Jefferson, *The Papers,* series 1, vol. 29 (September 7, 1803).

102. Madison, *The Writings,* vol. 7, 57–58 (James Madison to James Monroe, July 29, 1803).

103. Madison, *The Writings,* vol. 7, 54.

104. Henry Adams, *History of the United States of America During the Administrations of Thomas Jefferson,* 467–79.

105. This act authorized the president of the United States to set up as a separate district the coasts, waters, and coves of the Mobile Bay and River as well as those of other rivers and watercourses flowing into the Gulf of Mexico east of the Mobile River, and to choose a place in that district to become the entry port into it (see *Statutes at Large,* vol. 2, 254.)

106. Pierre-Clément de Laussat, *Memoirs of My Life,* trans. from the French 1831 edition (Baton Rouge, La., 1978), 88.

107. Jefferson, *The Writings,* Ford ed., vol. 8, 328 (Fourth Annual Message).

108. Madison, *The Writings,* vol. 7, 149 (James Madison to James Monroe, April 15, 1804).

109. Ibid., 141. (James Monroe to James Madison, April 15, 1804).

110. Clifford L. Egan, *Neither Peace nor War: Franco-American Relations, 1803–1812* (Baton Rouge, La., 1983), 147.

111. Jefferson, *The Writings,* Ford ed., vol. 8, 374, 376, 377, 379, 380 (Thomas Jefferson to James Madison, August 4, 1805; Thomas Jefferson to Albert Gallatin, August 7, 1805; Thomas Jefferson to James Madison, August 27, September 16, and October 11, 1805).

112. Ibid., 397–402 (confidential message regarding Spain).

113. Henry Adams, *History of the United States of America During the Administrations of Thomas Jefferson,* 674–703.

114. Jefferson, *The Writings,* Ford ed., vol. 9, 40 (Thomas Jefferson to James Bowdoin, April 2, 1807); 124 (Thomas Jefferson to James Madison, August 16, 1807).

115. Ibid., vol. 8, 433 (Thomas Jefferson to William Duane, March 22, 1806).

116. Whitaker, *The United States and the Independence of Latin America,* 61–70.

117. Bemis, *The American Secretaries of State,* vol. 3, 187.

118. Henry Adams, *History of the United States of America During the Administrations of James Madison* (New York, 1890, 1921), vol. 1, 307, 310, 326, 327.

119. Jefferson, *The Papers,* series 1, vol. 27, November 3, 1802.

120. Horsman, *Expansion,* 104–14. While Jefferson's thinking about Native Americans was often "ambivalent," it is impossible, however, to join in with Richard Drinnon's radical condemnation in *Facing West: The Metaphysics of Indian-hating and Empire-building* (New York, 1980), 96, where the author refuses to believe in Thomas Jefferson's authentic desire to help, and sees his philanthropy as masking a will to exterminate Native Americans. Conversely, one finds an overly optimistic vision of the relations between Jefferson and Native Americans in Claude Fohlen, *Thomas Jefferson* (Nancy, 1992), 122, 132.

121. Jefferson, *The Papers,* series 1, vol. 27 (February 16, 1803).

122. Horsman, *Expansion,* 119.

123. Jefferson, *The Papers,* series 1, vol. 27 (Thomas Jefferson to Cornplanter, Stinking Fish [. . .], February 11, 1803; Thomas Jefferson to the Seneca, Oneida, Onondaga nations, February 14, 1803).

124. Ibid. (Thomas Jefferson to Handsome Lake, November 3, 1802).

125. Horsman, *Expansion,* 151–53.

126. Jefferson, *The Writings,* Ford ed., vol. 8, 345.

127. Marienstras, *Les Mythes fondateurs,* 212: "For the organic character that was proclaimed and demanded for the future was defined according to the norm that issued from the British, Protestant majority, and which was then legitimately presented as 'natural.'"

128. *The Federalist,* no. 2, *op. cit.,* 7.

129. Jefferson, *The Papers,* series 1, vol. 29 (William Charles Coles Claiborne to Thomas Jefferson, Natchez, September 29, 1803; William Dunbar to Thomas Jefferson, January 16, 1804).

130. Ibid. (W. C. Claiborne to Thomas Jefferson, January 16, 1804). See also Ronald Creagh, *Nos Cousins d'Amérique: Histoire des Français aux Etats-Unis* (Paris, 1988), 238–40, for an analysis of the tense relations between the two communities after 1803.

131. Lewis William Newton, *The Americanization of French Louisiana* (New York, 1980), 17, 39–69.

132. *Treaties and Conventions,* 332.

133. Jefferson, *The Writings,* Ford ed., vol. 8, 250–51 (Thomas Jefferson to Horatio Gates, July 11, 1803).

134. Jefferson, *The Papers,* series 1, vol. 30 (Jean-Etienne Boré, Mayor of New Orleans, to Thomas Jefferson, February 20, 1804).

135. Newton, *The Americanization of French Louisiana,* 50–55, 65–68.

136. *Charleston Courier,* February 11, 1802: "An address by John Quincy Adams, delivered at Plymouth, Massachusetts."

Notes to Chapter 8

1. Franck C. Bowen, *America Sails the Seas* (New York, 1938), 192–95.

2. Larbi Mohamed Moncef, *La Jeune République Américaine face aux puissances barbaresques 1783–1830,* Ph.D. dissertation, Université Paris 7, 1981, 188–95.

3. Nyrop, *Algeria,* 27.

4. *Pennsylvania Gazette,* May 23, 1804; *Aurora,* May 17, 21, 22, 23, and 24, 1804.

5. *Aurora,* March 28 and May 23, 1804.

6. Ibid.

7. Donald H. Mugridge, ed., *Album of American Battle Art* (Washington, D.C., 1947), 73–75.

8. Marienstras, *Nous, le peuple,* 95.

9. *Boston Columbian Centinel,* July 8, 1807.

10. Stephen Howarth, *To the Shining Sea: A History of the United States Navy, 1775–1991* (New York, 1991), 85.

11. L. S. Kaplan, *Entangling Alliances with None: American Foreign Policy in the Age of Jefferson* (Kent, Ohio, 1987), 106.

12. James Stephen, *War in Disguise; or, the Frauds of the Neutral Flags* (London, 1805), 22.

13. Ibid.

14. Bemis, *The American Secretaries of State,* vol. 2, 108.

15. Bradford Perkins, *Prologue to War: England and the United States, 1805–1812* (Berkeley, Calif., 1963), 79.

16. Stephen, *War in Disguise,* 49.

17. Perkins, *The First Rapprochement,* 174.

18. Monroe, *The Writings,* vol. 4, 152 (James Monroe to Thomas Jefferson, March 15, 1804).

19. Ibid., 156.

20. Ibid.

21. *Aurora,* August 25, 1804. See also the issues of June 26 and August 2 and 16, 1804.

22. Jefferson, *The Writings,* Ford ed., vol. 8, 315 (Thomas Jefferson to the Secretary of State, August 15, 1804).

23. Ibid., 321 (Thomas Jefferson to the Attorney General, September 16, 1804).

24. Ibid., 323–24 (Fourth Annual Message, November 8, 1804). Captain Bradley, of the *Cambrian,* had been discharged after the incidents of the summer of 1804.

25. Monroe, *The Writings,* vol. 4, 233 (James Monroe to the Secretary of State, August 7, 1804); 218 (James Monroe to James Madison, July 1, 1804); 261 (James Monroe to the Secretary of State, October 3, 1804).

26. Donald R. Hickey, "The Monroe-Pinckney Treaty of 1806: A Reappraisal," *William and Mary Quarterly,* 3d series, 44(1) (1987), 71.

27. Perkins, *Prologue to War,* 18.

28. Stephen, *War in Disguise,* 5.

29. Ibid., 20.

30. Reginald Horsman, *The Causes of The War of 1812* (New York, 1962, 1979), 16, 18.

31. Monroe, *The Writings,* vol. 4, 335 (James Monroe to Thomas Jefferson, September 26, 1805).

32. Ibid., 337.

33. James Madison, *An Examination of the British Doctrine which subjects to capture a Neutral Trade not open in time of Peace* (Washington, D.C., 1806).

34. Monroe, *The Writings,* vol. 4, 345 and 348 (James Monroe to Thomas Jefferson, October 6, 1805).

35. Ibid., 355–56. The British denied that this new charge constituted a promotion; see Henry Adams, *History of the United States of America During the Administrations of Thomas Jefferson,* 634.

36. Jefferson, *The Writings,* Ford ed., vol. 8, 380 (Thomas Jefferson to the Secretary of State, October 11, 1805).

37. Ibid., 390.

38. Fletcher Pratt, *The Compact History of the United States Navy* (New York, 1957), 57.

39. Perkins, *Prologue to War,* 90.

40. Rufus King, *Despatches from U.S. Ministers to Great-Britain,* M30, Roll no. 3 (December

10, 1796, April 13, 1797), Roll no. 5 (January 9, 1798; January 25, 1799; July 15, 1799).

41. Monroe, *The Writings*, vol. 4, 8 (James Monroe to the Secretary of State, November 16, 1803); 112 (James Monroe to the Secretary of State, December 15, 1803).

42. Ibid., 192 (James Monroe to the Secretary of State, June 3, 1804); 229–30 (James Monroe to the Secretary of State, August 7, 1804).

43. Ibid., 402–3 (James Monroe to James Madison, February 2, 1806); see also dispatch no. 46, April 20, 1806, in *Despatches from U.S. Ministers to Great-Britain,* M30, Roll no. 3.

44. Jefferson, *The Writings,* Ford ed., vol. 8, 438 (Thomas Jefferson to Thomas Paine, March 25, 1806).

45. *Aurora,* October 16, 1805.

46. Ibid.

47. Perkins, *Prologue to War,* 25, 26, 27.

48. *Aurora,* April 29, 1806; see also Jefferson, *The Writings,* Ford ed., vol. 8, 445 ("Draft of Proclamation concerning *Leander,*" May 3, 1806).

49. Hickey, "The Monroe-Pinkney Treaty," 72.

50. Ibid., 5, 77, 84.

51. Ibid., 88.

52. Madison, *The Writings,* vol. 4, 493 (James Madison to John Randolph, November 2, 1806).

53. Perkins, *Prologue to War,* 136.

54. Pierre Léon, ed., *Histoire économique et sociale du monde* (Paris, 1977–78, 6 vols.), vol. 3, 378.

55. *Aurora,* October 16, 1805.

56. Glover, *The Napoleonic Wars,* 118. See also Harry L. Coles, *The War of 1812* (Chicago, 1965), 5.

57. Coles, *The War of 1812,* 6. For an exhaustive study of the continental blockade, see François Crouzet, *L'Economie britannique et le blocus continental,* 2d ed. (Paris, 1987).

58. *Aurora,* June 25, 1807.

59. *Boston Columbian Centinel,* July 4 and 8, 1807.

60. Ibid., July 4, 1807.

61. Ibid., July 8, 1807.

62. *Aurora,* June 30, 1807; *Boston Columbian Centinel,* July 18, 1807.

63. *Aurora,* August 6, 1807 (the citizens of the town of Chillicothe, Ohio), October 19, (letter from William Henry Harrison, from Vincennes), October 21 (patriotic meeting of the inhabitants of Washington County, in the Mississippi Territory).

64. Horsman, *The Causes of the War of 1812,* 225.

65. *Aurora,* June 29, 1807.

66. Glover, *Napoleonic Wars,* 122.

67. Jefferson, *The Writings,* Ford ed., vol. 9, 89–99.

68. Ibid., 103 (Thomas Jefferson to Thomas Cooper, July 9, 1807).

69. Ibid., 100 (Thomas Jefferson to the Vice President, July 6, 1807).

70. *Aurora,* July 3, 1807.

71. Jefferson, *The Writings,* Ford ed., vol. 9, 105 (Thomas Jefferson to Thomas Cooper, July 9, 1807); 116 (Thomas Jefferson to the American minister in France, July 17, 1807).

72. *Aurora,* July 14, 1807.

73. Jefferson, *The Writings,* Ford ed., vol. 9, 120 (Thomas Jefferson to William Duane, July 20, 1807).

74. *Aurora,* July 20, 1807.

75. Jefferson, *The Writings,* Ford ed., vol. 9, 136 (Thomas Jefferson to the Secretary of the Navy, September 3, 1807).

76. Ibid., 174.

77. Ibid., 167 (Thomas Jefferson to the governor of the Mississippi Territory).

78. Perkins, *Prologue to War,* 153–54.

79. *Aurora,* July 31, 1807.

80. Nelson, *Liberty and Property,* 147.

81. Albert Gallatin, *The Writings of Albert Gallatin,* ed. Henry Adams (Philadelphia, Pa., 1879, 3 vols.), vol. 1, 365 (December 18, 1807).

82. Perkins, *Prologue to War,* 168.

83. Glover, *Napoleonic Wars,* 131.

84. Perkins, *Prologue to War,* 168.

85. Ibid., 168.

86. William Bentley, *The Diary of William Bentley, D.D., Pastor of the East Church, Salem,* Massachusetts, vol. 3 (Gloucester, Mass., 1962), 337.

87. Ibid., 383 ; Perkins, *Prologue to War,* 171.

88. Perkins, *Prologue to War,* 173.

89. See Louis Martin Sears, *Jefferson and the Embargo* (New York, 1966), 108; Nelson, *Liberty and Property,* 136.

90. R. David Edmunds, *Tecumseh and the Quest for Indian Leadership* (Boston, Mass., 1984), 84–94.

91. Ibid., 113.

92. Perkins, *Prologue to War,* 167, 170–71.

93. Gallatin, *The Writings,* 401–2 (Albert Gallatin to Thomas Jefferson, August 5, 1808).

94. Ibid., 393 (Albert Gallatin to Thomas Jefferson, May 28, 1808); 402 (Albert Gallatin to Thomas Jefferson, August 6, 1808).

95. Ibid., 398 (Albert Gallatin to Thomas Jefferson, July 29, 1808).

96. Timothy Pickering, *Mr. Pickering's Speech in the Senate of the United States on the Resolution offered by Mr. Hillhouse to repeal the several acts laying an embargo, November 30, 1808* (Boston, Mass., 1808), 9.

97. Coles, *The War of 1812,* 11.

98. Bemis, *The American Secretaries of State,* vol. 3, 157–64.

99. Horsman, *The Causes of the War of 1812,* 150, 185, 186.

100. Donald R. Hickey, *The War of 1812: A Forgotten Conflict* (Urbana, Ill., 1989), 24.

101. Bemis, *The American Secretaries of State,* vol. 3, 216–19.

102. Horsman, *The Causes of the War of 1812,* 186, 207. Henry Adams, *History of the United States During the First Administration of James Madison* (New York, 1921), vol. 2, 67.

103. Horsman, *The Causes of the War of 1812,* 154–62.

104. Crouzet, *L'Economie britannique,* 524, 542, 571, 573, 581, 589, 649.

105. Henry Adams, *History of the United States of America During the First Administration of James Madison,* vol. 2, 210.

106. J. C. A. Stagg, *Mr. Madison's War: Politics, Diplomacy and Warfare in the Early American Republic, 1783–1830* (Princeton, N.J., 1983), 110.

107. Hickey, *The War of 1812,* 274–80.

108. The maritime causes constitute the chief topic of Horsman's study, *The Causes of the War of 1812.* Horsman does not agree with the thesis of an expansionist drive into the western states.

109. Hickey, *The War of 1812,* 1. For a bibliography of books and articles on the causes of the war of 1812, see Horsman, *The Causes of the War of 1812,* 269–93.

110. Watts, *The Republic Reborn.*

111. Coles, *The War of 1812,* 11.

112. Jefferson, *The Writings,* Ford ed., vol. 9, 213 (Thomas Jefferson to the governor of Louisiana, October 29, 1808).

113. Stagg emphasized that attempts at invading Canada still derived in part from the old idea of economic coercion: as long as Canada was in British hands, contraband could flourish between the northeastern states and Great Britain, via the British colonies in North America. Old republican ideas did not entirely yield to new ones, even after the outbreak of hostilities. See *Mr. Madison's War,* 38–47.

114. In Nelson's *Liberty and Property,* the chapter on "The Political Economy of Albert Gallatin" shows how, before the War of 1812, Gallatin developed the vision of a great domestic market destined to weld the nation in a union based on property and mutual exchange as guarantees for cohesion and political stability (*Liberty and Property,* 122).

Bibliography

Primary Sources

Diplomatic and Governmental Documents

Manuscripts

United States

National Archives, Washington, D.C. (Microfilm)
Despatches of American Ministers to Spain M31
Roll 2: August 15, 1792–February 2, 1795
Roll 3: February 13, 1795–December 10, 1795
Despatches from United States Ministers to France M34
Roll 5: October 20, 1793–September 18, 1794
Despatches from United States Ministers to Great-Britain M30
Roll 4: August 10, 1796–December 28, 1797
Roll 5: January 9–December 22, 1798 (includes the Gerry-Talleyrand correspondence)
Roll 6: January 3, 1799–December 18, 1800
Roll 9: July 19, 1803–October 10, 1807
Roll 11: April 24, 1806–December 29, 1808
Roll 12: January 23, 1809–June 26, 1810
Diplomatic and Consular Instructions of the Department of State M28
Roll 1: January 23, 1791–August 22, 1793
Roll 2: August 22, 1793–June 1, 1795
Roll 3: June 5, 1795–January 21, 1797

France
Archives du Ministère des Relations Extérieures, Paris
Correspondance Politique Etats-Unis
Volume 35: 1790–1791
Volume 36: 1792
Volume 37: January–June 1793
Volume 40: January–April 1794

Volume 41: May–September 1794
Volume 42: October–December 1794
Volume 46: June–December 1796
Volume 53: January–December 1801
Volume 54: January–September 1802
Volume 55: October 1802–June 1803
Volume 56: July 1803–March 1804
Volume 57: April–December 1804

Archives Nationales, Paris
AF III 21 A Rapport au Directoire Exécutif du 9 Thermidor an VI (on privateers)

Printed Matter

Government Publications

United States, *American State Papers, Foreign Relations,* 6 vols. Washington, D.C., 1834–56.

United States, *Annals of Congress, 1789–1824,* 42 vols. Washington, D.C., 1834–56.

United States, Continental Congress, *Journals of the Continental Congress, 1774–1789,* 34 vols. Washington, D.C., 1904–1937, 1968.

United States, The Public *Statutes at Large of the United States of America, 1789–1891,* ed. R. Peters, 27 vols. Washington, D.C., 1875–91.

Other Publications

Bouchary, M. ed. *La Déclaration des droits de l'Homme et du Citoyen et la Constitution de 1791.* Paris, 1946.

Dictionary of American Biography, under the auspices of the American Council of Learned Societies. 20 vols. New York, 1928–36.

Duvergier, J. B., ed. *Lois, Décrets, Ordonnances, Règlements et Avis du Conseil d'Etat.* Paris, 1825.

Kappler, Charles J., ed. *Indian Affairs, Laws and Treaties,* vol. 2. Washington, D.C., 1903.

Martens, M. de. *Recueil des Principaux Traités,* 11 vols. Göttingen, 1791–1808.

Parry, Clive, ed. *The Consolidated Treaty Series,* 221 vols. Dobbs Ferry, N.Y., 1969.

Treaties and Conventions Concluded Between the United States of America and Other Powers Since July 4, 1776. Washington, D.C., Government Printing Office, 1889.

Correspondence, Personal Papers, and Travel and Exploration Accounts

Correspondance and Personal Papers

Manuscripts

Jefferson, Thomas. *The Papers* (microfilm copy), series 1, Manuscript Division, Library of Congress, Washington, D.C.

Volume 26: April 1, 1802–August 1802
Volume 27: September 1, 1802–March 17, 1803
Volume 28: March 18, 1803–August 31, 1803
Volume 29: September 1, 1803–March 3, 1804
Volume 30: March 1804–August 20, 1804

Marshall, John. *Journal of John Marshall at Paris* (1797–98), Manuscript Division, Library of Congress, Washington, D.C.

Printed Matter

Adams, Abigail. *Letters of Mrs. Adams, the Wife of John Adams,* ed. Charles Francis Adams. Boston, Mass., 1841.

Adams, John. *The Works of John Adams,* ed. Charles Francis Adams, 10 vols. Boston, Mass., 1850–56.

Adams, John Quincy. *The Writings of John Quincy Adams,* ed. Worthington Chauncey Ford, 7 vols. New York, 1913–17.

Ames, Fisher. *The Works of Fisher Ames,* ed. W. B. Allen, 2 vols. Indianapolis, 1983.

Bentley, William. *The Diary of William Bentley, D.D., Pastor of the East Church, Salem, Massachusetts.* Gloucester, Mass., 1962.

de Laussat, Pierre-Clément. *Memoirs of My Life,* translated from the French edition of 1831. Baton Rouge, La., 1978.

Dunbar, William. *Life, Letters and Papers of William Dunbar, 1749–1810,* ed. Eron Dunbar Rowland. Jackson, Miss., 1930.

Gallatin, Albert. *The Writings of Albert Gallatin,* ed. Henry Adams, 3 vols. Philadelphia, Pa., 1879.

Hamilton, Alexander. *The Works of Alexander Hamilton,* ed. John C. Hamilton, 7 vols. New York, 1850–51.

———. *The Works of Alexander Hamilton,* ed. Henry Cabot Lodge, 9 vols. New York, 1885–86.

Jay, John. *The Correspondence and Public Papers of John Jay, 1794–1826,* ed. Henry P. Johnston, 4 vols. New York, 1890–93.

Jefferson, Thomas, *The Papers of Thomas Jefferson,* ed. Julian P. Boyd, 20 vols. Princeton, N.J., 1950–82.

———. *Notes on the State of Virginia,* ed. William Peden. New York, 1787, 1972.

———. *The Writings of Thomas Jefferson,* ed. H. A. Washington, 9 vols. Washington, D.C., 1853–54.

———. *The Writings of Thomas Jefferson,* ed. Paul Leicester Ford, 10 vols. Washington, D.C., 1892–99.

King, Rufus. *The Life and Correspondence of Rufus King,* Charles R. King, ed., 6 vols. New York, 1894–1900.

Madison, James. *The Writings of James Madison,* ed. Gaillard Hunt, 9 vols. New York, 1900–1910.

Monroe, James. *The Writings of James Monroe,* ed. Stanislaus Murray Hamilton, 7 vols. New York, 1898–1903.

Morris, Gouverneur. *The Diary and Letters of Gouverneur Morris,* ed. Anne Cary Morris, 2 vols. New York, 1888.

Sparks, Jared. *The Life of Gouverneur Morris,* 2 vols. Boston, Mass., 1832.

Washington, George. *The Writings of George Washington,* ed. John C. Fitzpatrick, 39 vols. Washington, 1931–44.

———. *The Writings of George Washington,* ed. Worthington Chauncey Ford, 14 vols. New York, 1889–93.

Travel and Exploration Accounts

Biddle, Nicholas, ed. *History of the expedition under the command of Captain Lewis and Clark, to the sources of the Missouri, thence across the Rocky Mountains and down the river Columbia to the Pacific Ocean.* Philadelphia, Pa., 1814.

Dunbar, William. *Documents Relating to the Purchase and Exploration of Louisiana.* Boston, Mass., 1904.

Jefferson, Thomas, ed. *Message from the President of the United States, communicating Discoveries made in exploring the Missouri, Red River and Washita by Captains Lewis and Clark, Doctor Sibley and Mr. Dunbar. . . .* Washington, 1806.

McKenzie, Alexander. *Voyages from Montreal on the River St Laurence, through the continent of North America, to the Frozen and Pacific Oceans, in the Years 1789 and 1793.* London, 1801.

Moreau de Saint-Méry, Médéric Louis Elie. *Moreau de Saint Mery's American Journey: 1793–1798,* ed. Kenneth Roberts, trans. Kenneth and Anna M. Roberts. New York, 1947.

———, *Voyage aux Etats-Unis d'Amérique: 1793–1798,* ed. Stewart L. Mims. New Haven, Conn., 1913.

Newspapers, Pamphlets, and Other Documents

Newspapers

United States

Aurora

Boston Columbian Centinel

Charleston Courier

Gazette of the United States

Minerva

National Gazette

New York Evening Post

Pennsylvania Gazette

Raleigh Register and North Carolina Gazette

Richmond Enquirer

Tennessee Gazette

FRANCE

Gazette de France Nationale
Le Moniteur Universel

Pamphlets

Hamilton, Alexander, James Madison, and John Jay. *The Federalist or the New Constitution, Papers by Alexander Hamilton, James Madison, John Jay.* New York, 1945.

Madison, James. *An Examination of the British Doctrine which subjects to capture a Neutral Trade not open in time of Peace.* Washington, D.C., 1806.

Morse, Jedidiah. *The Present Situation of the Nations of the World contrasted with our own.* Boston, Mass., 1795.

Osgood, David. *Some facts evincive of the atheistical, anarchical, and in other respects, immoral principles of the French Republicans.* Boston, Mass., 1798.

Paine, Thomas. *Common Sense, the Rights of Man and other Essential Writings of Thomas Paine,* introduction by Sydney Hook. New York, 1969.

Pickering, Timothy. *Mr. Pickering's Speech in the Senate of the United States on the Resolution offered by Mr. Hillhouse to repeal the several acts laying an embargo, November 30, 1808.* Boston, Mass., 1808.

Stephen, James. *War in Disguise; or, the Frauds of the Neutral Flags.* London, 1805.

Other Documents

Barbé-Marbois, François. *The History of Louisiana, Particularly of the cession of that colony to the United States of America,* translated from the 1828 (1830) French edition. Baton Rouge, La., 1977.

Cooper, James Fenimore. *The Prairie.* New York, 1827, 1864.

Edwards, Bryan, *An Historical Survey of the French Colony in the Island of Santo-Domingo.* London, 1797.

Garden, Comte de. *Traité Complet de Diplomatie.* Paris, 1833.

Warren, Mercy Otis. *History of the Rise, Progress and Termination of the American Revolution.* Boston, Mass., 1805.

Secondary Sources

Abénon, Lucien, Jacques Cauna, and Liliane Chauleau. *La Révolution aux Caraïbes.* Paris, 1989.

Abernethy, Thomas P. *The Burr Conspiracy.* New York, 1954.

———. *The South in the New Nation.* Baton Rouge, La., 1961.

Adams, Henry. *History of the United States of America During the Administrations of Thomas Jefferson* (1889–91). New York, 1986.

———. *History of the United States During the Administrations of James Madison,* vol. 1 (1890). New York, 1921.

Adams, Willi Paul, ed. "Gouverneur Morris, 'An Address, circa 1800.'" *Amerikastudien/American Studies* 21, 1976.

Agulhon, Maurice. "Aspects du nationalisme français." *Raison Présente* 103, 1992.

Anderson, Benedict. *Imagined Communities: Reflections on the Origin and Spread of Nationalism.* London, 1991.

Appleby, Joyce. *Capitalism and a New Social Order: The Republican Vision of the 1790s.* New York, 1984.

Bailyn, Bernard. *The Ideological Origins of the American Revolution.* Cambridge, Mass., 1967.

Banning, Lance. "Jeffersonian Ideology Revisited: Liberal and Classical Ideas in the New American Republic." *William and Mary Quarterly,* 3d series, 43(1), 1986.

———. *The Jeffersonian Persuasion: Evolution of a Party Ideology.* Ithaca, N.Y., 1978.

Beard, Charles A. *Economic Origins of Jeffersonian Democracy.* New York, 1929.

Beeman, Richard, ed. *Beyond Confederation: Origins of the Constitution and American National Identity.* Chapel Hill, N.C., 1987.

Bemis, Samuel Flagg, ed. *The American Secretaries of State and Their Diplomacy,* 10 vols. New York, 1927–29.

———. *The Diplomacy of the American Revolution.* New York, 1935.

———. *Jay's Treaty: A Study in Commerce and Diplomacy.* New Haven, Conn., 1923.

———. *Pinckney's Treaty: America's Advantage from Europe's Distress, 1783–1800.* New Haven, Conn., 1926, 1960.

Benot, Yves. *La démence coloniale sous Napoléon.* Paris, 1992.

Billington, Ray Allen. *Westward Expansion.* New York, 1949.

Bogart, Ernest L. *Economic History of the American People.* New York, 1942.

Bonnel, Ulane. *La France, les Etats-Unis et la guerre de course (1797–1815).* Paris, 1961.

Bowen, Franck C. *America Sails the Seas.* New York, 1938.

Boyd, Julian P. *Number 7: Alexander Hamilton's Secret Attempts to Control American Foreign Policy.* Princeton, N.J., 1964.

Bracey, John H., Jr., August Meier, and Elliott Rudwick, eds., *American Slavery: The Question of Resistance.* Belmont, Calif., 1971.

Bradley, Patricia. *Slavery, Propaganda, and the American Revolution.* Jackson, Miss., 1998.

Brant, Irving. *James Madison, Secretary of State, 1800–1809.* Indianapolis, 1953.

Breuilly, John J. *Nationalism and the State.* Manchester, 1982.

Brown, E. S., ed. "Documents. The Senate Debate on the Breckinridge Bill for the Government of Louisiana, 1804." *American Historical Review* 12(2), 1917.

Bruchey, Stuart. *The Wealth of the Nation: An Economic History of the United States.* New York, 1988.

Buel, Richard, Jr. *Securing the Revolution: Ideology in American Politics, 1789–1815.* Ithaca, N.Y., 1972.

Burdeau, George. *Le Libéralisme.* Paris, 1979.

Canny, Nicholas, and Anthony Pagden. *Colonial Identity in the Atlantic World, 1500–1800.* Princeton, N.J., 1987.

Carroll, Joseph Cephas. *Slave Insurrections in the United States, 1800–1865.* New York, 1938.

Césaire, Aimé. *Discours sur le Colonialisme.* Paris, 1950.

Chadwick, F. E. *The Relations of the United States and Spain.* New York, 1909.

Charles, Joseph. *The Origins of the American Party System.* New York, 1961.

Chartier, Roger. *Les Origines culturelles de la révolution française.* Paris, 1990.

Chastenet, Jacques. *Manuel Godoy et l'Espagne de Goya.* Paris, 1961.

Childs, Frances Sergeant. *French Refugee Life in the United States, 1790–1800: An American Chapter of the French Revolution.* Philadelphia, Pa., 1940, 1978.

Chinard, Gilbert. *Honest John Adams.* Boston, Mass., 1933.

———. *Les Origines historiques de la doctrine de l'isolement aux Etats-Unis.* Paris, 1937.

———. *Thomas Jefferson: The Apostle of Americanism.* Boston, Mass., 1939.

———. *Volney et l'Amérique, d'après des documents inédits et sa correspondance avec Jefferson.* Baltimore, Md., 1923.

Coatsworth, John H. "American Trade with European Colonies in the Caribbean and South America, 1790–1812." *William and Mary Quarterly,* 3d series, 24(2), 1967.

Coe, Samuel. *Mission of William Carmichael to Spain.* Baltimore, Md., 1928.

Coles, Harry L. *The War of 1812.* Chicago, 1965.

Cook, Warren L. *Flood Tide of Empire: Spain and the Pacific Northwest, 1543–1819.* New Haven, Conn., 1973.

Cotterill, R. S. *The Southern Indians: The Story of the Civilized Tribes Before Removal.* Norman, Okla., 1954.

Creagh, Ronald. *Nos Cousins d'Amérique: Histoire des Français aux Etats-Unis.* Paris, 1988.

Crouzet, François. *L'Economie britannique et le blocus continental,* 2d ed. Paris, 1987.

Cunningham, Noble E. *The Jeffersonian Republicans: The Formation of Party Organization, 1789–1801.* Chapel Hill, N.C., 1957.

Darnton, Robert. *The Great Cat Massacre and Other Episodes in French Cultural History.* New York, 1984, 1985.

Dauer, Manning J. *The Adams Federalists.* Baltimore, Md., 1953.

Davis, David Brion. *The Problem of Slavery in the Age of Revolution: 1770–1823.* Ithaca, N.Y., 1975.

———. *Revolutions: Reflections on American Equality and Foreign Liberations.* Cambridge, Mass., 1990.

De Conde, Alexander. *The Quasi-War: The Politics and Diplomacy of the Undeclared War with France, 1797–1801.* New York, 1966.

Delannoi, Gil, and Pierre-André Taguieff. *Théories du nationalisme. Nation, nationalité, ethnicité.* Paris, 1991.

Delanoë, Nelcya. *L'Entaille Rouge: terres indiennes et démocratie américaine.* Paris, 1982.

Drinnon, Richard. *Facing West: The Metaphysics of Indian-hating and Empire-building.* New York, 1980.

Durey, Michael. "Thomas Paine's Apostles: Radical Emigrés and the Triumph of Jeffersonian Republicanism." *William and Mary Quarterly,* 3d series, 44(4), 1987.

Duroselle, Jean-Baptiste, and Pierre Renouvin. *Introduction à l'histoire des Relations Internationales.* Paris, 1964, 1970.

Echeverria, Durand, ed. "General Collot's Plan for a Reconnaissance of the Ohio and Mississippi Valleys, 1796." *William and Mary Quarterly,* 3d series, 9, 1952.

Edmunds, R. David. *Tecumseh and the Quest for Indian Leadership.* Boston, Mass., 1984.

Egan, Clifford L. *Neither Peace nor War, Franco-American Relations, 1803–1812.* Baton Rouge, La., 1983.

Egnal, Marc. *A Mighty Empire: The Origins of the American Revolution.* Ithaca, N.Y., 1988.

Eley, Geoff. "Nationalism and Social History." *Social History* 6 (January 1981).

Faulkner, Harold Underwood. *Histoire économique des Etats-Unis d'Amérique des origines jusqu'à nos jours,* 2 vols. Paris, 1958.

Faÿ, Bernard. *L'Esprit révolutionnaire en France et aux Etats-unis à la fin du dix-huitième siècle.* Paris, 1924.

Fischer, David Hackett. *Albion's Seed: Four British Folkways in America.* New York, 1989.

Fiske, John. *The Critical Period of American History, 1783–1789.* Boston, Mass., 1888.

Fohlen, Claude. *Thomas Jefferson.* Nancy, 1992.

Foner, Eric. *The New American History.* Philadelphia, Pa., 1990.

Foucrier, Annick. *La France, les Français et la Californie avant la ruée vers l'or (1786–1848).* Ph.D. diss., Paris, E.H.E.S.S, 1991.

Furet, François. *Penser la Révolution Française.* Paris, 1978.

———, and Mona Ozouf, eds. *Dictionnaire critique de la Révolution française.* Paris, 1988.

Garnier, Michaël. *Histoire diplomatique de la France en Amérique du Nord (Louisiane), 1800–1803.* Ph.D. diss., EPHE, Université Paris 4, 1984.

———. "Louisiane," article from *Dictionnaire Napoléon,* ed. Jean Tulard.

Gaspar, David Barry. *Bondmen and Rebels: A Study of Master-Slave Relations in Antigua with Implications for Colonial British America.* Baltimore, Md., 1985.

Geertz, Clifford. "Ideology as a Cultural System." In *Ideology and Discontent,* ed. David A. Apter. London, 1964.

Gellner, Ernst. *Culture, Identity and Politics.* Cambridge, 1987.

Gilbert, Felix. *To the Farewell Address: Ideas of Early American Foreign Policy.* Princeton, N.J., 1961.

Girardet, Raoul, ed. *Mythes et Mythologies Politiques.* Paris, 1986.

———. *Le Nationalisme Français.* Paris, 1983.

Glover, Michael. *The Napoleonic Wars.* New York, 1978.

Godechot, Jacques. *La Grande Nation, L'expansion révolutionnaire de la France dans le monde de 1789 à 1799.* Paris, 1956.

Gordon, Colin. "Crafting a Usable Past: Consensus, Ideology and Historians of the American Revolution." *William and Mary Quarterly,* 3d series, 46(4), 1989.

Greene, Jack P. *Pursuits of Happiness: The Social Development of Early Modern British Colonies and the Formation of American Culture.* Chapel Hill, N.C., 1988.

Hall, Richard D. *Knowledge Is Power: The Diffusion of Information in Early America, 1700–1865.* New York, 1989.

Hay, Thomas Robson, and Morris-Robert Werner. *The Admirable Trumpeter.* Garden City, N.Y., 1941.

Heinl, Robert Debs, Jr., and Nancy Gordon Heinl. *Written in Blood: The Story of the Haitian People, 1492–1971.* Boston, Mass., 1978.

Henretta, James. *The Evolution of American Society: 1700–1815.* Lexington, Mass., 1973.

Hickey, Donald R. "The Monroe-Pinkney Treaty of 1806: A Reappraisal." *William and Mary Quarterly,* 3d series, 44(1), 1987.

———. *The War of 1812: A Forgotten Conflict.* Urbana, Ill., 1989.

Hobsbawm, Eric J. *Nations and Nationalism Since 1780: Programme, Myth, Reality.* Cambridge, 1990.

Hofstadter, Richard. *The Idea of a Party System: The Rise of Legitimate Opposition in the United States, 1780–1840.* Berkeley, Calif., 1969.

———. *The Paranoid Style in American Politics and Other Essays.* New York, 1963.

Horsman, Reginald. *The Causes of the War of 1812.* New York, 1962, 1979.

———. *The Diplomacy of the New Republic, 1776–1815.* Arlington Heights, Ill., 1985.

———. *Expansion and American Indian Policy: 1783–1812.* East Lansing, Mich., 1969.

———. *The Frontier in the Formative Years, 1783–1815.* New York, 1970.

Howarth, Stephen. *To the Shining Sea: A History of the United States Navy, 1775–1991.* New York, 1991.

Howe, John R. "Republican Thought and the Political Violence of the 1790s." *American Quarterly* 19(2), 1967.

Hunt, Alfred N. *Haiti's Influence on Antebellum America: Slumbering Volcano in the Caribbean.* Baton Rouge, La., 1988.

Hunt, Michael H. "Ideology." *Journal of American History* 77(1), June 1990.

———. *Ideology and U.S. Foreign Policy.* New Haven, Conn., 1987.

Iriye, Akira. "Culture." *Journal of American History* 77(1), June 1990.

Irwin, Ray W. *The Diplomatic Relations of the United States with the Barbary Powers, 1776–1816.* Chapel Hill, N.C., 1931.

Jackson, Donald, ed. *Letters of the Lewis and Clark Expedition, with Related Documents, 1783–1854.* Urbana, Ill., 1962.

———. *Thomas Jefferson and the Stony Mountains: Exploring the West from Monticello.* Urbana, Ill., 1987.

Jacobs, James Ripley. *The Beginnings of the United States Army, 1783–1812.* Princeton, N.J., 1947.

James, C. L. R. *The Black Jacobins: Toussaint Louverture and the San Domingo Revolution.* New York, 1938, 1963.

Jennings, Francis. *The Ambiguous Iroquois Empire.* New York, 1984.

Jensen, Merrill. *The New Nation: A History of the United States During the Confederation, 1781–1789.* New York, 1950.

Jones, Dorothy V. *License for Empire: Colonialism by Treaty in Early America.* Chicago, 1982.

Jordan, Winthrop. *White Over Black: American Attitudes Toward the Negro, 1550–1812.* New York, 1968, 1977.

Jusserand, Jean-Jacques. "La Jeunesse du Citoyen Genêt." *Revue d'Histoire Diplomatique* 44(3), 1930.

Kaplan, L. S. *Colonies into Nation: American Diplomacy, 1763–1801.* New York, 1972.

———. *Entangling Alliances with None: American Foreign Policy in the Age of Jefferson.* Kent, Ohio, 1987.

———. *Jefferson and France: An Essay on Politics and Political Ideas.* New Haven, Conn., 1967.

Kastner, Joseph. *A Species of Eternity.* New York, 1977.

Kehoe, Alice B. *North American Indians: A Comprehensive Account.* Englewood Cliffs, N.J., 1981.

Kerber, Linda K. *Federalists in Dissent: Imagery and Ideology in Jeffersonian America.* Ithaca, N.Y., 1970.

———. *Women of the Republic: Intellect and Ideology in Revolutionary America.* New York, 1980, 1986.

Klein, Rachel. *Unification of a Slave State: The Rise of the Planter Class in the South Carolina Backcountry, 1760–1808.* Chapel Hill, N.C., 1990.

Knox, Dudley W. *A History of the United States Navy* New York, 1936.

Koch, Adrienne. *Jefferson and Madison, The Great Collaboration.* New York, 1950.

Kohn, Richard H. *Eagle and Sword: The Beginnings of the Military Establishment in America, 1783–1802.* New York, 1975.

Kramnick, Isaac. "The 'Great National Discussion': The Discourse of Politics in 1787." *William and Mary Quarterly,* 3d series, 45(1), 1988.

Kurtz, Stephen G. *The Presidency of John Adams: The Collapse of Federalism, 1795–1800.* Philadelphia, Pa., 1957.

Lachance, Paul. "The 1809 Immigration of Saint-Domingue Refugees to New Orleans." *Louisiana History* 29(2), 1988.

Lacorne, Denis. *L'Invention de la République. Le modèle américain.* Paris, 1991.

———. "Une présidence hamiltonienne: la Politique étrangère de Ronald Reagan." *Revue Française de Science Politique* 39(4), 1989.

Lavender, David. *The Way to the Western Sea: Lewis and Clark Across the Continent.* New York, 1988.

Le Goff, Jacques, ed. *La Nouvelle Histoire.* Paris, 1978, 1988.

Léon, Pierre, ed. *Histoire économique et sociale du monde,* 6 vols. Paris, 1977–78.

Lilley, Charles R., and Michael H. Hunt. "On Social History, the State, and Foreign Relations: Commentary on 'The Cosmopolitan Connection.'" *Diplomatic History* 11, 1987.

Link, Eugene Perry. *Democratic-Republican Societies, 1790–1800.* New York, 1942.

Logan, Rayford W. *The Diplomatic Relations of the United States with Haiti, 1776–1891.* Chapel Hill, N.C., 1941.

Lowe, James Trapier. *Our Colonial Heritage: Diplomatic and Military.* Lanham, Md., 1987.

Lyon, E. Wilson. "The Directory and the United States." *American Historical Review* 42(3), 1938.

Maier, Charles S. "Marking Time: The Historiography of International Relations." In *The Past Before Us: Contemporary Historical Writing in the United States,* ed. Michael Kammen. Ithaca, N.Y., 1980.

Malkassian, Gérard. "Diaspora et question nationale." *Le Messager Européen* 5, 1991.

Malone, Dumas. *Jefferson and the Rights of Man.* Boston, Mass., 1951.

———. *Jefferson and the Ordeal of Liberty.* Boston, Mass., 1962.

Marienstras, Elise. *Les Mythes fondateurs de la nation américaine: Essai sur le discours idéologique aux Etats-Unis à l'époque de l'indépendance (1763–1800).* Paris, 1976.

———. *Naissance de la République Fédérale, 1783–1828.* Nancy, 1987.

———. *Nous, le peuple: Les origines du nationalisme américain.* Paris, 1988.

———. *La résistance indienne aux Etats-Unis du XVIe au XXe siècle.* Paris, 1980.

Marks, Frederick W. III. *Independence on Trial: Foreign Affairs and the Making of the Constitution.* Wilmington, Del., 1973, 1986.

Martin, Jean. *L'Empire renaissant, 1789–1871.* Paris, 1987.

Marshall, P. J., and Glyndwr Williams. *The Great Map of Mankind.* London, 1982.

Mathewson, Timothy M. "George Washington's Policy Toward the Haitian Revolution." *Diplomatic History* 3(3), 1979.

McCoy, Drew R. *The Elusive Republic: Political Economy in Jeffersonian America.* New York, 1980, 1982.

McDonald, Forrest. *E Pluribus Unum: The Formation of the American Republic, 1776–1790.* Indianapolis, 1979.

McLoughlin, William. *Cherokee Renascence in the New Republic.* Princeton, N.J., 1986.

Melton, Buckner F. *The First Impeachment: The Constitution's Framers and the Case of Senator William Blount.* Macon, Ga., 1998.

Merrell, James H. *The Indians' New World: Catawbas and Their Neighbours from European Contact through the Era of Removal.* Chapel Hill, N.C., 1989.

Mézière, Henri. *Le général Leclerc (1772–1802) et l'expédition de Saint-Domingue.* Paris, 1990.

Miller, John C. *Alexander Hamilton, Portrait in Paradox.* New York, 1959.

———. *Crisis in Freedom: The Alien and Sedition Acts.* Boston, Mass., 1951.

———. *The Federalist Era, 1789–1801.* London, 1961.

———. *Origins of the American Revolution.* Boston, Mass., 1943.

Millett, Allan Reed, and Peter Maslowski. *For the Common Defense: A Military History of the United States of America.* New York, 1984.

Millican, Edward. *One United People: The Federalist Papers and the National Idea.* Lexington, Mass., 1990.

Moncef, Larbi Mohamed. *La jeune République américaine face aux puissances barbaresques 1783–1830.* Ph.D. diss., Université Paris 7, 1981.

Morgan, Edmund S. *American Slavery, American Freedom: The Ordeal of Colonial Virginia.* New York, 1975.

Morris, Richard B. *The Peacemakers: The Great Powers and American Independence.* New York, 1965.

Mott, Frank Luther. *American Journalism: A History of Newspapers in the United States through 250 years, 1690 to 1940.* New York, 1942.

Mugridge, Donald H., ed. *Album of American Battle Art.* Washington, D.C., 1947.

Nelson, John R., Jr. *Liberty and Property: Political Economy and Policymaking in the New Nation, 1789–1812.* Baltimore, Md., 1987.

Newton, Lewis William. *The Americanization of French Louisiana.* New York, 1980.

Nobles, Gregory H. "Breaking into the Backcountry: New Approaches to the Early American Frontier, 1750–1800." *William and Mary Quarterly,* 3d series, 46(4), 1989.

Nora, Pierre. *Les lieux de mémoire: La République.* Paris, 1984.

North, Douglas C. *The Economic Growth of the United States: 1790–1860.* New York, 1961, 1966.

Nussbaum, F. L. "American Tobacco and French Politics." *Political Science Quarterly* 40(1), 1925.

———. "The French Colonial Arrêt of 1784." *South Atlantic Quarterly* 27(1), 1928.

———. "The Revolutionary Vergennes and Lafayette v. the Farmers General." *Journal of Modern History* 3(4), 1931.

Nyrop, R. F., ed. *Algeria: A Country Study.* Washington, D.C., 1979.

———. *Libya: A Country Study.* Washington, D.C., 1979.

O'Donnell, James H. III. *Southern Indians in the American Revolution.* Knoxville, Tenn., 1973.

Ozouf, Mona. *L'Homme régénéré. Essais sur la Révolution française.* Paris, 1989.

Palmer, R. R. . *The Age of the Democratic Revolution: A Political History of Europe and America, 1760–1800,* 2 vols. Princeton, N.J., 1964.

———. "A Revolutionary Republican: M. A. B. Mangourit." *William and Mary Quarterly,* 3d series, 10(4), 1952.

Pate, James Paul. *The Chickamauga: A Forgotten Segment of Indian Resistance on the Southern Frontier.* Ph.D. diss., Mississippi State University, 1969.

Paterson, Thomas G. "Explaining the History of American Foreign Relations." *Journal of American History* 77(1), June 1990.

Patterson, Orlando "The General Causes of Jamaican Slave Revolts" In *American Slavery: the Question of Resistance,* ed. John Barcey. Belmont, Calif., 1971.

Perkins, Bradford. *The First Rapprochement: England and the United States, 1795–1805.* Philadelphia, Pa., 1955.

———. *Prologue to War: England and the United States, 1805–1812.* Berkeley, Calif., 1963.

Perkins, Dexter. *A History of the Monroe Doctrine.* Boston, Mass., 1963.

Peterson, Merrill D. "Thomas Jefferson and Commercial Policy, 1783–1793." *William and Mary Quarterly,* 3d series, 22(4), 1965.

———. *Thomas Jefferson and the New Nation: A Biography.* New York, 1970.

Pfaff, William. *The Wrath of Nations: Civilization and the Furies of Nationalism.* New York, 1993.

Pluchon, Pierre. *Histoire de la colonisation française,* vol. 1. Paris, 1991.

———. *Toussaint Louverture.* Paris, 1989.

Pratt, Fletcher. *The Compact History of the United States Navy.* New York, 1957.

Pred, Allan R. *Urban Growth and the Circulation of Information: The United States System of Cities, 1790–1840.* Cambridge, Mass., 1973.

Price, Jacob M. *France and the Chesapeake: A History of the French Tobacco Monopoly, 1674–1791, and of its Relationships to the British and American Tobacco Trades,* 2 vols. Ann Arbor, Mich., 1973.

Price, Neal R. *The New England States: People, Politics and Power in the Six New England States.* New York, 1976.

Prucha, F. P. *The Great Father: The United States Government and the American Indians.* Lincoln, Nebr., 1984, 1986.

Ray, Thomas M. "'Not One Cent for Tribute': The Public Addresses and American Popular Reaction to the XYZ Affair, 1798–1799." *Journal of the Early Republic* 3(4), winter 1983.

Ronda, James P. "Dreams and Discoveries: Exploring the American West, 1760–1815." *William and Mary Quarterly,* 3d series, 46(1), 1989.

Rousseau, Jean-Jacques. *Oeuvres Complètes,* ed. Bernard Gagnebin and Marcel Raymond, 4 vols. Paris, 1964.

Ryan, Mary P. "Party Formation in the United States Congress. 1789 to 1796: A Quantitative Analysis." *William and Mary Quarterly,* 3d series, 28(4), 1971.

Salinger, Sharon V. "Artisans, Journeymen, and the Transformation of Labor in Late Eighteenth-Century Philadelphia." *William and Mary Quarterly,* 3d series, 40(1), 1983.

Sears, Louis Martin. *George Washington and the French Revolution.* Detroit, Mich., 1960.

———. *Jefferson and the Embargo.* New York, 1966.

Setser, Vernon G. *The Commercial Reciprocity Policy of the United States: 1774–1809.* Philadelphia, Pa., 1937.

Shaler, N. S. *Kentucky: A Pioneer Commonwealth.* Boston, Mass., 1884.

Shalhope, Robert E. "Toward a Republican Synthesis: The Emergence of an Understanding of Republicanism in American Historiography." *William and Mary Quarterly,* 3d series, 29(1), 1972.

Sheehan, Bernard W. *Seeds of Extinction: Jeffersonian Philanthropy and the American Indian.* New York, 1973, 1974.

Slaughter, Thomas P. *The Whiskey Rebellion: Frontier Epilogue to the American Revolution.* New York, 1986.

Smelser, Marshall. "The Federalist Period As an Age of Passion." *American Quarterly* 10(4), 1958.

Smith, James Morton. *Freedom's Fetters: The Alien and Sedition Laws of American Civil Liberties.* Ithaca, N.Y., 1956.

Sprague, Marshall. *So Vast, So Beautiful a Land: Louisiana and the Purchase.* Boston, Mass., 1974.

Stagg, J. C. A. *Mr. Madison's War: Politics, Diplomacy and Warfare in the Early American Republic, 1783–1800.* Princeton, N.J., 1983.

Sword, Wiley. *President Washington's Indian War: The Struggle for the Old Northwest, 1790–1795.* Norman, Okla., 1985.

Taylor, Alan. *Liberty Men and Great Proprietors: The Revolutionary Settlement on the Maine Frontier, 1760–1820.* Chapel Hill, N.C., 1990.

Thibau, Jacques. *Le Temps de Saint-Domingue: l'esclavage et la révolution française.* Paris, 1989.

Thompson, Isabel. "The Blount Conspiracy." *East Tennessee Historical Society Publications* 2, 1930.

Treudley, Mary. "The United States and Santo-Domingo: 1789–1866." *Journal of Race Development* 7, 1915–16.

Trevelyan, G. M. *A Shortened History of England.* Harmondsworth, 1942, 1979.

Trigger, Bruce G., ed. *Handbook of North American Indians,* vol. 15, *Northeast.* Washington, D.C., 1978.

Tucker, Robert W., and David C. Hendrickson, *Empire of Liberty: The Statecraft of Thomas Jefferson.* New York, 1990.

Tulard, Jean, ed. *Dictionnaire Napoléon.* Paris, 1989.

Turner, Frederick Jackson. "Documents on the Blount Conspiracy, 1795–1797." *American Historical Review* 10(2), 1905.

———. *The Frontier in American History.* Tucson, Ariz., 1920, 1986.

Turner, Katharine C. *Red Men Calling on the Great White Father.* Norman, Okla., 1951.

Van Alstyne, Richard W. *Empire and Independence: The International History of the American Revolution.* New York, 1965.

———. *Genesis of American Nationalism.* Waltham, Mass., 1970.

———. *The Rising American Empire.* New York, 1960, 1974.

———. "The Significance of the Mississippi Valley in American Diplomatic History: 1689–1890." *Mississippi Valley Historical Review* 36(2), September 1949.

Varg, Paul A. *Foreign Policies of the Founding Fathers.* Baltimore, Md., 1963, 1970.

Vattel, Emer de. *Le Droit des Gens,* 2 vols. Paris, 1758, 1863.

Vincent, Bernard. *Thomas Paine ou la religion de la liberté.* Paris, 1987.

Waldstreicher, David. *In the Midst of Perpetual Fetes: The Making of American Nationalism, 1776–1820.* Chapel Hill, N.C., 1997.

Walsh, James P. "'Mechanics and Citizens': The Connecticut Artisan Protest of 1792." *William and Mary Quarterly,* 3d series, 42(1), 1985.

Washburn, Wilcomb E. *The Indian in America.* New York, 1975.

Watts, Steven. *The Republic Reborn: War and the Making of Liberal America, 1790–1820.* Baltimore, Md., 1987.

Weber, David J. *The Spanish Frontier in North America.* New Haven, Conn., 1992.

Weinberg, Albert K. *Manifest Destiny: A Study of Nationalist Expansionism in American History.* Baltimore, Md., 1935.

Whipple, A. B. C. *To the Shores of Tripoli. The Birth of the U.S. Navy and Marines.* New York, 1991.

Whitaker, Arthur Preston. *The Mississippi Question, 1795–1803: A Study in Trade, Politics, and Diplomacy.* New York, 1934.

———. *The Spanish-American Frontier, 1783–1795.* Boston, Mass., 1927.

———. *The United States and the Independence of Latin America, 1800–1830.* Baltimore, Md., 1941.

White, Richard. *The Middle Ground: Indians, Empires, and Republics in the Great Lakes Region, 1650–1815.* New York, 1991.

Wiebe, Robert H. *The Opening of American Society.* New York, 1984.

Wilentz, Sean. *Chants Democratic: New York City and the Rise of the American Working Class, 1788–1850.* New York, 1984.

Williams, William Appleman. *The Contours of American History.* Cleveland, Ohio, 1961.

———, ed. *From Colony to Empire: Essays in the History of American Foreign Relations.* New York, 1972.

Wood, Gordon S. "Conspiracy and the Paranoid Style: Causality and Deceit in the Eighteenth Century." *William and Mary Quarterly* 39(3), 1982.

———. *The Creation of the American Republic, 1776–1787.* New York, 1969, 1972.

———. *The Radicalism of the American Revolution.* New York, 1992.

———. *The Rising Glory of America, 1760–1820.* New York, 1971.

Wood, Peter H. *Black Majority: Negroes in Colonial South Carolina From 1670 through the Stono Rebellion.* New York, 1974, 1975.

Young, Alfred F., ed. *The American Revolution: Explorations in the History of American Radicalism.* DeKalb, Ill., 1976.

Zelinsky, Wilbur. *Nation into State: The Shifting Symbolic Foundations of American Nationalism.* Chapel Hill, N.C., 1988.

Zuckerman, Michael. "The Power of Blackness: Thomas Jefferson and the Revolution in Saint-Domingue." In *Almost Chosen People: Oblique Biographies in the American Grain.* Berkeley, Calif., 1993.

Index

abolitionism/abolitionists, 120, 129, 133–34, 139
Adams, Abigail, 105
Adams, Henry, 145, 160, 188, 189, 190, 196
Adams, John, xiv, 5, 6, 29, 36–38, 40, 55–57, 59, 60–61, 65, 88–90, 93, 94, 99–106, 115, 125–26, 183, 190, 196
Adams, John Quincy, 38, 56, 104, 167
Adet, Pierre-Auguste, 58–59, 61, 93, 99–100, 143
African Americans. *See* blacks: in the United States
Alaska, 152
Aleutian Islands, 152
Algeria, 113–14
Algonquians, 9, 12. *See also names of individual tribes*
Alien and Sedition Acts. *See* exception laws
Allen, John, 101
America, Latin (South, Spanish), 80, 82, 88–89, 163–64, 189, 192
American Philosophical Society, 150
Ames, Fisher, 104–5
Amiens, Peace of, 127, 172, 184
Anderson, Benedict, xiii
Anglo-American treaties. *See* British-American treaties
Antilles. *See* Caribbean
Appleby, Joyce, 69
Aristides (newspaper columnist), 149
Armstrong, John, 163
Articles of Confederation, 3–5, 26, 28
Aurora, 55, 59, 64, 102, 133–34, 169–70, 177–78, 181–84
Austria, 174

Bache, Benjamin, 64
Banning, Lance, 45
Barbary Coast, xviii, 5, 94, 113–14, 170
Barbé-Marbois, François, 144, 148–49, 152, 159, 160
Bard, David, 130
Basle, Treaty of, 19, 143
Beard, Charles, 34
Beckwith, George, Colonel, 12–13, 30–32
Bellamy, Pierre, 61
Bemis, Samuel Flagg, xvi, 4, 13, 48–49
Bentley, William, 185
Berlin Decree, 180
Berthier, Alexandre, 142
Biddle, Nicholas, 159
Bill of Rights, 46, 63
blacks, 124, 126, 132, 156; in Haiti, xxi, 120–40, 142, 145; in the United States, xviii, 91, 125, 129–30, 134, 198
Bland, Theodorick, 72

Blockade, 178, 180, 184, 191
Bloody Fellow (Chief), 111
Blount, William, 22–23, 111
Blue Jacket (Chief), 13–14
Bonaparte, Napoleon, xv, 127, 139, 144–45, 148–49, 163, 171, 174, 180, 182, 184, 189, 197
Boré, Jean-Etienne, 167
Boston Columbian Centinel, xvii, 38, 102–3, 181
Bougainville, Louis-Antoine, comte de, 151
Boukman (leader of Haitian insurrection), 122
Bowdoin, James, 163
Brackenridge, Hugh Henry, 52, 83
Bradley (captain), 173, 175
Brant, Irving, 160
Brant, Joseph, 109–10
Breuilly, John, xi, xiii,
Britain. *See* Great Britain
broken voyage, practice of, 78, 172
Brown, Charles Brockden, 197
Brown, John, 21
Buffon, Georges Louis Leclerc, comte de, 158
Bunel, Joseph, 132
Burke, Edmund, 36, 38
Burr, Aaron, 24, 157, 163, 172

California, 152–53
Cambrian, 173, 175, 176
Canada, xviii, 4, 6, 13–14, 23, 87, 150, 156, 186, 190–91, 193; Lower, 47; Upper, 13–14
Canning, George, 188
Caribbean, 42, 47, 49, 60, 62, 70, 73–74, 78, 80–82, 84, 89, 103–4, 119–20, 122, 125, 138–39, 144, 171, 174–75, 182, 185, 200
Carmichael, William, 16–19, 31, 83, 86
Carolinas, 22. *See also* North Carolina; South Carolina
Carondelet, Francisco Luis Hector, baron de, 17–19
Carroll, Charles, 112
Carroll, Joseph Cephas, 129
Catawbas, xviii
censorship, 133–34, 140
Charles IV, King of Spain, 143
Charles, John, 28
Charleston City Gazette, 180
Charleston Courier, 147
Cherokees, 9, 11, 19–20, 22, 109–10
Chesapeake, xvii, 171, 181–82, 184, 188, 190
Chickamaugas, 20, 110, 112
Chickasaws, 9, 11, 15, 17–20, 110
Childs, Frances, 62
Chile, 82
China, 78, 83, 87
Chinard, Gilbert, 98
Chippewas, 112
Chisholm, John, 22–23
Choctaws, 9, 11, 15, 19–20, 110
citizens' addresses and resolutions, xvii, 40
Civil War, 200
Claiborne, William C. C., 145, 148, 162, 166
Clark, George R., General, 21, 86
Clark, William, 151, 154, 159
Coatsworth, John H., 82
Collot, Victor, 22, 143
Colnett, James, 153
Condorcet, Marie Jean, marquis de, 36, 121
Confederal Congress, 21
Confederation, xi, 5, 21, 94, 110. *See also* Articles of Confederation.
Congress, U.S., xv, 7, 10, 23, 27–28, 31–34, 38, 43–45, 47–48, 51, 53, 58, 60, 62–64, 71, 74, 76, 79, 87,

90–91, 95, 99–102, 108, 112–14, 124, 129, 130–31, 135, 137–38, 147, 149, 151–52, 155, 159, 162–64, 167, 170–71, 177–79, 182, 184, 188–89, 193, 196
Connecticut, 76, 101
Consolato del mare, 47
Constitution: Haitian, 133, 134; U.S., xii, xiii, 3, 25, 27, 33, 44, 50, 56, 64, 72, 76–78, 83, 121, 128, 166, 170, 198
Constitution (frigate), 191
Constitutional Convention, xii, xiv, xv, 3, 5, 22, 24, 121, 197
Consulate (French), 143
Continental Congress, xv, 3–4, 7, 20–21, 70
Cook, James, 83, 87, 151–52
Cook, Warren L., 152
Cooper, James Fenimore, 141, 197
Cornplanter (Chief), 108, 195
cotton, 133, 136, 140
Creeks, 9, 11, 15, 17–20, 22, 109, 112, 191–92
Creoles, 166–67, 198. *See also* Louisiana: French in
Cuba, 163
customs and tonnage duties, 27–28, 71, 74, 76

Davie, William R., 106
Davis, David Brion, 35
Decatur, Stephen, 169–70
Declaration of Independence: Haitian, 139; U.S., 35, 70, 97, 119, 138
Delaware (state of), 34, 130, 138
Delawares, 12, 112
democracy/democratic, xx, 27, 36, 40, 44–46, 54–55, 59, 62–65, 69, 84, 105, 120–21, 125, 129, 131–32, 135, 138, 168, 198, 199
democratic-republican societies, 41, 43, 50–52, 55, 137
Denmark, 70
Dessalines, Jean-Jacques, 120, 127, 129, 132, 134–35, 137
d'Holbach. *See* Holbach, Paul Henri, baron d'
Directory, The, 56, 58, 60–61, 99–101, 103, 143
discrimination laws, 71, 76, 92
Dorchester, Guy Carleton, Baron (Lord), 13–14, 29–30, 47
Duane, William, 64
Dunbar, William, 142, 154, 156–158, 166
Dundas, Henry, 90
Dupont de Nemours, Pierre Samuel, 145
Durey, Michael, 63

East(ern U.S.), 6, 50, 78, 83, 106, 181
Eaton, William, 169
Edwards, Bryan, 122
Ellsworth, Oliver, 106
embargo, 177–78, 180, 184–86, 188, 192
empire, xx, 82
England/English. *See* Great Britain
Enlightenment, xxi, 39, 81, 84, 107, 123, 142, 151, 159, 165, 195
Erskine, David M., 188
Erskine Agreement, 187–88
Essex, 172, 174–76
Europe, xiv, xvii–xviii, xx–xxii, 6, 18–19, 24, 35, 38, 39, 41, 45, 56, 64, 70–73, 78, 80, 82–83, 87–88, 93–94, 96–98, 101–3, 105–9, 112, 114–15, 120, 132, 135–36, 141, 147, 156, 158, 170, 173–74, 177–78, 180–83, 188–89, 192, 197. *See also* individual countries
Eustis, William, 191
exception laws, 45, 59, 62–64, 134

expansion(ism), xx–xxi, xxii, 24, 57, 69, 73, 80–87, 89, 91, 106–8, 110–11, 113, 135–36, 140, 141–68, 190, 192, 195, 197–200
Experiment, 125

Fallen Timbers, Battle of, 14, 24
Family Pact, 153
Far East, 80, 83
Fauchet, Joseph, 53, 57–58
Febvre, Lucien, xvii
Federalist, The, 3, 5, 25–28, 33, 35, 71, 88, 97, 166, 175
Federalists, xx, 34, 36, 40, 45–46, 48–57, 59–64, 69, 76, 87–88, 91, 93, 98–99, 101–3, 105–6, 110, 115, 119–20, 124–26, 129–30, 135, 138–39, 141, 146, 166, 172, 181, 185–87, 189, 190
Fenno, John, 36, 38, 55
Ferrand, Marie Louis, 137, 139–40
Fitzsimmons, Thomas, 76
Florida(s), xviii, xxii, 6–7, 15, 18, 22–23, 85–86, 89, 135–36, 145, 147–49, 154, 160, 162–63, 173, 175, 193, 199; East, 160, 162, 164; West, 160–62, 164, 190, 195, 198
Floridablanca, José Moñino, conde de, 15–16
Forrest, Uriah, 77
Fort Dearborn, 191
Fort Harmar, 12; Treaties of, 12, 112
Fort Miami, 14
Fort Nogales, 7
Fort Stanwix, 9; Treaties of, 9
Foster, Abiel, 77
Foster, Augustus, 188
Founding Fathers, xix–xx, 44, 121
Fox, Charles, 177–78, 180
France/French, ix–xii, xiv, 4, 6, 7, 12, 16, 19, 21–22, 28, 32–42, 44–50, 53–63, 65, 73–75, 78, 81, 83, 84, 86–88, 90, 92–93, 96–97, 99–105, 113–14, 119, 121–22, 124–28, 131–33, 135–37, 139–40, 143–50, 158, 160–63, 166, 169, 171–72, 174, 177, 180, 182, 185, 187–88, 190, 200
Franklin, Benjamin, 6, 82
Franklin, Jesse, 130
Franklin, state of, 11, 21
free trade, 70, 73–74, 80–82, 91
Fréneau, Philippe, 38
French and Indian War. *See* Seven Years' War
Friends of the Blacks, 121–22

Gabriel's Conspiracy, 129, 132, 134
Gales, Joseph, Jr., 134
Gallatin, Albert, 150, 184, 186
Gàlvez, José de, 152
Garden, Guillaume, comte de, xv
Gardoqui, Don Diego de, 7, 16, 18, 20–21, 87
Garnier, Michael, 142
Gaspar, David Barry, 132
Gates, Horatio, 167
Gazette of the United States, 36, 38, 55
Gellner, Ernst, xii
General Customs Tariff, 74–75
Genêt, Edmond-Charles, 21, 39–43, 51, 55, 57, 75, 85–86, 89
George III, King of Great Britain, 151, 187
Georgia, xiv, 15, 20–22, 72, 76–77, 137–38
Gerry, Elbridge, 60, 100, 103–4
Ghent, Treaty of, 191, 193
Girard, Stephen, 34
Girardet, Raoul, xi, 56
Godoy, Manuel, Duke of La Alcudia, 18–19
Grant (judge), 172–73, 177
Great Britain/British, x, xi, xiv, xviii,

xxii, 4–7, 9–16, 18–23, 26–31, 32–34, 37–40, 42–50, 52–53, 55–57, 59–63, 69–79, 82–85, 88–89, 95–96, 100, 113–14, 120, 122, 124–27, 136, 145, 147–48, 150–53, 158, 160, 163–64, 171–93, 196, 200
Greenville, Treaty of, 14
Grenville, William Wyndam, Lord, 23, 48–49, 90, 94, 126
Guadeloupe, 60, 74
Guerrière, 191

Haiti, xviii, xxi, 74, 82, 89–90, 92, 115, 119–40, 142–46, 148, 192, 197, 199
Hamilton, Alexander, 3–5, 12–13, 28–34, 37–43, 46, 48–49, 60, 62, 71, 76–80, 87–89, 91, 95, 97, 103–5
Hamilton, Paul, 191
Hammond, George, 13, 32, 42–43, 49, 53
Handsome Lake, 164–65, 195
Harmar, General, 12
Harmar, Fort. *See* Fort Harmar
Harrington, James, 26
Harrison, William Henry, 165, 186, 188, 191–92
Hauteval, Lucien, 61
Hawkesbury, Charles Jenkinson, Lord, 173
Heinl, Nancy Gordon, 132
Heinl, Robert Debbs, Jr., 132
Hereta-Bogota (expedition), 152
Hickey, Donald R., 178, 179, 190, 196
Hispanics, 153
Holbach, Paul Henri, baron d,' 81
Holland, 4, 70, 103, 145
Holston, Treaty of, 109
Horseshoe Bend, Battle of, 192
Horsman, Reginald, 110, 165
Hottinger, Jean Conrad, 60–61, 101
Hudson River School, 197
Hull, William, 190
human rights. *See* rights of man
Humboldt, Alexander von, 157
Humphreys, David, 31
Hunt, Alfred, 124, 128
Hunt, Michael, 65
Hunter, George, 156, 158
Hurons, 9, 12

impressment, 49, 176, 178, 180–81, 184, 190
India, 179
Indians, xiv, xviii, xxi, 6, 7, 9–15, 17–19, 21–22, 24, 30, 46–47, 84, 94, 107–13, 115, 121, 151–54, 156–60, 164–68, 186, 192, 195, 198–99. *See also names of individual tribes*
Indies, West. *See* Caribbean
Ireland, 63
Iriye, Akira, xix
Iroquois, 9, 109–10, 165, 198
isolationism, xvi, xxi, 92, 98, 106, 115, 170, 199

Jacobins, 89
Jackson, Andrew, 191–92
Jackson, Donald, 150–51
Jackson, James, 72, 76–77, 137–38
Jackson, John George, 131, 135
Jamaica, 90, 122, 138
Jaudenes, José de, 17
Jay, John, 6–7, 18, 20–21, 28–29, 37, 48–49, 52–54, 87, 166
Jay's Treaty, 14, 18, 23–24, 45–46, 48–50, 53–55, 58, 60, 143, 171, 177–79
Jefferson, Thomas, xiv, xx–xxi, 12–13, 15–17, 24, 27, 29–32, 34, 36–43,

46, 48, 55–57, 59, 63–65, 71, 73–76, 78, 80–84, 87, 89–91, 95, 113–15, 119, 121, 126, 129, 132, 135–36, 138, 141, 143–59, 161, 163–65, 167–70, 173, 175, 177–80, 182–84, 186–87, 189, 192–93, 195, 196, 199
Johnson, Andrew, 200
Jensen, Merrill, 4
Johnson, William, Sir, 9
Jordan, Winthrop, 139

Kaplan, L. S., xiv, 49, 87
Kendrick, John, 153
Kentucky, 20–22, 50, 64, 84–86, 146
Kentucky and Virginia Resolutions, 46, 64
Kerber, Linda K., 138
Key, Francis Scott, 191
King, Rufus, 23, 87–90, 143, 172, 176
Knox, Henry, 12, 28–29, 37, 42, 107–13, 165
Kurtz, Stephen J., 105

La Pérouse, Jean-François de, 87
Lafayette, Marie Joseph, marquis de, 35, 37, 73
Laussat, Pierre de, 162
Lawrence, John, 72, 76–78
Leander, 178, 190
Lear, Tobias, 126–27
Leclerc, Charles, Victor-Emmanuel, 127, 132, 144, 146, 148
Ledyard, John, 87
Lee, Richard Bland, 77
Leopard, 171, 181, 187
Lewis, Meriwether, 151, 153, 154, 158–59
Lewis and Clark (expedition), 87, 142, 150, 153–59, 163–64
liberalism (economic), xx, xxii, 76
liberty/liberties, 45–46, 119, 124, 129–31, 134, 136–38, 149, 186
Libya, 113–14
Link, Eugene, 41
Liston, Robert, 22
Little Belt, 188
Little Sarah, 42
Little Turtle (Chief), 13
Livingston, Robert R., 144–45, 148, 160
Logan, George, 137
Logan, Rayford W., 90, 134–35
Louis XVI, King of France, 39, 151
Louisiana, 18–19, 22–23, 57, 85–87, 89, 124, 127, 131, 136, 141–68, 198; French in, 160, 166 (*see also* Creoles); Upper, 86, 143, 158
Louisiana Purchase, 136, 141–68, 172, 192, 196, 197, 199, 200
Louverture (l'Ouverture), Toussaint. *See* Toussaint Louverture
Lowe, J. T., xiv
Lyon, Matthew, 64

Macedonian, 191
Macon, Nathaniel, 188
Madison, James, 13, 26–28, 32–33, 36, 38, 40–41, 46, 57–58, 64, 71–77, 79–80, 91–92, 127–28, 131–32, 143, 145–46, 156–57, 160, 162, 164, 175, 177–78, 196, 198–99
Maitland, Thomas, 89–90
Malkassian, Gérard, ix
Marienstras, Elise, xii, xiii
Marks, Frederick W., III, 25
Marshall, John, 60, 100–101, 103
Martinez de Yrujo, Carlo, 148, 151, 153
Martinique, 74
Maryland, 34, 50, 77, 112
Massachusetts, 28, 58, 102, 104, 181, 185, 189

Massillac (Club), 121
McDonald, Forrest, 4
McGillivray, Alexander, 11, 15, 17, 109
McKee, Alexander, 14
McKenzie, Alexander, 150
Meares, John, 152–53
Mercantile Advertiser, 133–34
mercantilism, 69–70, 73, 75–76, 81–82, 87, 90, 122
Mercer, John Francis, 36
merchant marine, 47, 74, 80, 99, 113–14, 135, 171, 185
Merry, Anthony, 172
Mexico, 86, 107, 153, 156–57, 163
Miami, Fort. *See* Fort Miami
Miamis, 9, 12–13, 109
Michaux, André, 86–87, 143, 150
Minerva, 55
Miranda, Francisco de, 88–89, 163
Miro, Esteban, 17, 20
Mississippi River, navigation of, xxi, 3–4, 7, 15–16, 18–23, 83–87
Mississippi Territory, 145–51, 166–67
Missouri River, 153
Mobile Act, 162
Mohawks, 109
Monroe, James, 52, 53, 54, 59, 99, 129, 131, 135, 143–44, 148–49, 162, 172–79, 188
Monroe-Pinkney Treaty, 176, 179–80
Montesquieu, Charles, baron de, 26
Montmorin, Armand Marc, comte de, 33, 74
Morales, Don Juan, 145, 148, 150
Moreau de Saint-Méry, Médéric Louis Elie, 92, 103, 142
Morocco, 4, 113
Morris, Gouverneur, 30, 32, 36, 37, 39, 54, 74–75, 92–95, 100, 110, 147, 190
Morris, Robert, 73, 95
Mortefontaine, Convention of, 62, 105–6
Moustier, Eléanor François Elie, comte de, 87
Mulgrave, Henry Phipps, Lord, 175

Napoleon. *See* Bonaparte, Napoleon
National Gazette, 38, 56
Native Americans. *See* Indians and *names of individual tribes*
Nelson, John R., Jr., 34, 76, 80, 184
Nelson, Horatio, Lord, 170, 174
Netherlands. *See* Holland.
neutrality, xvii, 38–39, 42–43, 46–47, 49, 60, 70, 75, 78, 85, 93, 98, 115, 137, 170, 173–74, 178, 180; Proclamation of, 39, 96
New England, xvii, 28, 56, 75, 97, 185, 187
New Hampshire, 77, 189
New Mexico, 153
New Orleans, 19–21, 84–86, 124, 143–50, 160, 162, 166–67, 195; Battle of, 191–92
New Spain, 152
New York, 13, 20, 28, 34, 52, 72, 76, 87, 109, 130, 163, 178, 181; Treaty of, 15
New York Evening Post, 146
Nicholson, James, 34
nonimportation, 177
nonintercourse, 177, 181–84, 187–88
noninterference, 90
Nootka Sound, 16, 27, 29–30, 38, 75, 95, 152–53
Nora, Pierre, xix
North Africa. *See* Barbary Coast *and names of individual countries.*
North Carolina, 11, 50, 130, 134
Northeast(ern U.S.), 186
Northwest (Old; Pacific), xxii, 4, 6, 8–13, 16, 46, 50, 83, 86–87,

109–10, 150–53, 158, 159, 165, 191–92
Northwestern tribes, Confederacy of, 12, 14, 17

O'Fallon, James, 21
Ogé, Vincent, 122
Ojibwas, 9
Oneidas, 9
Osages, 156, 158
Osgood, David, 57
Ottawas, 12, 112
Otto, Louis-Guillaume, 33
Ottoman Empire, 113

Pacific Ocean, 78, 82, 87, 150–53
pacifism, 110, 114, 160, 170, 177
Paine, Thomas, 35–36, 38, 70, 97
Paris, Peace of (1783), 5, 6, 10, 15, 30, 50, 85, 94, 161
Pattiwatimas, 112
Pennsylvania, 50, 52, 76, 130, 137
Pennsylvania Gazette, 35
Perez (expedition), 152
Perkins, Bradford, 62, 176, 179, 185
Perry, Olivier Hazard, 191
Petuns, 9, 12
Philadelphia (frigate), 169–70
Philadelphia Convention. *See* Constitutional Convention
Pichon, Louis-André, 103, 104, 126–28, 135, 143–44, 147–48
Pickering, Timothy, 53–54, 59–60, 82, 88–90, 100, 103, 125
Pierce, John, 178
Pike, Zebulon, 142, 157–58
Pinckney, Charles Cotesworth, 59, 60, 99–101, 103, 145
Pinckney, Thomas, 19
Pinckney's Treaty, xxi, 19, 23–24, 58, 146
Pinkney, William, 178, 188
Pioneers, 51, 57, 84–85, 89, 109, 111–13, 143–44, 154, 165, 185–86, 199
pirates/piracy, 60, 90, 94, 113–14
Pitt, William, 94, 153, 173–74, 177
Portugal, 31, 114, 173
Preble, Edward, 170
President (frigate), 188
privateers, privateering, 42, 60–62, 90, 103–4, 114, 125, 127, 163, 176, 191
Prussia, 4, 46, 182

quasi war, 61, 88, 90, 103, 106, 114, 125, 169

Rafinesque, Constantin Samuel, 157
Raleigh Register and North Carolina Gazette, 133–34
Rambouillet Decree, 188
Ramsay, David, 197
Randolph, Edmund, 28, 46, 48, 52–54
Raynaud, Phlippe, 35
Read, Jacob, 50
Republicans (U.S. political party), 34, 36, 38, 43, 45–46, 50–60, 63–65, 69, 76, 91, 96–98, 100–102, 105–6, 115, 119–20, 124–25, 128–31, 133–35, 137–39, 141, 145–46, 172, 177–81, 184–86, 188–90, 193, 197
republican(ism), 25–26, 36–37, 45, 64, 79, 92, 105, 183, 193
revolution(s)/revolutionary, 54, 57, 65, 72, 78, 129, 138, 163, 170; American (U.S.), xi, xiv, xix–xx, 7, 11, 15, 26–29, 34, 35, 41, 46, 51, 64, 69, 83, 87, 98, 119, 121–23, 131, 134–35, 138, 175, 182, 187, 196–97; French, xv, xix, 25, 35–38, 41, 44, 51, 56–57, 69, 73–74, 120,

122–25, 128, 134–35, 138, 163; Haitian, 119–40; Russian (1917), 134. *See also* War of Independence
Rhode Island, 189
Richmond Enquirer, xvii, 133, 134, 158
Rigaud, André, 125
rights of man, 121, 133, 135, 138
Ritchie, Thomas, 134
Rochambeau, Donatien Marie Joseph, vicomte de, 127–28
Rousseau, Jean-Jacques, 26, 81
Routledge, Edward, 81
Rule of 1756, 47, 171, 174
Russia, 83, 152, 182

Sacs, 112
Saint-Clair, Arthur, 12–13, 24, 113
Saint-Domingue. *See* Haiti
San Ildefonso, treaty of, 142, 160
Santo Domingo. *See* Haiti
Sauks, 12
Scott, William, Sir, 172
Selmer, Marshall, 55
Senecas, 108, 164, 165
Seven Years' War, 13, 142, 160
Sevier, John, 21
Seward, William H., 200
Shawnees, 12, 13, 14, 109, 165, 185
Sheffield, John Holroyd, Lord, 70
Sherman, Roger, 76–77
Short, William, 16–19, 31, 73–75, 81, 86
Siberia, 152
Simcoe, John Graves, Lord, 13
Slaughter, Thomas P., 52
slavery, xviii, xxi, 49–50, 89, 91, 94, 103, 113–14, 120–40, 156, 160, 197–98, 200
Smith, Adam, 70
Smith, John, 130
Smith, William Laughton, 77
Sonthonax, Léger Félicité, 124
South(ern U.S.), xviii, 6, 34, 72, 120–121, 124, 129, 136–37, 140, 160, 181, 186, 196–97
South Carolina, 21, 42, 50, 52, 72, 77, 81, 122, 124–25, 129, 138
Southwest(ern U.S.; also Old), 6, 7, 11, 15, 17–18, 20, 22, 109, 110, 158, 165
Spain/Spanish, xviii, xxi, xxii, 4, 6, 7, 9, 11, 14, 16–22, 24, 29–31, 42, 57, 70, 75, 78, 83–88, 95, 109, 113, 124–25, 137, 139, 142–46, 151–54, 156–57, 160–61, 164, 171, 176–77, 186
Stagg, Jay C. A., 189
Stanwix, Fort. *See* Fort Stanwix
states' rights, 64
Stephen, James, 172, 174–75
Stevens, Edward, 90, 126
Sweden, 4, 180

Taguieff, Pierre-André, ix
Talleyrand-Périgord, Charles Maurice de, 60, 61, 93, 101, 103–4, 109, 142–43, 148, 162–63
Tecumseh, 14, 20, 165, 186, 188, 191–92, 198–99
Tellico, Treaty of, 20
Tennessee, 11, 21–23, 84
Tennessee Gazette, 148–149
Tenskwatawa (Shawnee prophet), 165, 186
Ternant, Jean-Baptiste, 123
terror, 142–43
Texas, 153, 162–63
Thames, battle of the, 191–92
Thibau, Jacques, 121
Thornton, Edward, 151
tobacco, 73–75
Tone, Wolfe, 63
tonnage. *See* customs and tonnage duties

Toussaint Louverture (l'Ouverture), François Dominique, 89–90, 125–27, 132
Trade and Intercourse Acts, 112
trade, free. *See* free trade
Trans-Mississippian expeditions, 154
treaties: British-American, 7; Franco-American, 4, 42–43, 49, 60–61, 106, 166; Franco-British, 46; Spanish-American, 145. *See also names of individual treaties*
Tripoli harbor, 169
Tucker, Thomas Tudor, 72
Tunisia, 113, 114, 169
Turkey, 180
Turner, Frederick Jackson, 5–6
Turner, Katherine C., 109
Turreau, Louis Marie, baron de, 137
Tuscarooras, 9

United Provinces, 46
United States (frigate), 191

Van Alstyne, Richard W., xvi, 82
Vans Murray, William, 77–79, 103–4, 106
Vattel, Emer de, 39, 81
Venezuela, 163
Vergennes, Charles Gravier, comte de, 73
Vermont, xi, xiv, 20–21, 64, 189
Viar, Josef Ignacio de, 17
Victor, Charles Perrin, 145
Virginia, 28, 50, 64, 72, 75, 77, 124, 129, 131–32, 134
Virginia and Kentucky Resolutions, 46, 64
Volney, Constantin, comte de, 143, 157

War of Independence, 6–7, 9, 26, 50, 52, 86, 91, 113, 196–97, 199. *See also* Revolution: American
War of 1812, xviii, 14–15, 20, 169, 174, 188–93, 196, 200
Warren, Mercy Otis, 106, 197
Washington, George, 12, 21–22, 27, 29–31, 33, 35–40, 43–44, 46, 48, 50–55, 58, 88, 92–99, 106–12, 114, 121–23, 137, 168, 178, 190, 195–96, 199
Watts, Steven, 190
Wayne, Anthony, 14, 110, 113, 195
Webster, Noah, 55, 197
Weinberg, Albert K., 83
West(ern U.S.), xxi, 22, 24, 50, 52, 83, 86–87, 106, 141–42, 146–47, 153, 181, 186, 196, 199, 200
West Indies. *See* Caribbean
Whisky Rebellion, 45, 50–53, 55, 65, 87
Whitaker, Arthur Preston, 19
White, James, 20
White, Samuel, 130, 138–39
whites, xxii, 5, 91, 120, 124–25, 132, 135; in Haiti, 128, 133–34; in the U.S., 134, 164, 198, 200
Whitney, Eli, 136
Wilkinson, James, 20, 23
Wilkinson, General, 157, 162, 191
Williams, William Appleman, xvi, 76
Wistar, Caspar, 150
Wolcott, Oliver, 103, 125
Wyandotts, 112

xenophobia, x, 63, 100–101, 103
XYZ affair, xvii, 57, 60–62, 93, 99–101, 103, 105, 109, 114

Yrujo. *See* Martinez de Yrujo, 22

www.ingramcontent.com/pod-product-compliance
Lightning Source LLC
La Vergne TN
LVHW091030080826
845145LV00002B/427